Excavation at Fengate Peterborough, England: The Fourth Report

Excavation at Fengate Peterborough, England: The Fourth Report

Francis Pryor

With principal illustrations by Robert Bourne, Charles French, Robert Powell, Maisie Taylor and the Author

and
major contributions by Kathleen Biddick, Paul Craddock, Charles French, John Hayes, Faye Powell and Gay Wilson.

Northamptonshire Archaeological Society Monograph 2
Royal Ontario Museum Archaeology Monograph 7
1984

ISBN: — 0 9507151 1 5
ISSN: — 0144-5391

This book is published jointly by the Northamptonshire Archaeological Society and the Royal Ontario Museum. A generous grant towards the cost of publication from the Department of the Environment is acknowledged.

The Royal Ontario Museum publishes two series in the field of archaeology: Monographs, a numbered series of original publications, and Papers, a numbered series of primarily shorter original publications. All manuscripts considered for publication are subject to the editorial policies of the Royal Ontario Museum, and to review by persons outside the museum staff who are authorities in the particular field involved. (The Royal Ontario Museum, 100 Queen's Park, Toronto, Canada, M5S 2C6.)

Cover illustration by David Crowther

It is distributed in the United Kingdom by the Northamptonshire Archaeological Society.

To George Dixon, Project Accountant, who did so much for so little — so often.

CONTENTS

FOREWORD

This is the last report of the Fengate series, in line with the revised publication plans discussed in the Foreword to the Second Report (FNG 2, ix). Throughout the series we have kept publication costs to a minimum, so students and others could purchase Fengate volumes for their own use. The volumes have, however, become progressively larger and this reflects the quantity of archaeological material from later prehistoric and Romano-British contexts. The Fourth Report would be almost three times the size of the Third Report were not certain, mainly descriptive passages, placed on microfiche. The arrangement of the microfiche follows recent suggestion of the DoE/CBA publication working party (*The Publication of Archaeological Excavations*, CBA/DoE, December 7, 1982). Microfiche'd passages in the present volume are discussed in the Introduction, below. The reader is also advised to consult the Microfiche Contents, at the end of this report.

ACKNOWLEDGEMENTS

It would be impossible to acknowledge everyone who has helped the Fengate project in one way or another. Nevertheless, some attempt must be made. Many helpers have been acknowledged in the first three reports and this particularly applies to experienced volunteers and supervisors all of whom are mentioned in Reports Two and Three. Certain individuals have shown a continued interest in our work and these I would like to thank especially. First, from 1971 our finances have been managed by Mr George Dixon, to whom this volume is gratefully dedicated. I am also endebted to the following for their continued, lively interest in the academic side of the project: Richard Bradley, David Coombs, Ian Kinnes, Paul Craddock, Geoff Dannell, John Peter Wild, Tony Fleming and Tony Gregory. Professor W F Grimes, then Chairman of the Nene Valley Research Committee, was particularly encouraging in the first two seasons of the project and its successful outcome is due, in no small measure, to this encouragement.

Next I must thank those who kindly contributed reports to this volume, many of which took months to prepare: Kathy Biddick (animal bones); Bernard Denston (Neolithic human bones); Faye Powell (Iron Age human bones); Charles French (molluscs and sediments); Paul Craddock (soil phosphates and slags); Gay Wilson (palaeobotany); Maisie Taylor (wood and charcoals); John Hayes (Roman pottery); David Williams (pottery fabrics); Donald Mackreth (brooches); Richard Reece (coins); Martin Henig (finger ring); Stephen Green (Neolithic arrowhead); Felicity Wild (with Brenda Dickinson) (samian ware); Kay Hartley (mortaria). I would also like to acknowledge the help we received from Bernard Denston and Pat Smith, both of Cambridge, when we undertook the very difficult task of lifting the Neolithic grave group intact (our trials are informally reported in *Durobrivae*, 8, 1980 'Raising the Dead'). Sara Lunt prepared additional pottery drawings, and thanks are also due to Martin Howe, Curator of Peterborough Museum, who has kindly undertaken to store the site records, plans and finds. Tony Brown has been a model Editor throughout the production of the last two reports, and what successes there have been are in great measure due to him. The Peterborough Development Corporation, owners of most of Fengate, have cooperated with the excavations in the fullest possible sense; indeed the fact that not one feature had to be hurriedly dug, or abandoned half dug, is a tribute to all concerned and most particularly to David Bath, Chief Planning Officer.

Dr Jay Butler did much to help me on my research trip to Holland and I am particularly endebted to him and Dr Willy Groenman-van Waateringe for their kindness and generosity.

An Apple II microcomputer was bought to process the Iron Age pottery and the Apple Writer Text Editing System was used in the production of this manuscript. I will forever be indebted to Bridget Todd who unflinchingly spent many tedious weeks expertly interpreting, editing and typing my all too inadequate first draft (and who kindly wrote her own acknowledgement). The Iron Age pottery program was written by Faye Powell and extended by Ben Booth; special thanks are due to Peter Wolfenden and the staff of Digitus, Covent Garden who, with David Russell of Peterborough Technical College, did so much to help us master the micro.

The preparation of this report would have been impossible without the willing assistance of many people, but most especially I wish to thank David Cranston, Maisie Taylor, Bob Powell, Faye Powell, Charles French, Bob Bourne and latterly David Crowther.

The excavations were funded by the Department of the Environment and the Royal Ontario Museum.

Post-excavation grants and publication subsidies were provided by both bodies, and I particularly wish to thank Doug Tushingham, until recently Chief Archaeologist of the Royal Ontario Museum for his encouragement throughout the project. John Campsie, Royal Ontario Museum Publications Officer, provided a grant towards the production costs of this volume.

Peterborough, January 1981

FENGATE THIRD REPORT ERRATA

FIG 73 (lower left histogram) Non-cortical values should read: 0; 13; 17; 8; 3; 1. Cortical values should read: 0; 13; 15; 8; 2; 1.

FIG 74 (lower left histogram) Caption should read: Late Neolithic Breadth:Length Ratios, All Complete Flakes (1361)

FIG 74 (lower right histogram) Non-cortical values should read: 2; 20; 34; 35; 36; 79

LIST OF FIGURES

NOTE: Microfiche'd figures are not listed below. They are distinguished by the prefix ''M'' and are listed separately in the Table of Microfiche Contents, at the back of the report.

LIST OF PLATES

LIST OF TABLES

NOTE the microfichéd tables are not listed below. They are distinguished by the prefix 'M' and are listed separately in the Table of Microfiche Contents, at the back of the report.

TERMINOLOGY, CONVENTIONS AND ABBREVIATIONS

The linear measurements are given in the metric system (wherever possible) and metres are used as the basic unit. In the running text the metre abbreviation (m) is used, but in the catalogues of pottery sherds and flints it is omitted.

Throughout this report radiocarbon dates are given using the 'Libby' half-life for radiocarbon (5,568 years), correct to one standard deviation. Dates in 'radiocarbon years' are indicated by the use of the letters 'ad' and 'bc' to distinguish them from calendar years AD and BC.

The depths of finds in this report are given below the stripped surface (in metres), that is about 0.75 m below the modern ground level (the problem is discussed in the Second Report Appendix 1). Similarly, sections are drawn with the original ploughsoil removed, as it was thought undesirable to 'reconstruct' the modern soil profile after it had been removed mechanically. The representation of soil types used in this report follows the standard scheme introduced in 1972 by D F Mackreth, Nene Valley Research Committee, Director of Excavations. A few minor modifications have been introduced, however, and these are given below in FIG. 6.

The previous Fengate reports are denoted by the abbreviations FNG 1 (Pryor 1974c), FNG 2 (Pryor 1978a) and FNG 3 (Pryor 1980a).

INTRODUCTION

ABSTRACT

This report is mainly devoted to a detailed description and analysis of features and finds from a Mid-Iron Age to Romano-British settlement on the Cat's Water subsite. This area produced extensive evidence for settlement, including numerous round buildings, a few rectilinear buildings and a hitherto unrecognised class of round structure defined by one or more arcs of discontinuous ring-ditch. A large pottery assemblage and numerous animal bones are discussed at length. The Cat's Water subsite also produced an earlier Neolithic multiple burial. Smaller, or partially preserved, Iron Age and Romano-British settlements are described from the Storey's Bar Road, Vicarage Farm and Padholme Road subsites; specialists' reports include a discussion of a collection of Romano-British pottery from Fengate in Peterborough Museum, palaeoenvironmental papers and a detailed discussion of soil phosphate analyses. Finally, an attempt is made to draw together the various archaeological periods represented at Fengate, and the changing Fen-edge economy is considered in the context of similar sites in lowland Britain and the southern North Sea basin.

ARRANGEMENT OF THE REPORT

The layout of this volume is essentially the same as reports Two and Three, but as the subject matter treated is more heterogeneous, the structure of this report has had to be more flexible. Chapter 1 considers Iron Age and Romano-British features from the Padholme Road subsite, some of which have already been briefly discussed in the First Report (FNG 1, 15-22; 37-38). Chapter 2 considers Iron Age features from the Padholme Road subsite, some of which, again have been described in the First Report (FNG 1, 22-29; 37-38). Iron Age and Romano-British features from the Storey's Bar Road subsite are discussed in Chapter 3 and features of Neolithic to Romano-British date are considered in Chapter 4. Finds are treated in Chapters 5 (Neolithic and Early Bronze Age), 6 (mainly Late Bronze and Iron Age) and 7 (Romano-British). The final chapter, 8, attempts a synthesis of the various settlements and economies, of all periods, found at Fengate and concludes with an assessment of the site's significance in the Fenland region and in the wider context of the southern North Sea basin.

Certain portions of the report have been placed on microfiche which are stored inside the back cover (see Foreword, above). Passages placed on microfiche are either of specialised interest or include lengthy, detailed descriptions or tabulations. As a general rule the site's importance lies in the spatial distribution of features and finds. Soils are often homogenous and consequently only the most important section drawings appear in the body of the text. Section conventions are given in FIG 6.

The fiche are arranged by chapter and are integrated so that text, relevant illustrations and tables appear together. All fiche figures and tables are denoted by the prefix 'M' and the page reference of each M Figure or Table is given in the Table of Microfiche Contents at the back of the report. Summaries of microfiche Appendices are given on pages 258 to 260.

THE SITE AND ITS SETTING (FIGS 1 and 2)

The site's topographical and geological setting has been quite fully reviewed in previous reports (FNG 2, 1-6; FNG 3, 1-3) and an updated discussion of Fen Flandrian deposits is given in Part I of Chapter 8, below. Only a brief resumé, therefore, need appear here. The site is a large one, extending along the extreme east side of Peterborough from the Nene just north of Stanground (TL 205982), north-eastwards for some 3.5km towards Oxney 'island' (TF 225010). Only the central part of this area is currently under threat

(FIG 3), and forms the subject of this and previous reports. Plans of crop marks have appeared in all earlier reports (FNG 1, FIG 1; FNG 2, FIG 3; FNG 3, FIG 4) and it is not considered necessary to repeat them here — the simplified version given in the Third Report should be considered the most reliable, as it incorporates material from all eight seasons of excavation (1971-8) with non-archaeological features omitted. Cropmarks generally show up well, as the subsoil over most of the site is freely draining gravel of the Nene first terrace

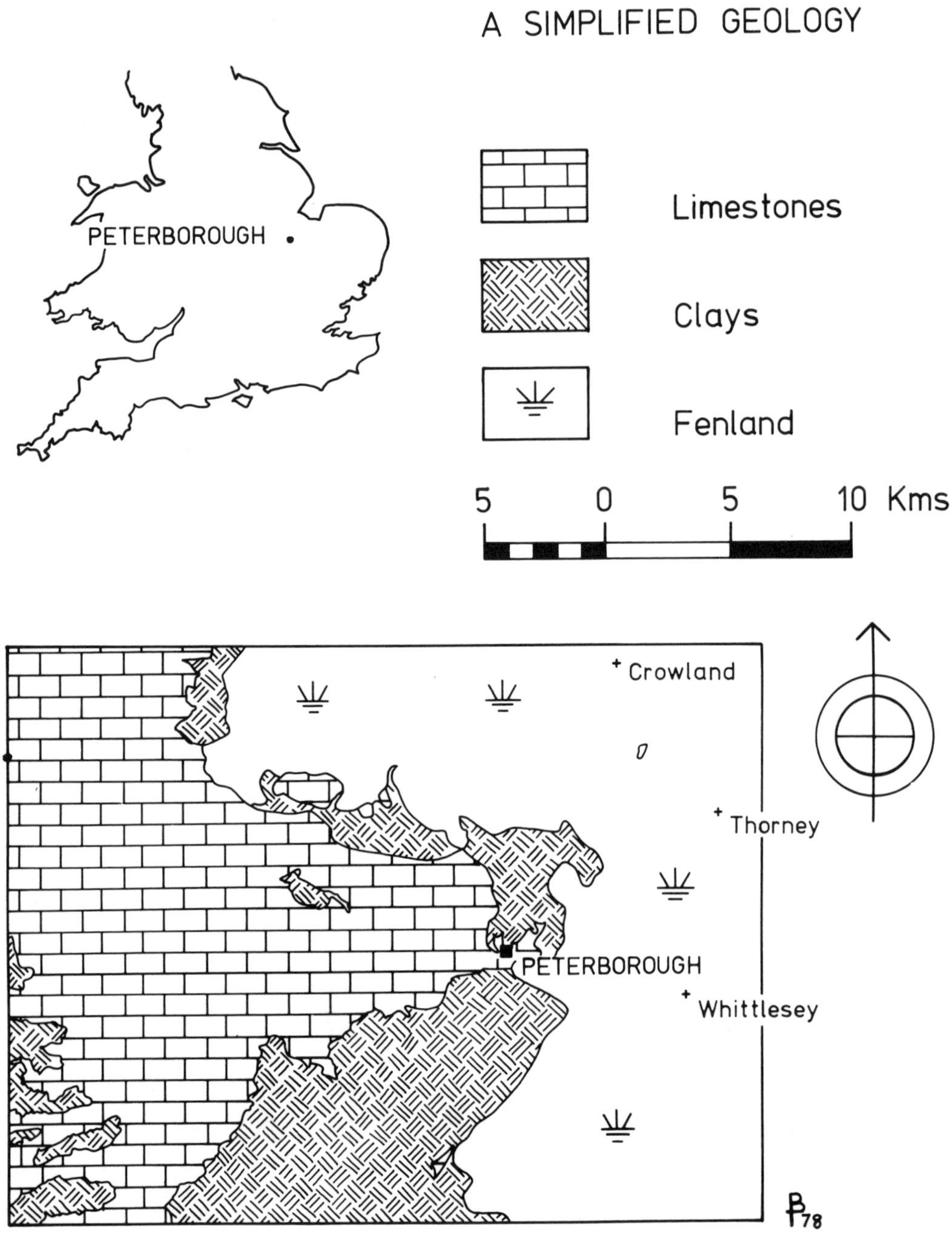
A SIMPLIFIED GEOLOGY
PETERBOROUGH
Limestones
Clays
Fenland
5
0
5
10 Kms
Crowland
Thorney
PETERBOROUGH
Whittlesey
B 78

Fig. 1 *A simplified map of the solid geology of the Peterborough area (after Horton et al* 1974).

series (Horton *et al* 1974). The extreme western edge of the site is however, directly underlain by solid geology, in this case the weathered limestone of the Upper Jurassic Cornbrash series. Further to the east, at about the ten or twelve foot contour OD more recent alluvial and Fen deposits overlie the gravels. Cropmarks are principally confined to the land defined by the 10 and 25-foot contours; this in part reflects the distribution of the gravel subsoil, but also reflects the dispersal of modern, mainly industrial, buildings. More low-lying parts of the site, particularly the Fourth Drove and Cat's Water subsites (FIG 3), are covered by an unusually thick topsoil (A horizon) which is in part composed of Roman fresh-water flood clays. These superficial clay-rich deposits affect the whole of Fengate, excepting Vicarage Farm, to a greater or lesser extent, and help to account for the site's excellent preservation, as the plough could not penetrate far below the thick topsoil. The blanketing effect of so thick a soil cover has made it impossible to carry out detailed surface collection. Soil phosphate survey has happily proved an excellent substitute for more conventional prospecting techniques (see Appendix 4).

Finally it has become apparent that the original course of the river Nene was not along the Cat's Water which is now best interpreted as a post-Roman catchwater drain, similar in function, perhaps, to the Lincolnshire Car Dyke (Simmons 1979; R Evans 1979; A Pryor 1978). The precise edge of the Fen south and east of Fengate would have varied at different periods, and estimates of its location must await the completion of David Hall's current research programme (Mr Hall is the Cambridgeshire Archaeological Committee Fenland Field Officer) The excellent bare-earth aerial cover of the region does not show a suitably-sized rodden north of Whittlesey 'island' and there is a strong probability that the river Nene originally flowed to the south (R Evans 1979). Thus the suspicions voiced in the Third Report (FNG 3) do seem to have been justified, and Fengate can no longer be seen as a settlement site in close proximity to a major river (Whittle 1977, FIG 4, 2).

NOTES ON THE ARCHIVE

From time to time there will be references in this report to the Archive. This consists of the site layer cards, finds cards, plans and photographs stored with the finds, bones and soil samples in Peterborough Museum. Those who wish to make use of the archive should note that, inevitably, certain feature numbers and excavated area numbers used in this or previous reports will differ from the archive. Concordance lists are given in the Second Report (FNG 1, Appendix 11), in the Third Report (FNG 3, 246-7) and in this report the only significant alteration refers to the Cat's Water excavations of 1975 (FNG 75 code in archive) where all feature numbers have been increased by 1000 — thus feature 86, as dug, will appear in this report as F1086. Unfortunately it was not possible to devise a uniform grid for the whole site and most subsites are excavated and planned on their own grids, which are illustrated in the appropriate chapters. Only the Cat's Water and Fourth Drove subsites have a common grid, based on the Ordnance Survey, with a false origin in the Fen to the south-east. In order to facilitate cross reference to the archive, all section line orientations, as printed, refer to the relevant subsite grid north. In this report section numbers correspond with those in the archive, and are placed within square brackets ([]).

A NOTE ON THE PUBLICATION OF PREVIOUS FINDS FROM FENGATE

The finds from a site which has been extensively excavated for so many years must inevitably find publication in a diversity of sources. In addition to the material from the present series of excavations which is published in the four reports, the reader's attention is drawn to earlier publications, most notably those by G Wyman Abbott (1910), the original discoverer of the site, E T Leeds (1922) and Hawkes and Fell (1945). These three reports were specifically devoted to the site, but additional Beaker material was also published by D L Clarke in his corpus (1970, 490-1); the large quantities of 'domestic' Beaker material from Fengate in Peterborough Museum was published by Alex Gibson in the Third Report (FNG 3, Appendix 10). Neolithic pottery has been comprehensively treated by I F Smith (1956) and a recent note (Gibson 1979) considers non-Beaker Bronze Age pottery from Fengate, and other locations in the area, in Peterborough Museum. Dr John Hayes completes the study of previous finds from Fengate in this report (Appendix 10), below.

POSTSCRIPT

Fenland archaeology is a rapidly growing subject. The following important papers have appeared since the completion of this report.

de Bakker, H, and van den Berg, M W, (eds) 1982 *Proceedings of the symposium on peat lands below the sea level*, International Institute for Land Reclamation and Improvement (Wageningen). Mainly environmental, but contains good syntheses of Dutch and German coastal sequences, also an account of the East Anglian Fens by Ravensdale (based on Hall's recent work).

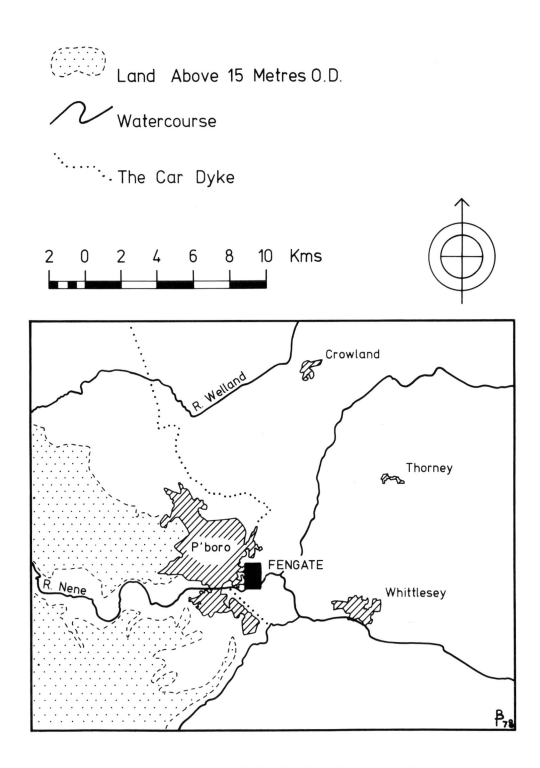

Land Above 15 Metres O.D.

Watercourse

The Car Dyke

2 0 2 4 6 8 10 Kms

Crowland

R. Welland

Thorney

P'boro

FENGATE

R. Nene

Whittlesey

β78

Fig. 2   Topography of the Peterborough area. The location of FIG 3 is shown in black.

4

Bamford, H M, 1982
Beaker domestic sites in the Fen edge and East Anglia, *East Anglian Archaeology*, Report No 16. Numerous references to Fengate (see Index), especially FIGS 36 & 37.

Booth, S J, 1982
The sand and gravel resources of the country around Whittlesey, Cambridgeshire, *Miner Assess Rep Inst Geol Soc*, 93. The term 'Fen Gravel' is dropped; the deposit is now seen to be of the Nene and Welland 1st and 2nd terrace.

Gibson, A M, 1982
Beaker domestic sites, 2 vols, British Archaeological Reports 107(i) and (ii). Very comprehensive treatment of Fengate beakers, following the author's contribution to FNG 3 (pp 234-45); see vol i, pp 97 (America Farm), 151-4; vol ii, pp 383-399.

Hall, D N, 1982
The changing landscape of the Cambridgeshire silt fens, *Landscape History*, 3, 40-49. The paper summarises some of the author's recent work in the Cambs Fen around Wisbech. It also contains many useful references to his other recent work.

Potter, T W and C W, 1982
A Romano-British village at Grandford, March, Cambridgeshire, British Museum Occ Paper 35 (London). Definitive account of an important site which was excavated while still an earthwork. Most exposed Fen sites are now seriously plough-damaged.

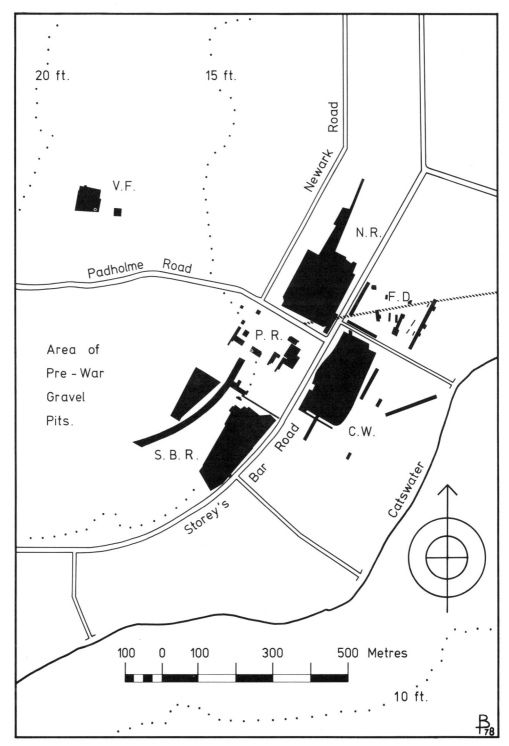

Fig. 3   Areas excavated 1971-78. Key to subsites: VF, Vicarage Farm; NR, Newark Road; FD, Fourth Drove; PR, Padholme Road; CW, Cat's Water; SBR, Storey's Bar Road. The Fen Causeway (Roman road) is shown by a slashed line.

6

CHAPTER 1: THE VICARAGE FARM SUBSITE

1. INTRODUCTION

The Vicarage Farm subsite was excavated in the summer of 1972, immediately in advance of factory building. It has been extensively considered in the First Report (FNG 1, 15-22; 37) that account was confined to a rectangular portion of Area 1 (within the broken line in FIG 5; shaded in FIG M9) and other parts of the subsite were only mentioned in passing. This small area was selected for publication because the majority of non-linear features within it contained early Iron Age pottery of Group 1 types (see Chapter 6 for a detailed discussion of this material).

Six rock-cut pits were shown (FNG 1, FIG 13, features 6, 9, 12, 13, 22 and 26), and it should be noted that the illustrations were made before the introduction of the Nene Valley Research Committee's standard scheme of soil conventions. The detailed textural descriptions provided, however, should allow adequate comparison to be made with the features described in detail below (FNG 1, caption to FIG 13).

The geology of this subsite is more complex than elsewhere at Fengate; Vicarage Farm, Area 1, is the only excavated area with a non-drift subsoil, in this case, the upper Jurassic Cornbrash Limestone overlying Blisworth Clay (discussed in FNG 2, 3). The transition from solid to drift geology is approximately half-way across Area 1, where First Terrace Nene Gravels are superimposed on the limestone (FIG 5). The transitional zone is uneven in width (10-20m) and crosses the excavated area diagonally, from SW-NE (see also FNG 1, PL 2). The gravel forms a thin layer in Area 1, where the deeper features (for example nos 37, 83 etc) penetrate through it, to the limestone beneath. Area II, to the west is, however, entirely formed of gravel and the typical Fengate tripartite soil profile is clearly seen (FIG M6, E; see also FNG 2, Appendix 1; FNG 3, Appendices 2 and 3). A disturbed ploughsoil of varying thickness, with no clearly evident B horizon (as defined in FNG 2, Appendix 1), directly overlay the Cornbrash in Area 1.

A feature-by-feature description (Part 1) of the excavation of Areas I and II has been placed on microfiche. Part II below, is a discussion of these excavations. Features mentioned in this discussion are illustrated in FIG 5 (also FNG 1, FIG 12).

2. DATING AND DISCUSSION
(SEE MICROFICHE PAGES 1-14)

The dating of features within Area I must depend largely on pottery typology, as stratigraphic relationships are few. Only one feature (the large pit F68 at Grid 7E/35N) produced pottery of pre-first millennium BC date, in this case a few weathered scraps of comb-impressed Beaker ware. The only other artifact of first millennium date was a flake of Group VI (Langdale) polished stone, presumably from an axe; this was found with Iron Age pottery in the small pit F10 at Grid 4E/77N (identification by Dr F S Wallis, pers comm). It is most unfortunate that despite their near total excavation, the ditches of the main diagonal drove, together with the related ditches F39 and F21, produced no dateable material. Stratigraphically, they must pre-date ditches F81 and F76 and the upper, tertiary, filling of the large pits F6, F9 and F22. This would suggest that they are earlier than the Iron Age. The spatial arrangement of pits F6, F9 and F22, however, does indicate at least a degree of spatial association, but the absence of domestic debris, so common in the lower layers of the pits, still requires explanation.

The alignment of ditches F14, F17, F21 and F39 is significantly different from that of the main ditched enclosure system of the second millennium and an association seems most doubtful. On the other hand, bearing in mind that the ditches were almost completely excavated, and that Iron Age domestic debris is commonly found on the subsite, the absence of first millennium pottery is very unusual. Factories now cover the subsite, so the problem will never be satisfactorily resolved, but a Neolithic date should not necessarily be ruled out. Early first millennium pottery was found in primary contexts in pits F6 and F26 (FNG 1, FIG 14, nos 1-21; FIG 15, nos 11-12); generally similar pottery was also found in pits F9, F12, F20 and F58 (FNG 1, FIG 14, 22, 26-32; FIG 15, 16-17). This material is considered in detail in Chapter 6, but the radiocarbon date (UB-822) 340+125bc, taken from waterlogged twigs from the layer that yielded the vessel with the wrapped wooden handle (F6, layer 4; FNG 1, FIG 14, no 3), is younger than expected.

Hand made pottery of Iron Age Group 2 type (see Chapter 6) was found in the pits F10 (FNG 1, FIG 14, nos 23-5), F22 (FNG 1, FIG 15, nos 1-10) and, probably, in F84.

Features of the earlier and middle Iron Age are entirely confined within the area studied in detail in the First Report. Outside this area, features tend to be later. Thus wheel-made pottery of Iron Age type (Chapter 6, Group 3) was found in the NE-SW ditch F76, and early Romano-British sherds came from features 36, 37, 77, 81 and 83 (see report by Dr Wild, Chapter 7). The distribution of these later features tends towards the south and east of the area excavated, suggesting, perhaps, a degree of 'settlement drift' (FNG 1, 37) across the subsite during the last millennium BC. Area

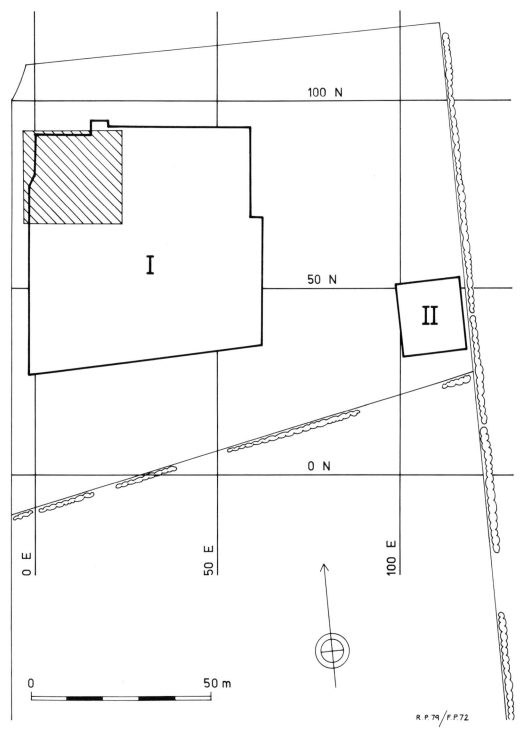

I

II

100 N

50 N

0 N

0 E

50 E

100 E

0   50 m

R.P.79/F.P.72

Fig. 4   Vicarage Farm subsite: plan showing location of excavated areas and subsite Grid. The shaded portion of Area I is published in the First Report, FIG 12.

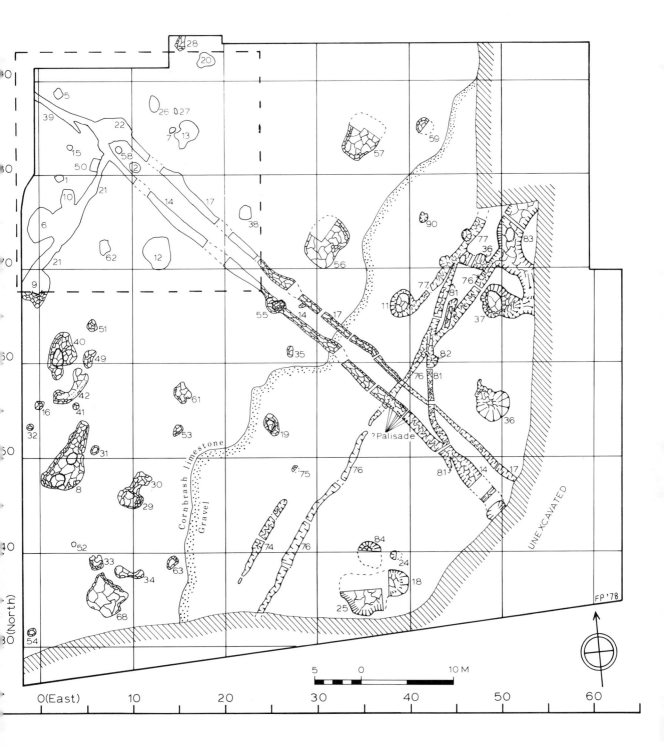

Fig. 5   Vicarage Farm subsite: general plan of Area I. Features outlined, at top left, are shown in detail in the First Report, FIG 12.

II, to the SE, only produced late Iron Age pottery; all the features of this small trench are therefore probably broadly contemporary.

A few points of general interest arise from the Vicarage Farm excavations. First, laying aside the question of the date of the two ditches which cross Area 1 from NW-SE, there is no good evidence for extensive occupation prior to the first millennium BC. Second, the 'settlement drift', referred to above, indicates some continuity of settlement and land use; long periods of abandonment would seem, on the whole, improbable.

Third, the limited excavations of Area II provide grounds for believing that the rectilinear ditched enclosures to the S and E of the area excavated, are of later Iron Age date. The shift 'inland', away from the peat Fens, perhaps to ground not previously exploited (although the use of the subsite for grazing cannot be discounted), in the early part of the first millennium, is consistent with the general explanation of land-use advanced here (Chapter 8) and in the Third Report (Chapter 5).

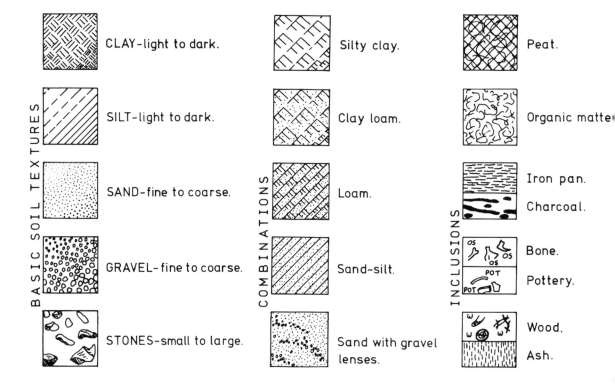

Fig. 6   Conventions used in the section drawings.

CHAPTER 2: THE PADHOLME ROAD SUBSITE

1. INTRODUCTION

The Padholme Road subsite was excavated in the first two seasons of the project (1971-2); much of this material has, therefore, been described in the First Report (FNG 1, 22-29). This chapter will consider the remaining material, which is of Iron Age date, and a brief discussion (Part II) of all periods will follow the detailed description (Part I) which has been placed on microfiche (pages 15-20).

2. DISCUSSION (SEE MICROFICHE PAGES 15-20)

Area XI (FIG M7; FNG 1, FIG 17)

This Area was placed near the centre of the subsite, where it was hoped to locate the second millennium ditches 3 and 4. Ditch 3 was located at the southern part of the Area and is discussed in the Third Report, chapter 1; ditch 4 terminated in Area VII, to the NW. The northern part of the trench exposed the corner of a large Iron Age back-filled pit, and the excavation was enlarged to reveal two pits, a well (F3) and a large quarry pit (F1) which had been filled-in with gravel and domestic rubbish; the well deposits contained sherds which joined with those from the large pit, and clearly had accumulated after the latter had been completely filled-in. The well and its filling are described in the First Report (pp 22-29).

Area XII (FIGS M8-M10; PL 4)

1. The 'Pit Complex'

This Area was located immediately NE of Area XIII (FIG 7) in the hope of revealing further earlier Neolithic features, which it failed to do. A large Iron Age 'pit complex' was, however, found (FIG M9, b) and excavated. The 'pit complex' filling was somewhat darker and less stony than the silts and gravels of the natural subsoil, but individual features within it could not be differentiated from the stripped surface. The irregular plan of the complex strongly indicated that more than one feature/period was involved, and as time and resources would not permit the upper layers of filling to be removed in hand-trowelled arbitrary levels, it was decided to subdivide the complex into numbered arbitrary 'features' on the basis of slight soil colour changes, and other largely intuitive criteria. These 'features' are shown in FIG M9, which also indicates the lines of the sections described in greater detail below (FIG M10). In general the intuitive placing of the section lines seems to have been successful, as a comparison of the section drawings (FIG M10) with the two plans (FIGS M8-M9) will attest.

Pottery from the pit complex was all in the mid-Iron Age 'scored ware' tradition and there was no wheel-thrown pottery (Chapter 6); this, together with the homogeneity of the fillings of the features comprising the pit complex, tends to suggest that the complex was in use at more or less the same time. There are no obvious signs of re-use of the pit complex after its final abandonment, nor are there clear indications that any of the material found filling the features had been deliberately dumped in. The two largest, deepest, pits (FIG M8, A and B) are probably wells as they extended below the modern (1972) water table in the lower 0.4m, or so, of their primary filling. Both these features, at a point *c* 1m below the stripped surface, where their plans could be appreciated undisturbed by shallower features of the pit complex, had the steep-sided, approximately circular plan of known wells (eg FNG 1, FIG 17, F3). Much decayed remnants of the upright of a wooden lining in the pit provide support for this hypothesis.

The function of other features belonging to the complex must remain obscure and it is by no means certain whether the other 'features' are, indeed, man-made. Perhaps the 'pit complex' represents the much truncated remains of a once undulating land surface, rich in settlement debris which had accumulated while people and/or animals had gathered around the well(s). The subsoil in this part of the subsite was noticeably soft and drained poorly after rain, and it is not entirely improbable that the undulations formed as the result of trampling. This interpretation would accord best with the stratigraphy which does not show the probable wells either to have been covered by, or cut through, the sand-silts of the shallower 'pit complex' features; it would also account for the way in which certain edges of the pit complex were impossible to define accurately (eg around Features 7, 10 and 35 (FIG M9). This 'feathering out' effect would be the expected pattern on the periphery of deeply trampled areas.

2. Isolated Features (FIG M9)

A group of seven very small pits or postholes was located E and SE of the 'pit complex', and is probably associated in some way with it, despite the fact that dating evidence was not found. The circular, shallow, dished feature F26/11/16, around which cluster the postholes F13-15, also revealed no dating evidence. With the exception of the latter larger pit, which had a pale filling, most of the small pits or postholes had fillings somewhat darker than those associated with the earlier Neolithic house of Area XIII. It has frequently been observed that paler fillings are often earlier than darker fillings (a point briefly discussed in Pryor 1976b) and this would tend to suggest that the pits described below are, in fact, post-Neolithic; given their location, an Iron Age date would seem appropriate.

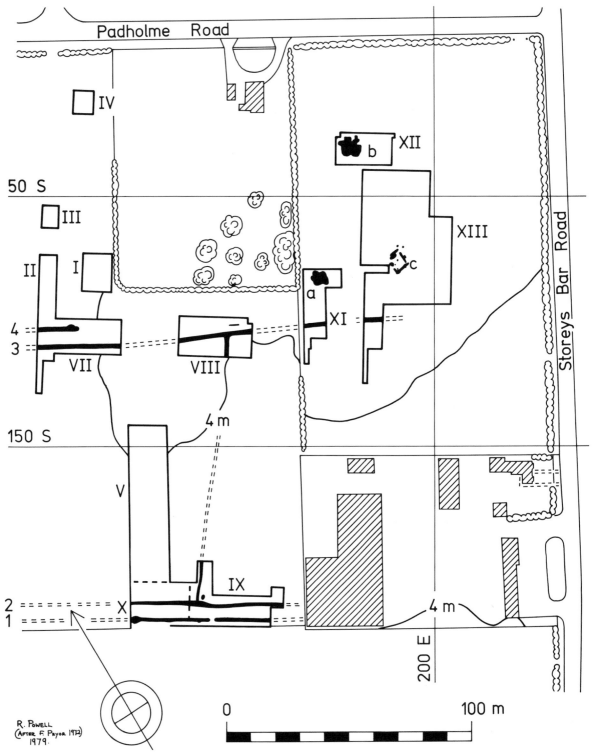

Padholme Road

50 S

150 S

Storeys Bar Road

IV

XII

b

III

XIII

II   I

a

c

4
3

XI

VII   VIII

4 m

V

IX

2
1

X

4 m

200 E

R. POWELL
(AFTER F. PRYOR 1972)
1979.

0   100 m

Fig. 7   Padholme Road subsite, summary plan showing principal excavated features. Second millennium ('Bronze Age') ditches are numbered; other features are: a, b, Iron Age pits; c, the earlier Neolithic house.

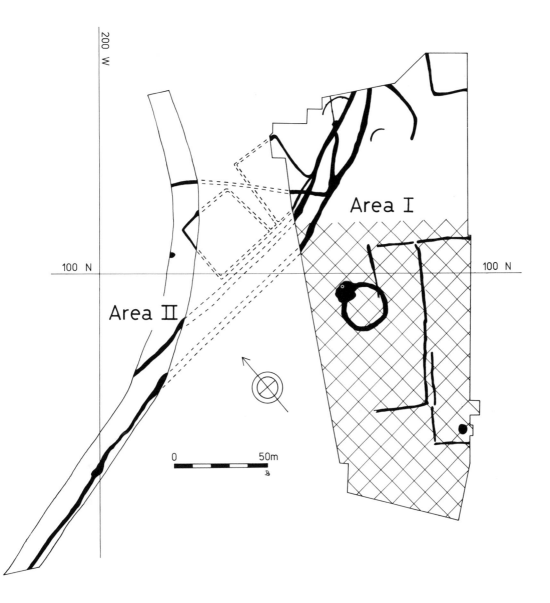

Fig. 8   Storey's Bar Road subsite, Areas I and II: plan of principal excavated features. Features in cross-hatched areas are mainly of Late Neolithic date and are described in the Second Report (FNG 2: chapter 2).

Fig. 9   Storey's Bar Road subsite, Area I, northern part: general plan showing extent of excavated features (in black).

INTRODUCTION AND SUMMARY
(SEE MICROFICHE PAGES 21-38)

The Storey's Bar Road subsite was excavated in three seasons. Area II was excavated in 1971 as a southerly extension of Padholme Road subsite Area V/X (FIG 7). Its gently curving plan was to anticipate the course of what is today the Newark Road Extension south of Padholme Road. Area I was excavated in 1973 and 1974. The former season saw the stripping and cleaning of Area I between Grid 0N and 120N; the latter season completed the remaining area (FNG 2 FIG 6). Occupation on the subsite is represented by a number of quite clearly defined groups of features,

1. Late third and second millennia BC. These features can be further sub-divided into two groups:

  a) Features associated with the large ring-ditch and rectilinear enclosures described at length in the Second Report. These are almost entirely confined within the 1973 excavation limits (Grid 0 to 120N) in Area I, and need not be considered any further here.

  b) Two possible second millennium BC ditches in the northern part of Area I (FIG 10, N1 and P18) and a possible extension in Area II (FIG 12, R1; see FIG 8 for a suggested alignment).

2. A possible Early Iron Age ditch in the northern part of Area I (FIG 10, N19).

3. Later Iron Age features fall into two groups,

  a) Structures 1 and 2 at the north end of Area I (FIGS 9 and 10). These structures are considered in their wider contexts in the general discussions of Iron Age buildings, Chapters 4 and 8 below.

  b) Two sub-rectangular ditched enclosures, that to the west being defined by Area II feature R2 (FIG 12) and that to the east by Area I features P28 and P17 (FIG 10). The possible relationship of the two enclosures is shown in FIG 8 by broken lines (based on aerial photographs).

4. A second century Romano-British droveway defined in Area II by ditches R4 and R5 (FIG 12) and in Area I by ditches P12 and P13 (FIG 10). The alignment of the two Romano-British drove ditches between Areas I and II (FIG 8) showed more clearly on the aerial photographs than the two sub-rectangular Iron Age ditched enclosures just mentioned. This was almost certainly due to the thick accumulations of third century AD flood clays in the upper levels of the Roman ditches, a deposit that was not encountered in the Iron Age ditches. Detailed descriptions of the various features that comprise these four groups may be found in Part II, on microfiche (pages 21-38).

CHAPTER 4: THE CAT'S WATER SUBSITE

INTRODUCTION

The Cat's Water subsite (for location see FIG 3) contained the most complex palimpsest of settlement and funerary features yet found at Fengate. Most later prehistoric periods are represented on the subsite and

will be described under the following phase headings:
1. Earlier Neolithic
2. Second Millennium BC (Late Neolithic and Early/ Middle Bronze Age)
3. The Iron Age and Romano-British settlement
The Grid is aligned along the Ordnance Survey North,

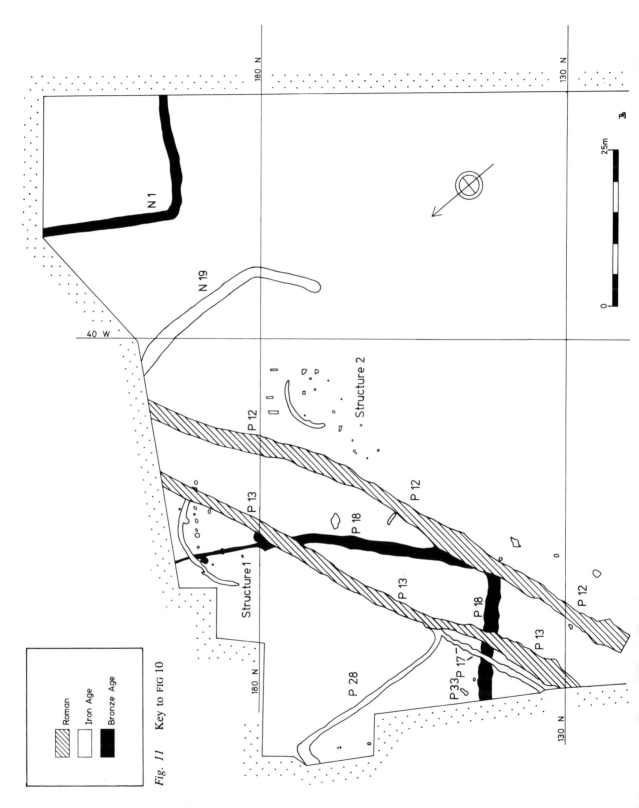

Fig. 11   Key to FIG 10

N 1

N 19

40 W

180 N

130 N

180 N

130 N

P 12

Structure 2

P 13

P 18

P 12

Structure 1

P 13

P 18

P 12

P 28

P 13

P33 P 17

25m

0

Roman
Iron Age
Bronze Age

16

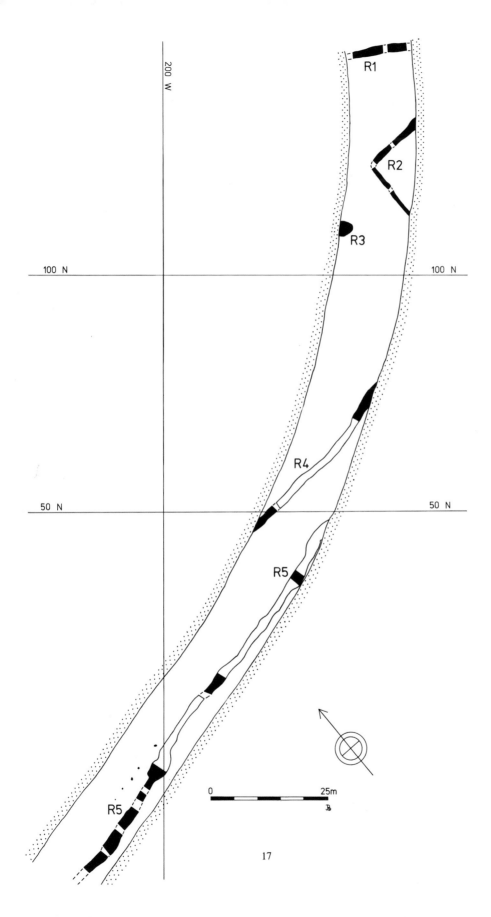

Fig. 12 Storey's Bar Road subsite, Area II: general plan showing extent of excavated features (in black).

17

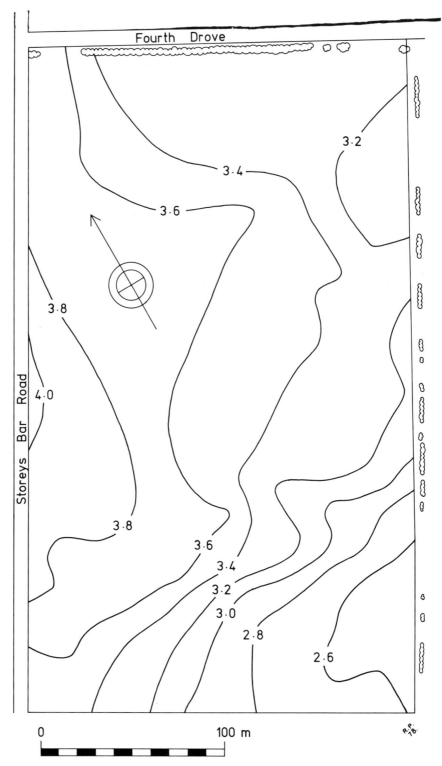

Fig. 13   Cat's Water subsite: surface contours in metres above OD.

and Cat's Water Grid References are given in metres west and north. The Grid is shown in FIGS 16 and 18.

The detailed descriptive passages that follow are best understood if the general sequence of events is first outlined in very general terms. The earliest evidence for occupation on the subsite is provided by a multiple burial which probably dates to the third millennium BC. This burial could possibly be associated with the earlier Neolithic house of the Padholme Road subsite nearby (see FNG 1, 6ff; also this volume Chapter 2 and FIG 7). Good evidence for Late Neolithic occupation — in the form of Peterborough or Grooved Wares — is lacking, but this may well be due to the continued use of features throughout the second millennium BC, for this is the period which sees the construction and use of the main ditched enclosure system described at length in the Third Report. The Cat's Water subsite contains many ditches of this system and at least one structure (46) can be related to it with some confidence.

The ditched enclosures of the second millennium system were abandoned at the start of the first millennium. This period, the early first millennium, sees only slight occupation on the subsite, although this, again, may be a false impression caused by the continued use of earlier features, such as drainage ditches. Neither the earlier first millennium features, nor those of the large later Iron Age settlement which follows, respect the layout of the second millennium ditch system. The main period of occupation appears to have been in the latter three (or four) centuries prior to the Roman conquest when the subsite was the scene of a substantial community. The features of this large settlement fall into two general phases: an earlier period characterised by pottery in the middle/later Iron Age 'scored ware' tradition, and a later period which sees the first use of wheel-made wares. The subsite then appears to have been abandoned at a time roughly coincident with the Roman Conquest (and an association of the two events seems improbable) before being re-occupied, briefly, in the latter half of the second century AD. Finally, the Cat's Water subsite, in common with all of Fengate below the 15-foot contour, was not occupied on a permanent basis during Late Roman, Saxon or Medieval times and it was not until the wide-spread Fen drainage work of the seventeenth and eighteenth centuries that year-round settlement again became possible.

1. THE NEOLITHIC MULTIPLE BURIAL
(FIG 19; PLS 12-13)

Description
The only feature that can be dated to this period with any confidence is the multiple burial, feature 1283 at Grid 426W/695N. This large oval pit (length 4.0m; breadth 2.0m; depth 0.60m) was cut by the late Iron Age ditch F1267. The filling of the grave pit was of homogeneous sand-silt with very few scattered gravel pebbles (c10YR 3/3) and there were no traces of rapid silting; the grave had, presumably, been filled-in (largely with topsoil) shortly after being dug. This would argue against the pit having been originally dug for some other, non-funerary, purpose).

The large pit contained the bones of four individuals which lay on the clean subsoil of its flat bottom. Body 1 was an adult male, aged 25-30 years; he was buried in the crouched position and lay on his right side, with his head to the SW (see FIG 19 for a plan of the burials). Body 2 lay immediately NE of Body 1 and consisted of the much disintegrated bones of an infant aged between 3-4 years. Bodies 3 and 4 lay immediately NE of the infant; these largely disarticulated and semi-disarticulated bones could be seen to come from at least two individuals: a female aged 25-30 years, and a child of some 8-12 years. Mr C B Denston's report on the skeletal remains appears below as Appendix 8.

The dating of the grave group depends on Stephen Green's detailed consideration of the leaf-shaped flint arrowhead which was found lodged between the 8th and 9th ribs of Body 1. If it is assumed that this arrowhead was the cause of Body's 1 death and that it was not a re-used or residual item, then Dr Green's study (which appears immediately below) would suggest a Neolithic date for the grave group as a whole. Such a date would be entirely consistent with the pale colour of the grave's filling and the limited stratigraphic evidence — the fact that the filled-in grave was cut by an Iron Age ditch.

The leaf arrowhead from the burial
group in Cat's Water F1283
by Dr H Stephen Green

The arrowhead falls into my type 4C (Green 1980) which is characterized by small slender leaf arrowheads. No particular chronological position or cultural affinity may be recognized for leaf arrowheads of this type beyond a dating somewhere between the beginning of the Neolithic and the end of the Middle Bronze Age. However, the placing of leaf arrowheads with inhumation burials, often disarticulated, is characteristic of the Towthorpe tradition burials of northern England (Green 1980). On present evidence, these seem to date between around 3,000 and 1,500 bc.

The interpretation of the arrowhead as the cause of death is dependent on the excavator's evidence of its precise position in the skeleton. Instances of injuries from leaf (or probable leaf) arrowheads are rare in Britain and one may point with confidence only to the chamber tombs of Ascott-under-Wychwood (Oxon)(1) and Tulloch of Assery B (Caithness)(2). Analysis of the position of leaf arrowheads with articulated inhumations indicates that where arrowheads were placed as grave offerings they may occur in proximity to any part of the

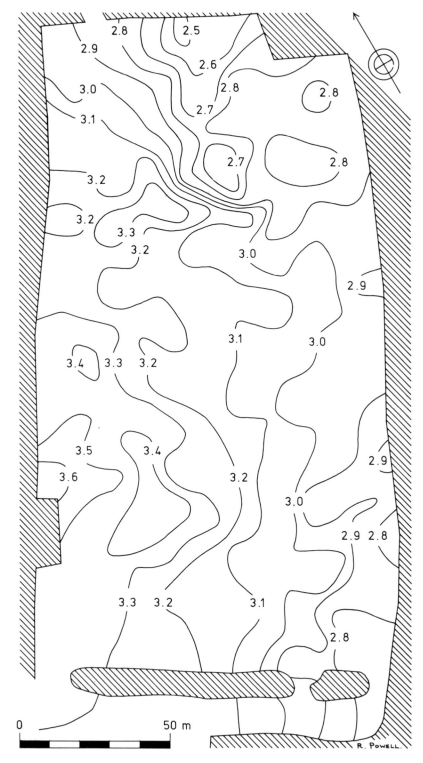

Fig. 14 Cat's Water subsite, main area: contours of stripped surface in metres above OD.

20

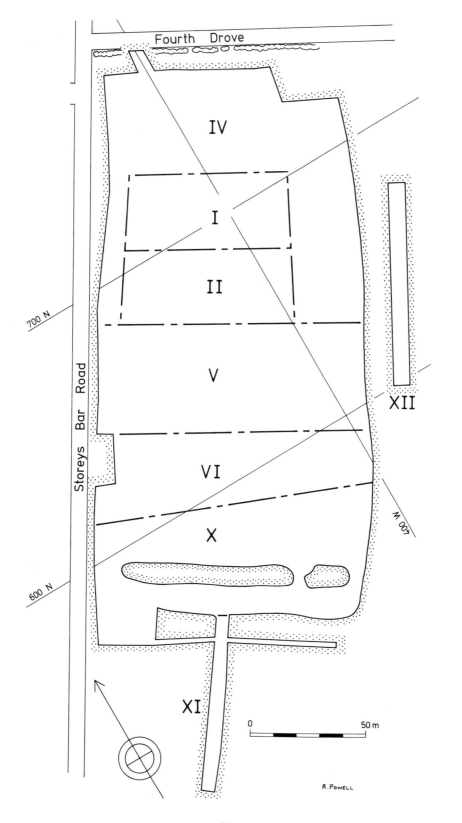

Fig. 15   Cat's Water subsite: location of excavated areas (Roman numerals).

21

trunk of the body and that no 'preferred situation' can be inferred (Table 1). This picture is complicated by the possibility that the arrowheads tabulated may not all have been grave goods but may rather have been the cause of death in some instances, as here. Piggott (1962, 25) has suggested this in the case of the arrowhead found at the neck of a skeleton in the West Kennet long barrow (Wiltshire). The fact that this skeleton (Burial ii) also preserved possible evidence of an earlier healed wound might lend support to such an interpretation, although Brothwell (1967, 342) has suggested that a tumour may have been responsible for the apparent injury.

Significance
The small number of instances of certain or probable death from leaf arrowhead wounds can hardly lead directly to inferences on the importance of warfare in the British Neolithic. However, the limited evidence for hunting is worth restating (I F Smith 1974, 104) and some recent suggestions of the importance of leaf arrowheads in hunting are capable of alternative interpretation(3). The Fengate find goes some way to supporting Case's (1970, 111) suggestion of the importance of warfare among 'stably adjusted Neolithic communities' in Britain. This suggestion has recently found some direct support from evidence of an attack, using arrows, at Crickley Hill causewayed camp (Gloucestershire)(4).

Discussion
The burial is of interest for a number of reasons, some of which have already been discussed in a short note (Pryor 1976b). First, the arrowhead was only revealed once the removal of the bones had begun. It was found sealed beneath much-decayed pieces of sternum which had collapsed across the ribs of the body's right side. Its use as a pendant or as an accompanying piece of grave furniture can therefore probably be discounted. Second, the grave pit lay beneath a temporary NE-SW baulk and there was no evidence in the section for a significant-sized mound or barrow, nor was there a contemporary ring-ditch or quarry-pit in the vicinity. The bodies had been buried in a simple, apparently unmarked, communal grave.

Turning to the interpretation of the intermixed bones of Bodies 3 and 4, two explanations seem possible. The first, and perhaps least attractive, is that Bodies 3 and 4 had been laid out for some time before they were pushed to one end of the pit to make room for Bodies 1 and 2. There are two objections to this hypothesis. Had the bodies been allowed to rest for any length of time, rapid silts would have accumulated around and even over them; this, however, did not happen: the homogeneous sand-silt of the gravel filling lay directly over the bones and grave bottom and walls, with no intervening 'rapid' deposits. Further, had Bodies 3 and 4 been pushed to one side, it is probable that a few bones would have escaped notice and these would now be found with Bodies 1 and 2; it is also probable that more bones would have survived than were actually found and that parts of the body — the head or feet — could have remained in the position in which they were originally buried. At this point it should be emphasised that disturbance caused by recutting of the grave is improbable (a) because of the pit's even plan and uniform flat bottom and (b) because of the extremely uniform nature of the grave filling, which showed no evidence for re-digging.

The alternative explanation for the presence and state of Bodies 3 and 4 is that they had either been buried or exposed elsewhere before they were placed in the same grave as Body 1, probably shortly after the latter's death. This hypothesis explains the neat arrangement of the four bodies in the grave and does not conflict with stratigraphic evidence.

Finally, it is perhaps of some interest to note that, despite a most careful search which included the use of ½ inch sieves, only one broken flint flake was found in the grave filling. No other finds were encountered and charcoal was extremely scarce. This suggests that the site selected for the grave was removed from areas of settlement. The use of unmarked graves placed away from habitation sites might help account for the otherwise remarkable absence of Neolithic burials in East Anglia (a problem recently discussed by Whittle (1977, 218-9).

Notes
1. Site number 173 in Green (1977). I am indebted to Don Benson for access to the Ascott-under-Wychwood material
2. *Proceedings of the Society of Antiquaries of Scotland*, 98, 1964-6, 44 and plate XIV
3. For example, Coles and Hibbert (in Fowler, P J (ed) *Recent Work in Rural Archaeology*, 1975, 16-17) suggest that the probable presence in antiquity of plentiful fish and wildfowl in the Somerset Levels, combined with discoveries of flint arrowheads and wooden bowls, 'must point to a great interest in hunting food of this kind'. However, one might suggest, with as little direct evidence, that the bows and arrows relate to disputes over the use of the Somerset moors for intercommoning animals and to conflict over land and food resources during the wet season or over the first use of the rich grazing of the 'hangings' as the flood waters began to subside.
4. *The Times* newspaper, December 7th, 1977.

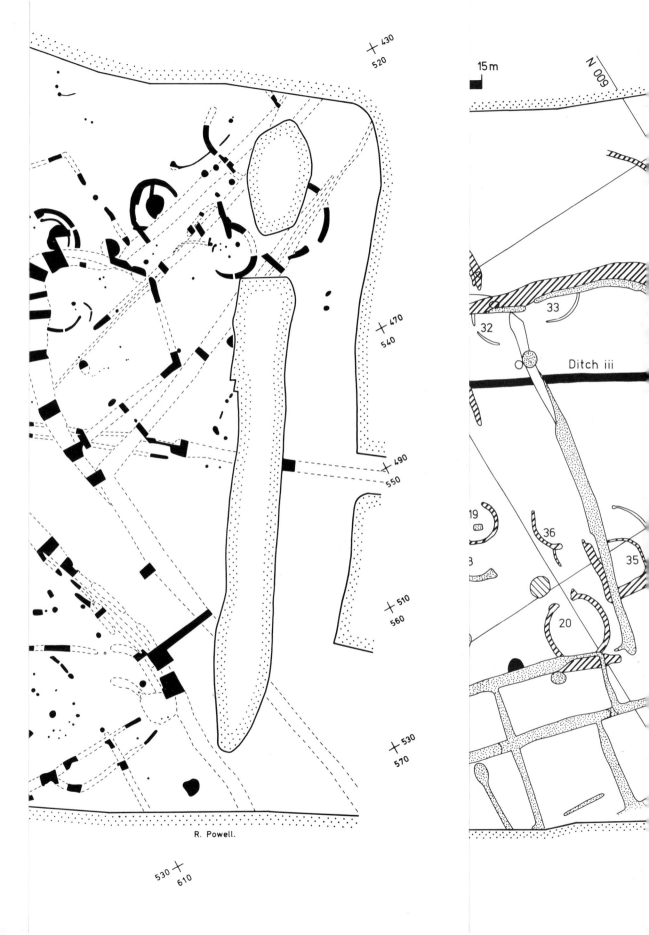

15 m

N 600

+ 430
520

+ 470
540

+ 490
550

+ 510
560

+ 530
570

530 +
610

R. Powell.

33

32

Ditch iii

19

36

35

20

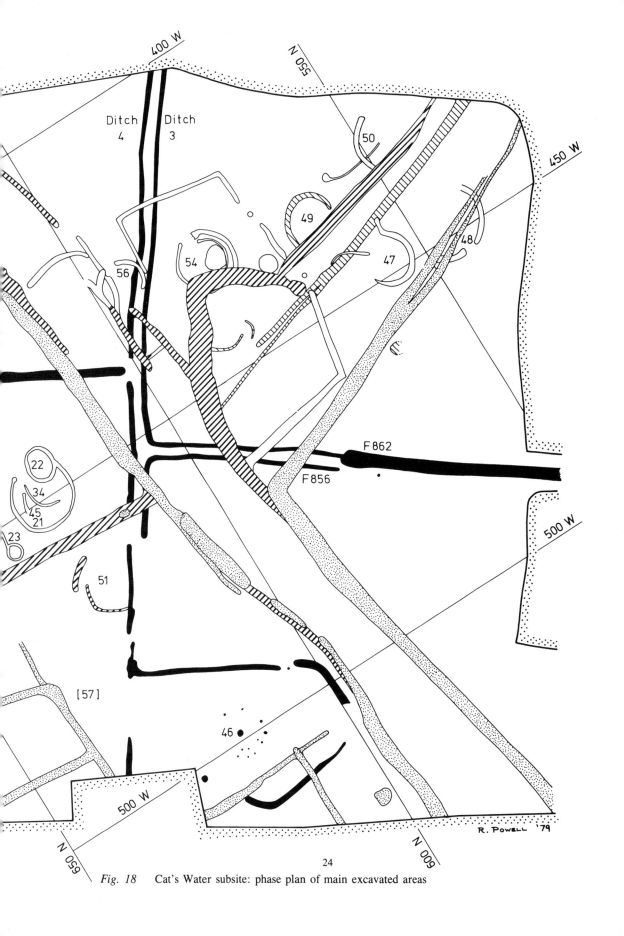

400 W

N 550

Ditch 4

Ditch 3

50

450 W

49

48

54

47

56

F 862

F 856

500 W

22

34

45
21

23

51

500 W

[57]

46

650 N

600 N

R. POWELL '79

24

Fig. 18   Cat's Water subsite: phase plan of main excavated areas

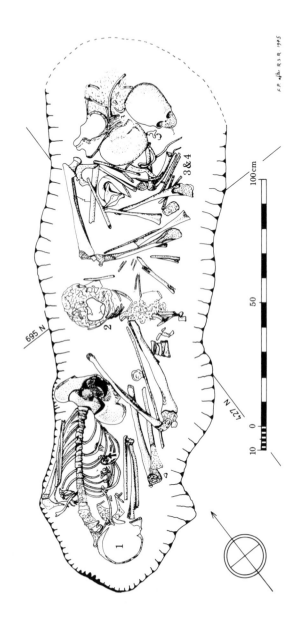

Fig. 19 Cat's Water subsite: earlier Neolithic multiple burial, F1283 (Grid 426W/695N).

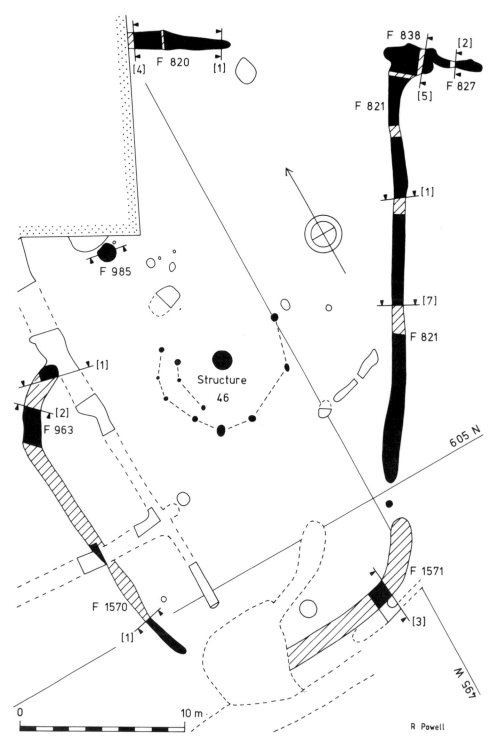

Fig. 20 Cat's Water subsite: probable second millennium BC features associated with Structure 46 and its enclosure. Later features are indicated by dashed lines; second millennium features are hatched; excavated second millennium features are shown in black.

TABLE 1.
The positions of leaf arrowheads with articulated inhumations from British Neolithic/Bronze Age burials

	In front of	In or on	Behind	Near	Totals
Skull				3	3
Neck	1				1
Shoulders			2	2	4
Ribs	1	3			4
Pelvis		1	2		3
Knees				1	1
Foot				1	1
Hand				1	1
Totals	2	4	4	8	18

2. FEATURES OF SECOND MILLENNIUM BC DATE
(FIGS 20; M23 TO M32)
(SEE MICROFICHE PAGES 39-52)

Introduction
Features of probable second millennium date will be considered under three headings: structural; linear; non-linear. The non-linear features cannot be associated with the main second millennium ditched enclosure system (described at length in the Third Report), by vertical or horizontal stratigraphy and are dated to this period on the basis of material found in their fillings. The linear features, on the other hand, are ditches which can clearly be seen to form an integral part of the larger enclosure system. Finally, the finds are considered in detail in Chapter 5, below. In view of the extended treatment accorded to the second millennium BC ditched enclosures in the Third Report, those of the Cat's Water subsite are described in detail on microfiche (for a general account see FNG 3, chapter 4). The enclosed post-built round-building, Structure 46, is, however, of sufficient interest to warrant description in the text. Sections through the enclosure ditch are considered on fiche, together with non-linear features of probable second millennium date.

Structural and Associated Features (FIGS 20; M23-M24)
Structure 46 was a post-built round building located at Grid 500W/605N, *c* 15m SE of ditch 4 (FIGS 18; 20). The building itself was considered in detail in the Third Report (FNG 3, FIGS 94-96) and an outline plan is given here (FIG 20). It was composed of two concentric rings of posts (dia 7.2 and 5.0m), the outer one of which survived for over two thirds of its circumference. A very shallow circular pit or depression was located in the centre of the building, and none of the postholes showed evidence for recutting or replacement. This report will be mainly concerned with the ditches of the small enclosure in which the building stood.

The ditches which enclosed Structure 46 formed a roughly oval enclosure to the SE of the discontinuous alignment of ditch 4, discussed above. The ditch 4 alignment is here represented by features 820, 827 and 838 (FIG 20). The enclosure ditches are laid out in three

quite distinct lengths, separated by entranceways of varying width. The main NE-SW ditch, F821, curves round at its NE end to meet F838 and both features appear to have filled-in at the same time (FIG M23, bottom). The SE side of the enclosure is broached by an entranceway at Grid 495W/605N between ditch F821 and F1571; this gap is 2m wide (the posthole midway between the two ditch butt-ends is Iron Age). Ditch F1571 was much disturbed by Iron Age and Roman activity and its westerly termination has been lost. There is, however, another entranceway between F1571 and feature 1570/963 which forms the south-westerly side of the enclosure. The north end of this ditch was found to have a clear rounded butt-end beneath the Romano-British yard ditch which cuts it. This area was unfortunately much disturbed by modern sewer construction, but nonetheless there was no evidence for a substantial ditch which could have linked the ditch just described with F820, in order to complete the enclosure. The shallow pit, 985, is on the correct alignment and was filled with suitably pale sand-silt (later features in this area have noticeably darker fillings, often with a high clay content) and could, perhaps implausibly, be seen as a boundary feature. It should, once again, be stressed that this was a severely disturbed area in which perhaps 0.3m of C soil horizon had been lost through recent activity.

3. THE IRON AGE AND ROMANO-BRITISH SETTLEMENT

Introduction
The features of this long-lived settlement occupied the greater part of the main excavated area on Cat's Water. The limits of the settlement have generally been satisfactorily determined. The northern edge appears to be defined by a number of Iron Age ditches which run approximately parallel to, and south-west of the second millennium ditch 5. A long trench (FNG 3, FIG 78, Area I) immediately NE of the Fourth Drove, which separates the Fourth Drove and Cat's Water subsites, proved to be largely sterile, and the true northern edge of the settlement appears to have been satisfactorily located, as Area XII (FIG 15) was also largely sterile. The south-western limit is established by excavation in Areas X and XI, and only the north-western limit remains unproven. The excavation of a modern sewer trench along the NW edge of Storey's Bar Road, on the Padholme Road subsite proved to be sterile, and although Iron Age features were located at the centre of that subsite they are separated from the Cat's Water settlement by at least 60m of clear ground (much of it stripped, as for example Padholme Road Area XII; FIG 7). They are unlikely, therefore, to have formed part of the main Cat's Water settlement. The general spread of Iron Age structures on the western edge of the settlement is approximately N-S, and of these only perhaps Structures 4, 14 and 15 suggest, by their

location, that the settlement may have once continued further to the NW. Bearing in mind that the extreme SE corner of the nearby Newark Road subsite was extensively excavated, it does not appear probable that Iron Age structures belonging to the Cat's Water settlement ever extended appreciably to the NW of Storey's Bar Road. Perhaps the remains of about 1-5 buildings were destroyed when the modern road was built.

The Cat's Water settlement thus represents a virtually complete dwelling site of considerable importance, and the discussion that follows is necessarily complex. It falls into two parts. Part I is devoted to a detailed description of the excavations; features will be described, as above, in three groups: structures; linear features; non-linear features. Part II will be given over to a discussion of the function and phasing of the various features. Discussion of broader issues will be reserved for Chapter 8.

The most important aspect of the Cat's Water settlement is the functional analysis of the structures, which are described in the text, complete with plans and finds' distributions (part 1). In common with practice elsewhere in this report (see Introduction), sections are generally placed on microfiche; similarly sections and detailed plans of linear features (part 2) and some non-linear features (part 3) are also placed on fiche; burials have been treated in the text.

I THE EXCAVATIONS

1. STRUCTURES
(SEE MICROFICHE PAGES 53-114)

Introduction
The structures described below appear in numerical order. The numbering follows, in part, the typological classification discussed briefly in the Interim Report (Pryor and Cranstone 1978, 18-24). It is intended for ease of reference only and has no functional or chrono-logical significance. The position of each structure is shown in FIG 18. Special attention is paid to the fillings of structural features which may be expected to offer clues as to the original function of the features in question. Thus, the presence or absence of clay, char-coal, burnt stones is of some importance, as is the presence/absence of 'rapid' silting or tip lines. Descriptions of structural features, and particularly their filling, will, therefore, be more detailed than those of isolated non-linear features and main drainage ditches.

Section numbers, as was noted above, are those given in the field. Field drawing numbers selected for illust-ration are indicated in square brackets and the section lines chosen are shown on relevant structure plans, but not on finds distribution plans.

Structure 1
Plan (FIG 22, right): A round building centred on Grid 423W/717N. Consists of a ring-gully, F1056, dia *c* 7.0m; near central roof-support posthole. F1057; single door posthole, F1064.

Relations/phasing: The ring-gully cuts the nearby drainage ditch F1084 which is, in turn, an early phase of the main drainage ditch F1006 (Late Iron Age). Pottery and stratigraphy suggest that Structure 1 is of Middle Iron Age date, ie earlier than F1006.

Finds distribution (FIG 23): Although a fairly substantial feature, the ring-gully produced few finds, in marked distinction to the main drainage ditches of the Middle and Late Iron Age nearby. There is no obvious explanation for this unusual distribution.

Structure 2
Plan (FIG 24, left): A round building centred on Grid 374W/660N. Consists of a ring-gully (F131), dia *c* 8.0m. and no clear internal features (although two possible door postholes were seen briefly during the wet weather after excavation — *cf* Structure 8, FIG 24). Two slightly offset pits outside the entranceway, F472 and F476, may be associated with a porch. The scatter of pits shown outside the structure itself clearly respects its existence and may well be contemporary with it.

Relations/phasing: Pottery was all of Middle Iron Age type and its location near the well dated Structures 3 and 8 would support this impression. Its size and orientation are almost identical to that of Structure 8, to the north.

Finds distribution (FIG 25, left): Two points of interest emerge, first, the slight concentration of pottery around the entranceway; second the presence, to the NW, of flints in both F781 (a pit) and the ring-gully. No flints occur around the building's doorway; this suggests that the flints derive from an earlier feature which has contributed to the filling of the ring-gully and F781/797. The lack of finds from the suggested porch postholes, F472 and F476, perhaps implies that they are not contemporary with the building at all.

Structure 3
Plan (FIG 26): A round building, centred on Grid 375W/673N, enclosed within an approximately circular (dia 15.5m) ditched enclosure. The principal structural ring-gully, F82, has a diameter of *c* 9.5m. A number of postholes are distributed within the ring-ditch interior; these do not appear to form a coherent pattern, with the obvious exceptions of the four-post internal porch defined by features 117, 118, 119 and 122; features 120, 121 and 197 could, perhaps be seen to form an aisle or 'corridor' leading towards the clay-lined central pit F152. This feature had been deliberately lined with unfired blue clay and is best interpreted as a small water container, perhaps akin to a modern sink or basin. The four-post porch is marked by a gap in the ring-gully to the SW. The enclosure ditch plan clearly shows evidence for several phases of recutting, only one of

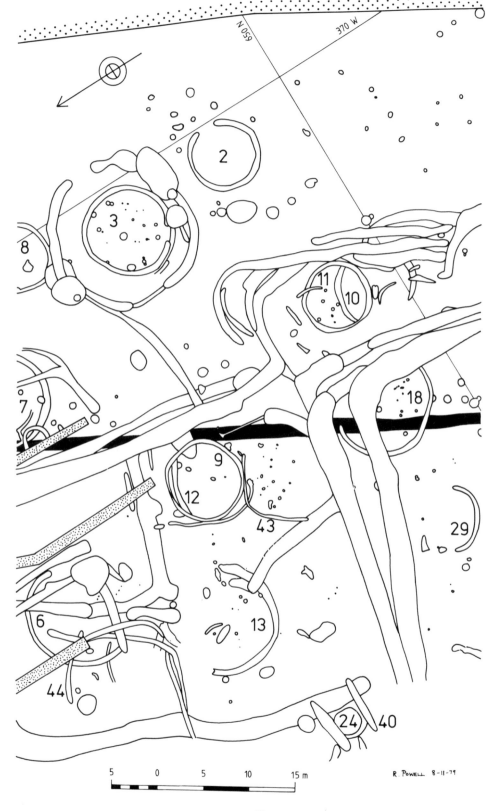

Fig. 21 Cat's Water subsite: plan showing stratigraphic relationship of features in the east-central settlement area. Second millennium ditch iii in black; baulks stippled.

N 059

370 W

2

3

8

11

10

7

18

9

12

43

29

6

13

44

24

40

5   0   5   10   15 m

R. POWELL 8-11-79

29

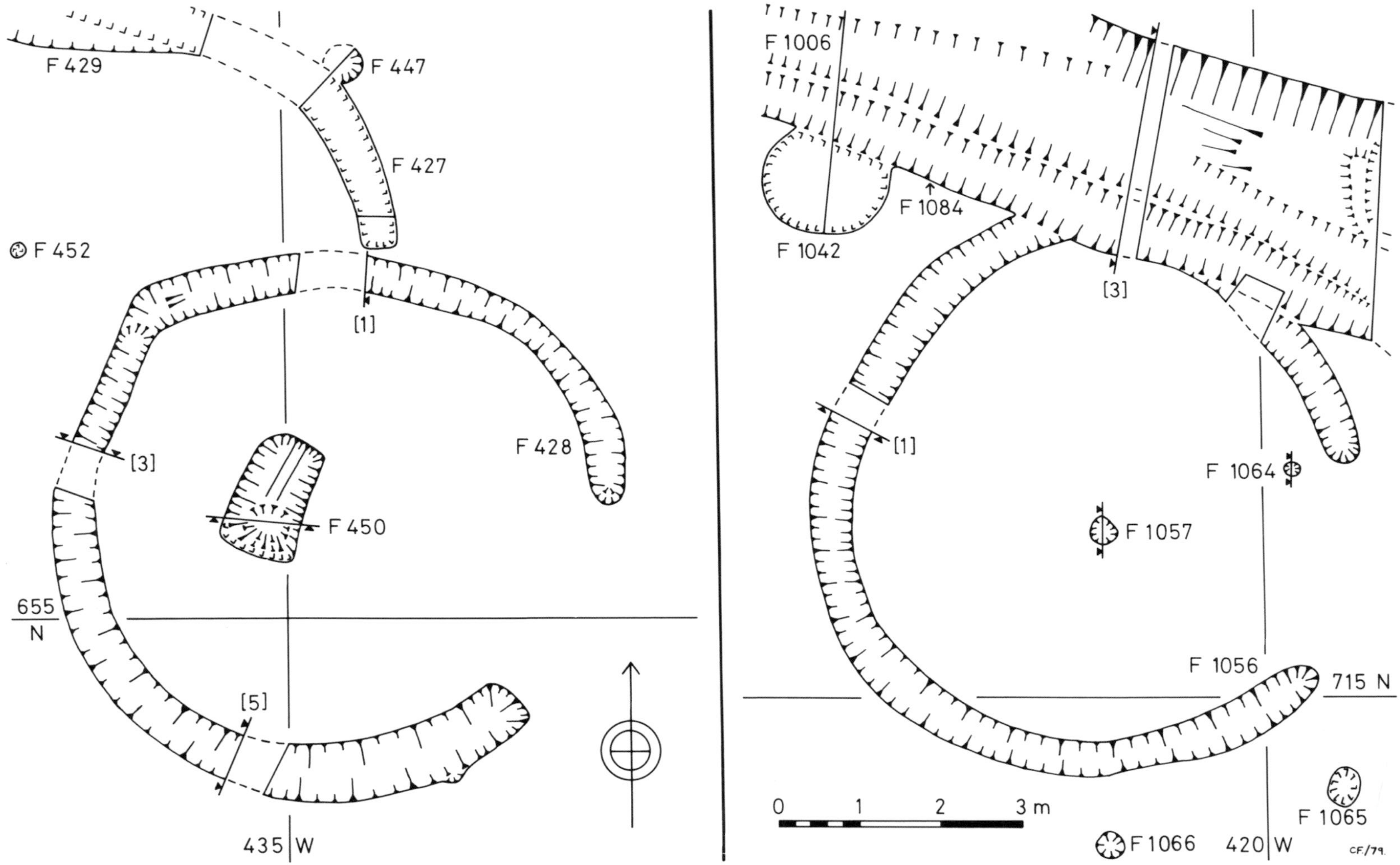

Fig. 22 Cat's Water subsite: Structures 19 (left) and 1 (right).

30

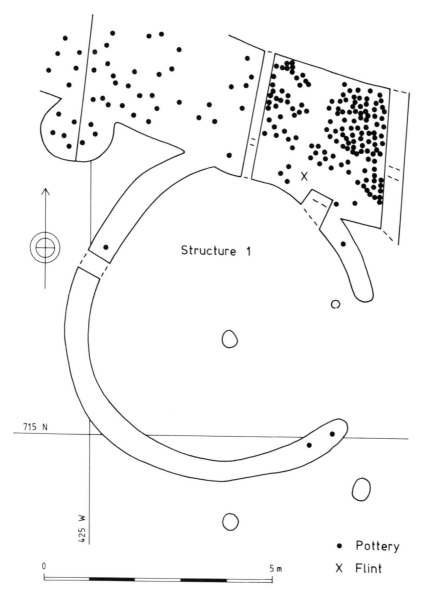

715 N

425 W

Structure 1

0   5 m

• Pottery

X Flint

R. POWELL.

Fig. 23   Cat's Water subsite: Structure 1, finds distribution.

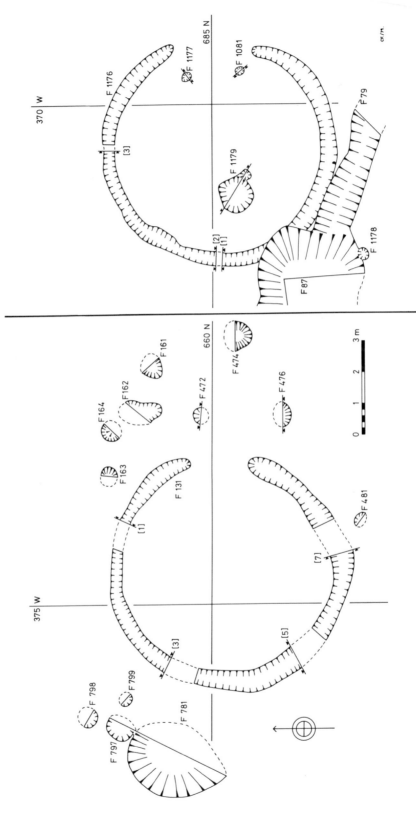

685 N

370 W

F 1176

[3]

F 1177

F 1081

F 1179

F 79

[2]
[1]

F 87

F 1178

660 N

F 161

F 162

F 164

F 474

F 472

F 476

375 W

F 163

F 131

[1]

F 481

[7]

[3]

[5]

F 798

F 799

F 797

F 781

0   1   2   3 m

Fig. 24   Cat's Water subsite: Structures 2 (left) and 8.

32

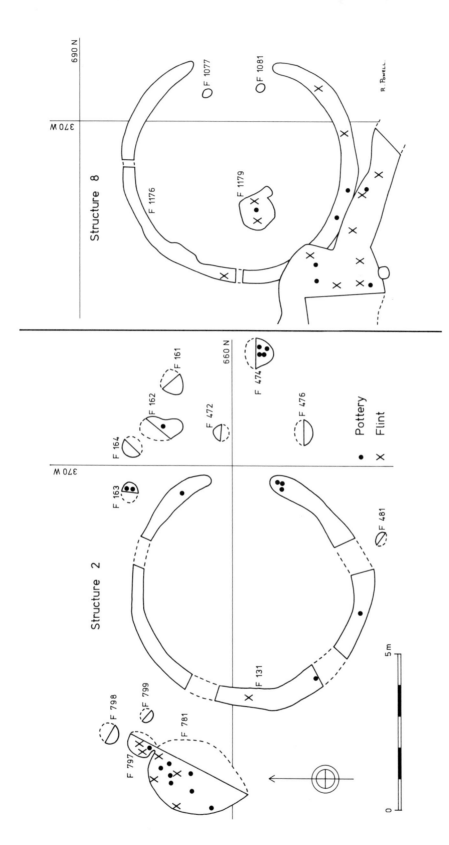

Fig. 25   Cat's Water subsite: Structures 2 (left) and 8, finds distribution

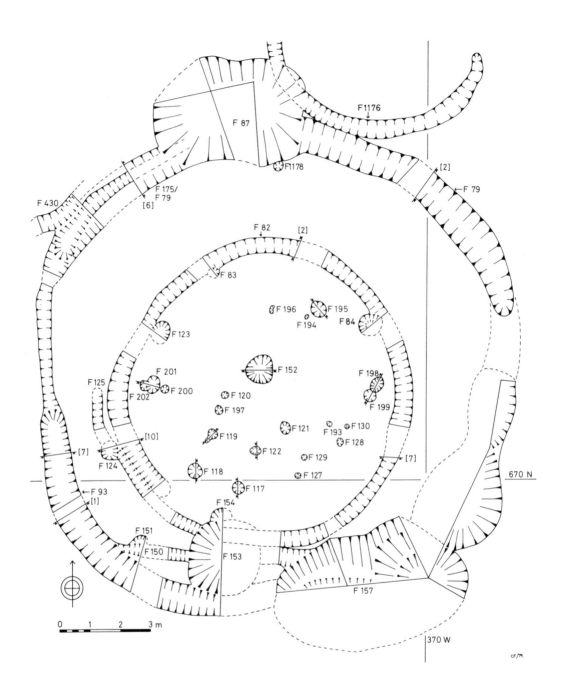

Fig. 26 Cat's Water subsite: Structure 3.

which is convincingly demonstrated in section (that to the NE). The interpretation of this feature is further complicated by the presence of several large back-filled pits, F87, F153, F157 which are probably best interpreted as water holes or wells. Neither the house ring-gully (in the case of F53) nor the external ditch could be shown to cut through these back-filled pits which, on spatial grounds alone, are almost certainly contemporary with one or more phases of the structure's period of use. The enclosure ring-ditch is connected to the main ditch system by an E-W ditch, F430. There can be no doubt that F430 is associated with the enclosure ditch, but its phasing is not altogether clear. At its western end its filling cuts, or rather overlies that of F436, the earliest demonstrable phase of this main drain, but is cut by the Late Iron Age final phase, represented by F439. It does not continue westwards beyond the main drain and it would appear that it originally drained into it.

Relations/phasing: This structure and its enclosure provides the best evidence for multi-period use of a building at Fengate. Three phases can be demonstrated with some confidence. The first is represented by an entranceway to the east; here the ring-gully (F125) lies slightly outside F82, which cuts it (FIG M35, F82. [10]). Possible door posts of this period are features 123, 200, 201, 202 which clearly respect the butt-end of F125; this butt-end aligns well with a butt-end in the enclosure ditch which was cut through in a later phase. It is interesting to note that the external enclosure ditch suddenly becomes deeper immediately south of F430 (which connects the enclosure ditch to the main drain system); if this is accepted as the other side of a subsequently blocked causeway across the enclosure ditch, it could be argued, on grounds of ditch depths alone, that the earliest phase of the enclosure was not connected to the main drainage network. The second phase of the structure is represented by the four internal porch posts described above (F117, F118, F119, F122) and the main ring-gully, F82 which has a clear butt-end to the SW. The second, SW, phase is replaced by a third phase with an entranceway to the east. This phase is less apparent than the previous two and its existence is more implied than proved; nearby, Structures 2 and 8 have entranceways facing due east and the enclosure ditch surrounding Structure 3 has a clear butt-end, stratigraphically late, which could have provided an eastwards-facing causeway across filled-in earlier phases; only the NE side of the causeway has survived, that to the south being removed by the large pit complex F157. Perhaps the northern end of the pit (F157) may be an enlargement of the late recut. Finally, Structure 3, immediately to the north (FIG 26, F1176) cuts the enclosure ditch and the large pit F87.

Finds distribution (FIG 27): The distribution of finds is, on the whole, even. The ring-gully shows no concentration around any of the three phases' doorways and the only predictable concentration is that around the enclosure ditch late recut causeway (NE) terminal. The absence of finds and small features in the area between the building and the ring-gully and the encircling enclosure ditch is of considerable interest, and in pronounced contradistinction to the scatter of post- and stake-holes in the yard surrounding Structure 16 (FIG 43). Structure 16 provides a useful comparison, for it is also enclosed and of approximately the same size, and sits on the eastern edge of the settlement area, with its entranceway also facing eastwards. Unlike Structure 3, however, Structure 16 appears to have been built and used in one period and its finds distribution is accordingly less homogeneous, showing a pronounced concentration of material on either side of the house doorway and the yard enclosure ditch. In cases where other evidence is lacking, markedly patterned finds distributions could be taken to indicate short or single-phase use of structures. Thus apparently undiagnostic finds distributions are of considerable interpretive importance.

Structure 4

Plan (FIG 28, left): An arc of ring-gully formed by features 556 and 1101, centred on Grid 445W/710N. Posthole (F1106) could be associated with the structure. The structure's estimated diameter (if it was originally circular) would be *c* 12m.

Relations/phasing: Sherds of wheel-made pottery indicate a Late Iron Age date.

Finds distribution (FIG 29, left): The concentration of finds around the eastern butt-end of F1101 suggests that this was near an entranceway. The large quantities of domestic refuse (including triangular loomweight) strongly suggest that this structure had a domestic function. This interpretation differs from that of Jackson (Jackson and Ambrose 1978, 140) and it would seem reasonable to suppose that these commonly occurring features have a number of functions.

Structure 5

Plan (FIG 30): An arc of (?) ring-gully centred on Grid 398W/706N, of approximate diameter 9m. No other features can be associated with this structure.

Relations/phasing: Pottery of wheel-made type indicates a Late Iron Age date. The SW end of the ditch just touches the edge of the main (Late Iron Age) drain F1008; the relationship of the two features was not at all clear, but slight surface indications suggested that the ring-gully was perhaps later than the drain.

Finds distribution (FIG 30): Both ends of this feature were deep, steep-sided and rounded; there can, therefore, be no grounds to believe that the gully is the ploughed-out remnant of a complete ring-gully. Flint was found in most neighbouring features, but not in the gully arc, which is unusual and might suggest that the filling of the latter feature did not derive from the soil of the immediate vicinity. The concentration of finds towards the SW end of the gully arc suggests a possible entranceway or area of rubbish disposal; otherwise, the

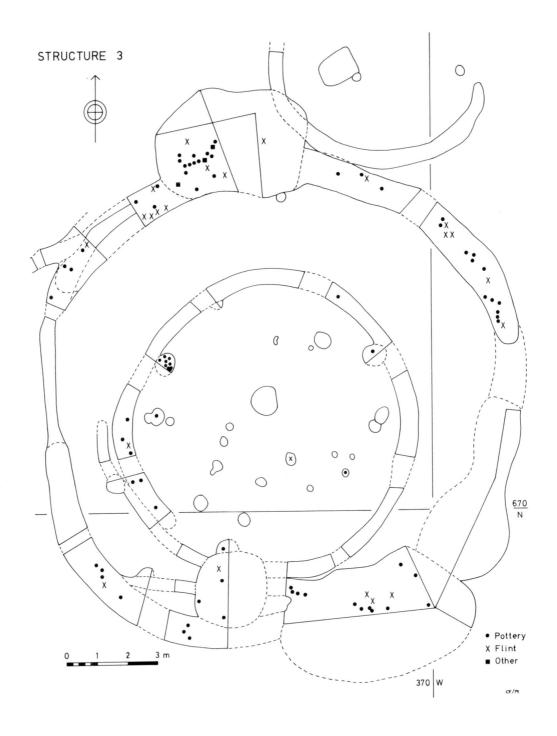

STRUCTURE 3

670
N

370 W

● Pottery
X Flint
■ Other

0 1 2 3 m

CF/M

Fig. 27   Cat's Water subsite: Structure 3, finds distribution

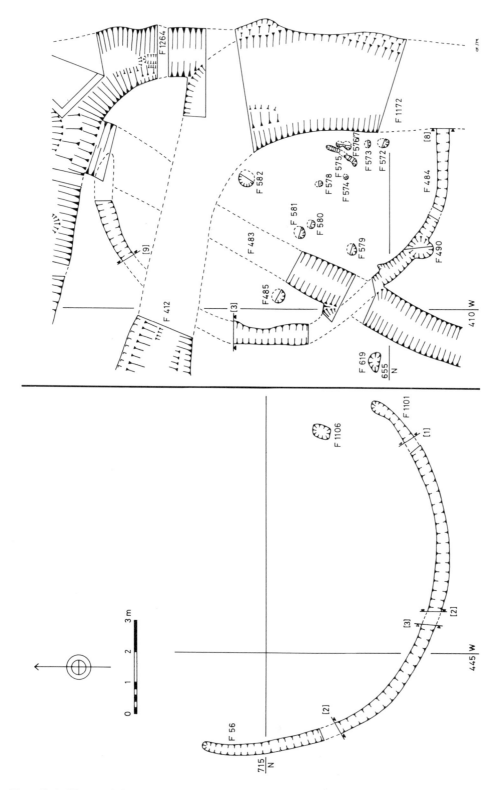

Fig. 28 Cat's Water subsite: Structures 4 (left) and 18.

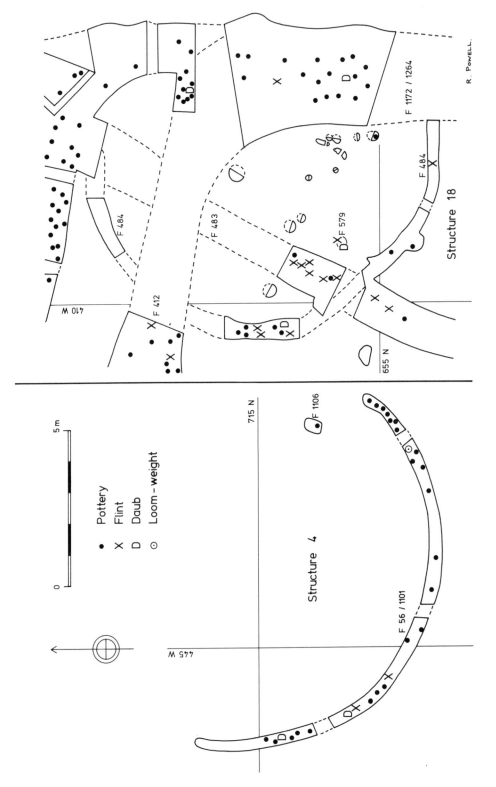

Fig. 29 Cat's Water subsite: Structures 4 and 8, finds distribution

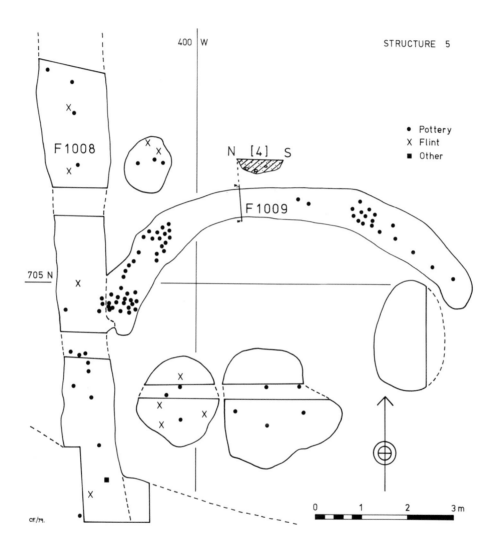

Fig. 30   Cat's Water subsite: Structure 5, finds distribution. One section (4) is shown immediately north of the ring-gully.

absence of daub and other remains of domestic life is unusual. The large pits apparently inside this structure could possibly be contemporary with it; certainly their fillings and finds were very similar.

Section (FIG 30): F1009 [4] layer 1: Sand-silt with scattered gravel pebbles; patches of charcoal. This feature was extremely regular in profile and only one section is shown here.

Structure 6

Plan (FIG 31): A circular building defined by a ring-gully (F1044) of 12m diameter and centred on Grid 407W/669N. Only one butt-end is visible, that to the W, between later ditches F1008 and F1037. It is apparent from the plan that the area has been intensively used since the construction of Structure 6 and its course to the south-west has proved impossible to trace beneath later features. A short length of gully could be discerned immediately south and east of the large pit (or well), F1058. No internal features could be satisfactorily defined, again due to later activity.

Relations/phasing: The ring-gully, F1044, is certainly cut by features 1037, 1038, 1058, 1082, 1089, and 1199 and probably cut by 1008, 1095, 1170, 1191, 1193 and 1200. In short it is early in the sequence, and probably of Middle Iron Age date (on pottery evidence). For purposes of record, the sequence of features is as follows, 1044 - F1058/F1199, F1200 - F1037/F1089 - F1038, F1186 - F1008, where the dashes represent stratigrapically proven distinct phases (of unknown duration).

Finds distribution (FIG 32): Flint and pottery show different distribution patterns. Flint appears to be evenly spread along the gully but pottery is concentrated near the only preserved butt-end, to the east. A slight concentration of pottery in the adjacent Late Iron ditch could consist of residual material derived from the earlier house gully.

Structures 7 and 25

Plan (FIG 33): Structure 7 is a round building (centred on Grid 383W/694N) defined by two concentric ring-gullies; the outer (F1020) was deeper and wider than the inner and had an external diameter of 11.0m. Its function was probably that of an eaves-drip gully. The plan shows evidence for a causeway across F1020 immediately west of the suggested doorway in the inner, wall foundation, gully F1069; a narrow extension of the eaves-drip gully either pre-dates or post-dates the causeway, the southern terminal of which has been cut away by the later ring-gully of Structure 25 (F1015). The inner ring-gully (F1069) survives in two arcs north south of the entranceway just described (width 1.3m). Both arcs have an approximate diameter of 7.8m and the distance from the centre of the wall foundation trench to the centre of the eaves-drip gully (ie the probable eaves width) is 1.0m to 1.2m. The northern arc of F1069 survives for approximately ⅓ of its original circum-

ference and showed evidence during excavation for having once held upright posts (two are visible as off-centre enlargements in the plan); at its SW (doorway) end the gully was deeper and wider than elsewhere, suggesting, perhaps the presence of a door-post; its NE end petered out into the overlying B soil horizon. The southern arc was shorter than the northern arc (c 2.8m); it too petered out at one (SE) end and also seemed to show evidence for a post at the doorway; evidence for wall posts was slighter than before; a probable (ancient) animal burrow linked the inner to the outer ring-gully immediately south of the doorway. Non-linear features of note include F1016, a substantial posthole which seems to have been used to block the doorway; this feature may, therefore, be contemporary with the recutting of the causeway in the external ring-gully, discussed above. The internal postholes and the small oblong pit F1094 are probably connected with the structure in one of its phases, but do not form a coherent pattern; the rarity of postholes and small pits outside the eaves-drip gully tends to support this view.

Structure 25 consists of a small ring-gully (F1015) of diameter 3.2m; it is located west of Structure 7 and partly overlaps it.

Relations/phasing: Pottery from the filling of the eaves-drip gully indicates a Middle Iron Age date for Structure 7, a *terminus ante quem* for which is given by the Late Iron Age drainage/soak away ditch F1017/1019 which clearly cuts the eaves-drip gully. Indeed, this latter feature could, possibly, provide a reason for the building's abandonment. The dating of Structure 25 is more problematical, it cuts the eaves drip-gully of Structure 7 and must have been in use at some time after the latter's complete disappearance. Although disturbed on its western side by Roman flood clays, its location near a Late Iron Age drainage ditch may be functional (if the stack-stand hypothesis of Chapter 8 be accepted) and a Late Iron Age date is accordingly suggested here.

Finds distribution (FIG 34): The majority of finds are distributed in the SE portion of the eaves-drip gully over a length of some 5.0m. These are unlikely to have derived from Structure 7 itself, as there is no evidence for an entranceway at this point, nor is there any gap in the linear spread of material. A more plausible hypothesis is that the finds derived from rubbish (perhaps used to consolidate wet ground) deposited between Structures 3/8 and 7, perhaps around, or on either side of, a pathway. The large pits in the enclosed ditch around Structure 3 (FIG 26) provide another contemporary source for this material.

Structure 8

Plan (FIG 24): A circular building (centred on Grid 371W/684N) defined by ring-gully 1176 (dia c 7.5m). The doorway faces eastwards and is marked by a break in the ring-gully and two internal door postholes, F1177 (north) and F1081 (south); the doorway width is 1.40m. A shallow pit or scoop with offset stake or posthole is

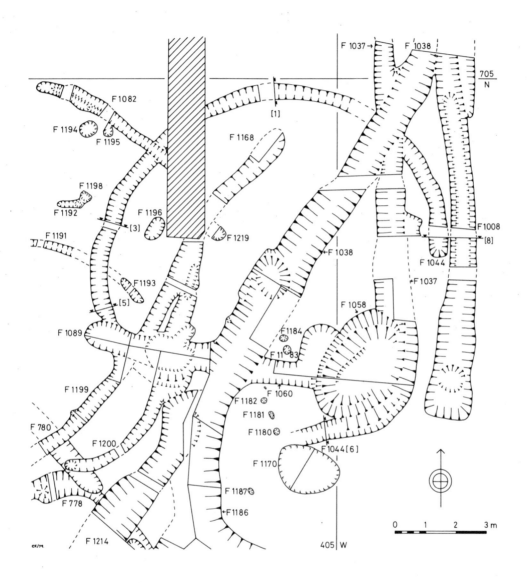

F 1037→ F 1038

705
N

F 1082

F 1194 F 1195

F 1168

[1]

F 1198
F 1192

F 1196

F 1191

[3]

F 1219

F 1008

[8]

←F 1038

F 1044

F 1193

[5]

←F 1037

F 1089

F 1058

F 1184

F 11 83

F 1199

F 780

F 1060
F 1182

F 1181

F 1200

F 1180

F 1044[6]

F 778

F 1170

F 1187

F 1186

F 1214

405 W

CK/79.

0   1   2   3 m

Fig. 31   Cat's Water subsite: Structure 6 (unexcavated baulk shaded).

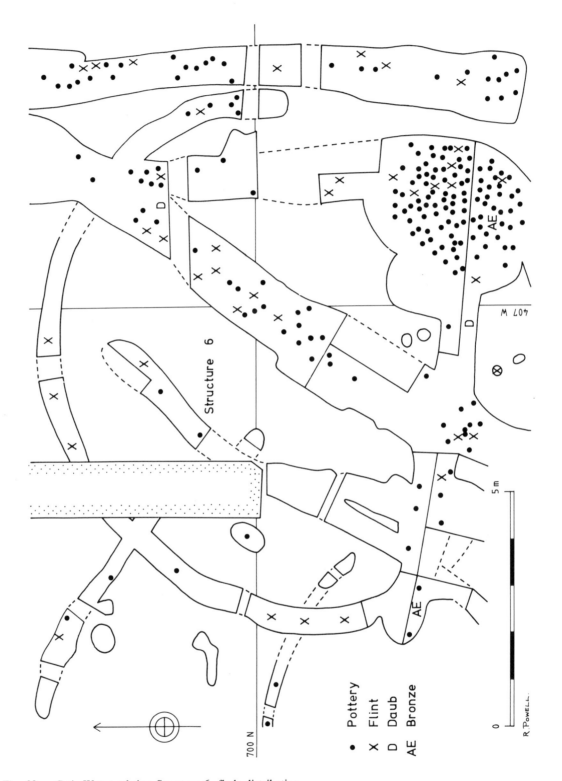

Fig. 32 Cat's Water subsite: Structure 6, finds distribution.

42

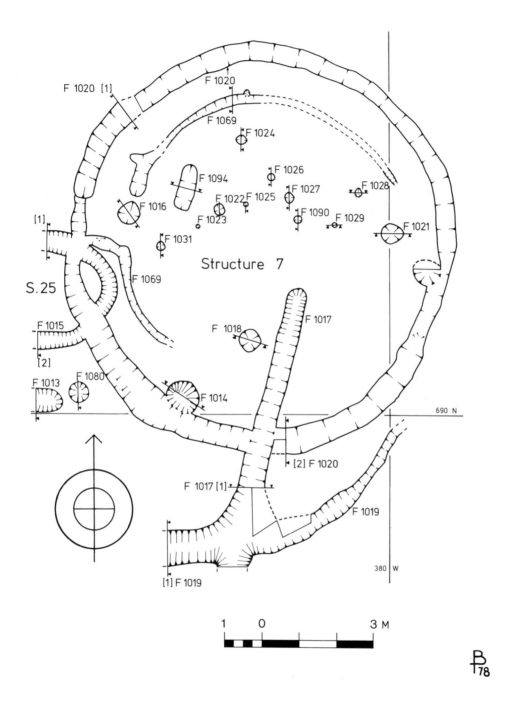

F 1020 [1]

F 1020

F 1069

F 1024

F 1094

F 1026

F 1016

F 1022 F 1025

F 1027

F 1028

F 1023

F 1090

F 1029

F 1021

F 1031

[1]

Structure 7

S.25

F 1069

F 1015

F 1018

F 1017

[2]

F 1013

F 1080

F 1014

690 N

[2] F 1020

F 1017 [1]

F 1019

380 W

[1] F 1019

1   0   3 M

B
78

Fig. 33   Cat's Water subsite: Structure 7.

43

located within the area enclosed by the ring-gully and may be associated with the structure.

Relations/phasing: The location of Structures 8, 3 and 2 on the east side of the settlement, with entrances facing eastwards, suggests contemporaneity in at least one phase and in this respect it is important to note that the ring-gully of Structure 8 clearly respects the enclosure ditch around Structure 3 but cuts through the large pit (Feature 87). Although impossible to prove stratigraphically, it would appear that Structures 8 and 2 are contemporary with the third, and final, phase of Structure 3 (that represented by an eastwards-facing entranceway and the recut causeway through the external enclosure ditch).

Finds distribution (FIG 25, right): The few finds from the ring-gully filling all occur in its southern half, suggesting, perhaps, an origin in the area around Structure 3. Most, if not all, of this material is, therefore, residual and offers no clues as to the building's original function(s). Finally, the few finds and very rare charcoal argue against this building's use as a house.

Structures 9, 12, and 43
(Grids 402W/680N; 402W/679N respectively)

Plan (FIG 35): Structures 9 and 12 are round buildings defined by ring-gullies of 8.5 to 8.8m and 9.5m diameters respectively. Structure 9 survives as a complete ring (with no apparent entranceway), F1108. Structure 12 is less straightforward. Its linear elements consist of an approximately semi-circular ring-gully (F1109 and F115). This feature clearly formed the principal component of the building. Two other features of interest should also be noted; first a very shallow gully, F1112, which ran NE and cut the upper layers of a main Middle Iron Age drain before becoming impossible to trace further and, second, a N-S gully, F1140, which connected with a main Late Iron Age drain 5.5m due south. Feature 1140 is probably best interpreted as a small drainage ditch; its northern end was marked by a T-shaped enlargement which clearly diverged from the alignment of Structure 9 (F1108) but which seems approximately to follow that of Structure 12 (F1115). Non-linear features, probably associated with Structure 12, include the slot F1155 which can be seen to link the northern T-shaped end of F1140 and the main semi-circular ring-gully, F1115. The southern terminal (an entranceway?) of the latter feature is marked by a group of postholes represented by F1207 and F1208; finally, the group of postholes F1212, F1141 and F1142 could be associated with both structures, probably as doorposts, since east-facing entranceways are commonly found on Cat's Water. Structure 43 (Grid 406W/671N) is exeptionally amorphous and difficult to interpret. It consists of a curving L-shaped gully, F1116 which encloses a group of post- or stake-holes (features 1116-38, 1171, 1174). These postholes were arranged in three slightly curving lines, running approximately

N-S towards the corner of F1116 (the general pattern can be seen in FIGS 16 and 18; the northern postholes are shown in FIG 35). The association of the gully with the postholes may be entirely fortuitous and the apparent structure could, perhaps, best be seen as a stock compound in the south-eastern corner of a Late Iron Age yard.

Relations/phasing: Structure 9, the complete ring-gully, cuts Structure 12, but is, in turn, cut by the gully of Structure 43 (F1116, the gully of Structure 43, also clearly cut F1115, the gully of Structure 12). The sequence is thus Structure 12, followed by 9 and 43. Phasing within the settlement sequence is less straight-forward, and finds are of no assistance. The location of Structure 12 would, perhaps, suggest a date within one of the phases of the Middle Iron Age period, despite the fact that the NE gully, F1112, cut a filled-in Middle Iron Age main drain (F1039). The main drain in question is stratigraphically early and was probably deliberately filled-in at this point. The relationship of the southern gully, F1140 to the later Iron Age ditch immediately south of it was not apparent, either in plan or section. Finally, the gully of Structure 43 (1116) clearly cut a Middle Iron Age main drainage ditch (1277) to the SW. The latter intersection, it should be noted, is the only one which plainly accords with the sequence suggested above and serves to illustrate the problem of interpreting detailed stratigraphies on sites where ditches have been recut or cleaned out repeatedly over the years.

Structures 10, 11, 30, 31

Plan (FIG 36): Structure 10 (Grid 394W/652N) consists of two crescentic gullies (F1237 and F522) cut to the east, but still visible beneath the Late Iron Age drainage ditches (F554-6, F567) that form the settlement's eastern boundary at this point. Butt-ends of both gullies are clearly defined, steep and would indicate that the building (dia c 9.2m) was originally constructed with two entranceways. It should also be noted that although deep, both gullies are not of the same depth, that to the south (F522) being approximately half as deep as that to the north. The latter is a matter of considerable importance to the interpretation of structures, apparently only defined by a single arc of ring-gully, where the ditch can be shown to have clear, sharply defined butt-ends. Structure 11 (Grid 393W/657N) was a round building defined by a ring-gully (F1233) of diameter 7.8m. It overlapped Structure 10 to the NE, and showed no clear indications of an entranceway, although the expansion immediately north of section 9 may mark the southern edge of an east-facing doorway. The dashed line indicates the probable course of F1233 to the NW, where it was particularly difficult to trace. The postholes within the area enclosed by the ring-gully are probably best interpreted as being part of Structure 31. Finally, it should be noted that the Late Iron Age drainage ditch F555 terminates due east of the suggested entranceway, thus providing access to

STRUCTURE 7

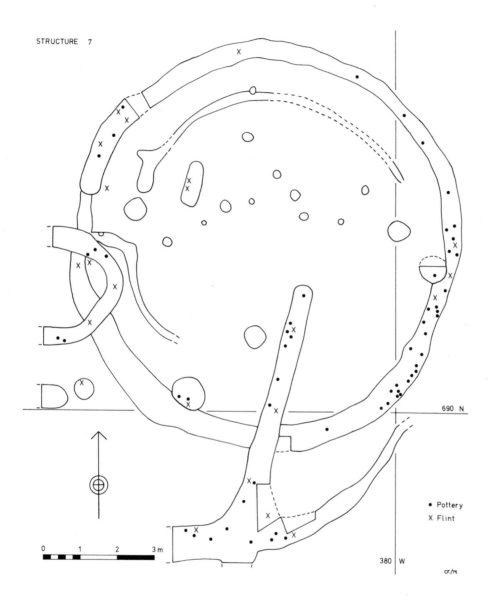

690 N

• Pottery
X Flint

380 W

Fig. 34   Cat's Water subsite: Structure 7, finds distribution.

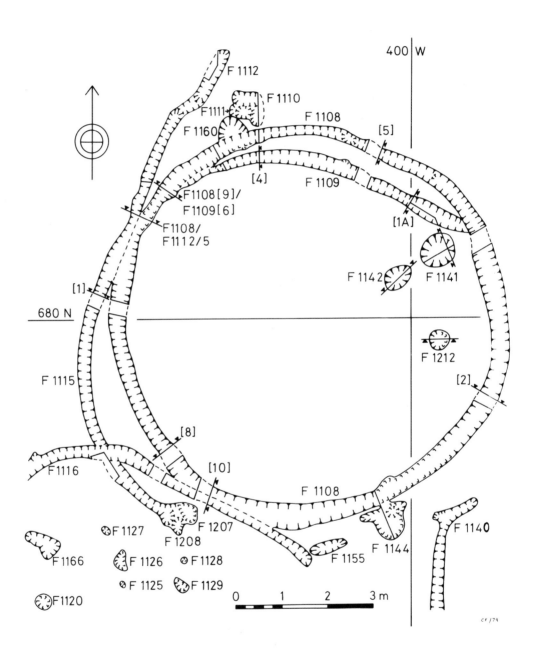

Fig. 35   Cat's Water subsite: Structures 9 and 12 (and part of the possible Structure 43).

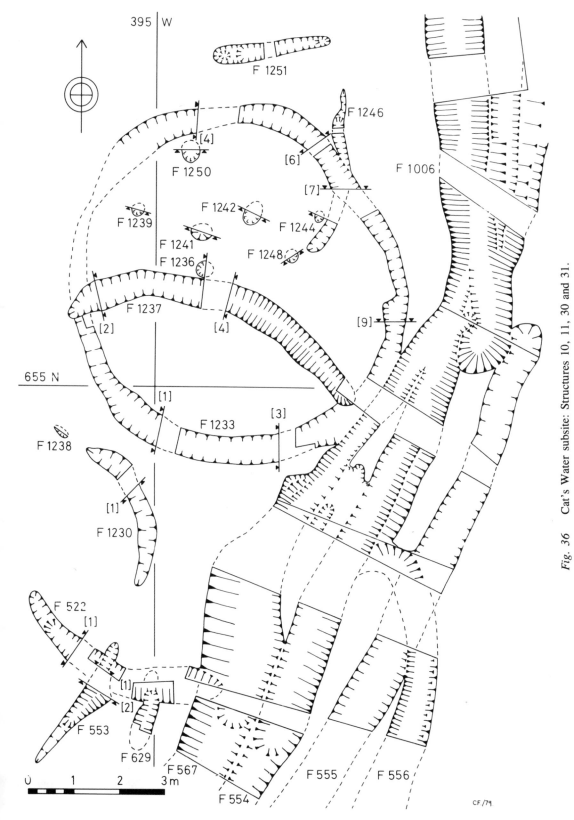

395 | W

F 1251

F 1246

[4]

F 1250

[6]

F 1006

[7]

F 1242

F 1239

F 1244

F 1241

F 1248

F 1236

[2]

F 1237

[4]

[9]

655 N

[1]

F 1233

[3]

F 1238

[1]

F 1230

F 522

[1]

[1]

F 553

[2]

F 629

F 567

0   1   2   3 m

F 555   F 556

F 554

CF./79

Fig. 36   Cat's Water subsite: Structures 10, 11, 30 and 31.

the open land outside the main settlement area.

Structure 30 (Grid 399W/650N) consists of two short lengths of gully (F1230 and F553) and a possible posthole, F1238. No explanation of the form or purpose of this apparent structure is offered here, but the precise alignment of all the features was most noticeable.

Structure 31 (Grid 394W/659N) consists of short lengths of gully (F1246 and F1251) and a group of postholes (F1236, F1239, F1241, F1242, F1244, F1250 and F1255). This structure, like 30, above, is most difficult to define, but a short length of ring-gully immediately north of F1251 (not shown in FIG 35) continued the line of F1246, to form a poorly-defined round building of c 7.0m diameter.

Relations/phasing: Structure 10 was clearly cut by the ditches of Structure 11 and by all the Late Iron Age drainage ditches to the east; its western entranceway does, however, provide access to a late phase causeway across the Middle Iron Age drainage ditch immediately to the west, and a date within that period would seem appropriate. Structure 11 clearly forms part of the Late Iron Age ditch system which it respects, and Structures 30 and 31 both post-date it (but on spatial grounds are probably Iron Age rather than Roman in date).

Finds distribution (FIG 37): The finds distribution within the filling of the four structures is on the whole uniform and undistinctive. The principal point of interest is the contrast in finds density between the earliest structure, 10, and the complete ring-gully (Structure 11) which follows it. The domestic rubbish from the two crescentic gullies of the earlier feature (pottery and burnt clay daub) could not have derived from any of the later features, and the general rarity of debris in the filling of these later features supports the hypothesis that much of the material from the Late Iron Age drainage ditches nearby (F554-6, F567) is residual. A similarly high density of occupation debris was found in the filling of the Middle Iron Age ditches just west of the structures discussed here. This example illustrates a major difficulty in interpreting pottery assemblages on sites where quantities of residual sherds are high.

Structure 11 — see Structure 10

Structure 12 — see Structure 9

Structure 13

Plan (FIG 38): A circular building (Grid 416W/685N) defined by ring-gully F491 (dia c 12.0m); the ring-gully survives for about ⅔ of its presumed original circumference and shows evidence for re-aligned recuttings at its SE terminal; its NW terminal could not be traced, the ditch merely becoming shallower and eventually proved impossible to excavate. A number of postholes were located in the area enclosed by the ring-gully, but these showed no obvious pattern, and as the area around the structure was the scene of considerable activity, they

have been omitted from the section drawings; their association with the structure is possible, but not probable, and all had fillings considerably darker than that of the ring-gully. Two ditches of the neighbouring complex of Middle Iron Age drainage ditches could have connections with phases of Structure 13: the short butt-end of ditch F1440 could be seen as forming the NE side of an entranceway with the enlarged ring-gully, F500; similarly, the slighter gully F778 could form a northern entranceway with F491.

Relations/phasing: The relationship of Structure 13 to the neighbouring Middle Iron Age drainage ditches has already been discussed and a connection seems, on balance probable. The multi-period recuts at the SE end of the ring-gully were difficult to disentangle owing to the homogeneity of the fillings involved, but F631, a short gully immediately SE of F491 was clearly later than it. The section of F491 [9] illustrates all the stratigraphic relationships that could be proved beyond reasonable doubt (note that the relationship of F491 to F496 was obscured by the later posthole, F495). A *terminus ante quem* for the structure is provided by the well-dated Middle Iron Age main drainage ditch F1277 which cuts the ring-gully in all its principal phases. A date early in the Cat's Water Middle Iron Age succession is indicated.

Finds distribution (FIG 39): The finds distribution is particularly interesting. We have seen above, that on purely spatial grounds (size, orientation, location), the SE entranceway is best defined by features 1440 and 500. The finds distribution, however, indicates that F1440 and F449 (in both its phases) to the SW, have finds densities that are closely comparable and that F500 is most probably not associated with F1440. Furthermore, the finds distribution (but not the composition of the section which was homogeneous) of F1440 indicates at least two phases of use, of which the most westerly had the greatest concentration of finds. Similarly, on the other side of the entranceway, the westerly phase of F499 contained more finds than that to the east (or, indeed, the short, late gully, F631). Finds distribution also indicate (a) that if F500 is part of a rebuilding, then the function of the structure has altered between this phase and that just discussed and, (b), F500 may antedate the entranceway formed by features 1440 and 499, since residual material would otherwise have found its way into the open gully. It should also be noted that the possible NW entranceway (between F491 and F778) has a low finds density and may, therefore, possibly be contemporary with F500; alternatively it may be the result of post-depositional factors and is not an entranceway at all (a more reasonable suggestion?). Finally, the spaced distribution of finds in the Middle Iron Age main drain that cuts the ring-gully on its southern side (F1277) suggests that many of these sherds have been mixed evenly throughout the ditch filling by frequent recutting and cleaning out; they probably originally derived from F499.

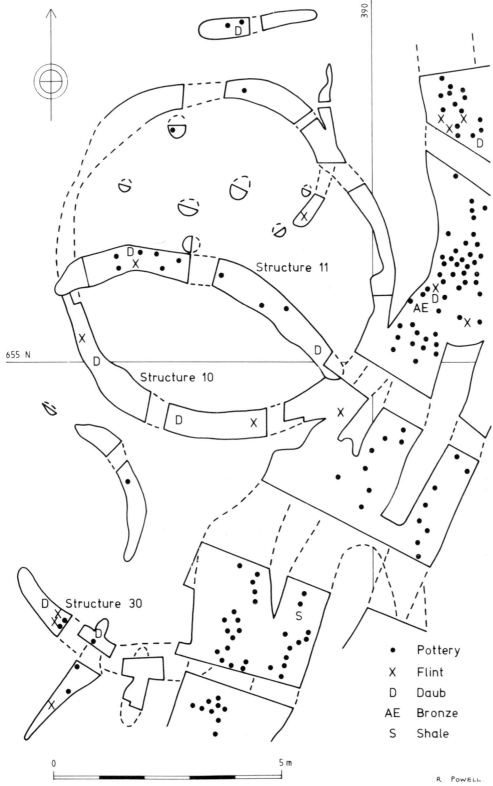

Fig. 37 Cat's Water subsite: Structures 10, 11, 30 and 31, finds distribution.

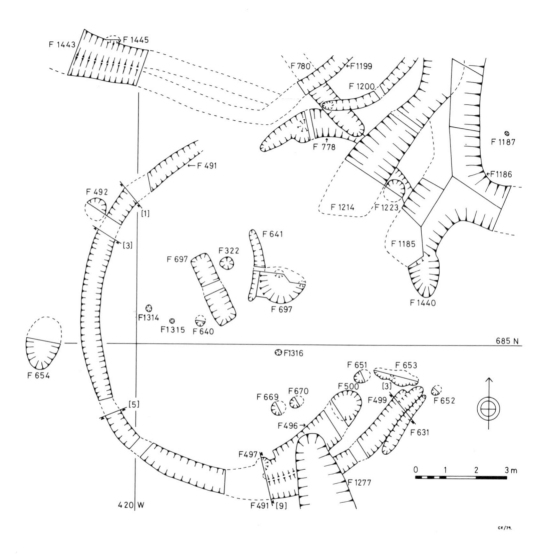

Fig. 38   Cat's Water subsite: Structure 13.

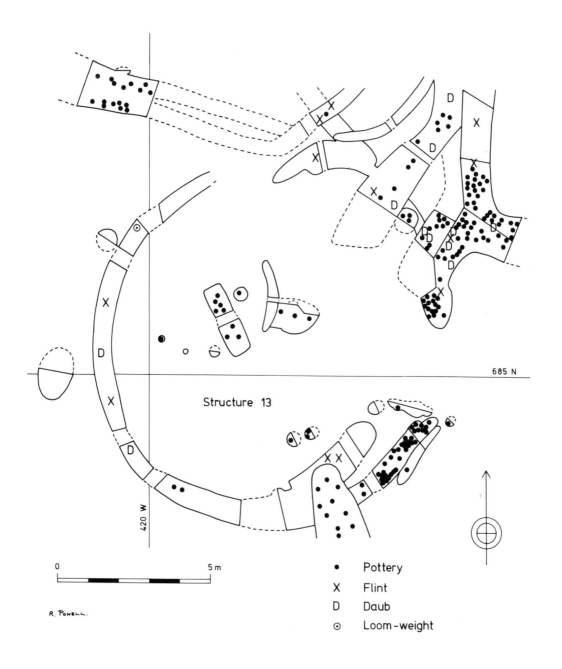

685 N

Structure 13

420 W

0   5 m

R. POWELL.

-   Pottery
X   Flint
D   Daub
⊙   Loom-weight

Fig. 39   Cat's Water subsite: Structure 13, finds distribution.

Structure 14

Plan (FIG 40): A round building (Grid 417W/755N) defined by two ring-gullies; an outer, or eaves-drip, gully (F1) of *c* 8.5m diameter and an inner, or wall-foundation, gully (F2) of *c* 6.2m diameter. The distance between the centre of each ring-gully (eaves width) was 1.5m. A concentration of postholes on the interior may well be associated with the structure and those between the two ring-gullies (F4, F53 and F350) could, perhaps, be seen as wall props or buttresses. Gully terminations could not properly be defined, either through later activity or because of problems in definition; the only exception to this being the SE end of F2 which was steep, rounded and slightly expanded, suggesting, perhaps, the presence of a door post. The other side of the doorway may have been supported by a post in F361 (or F8) and the short slot, F3, might be a truncated remnant of the wall bedding trench to the east. Supporting evidence for the NW side of the doorway is provided by a terminal-like enlargement of the external (eaves-drip) gully, F1, 0.4m south-east of section 5; the slighter easterly continuation of F1 is clearly distinct from the more robust northerly length (compare FIG M42: sections 3 and 5). Only three external features, the triangle of postholes, features 17, 18, 349, could, on spatial grounds, be associated with Structure 14.

Phasing and relations: The pit F420 is of pre-Iron Age date and the pit complex F402/407/775 cuts the inner ring-gully and is therefore later; the large pits F119 and F20 would also be out of place in a structural setting, and the high clay content of their upper fillings suggest a Late Iron Age date. Pottery from the eaves-drip gullies of Structures 14 and 15 (below) suggests a Middle Iron Age date, and the positioning of Structure 14 so near a Late Iron Age ditch (which must cut it if the arc of the outer ring-gully is produced to the NE) indicates a date prior to that. The Late Iron Age ditch in question (F114) shows no good evidence for having had an earlier, Middle Iron Age, phase. Finally, the location of Structures 14 and 15 with neighbouring, almost inter-communicating, entrances suggests contemporaneity, a hypothesis that finds some support in the positioning of Burial 1 north of, and between, the two buildings. Clearly the relationship of the two structures (or indeed the burial) cannot be proved, but both seem to respect each other, in all their phases.

Finds distribution (FIG 41): The distribution of finds within the features comprising Structures 14 and 15 is generally uniform: Structure 14 is almost devoid of material, but Structure 15 shows an even spread of finds with an unusually high concentration of flints; these could have derived from activity associated with the second millennium pit F420, but the absence of flints from neighbouring features of Structure 14 makes this hypothesis improbable. It should be noted that the finds from F420 have not been plotted in FIG 40.

Structure 15

Plan (FIG 40): A round building (Grid 428W/752N) defined by a two-phased ring-gully (F101, F102, F335) of *c* 11.8m diameter. The ring-gully passes out of the excavated area at Grid 426W/758N, to the NW, and Grid 431W/748N, to the SW. It is broken by an entranceway gap (width 2.9m) to the SE. The two phases are clearly visible in the northern arc of ring-gully (where F101 cuts F102); in the southern arc the two phases are only implied by the ditch's stepped profile (F335), no change of infilling, however, can be discerned (FIG M42). Two postholes (F383 and F334) are set back from the gap in the gully and probably represent door posts. The cluster of stakeholes to the SW are difficult to interpret, as are the external postholes F16, F385, F390, F768-71 and F774.

Relations/phasing: See Structure 14, above.

Finds distribution: See Structure 14, above.

Structure 16

Plan (FIG 42): Structure 16 is a round building (Grid 376W/724N) defined by a penannular ring-gully (F42/F43) of *c* 9.8m diameter. It contains a number of post- and stake-holes in its interior, of which four can be interpreted as door or porch posts (F132, F133, F141, F142) and three (F134, F135 and F144) as possible wall posts. The remaining interior postholes cannot be easily interpreted. The building is enclosed by a sub-rectangular arrangement of ditches: the western side consists of ditch F207/242, a multi-period main drainage ditch with good stratigraphic evidence for frequent recuts, the last of which was in Late Iron Age times. The north, south and east enclosure ditches (F32, F40 and 34 respectively) were all cut by the latest recut of the main drain F207/242. The building's entrance-way (width in the ring gully 2.2m) faces slightly south-east of the enclosure entranceway (width 2.2m) between features 32 and 4. A small gully (possibly earlier than the main ditch F34), F33, may have held a fence or screen across the SE part of the enclosure entranceway. A group of 21 postholes form a cluster *c* 8.0m (E-W) by 7.0m (N-S) between the building and enclosure entranceways. The latter features are probably best seen in terms of sporadic activity (temporary structures, drying racks etc) in the yard, rather than the components of a permanent building; some (from E-W, F191, F190, F185, F183, F182, F180/1) may have been located along a pathway from the building's doorway to the enclosure causeway.

Relations/phasing: Large quantities of Middle Iron Age pottery were found in the filling of the ring-gully and the enclosure ditch and this accords well with the stratigraphic evidence which shows both north and south enclosure ditches cut by the latest (Late Iron Age) phase of the main drainage ditch, F207/242. The house ring-gully, however, cuts a stratigraphically early (probably Middle Iron Age) phase of the main drain. The eastern edge of the main drain curves to respect the house ring-

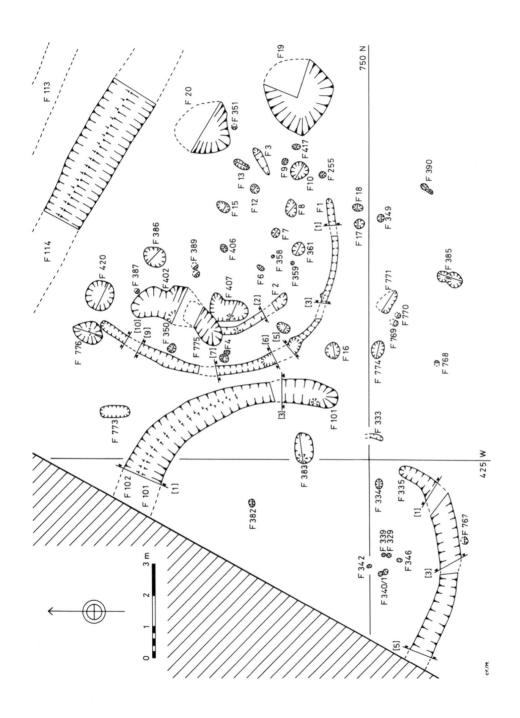

Fig. 40   Cat's Water subsite: Structures 14 (right) and 15 (left).

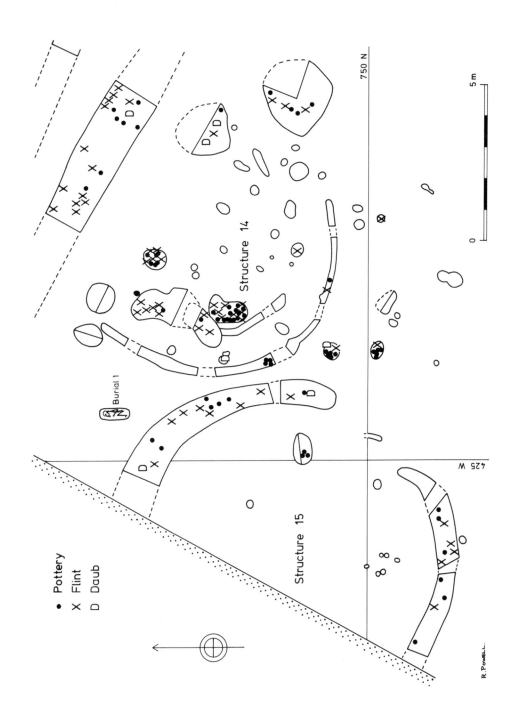

Pottery •
Flint X
Daub D

Structure 14

Structure 15

Burial 1

750 N

425 W

5 m

R. Powell.

Fig. 41   Cat's Water subsite: Structures 14 (right) and 15 (left), finds distribution.

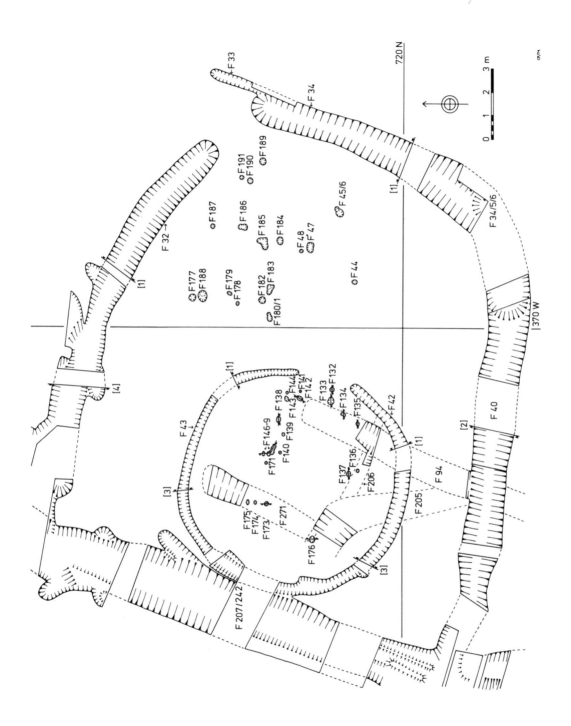

Fig. 42 Cat's Water subsite: Structure 16.

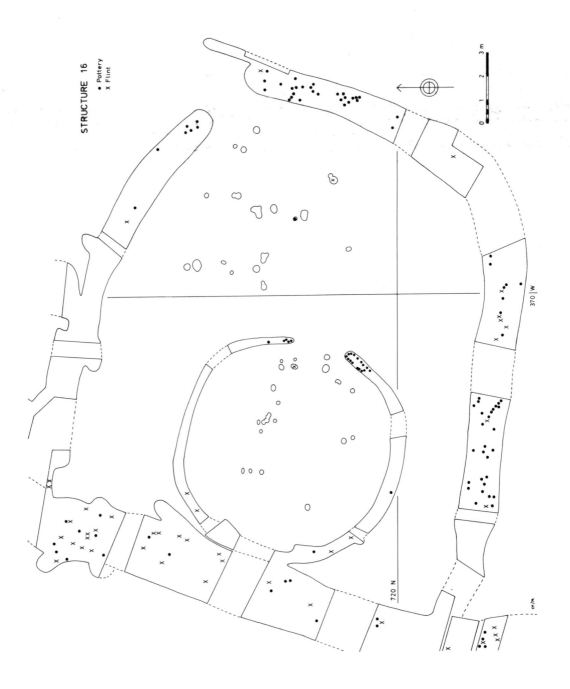

STRUCTURE 16
• Pottery
x Flint

Fig. 43 Cat's Water subsite: Structure 16, finds distribution.

56

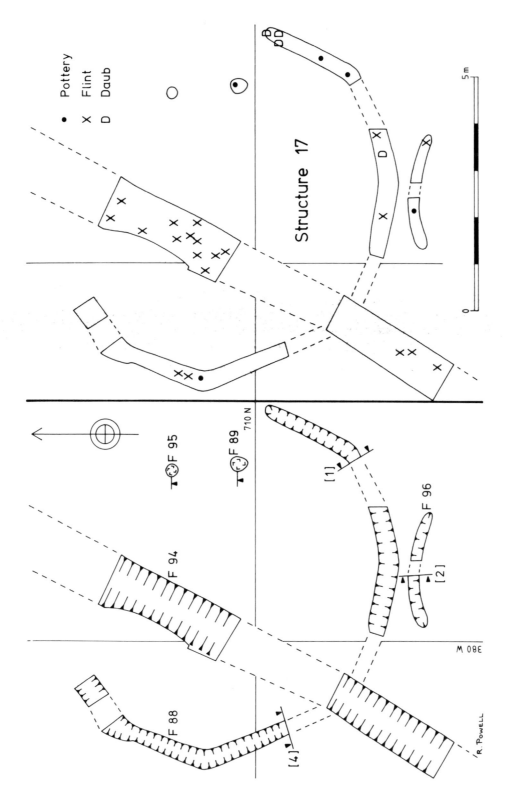

Fig. 44   Cat's Water subsite: Structure 17, plan and finds distribution.

gully at this point which, again, would imply that the earlier phases of this ditch were of Middle Iron Age date. Finally, the building and its enclosure ditch are superimposed upon two second millennium boundary ditches, F94 and F271; the anomalous feature, 205, may not be man-made. All non-Iron Age features have been omitted from the finds distribution plan (FIG 43).

Finds distribution (FIG 43): The finds distribution raises some important points. First, the distribution shows patterning and this would accord well with a comparatively short use-life for the structure and enclosure ditch. The finds have not been spread by frequent recuts (compare, for example Structure 3, FIG 27), either in the building or its associated enclosure ditch. The main drain to the west, however, has good stratigraphic evidence for recutting, and a con-comitantly uniform finds distribution. The distribution of finds in the enclosure ditch shows a clear concentration around the entrance causeway and few finds along the rest of the northern ditch (F32). The southern ditch (F40), on the other hand, shows a second marked concentration in the 9m, or so, west of Grid line 370W. This concentration is difficult to explain in terms of Structure 16, and is more probably connected with Structure 17 immediately to the south. Non-linear features, both inside and outside the building, yielded few finds. The finds' distribution in the ring-gully shows a clear and pronounced concentration around the entranceway, and the distribution pattern of flint and pottery, in building and enclosure ditch, shows a clear distinction. Much of the flintwork in the main drainage ditch (F207/242) and the western portion of the ring-gully probably derived from features associated with the second millennium ditches F94 and F271; indeed the quantities of flint in the NW corner of the enclosure hint at a lost settlement area of that period.

Structure 17

Plan (FIG 44): Structure 17 was a round building (Grid 378W/711N) defined by a polygonal ring-gully (F88) of c 7.8m diameter. Over two thirds of the ring-gully were preserved and one butt-end, that to the east, could be clearly defined; the western end of the gully became impossible to trace, but its probable course north and eastwards would have respected the southern edge of the enclosure ditch around Structure 16 (FIG 42, F40). Two door posts, F89 and F95 are set back from the SE terminal of the ring-gully to give an east-facing entranceway (width 1.1m), on the same alignment as many others in the area (eg Structures 1, 2, 8). A small length of curved gully, F96 might represent the remains of a structure that could have been built on the apparently unoccupied land between Structures 7, 17, and 42. The principal interest of Structure 17, however, lies in the layout of the polygonal ring-gully which is composed of straight lengths of c 2.0-2.5m. If the plan shown here is produced north-east to complete the original penannular ground-plan, then the polygon

would be nine-sided; such polygonal construction is interpreted by Drury (1978, 161 and FIG 68) as evidence for wall-plate construction.

Relations/phasing: The ring-gully, F88, cut the main second millennium ditch iii (F94), but produced insufficient pottery for reliable dating. No wheel-made vessels were found, and the building's location immediately south of the Middle Iron Age enclosure ditch around Structure 16 (which it respects) suggests contemporaneity. If the concentration of finds in the nearby enclosure ditch (FIG 43, 24) derives from Structure 17, then the two features are either contemporary, or Structure 17 could antedate the enclosure ditch, in which case the finds from the latter would be residual. In sum, available information indicates that Structures 16 and 17 are probably contemporary.

Finds distribution (FIG 44): The distribution of finds in the second millennium ditch F94 is plotted to show the spread of residual material in later features. It will be seen that the earlier ditch does not appear to have had a 'concentrating' effect on the flints, which are widely spaced through the ring-gully filling. Pottery and burnt clay daub tend to be concentrated around the entrance-way, but this was not very marked.

Structure 18

Plan (FIG 28, right): Structure 18 was a round building defined (Grid 405W/658N) by the ring-gully F484 (diameter c 11.6m). One terminal to the north, cut into the second millennium ditch iii (F483), was clearly defined; to the south the gully was truncated by the Late Iron Age ditch F1172. It could not be traced east of the latter ditch and may originally have swung north along its course, as its surviving plan is very irregular, with clear straight sections and corners. The Middle Iron Age ditch F1264 passes through a rounded right-angled corner immediately east of the ring-gully terminal and may, perhaps, be functionally connected with the structure; a similar arrangement can be seen in the ditches east of Structure 53 (FIG 73). A scatter of postholes is enclosed by the ring-gully and many are probably connected with the structure, although it is hard to discern any regular pattern (the small pit F582 could, perhaps, be seen as a central roof-support pole).

Relations/phasing: The ring-gully F484 cuts the second millennium ditch iii and is cut by the Late Iron Age ditch F412/1172. A date in the Middle Iron Age would accord with the stratigraphy and meagre pottery evidence.

Finds distribution (FIG 29, right): The main drain and boundary ditches show on the whole, a uniform spread of material in contrast to the localised pattern of the ring-gully, but the latter could merely be the result of post-depositional factors, for example the concentration of finds in the western part of the gully probably reflects the ditch's better preservation at that point (perhaps due to a bank south of F412?).

58

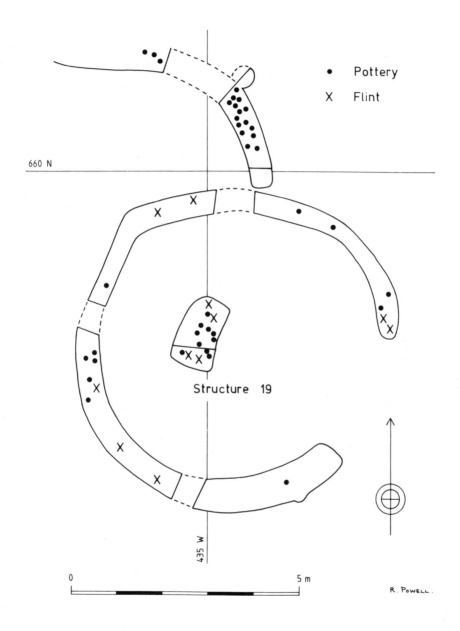

660 N

Pottery

X Flint

Structure 19

435 W

0   5 m

R. POWELL.

Fig. 45   Cat's Water subsite: Structure 19, finds distribution.

59

Structure 19

Plan (FIG 22, left): An approximately round building (Grid 434W/656N) defined by the penannular ring-gully F428 (dia 7.0m). The entranceway causeway is 2.6m wide. No other features can be attributed to this structure (F427 and F450 belong to Structure 28).

Relations/phasing: Pottery suggests a Late Iron Age date and a *terminus ante quem* is provided by the pit of Structure 28 (Romano-British) which overlaps Structure 19.

Finds distribution (FIG 45): This building is of particular interest in that it shows evidence for substantial modification. The first phase was defined by two opposed arcs of ring-gully (in the manner of Structure 10 — FIG 76) forming a building with two entranceways, one to the SE and one to the NW. The second phase saw the blocking of the NW entranceway by a straight and slightly narrower length of ditch (FIG M33, F428).[3] This blocked entranceway is reflected in the finds distribution by the local concentration of material immediately south of the section 3 baulk. A similar concentration, on the northern side of the SE entranceway, is also clearly visible.

Structure 20

Plan (FIG 46): Structure 20 was a round building (Grid 457W/651N) defined by the penannular ring-gully F449 (diameter *c* 10.2m). The entrance causeway was marked by expanded terminals, that to the north being approximately oval, and that to the south elongated and orientated NW-SE. There was no indication that either pit-like expansion had ever held uprights. Two door postholes (F512 and F514) were the only internal features that could reliably be associated with the structure; the width of the doorway was 1.2m.

Relations/phasing: The stratigraphic relationship of the ring-gully to the main Late Iron Age drainage ditch to the west (F445) could not be discerned, but the ring-ditch's flattened course at this point strongly suggests that both features were open at the same time. The siting of the structure in the corner of a large Late Iron Age yard, close to an entranceway, also suggests such a date. A *terminus ante quem* is provided by a narrow Romano-British ditch (F453) which continues SW from the rounded butt-end of a larger Romano-British ditch, F422, before swinging westwards to link up with the main yard system of the final phase (the relationship of the large and small Romano-British ditches was not clear).

Finds distribution (FIG 47): The distribution of finds in the ring-gully shows two pronounced concentrations on either side of the entranceway causeway; the relative scarcity of finds from elsewhere in the ring ditch (flints are probably residual) is most marked, especially in view of the feature's size and depth.

Structures 21-23, 34, 35

Plan (FIG 48): This group of structures is centred on Grid 450W/630N, in the western portion of a ditched yard which was maintained in use from Middle Iron Age to Roman times. The main drainage ditches therefore show considerable evidence for recutting and realignment over time; this may also apply to the structures discussed here, whose layout would be difficult to explain otherwise. Structure 21 consists of an approximately oval gully F270 (10.0m E-W; 11.2m N-S). Its south-east end joins Structure 22 with which it is most probably contemporary and functionally related (perhaps as a fenced yard — *cf* Richmond 1968, FIG 13); its other, north-east, end finishes in a large, vertical-sided, flat-bottomed posthole (dia 0.8m; depth 0.6m). The western part of the gully was difficult to trace and showed signs of disturbance, perhaps associated with the digging of the gully F855. A pit (F732) and a large posthole (F733) blocked the gap (width 1.6m) between Structures 21 and 22; a small posthole (F747) set into the side of the Structure 22 ring-gully (F738) could have formed the south side of a doorway into the yard enclosed by Structures 21 and 22.

Structure 22 has already been mentioned in passing; it was composed of a roughly circular gully (F738) (5.0m N-S, 6.0m E-W) which was continuous, but showed indications of once having had an entranceway facing east (the north terminal could be seen in plan, immediately south of F736).

Structure 23 is clearly closely related morphologically to Structures 21 and 22. It consists of a small ring-gully, F710 (dia *c* 2.6m) connected to a gently curving gully (F711) which extends ENE for 8.5m and ends in a small pit or posthole (F704) 0.3m deep.

Structure 34 is a very shallow arc of gully in the enclosure formed by the gully of Structure 21; it is clearly related, either functionally or chronologically, to Structures 21 and 22, perhaps the pit F750, set into the gully of Structure 22 could be the south side of a doorway, in the manner of F747 2m to the east. The gully F735 and connected posthole (F737) between Structures 21 and 34 is plainly a part of the structure complex and its close similarity to Structure 21 suggests a chronological, rather than functional relationship; unfortunately it was extremely difficult to excavate, being pale and shallow, and could not be traced further west.

Structure 35 is an arc of gully *c* 9.0m long between two main drains, F649 to the north, and F479 to the west. It is difficult to interpret, but would appear, on morphological grounds alone, to be associated with the structures further south.

Relations/phasing: Only one Structure of this complex can be tied into the main ditch system directly. The curved gully of Structure 35 is cut to the north by the Romano-British drainage ditch F649; its western end curves sharply north-west to respect the Late Iron Age drain, F479 — the filling of the two features was closely similar and they are both probably contemporary. Quantities of wheel-made pottery were recovered from ditch

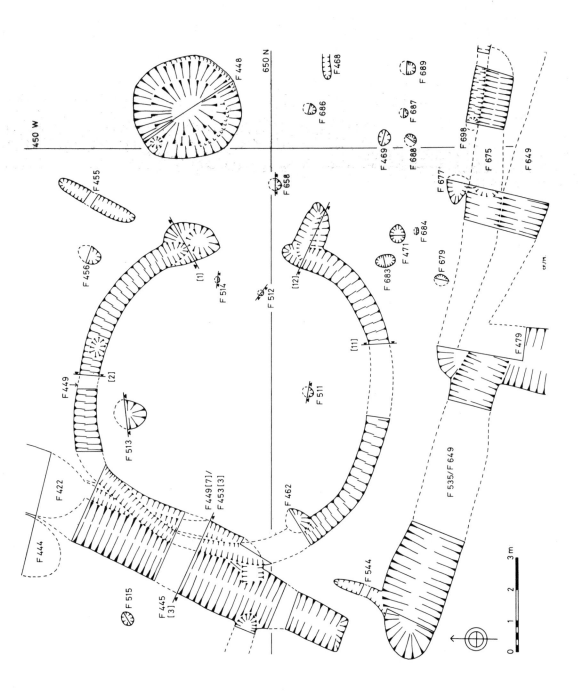

Fig. 46 Cat's Water subsite: Structure 20.

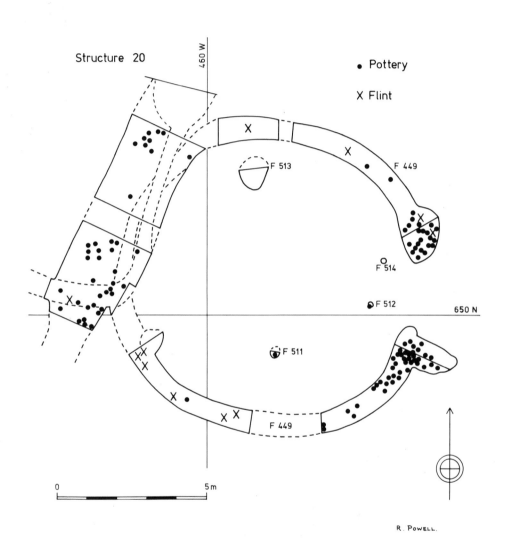

Structure 20

460 W

• Pottery

X Flint

F 513

X

X

F 449

•

F 514

F 512

650 N

F 511

X X
X

X

•

X X

F 449

0   5 m

R. POWELL.

Fig. 47   Cat's Water subsite: Structure 20, finds distribution.

62

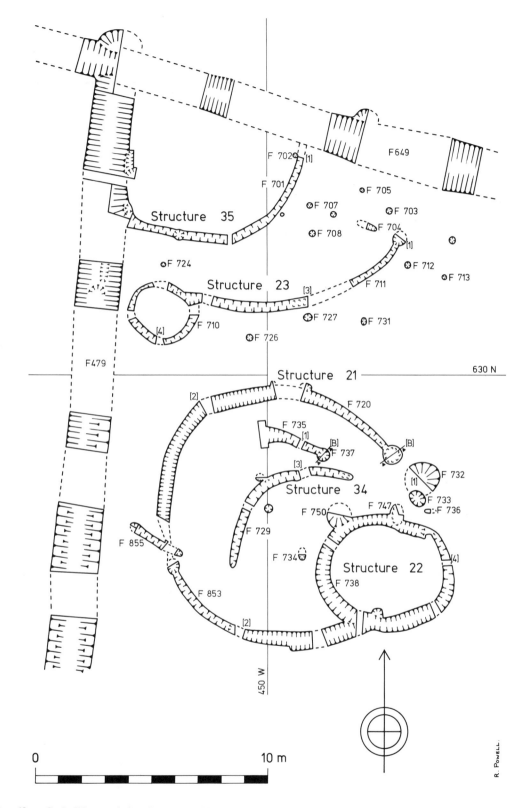

Fig. 48 Cat's Water subsite: Structures 22, 23, 34 and 35.

F479, but none was found in the gullies of Structures 21-23 and 34 and they are accordingly placed in the Middle Iron Age — a date that would accord with the few sherds of diagnostic pottery found. It is not at all improbable that the Late Iron Age ditch had an earlier phase totally removed by later recuts.

Finds distribution (FIG 49): The contrast between the finds density in the structural features and the main drainage ditches is immediately apparent. This must reflect the different size of the two types of features, but only in part, and such a disparate distribution requires further explanation. The absence of proven structures to the west of those discussed here must imply that the finds in the main drainage ditches originated from the latter structures — if indeed they came from any archaeologically demonstrable building. This hypothesis finds some support from the way in which the finds density increases as the area of the structures is approached (ie there is a decrease to the south, in F479, and east, in F649). The gradual increase implies that the material originated locally and was not transported from elsewhere and dumped in the ditches. Perhaps the disparity in finds density discussed here is a reflection of reality: the buildings were kept clean and rubbish was allowed to accumulate in the nearest convenient large ditch.

Structures 24, 37-40

Plan (FIG 50): The structures of this complex have two foci, Structures 24 and 40 are centred on Grid 332W/680N and structures 37-39 on Grid 440W/680N. Structure 24 consists of a small (dia 3.6m) ring-gully, F1281, and a posthole F1275 which may or may not be associated with the structure (or the adjacent Structure 40). In plan, this small ring-gully is approximately pentagonal, has no apparent entranceway and has a markedly flattened east side, respecting a phase of the nearby main drain, F1086.

Structure 37 is the most northerly of the three structures (37-9) NW of 24 and 40; each consists of an irregular arc of gully of varying length, but none overlap and all are morphologically very similar. Structure 37 shows some evidence for modification; the main gully (F1278) cuts an earlier gully, F1273 near its eastern butt-end, to give the impression of a long, expanded terminal; F1273 may also have continued further west along the course of F1278. A second, much shorter gully, F1282, cuts the main gully and may, perhaps be associated with another short gully, F1300, some 2.4m to the SSW.

Structure 38 is represented by an arc gully, F1284, which appears to curve around F1300; this gully, unlike that of Structure 37, does not show evidence for recutting.

Structure 39 is the most southerly of the group. It consists of an irregular, ?-shaped gully (F1285/1325) which either butts just short of F1281 (the ring gully of Structure 24) or is continued into it by a shallow

extension — it was very difficult to interpret in the field. The pronounced change in direction, from E-W to NW-SE at Grid 438W/682N, may indicate modification, with one phase terminating on line with the eastern butt-ends of Structures 37 and 38.

Structure 40 consisted of two E-W steep-sided gullies, F1274 (length 5.8m) and F1279 (length 6.5m) located immediately north and south of Structure 24 which they both cut.

Relations/phasing: The features discussed here can best be considered in three groups, the multi-period main drain, F1086; Structures 24 and 40; Structures 37-39. The location of the structures so close to the southern butt-end of the important drain and boundary F1086 is most probably for a functional and, therefore, chronological reason. Structure 24 clearly respects the west edge of F1086 (hence its flattened east side), but is cut by its latest (Late Iron Age) recut. Structure 40, on the other hand, seems to respect Structure 24, but cuts it in two places and clearly post-dates the last phase of the main drain, F1086. This would suggest that later phases of Structure 24 did not require deep foundations and that the main drain filled-in rapidly. Turning to Structures 37-39, their layout suggests contemporaneity with the features just discussed, but direct stratigraphic evidence is lacking.

Finds distribution (FIG 51): The distribution of finds in these features in most informative. First, the concentration of material in the two gullies of Structure 40 supports the stratigraphic evidence that it cut the ring-gully of Structure 24. Second, the rarity of finds in Structure 24 and, by contrast, the concentration of material around the eastern butt-end of F1325 (Structure 39) suggests that the two features are probably not associated in the manner, for instance, of Structure 23 (FIG 48). This would imply that Structures 39 and 40 are functionally and chronologically related. Turning to the remaining three structures, these are best interpreted sequentially, Structures 37 and 38 are clearly not contemporary, as their layout to the west (where they almost touch) makes clear.

Similarly, the eastern butt-end of Structure 37 is too close to Structure 40 for contemporaneity but could be associated with Structure 24; the gap (c 0.8m) between the two structures would be narrow, but usable. The wider gap between Structures 24 and 38 may perhaps reflect a change in livestock management methods, but whether before or after the construction of Structure 37, is not clear. It was noted above that Structure 39 could be two-phased; if this is accepted, the first phase would be associated with Structure 24, the second with Structure 40. Two points, perhaps reflecting a common function, unite the features of Structures 37-39: first their western butt-ends (which, like their eastern butt-ends were steep and well-defined) terminate on a clear NW-SE line and finds are virtually absent; second, their western butt-ends are marked by a pronounced increase in finds density. Finally, the strong resemblance of these

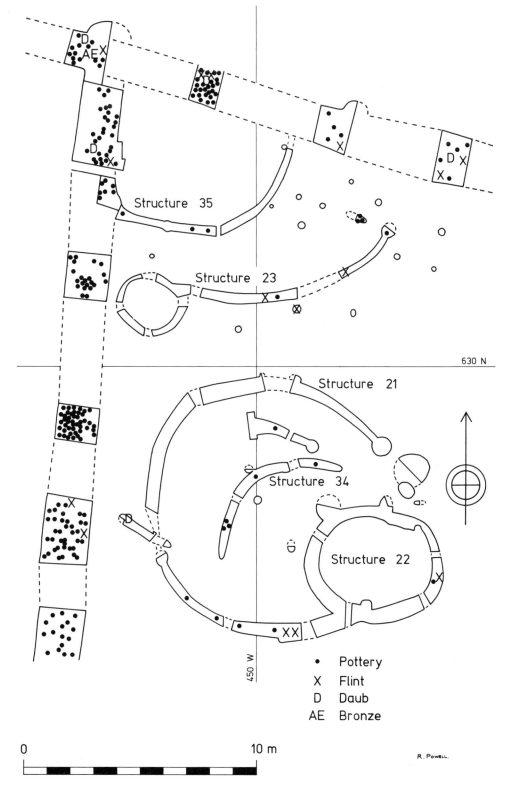

• Pottery
X Flint
D Daub
AE Bronze

0   10 m

R. Powell.

Fig. 49   Cat's Water subsite: Structures 22, 23, 34 and 35, finds distribution.

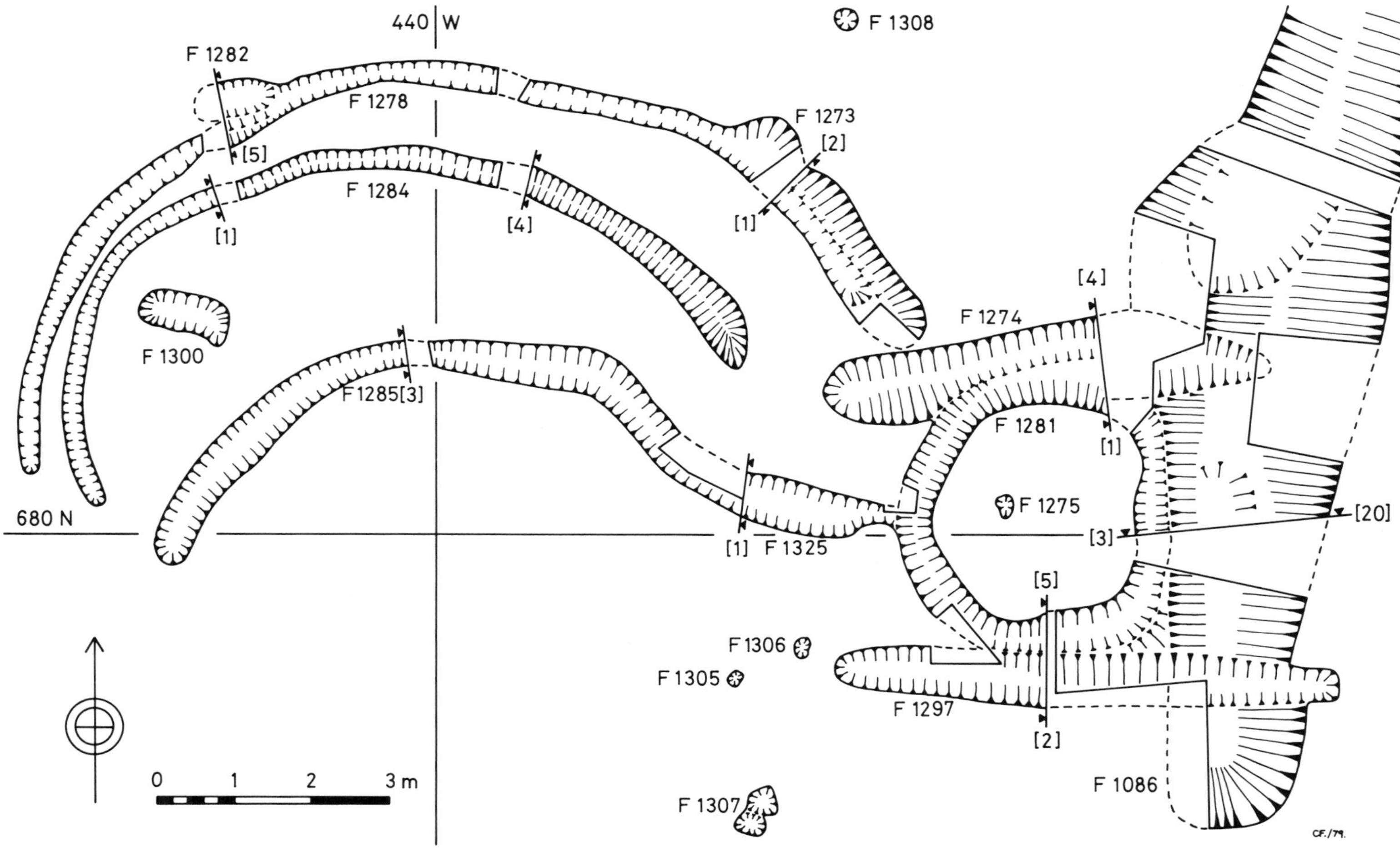

Fig. 50 Cat's Water subsite: Structures 24, 37, 38, 39 and 40.

66

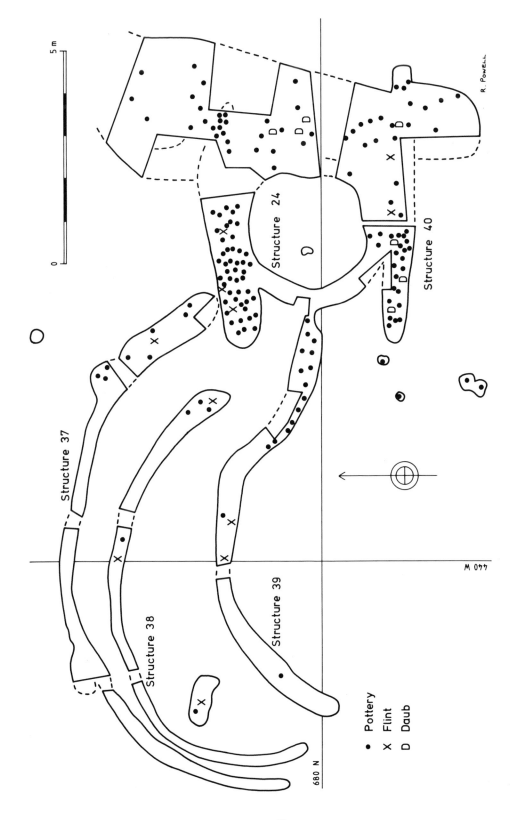

Fig. 51 Cat's Water subsite: Structures 24, 37, 38, 39 and 40, finds distribution.

Pottery •
Flint X
Daub D

R. Powell

5 m

680 N

M 077

Structure 24

Structure 40

Structure 37

Structure 38

Structure 39

67

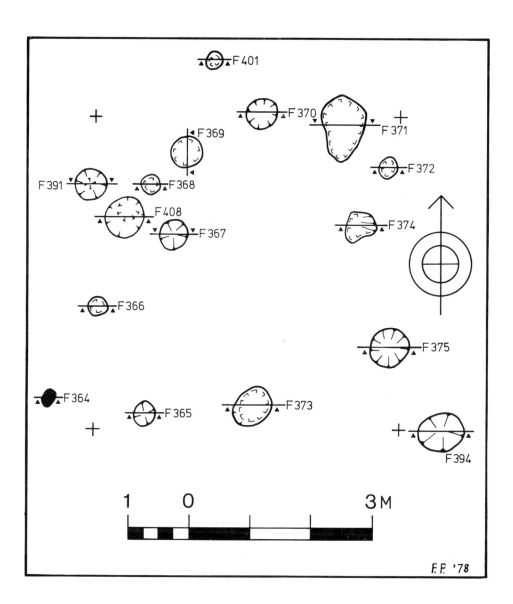

Fig. 52   Cat's Water subsite: Plan of possible Structure 26; one dubious feature is shown in black.

features to those described above (Structures 21-23, 34) suggests a similar function, probably associated with animal management.

Structure 25 — see Structure 7

Structure 26

Plan (FIG 52): This structure was unlike any other found on the subsite. In form it was amorphous, but had an open space *c* 3.0m by 3.0m at its approximate centre (Grid 407W/737N) and was composed of unusually large and deep, steep-sided postholes, many of which contained charcoal. Only one posthole was dubious (probably natural) and this has been shaded black on the plan. Attempts were made in the Iron Age interim report (Pryor and Cranstone 1978, 22) to reconstruct this building, if such it was, but these were not successful and will not be advanced again here.

Relations/phasing: The postholes of Structure 26 did not yield any datable material, but the general spread (NW-SE) of pits and other non-linear features, of which the structure seems to form a part, are of later Iron Age date. The high clay content of some of the posthole fillings (eg F367, F369, F391, F408) might be associated with the wetter conditions that prevailed in the latter years of the Iron Age occupation, but this cannot be considered sound dating evidence. Although an Iron Age date would fit the available data, the absence of pottery would be remarkable in so substantial an Iron Age building at Fengate.

Structures 27 and 28

Plan (FIG 53): These two buildings are located north and slightly east of Structure 19, Structure 27 is centred on Grid 436W/667N; Structure 28 on 438W/659N.

Structure 27 consists of two arcs of ring-gully, features 426 and 429, of *c* 9.0m-10.0m diameter. Both arcs are cut by the steep-sided gully (F427) of Structure 28 and their relationship is thus not clear, but F429, the easterly gully, appears to butt immediately south of Structure 28. The westerly arc of the gully must have terminated beneath F427, as it does not reappear south of it. The northern terminals of each gully are steep and well-defined, that of F429 being slightly expanded, perhaps to accommodate an upright.

Structure 28, although superficially similar in plan to Structures 19 (in its first phase) and 27, is quite distinct in its technique of construction. It consists of a semi-circular gully, F427 of *c* 9.0m-10.0m diameter and (probably) a rectilinear pit, F450, in the interior of Structure 19, some 2.5m due south-east. The pit is deep and steep-sided and has a filling highly reminiscent of the main gully (see FIG 18 for an overall view; FIGS 22 and 45 for detailed plans of the eastern portion of Structure 28). The other (western) end of the gully was marked by a deep pit-like enlargement which probably held the upright that took the weight of the long open side of this structure; the other upright would have been located in the pit F450.

Relations/phasing: Both pit (F450) and ring-gully (F427) of Structure 28 have produced Roman pottery, and this would accord with its location at the centre of a large ditched Romano-British yard. The gully of Structure 28 clearly cuts both gullies of Structure 27, and it is also probably later than Structure 19 (see the discussion of that building above). Structure 19 has been dated to the Late Iron Age and Structure 27 is probably of that period as well; its location, with, perhaps, a narrow pathway between the two buildings, suggests contemporaneity; the hint of an entranceway facing southwards, towards the postulated first phase entrance-way of Structure 19, also suggests a functional association.

Finds distribution (FIGS 45 and 54): The finds from Structure 27 are too few for comment, but those from Structure 28 strongly support the association, discussed above, of gully (F427) and pit (F450); the absence of finds from the other end of the gully is, however, striking. Perhaps the entranceway to the east — which may have been used by people rather than livestock — was consolidated with 'hard core' which included pottery. The open south of the building — which would have been used by animals — might perhaps have been covered with straw, as on a modern farm.

Structure 29

Plan (FIG 55): Structure 29 consisted of an arc of gully (length 7.2m approximate diameter 7.5m-8.0m), F541, centred on Grid 419W/659N. Both butt-ends were steep-sided and clearly defined and the course of the gully was angular — not smoothly curved.

Relations/phasing: Pottery from the gully filling included wheel made sherds of Iron Age type.

Finds distribution: Finds were too rare to form significant patterns, but finds (and charcoal) around the northern butt-end suggest the one-time presence of an entranceway.

FIG M50, bottom: F541 [1, 3] layer 1 (Gully): Sand-silt with patches (lumps) of blue clay, burnt daub (10YR 4/2); charcoal common, dense around northern butt-end and associated with clay patches. Burnt stones were also found, and the natural sub-soil had been reddened by heat.

Structure 30 — see Structure 10

Structure 31 — see Structure 10

Structures 32 and 33

Plan (FIG 57): Structures 32 and 33 are located in an area rich in evidence for multi-period occupation (Grids 408W/634N and 416W/628N respectively). Structure 32 is represented by an arc of gully, F603, of very approximate diameter 6.5-7.0m. It survives in two lengths, apparently giving access to a narrow entrance-way, but the gully was very shallow and its survival

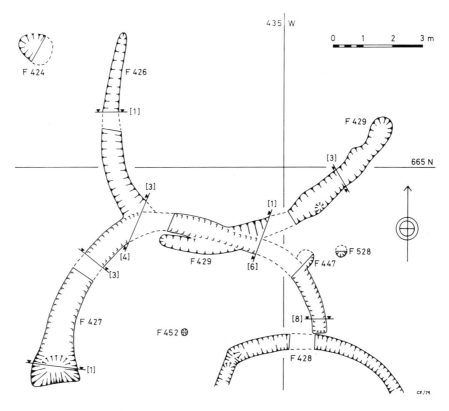

Fig. 53 Cat's Water subsite: Structures 27 and 28.

consequently uneven; the gap is probably the result of post-depositional damage. Structure 33 is even more difficult to trace; it consisted of an arc of gully aligned approximately N-S (F636). Its northern butt-end was, however, quite well-defined and the two shallow post-holes immediately to the north may, perhaps, be the remains of a door or porch. Its SE course was extremely difficult to follow, but an examination of the surface clearly indicated that the gully was cut by the main drain, F633/548.

Relations/phasing: If it is assumed that both structures were originally round buildings, then (a) they cannot be strictly contemporary, as their projected courses interlock and (b) they cannot be contemporary with any phase of the main drainage ditches in the vicinity. The earliest proven drain in the area is F624 which is of Middle Iron Age date. This feature stops short of the main NE-SW drain complex (F548, F600, F633 etc) and probably originally formed a corner entranceway with it; the latter features, which are of Late Iron Age date cut Structures 32 and (probably) 33. It is interesting to note that the two structures' gullies do not appear to the east of the main drain and it is possible that they owe

their survival to the protection afforded by a bank along the drain's west side.

Finds/distribution (FIG 58): No obvious pattern can be discerned, but the quantity of flintwork is notable; the many fragments of daub in the northern section of the main NE-SW drain come from a clay oven which was discarded in the ditch at this point.

Structure 33 — see Structure 32

Structure 34 — see Structure 21

Structure 35 — see Structure 21

Structure 36

Plan FIG 55, above: An arc of gully (F467) of approximate diameter 8.5m and centred on Grid 442W/644N. This feature has the same slightly angular plan as Structure 19. Both butt-ends were steep and clearly defined. The small gully F468 is probably associated with the structure — perhaps as an entranceway screen — and its filling blended into that of the main gully.

Relations/phasing: The large gully (F467) contained

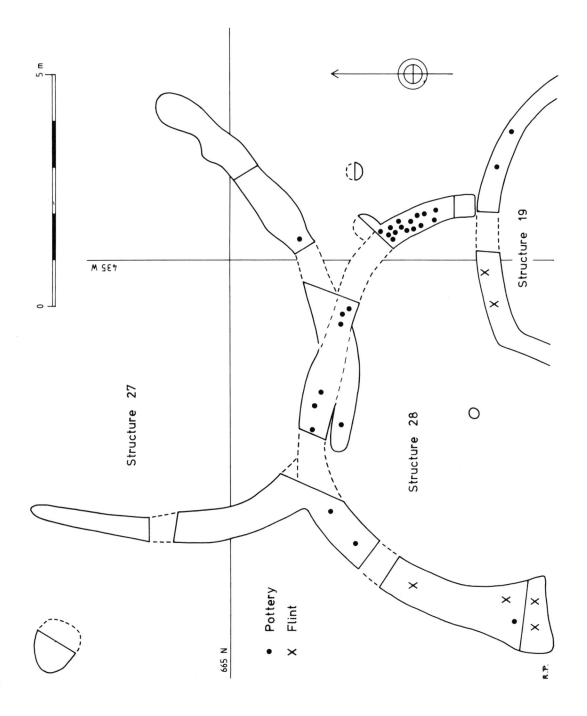

Fig. 54 Cat's Water subsite: Structures 27 and 28, finds distribution.

71

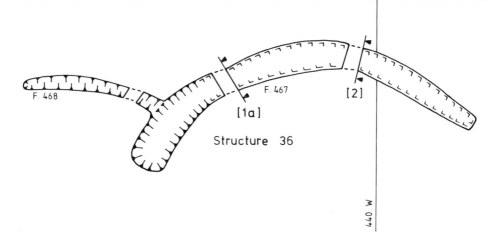

650 N

F. 468

F. 467

[1a]

[2]

440 W

Structure 36

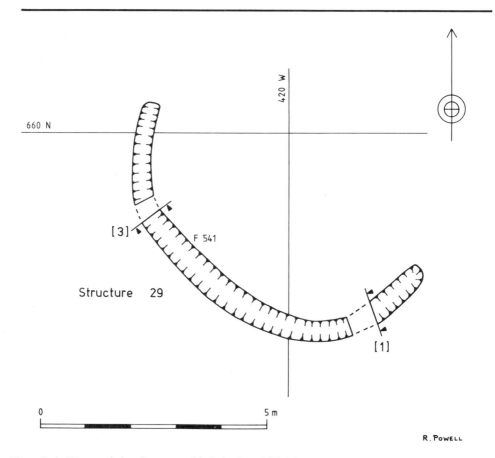

420 W

660 N

[3]

F 541

Structure 29

[1]

0   5 m

R. POWELL

Fig. 55   Cat's Water subsite: Structures 29 (below) and 36 (above).

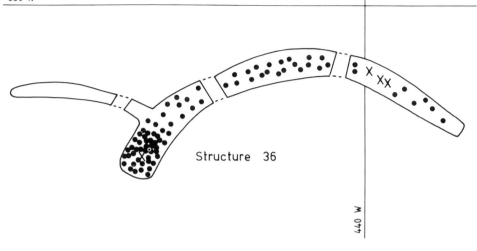

Structure 36

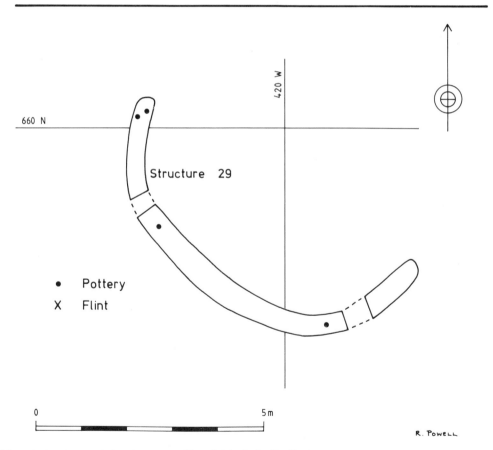

Structure 29

• Pottery

X Flint

0   5 m

R. POWELL

Fig. 56   Cat's Water subsite: Structures 29 and 36, finds distribution.

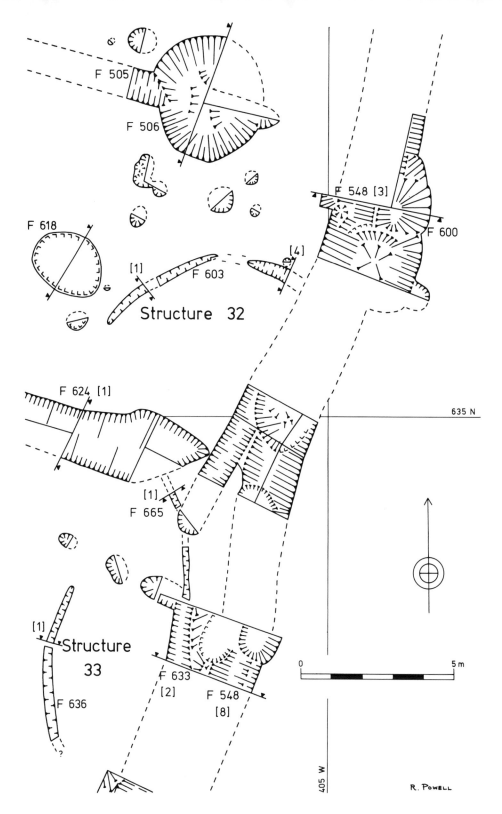

Fig. 57 Cat's Water subsite: Structures 32 and 33 and associated features.

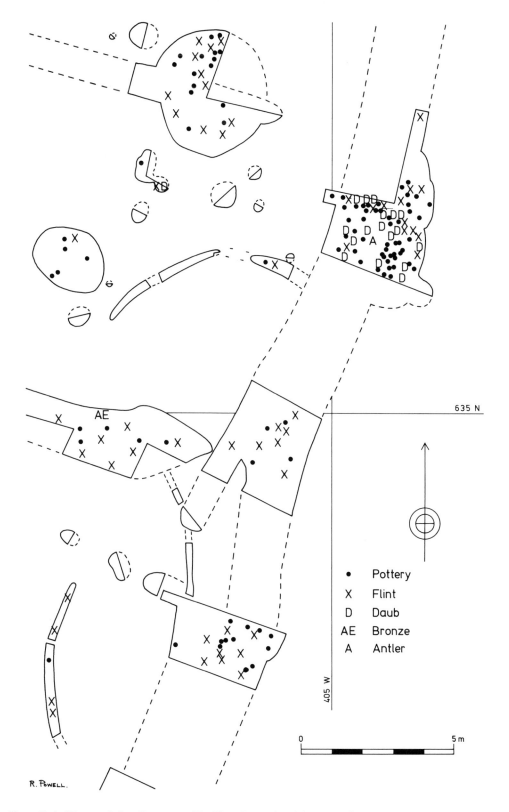

Fig. 58   Cat's Water subsite: Structures 32, 33 and associated features, finds distribution.

75

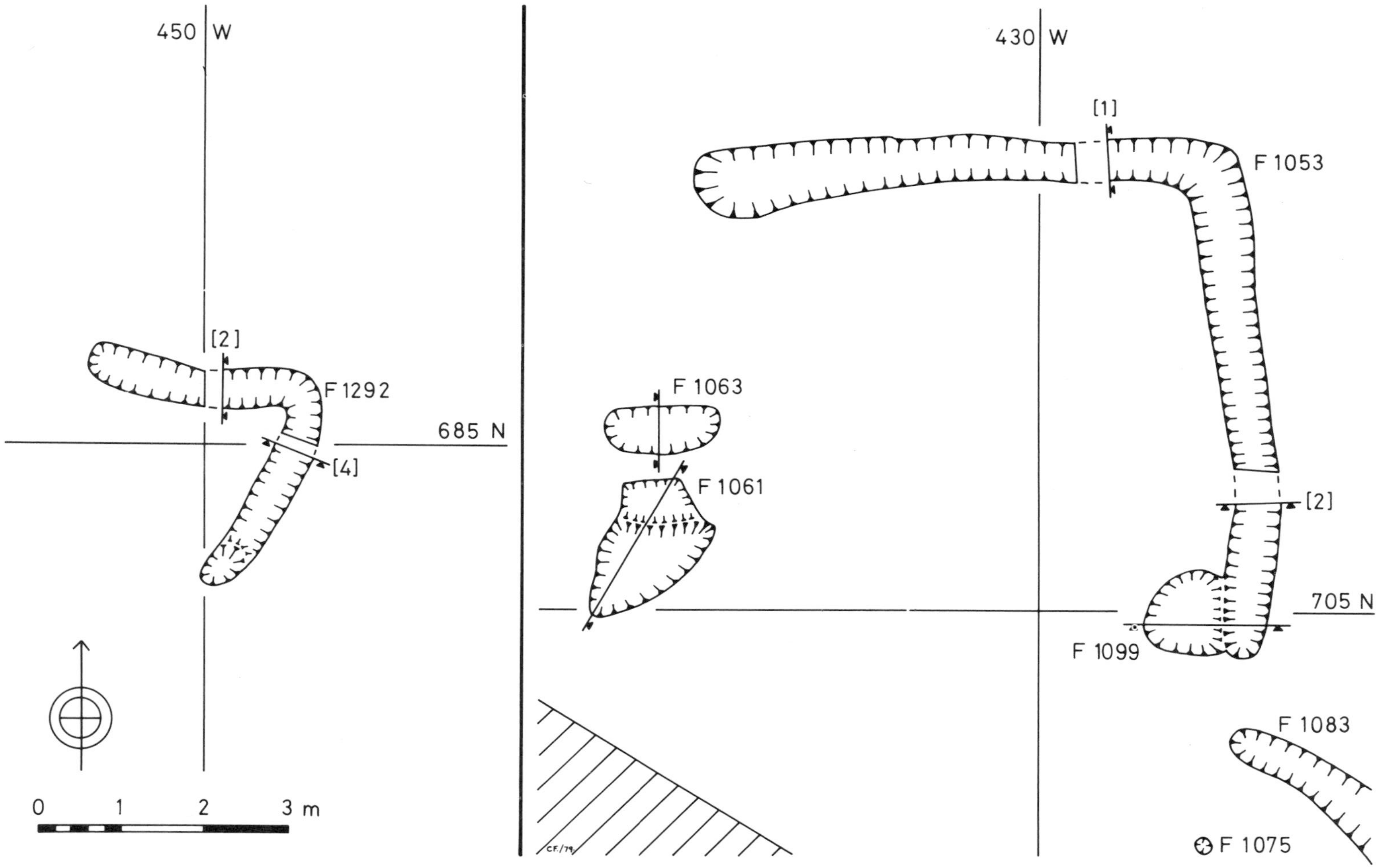

Fig. 59 Cat's Water subsite: Structures 41 (right) and 45 (left).

76

quantities of wheel-made Iron Age pottery, indicating a Late Iron Age date; the small gully (F468) pointed directly towards the entranceway of nearby Structure 20 and an association seems probable (FIG 18). The small gully also runs precisely parallel to the main Late Iron Age drain/enclosure ditch some 5m to the south. Structures 20, 35 and 36 seem to form a coherent group around the offset entranceway of a major Late Iron Age ditched yard.

Finds distribution (FIG 55, above): The finds distribution shows a gradual, but most pronounced concentration of material around the gully's western butt-end. The absence of finds from the small gully is probably a reflection of that feature's small size.

Structure 37 — see Structure 24

Structure 38 — see Structure 24

Structure 39 — see Structure 24

Structure 40 — see Structure 24

Structures 41 and 45

Plan FIG 59: These two structures are the only two possible post-Neolithic buildings of rectilinear plan at Fengate. Both are difficult to interpret, but of the two, Structure 41 is more convincing as a building than are the slight remains of Structure 45. Structure 41 (FIG 59, right) is centred on Grid 431W/707N and is composed of the L-shaped gully F1053 and three recut postholes, features 1061, 1063, and 1099. The L-shaped gully is consistent in depth (0.45m), is steep-sided and regular in plan; its E-W arm is 6.6m long and its N-S is 6.3m long. Its south butt-end is cut by the shallow feature 1099 (this may represent replacement of a post and would not necessarily remove the posthole from the structure) and, like the north-eastern butt-end, it is steep-sided and well-defined. The south-western post-holes are not ideally situated to act as corner supports, assuming, that is, that the steep-sided L-shaped gully is a wall slot and not an eaves-drip gully. F1061, for example, appears to have been placed too far north and west for correct alignment on the two butt-ends of the gully. If F1061 had been placed further south-east, then the elongated posthole or slot, F1063 could have been used as, perhaps, a short partition wall midway along the building's open west side; as it stands, however, it makes little sense in a structural context. The filling of features 1099 and 1061 was dumped-in and their undulating profiles suggest more than one period of use; the filling of the main gully, too, appears to have been dumped in, although evidence for recutting here is not apparent. F1063 could be variously interpreted as a recut posthole or small gully. If Structure 41 is accepted as a building, its south and west sides would have been open, and the roof would be supported by post(s) set in F1061, together with the north and east walls (set in the

gully F1053). The floor area available would have been about 25 sq m.

Structure 45 is represented by the small L-shaped gully F1292 centred on Grid 450W/685N (FIG 59, left). It measures 2.8m E-W and 2.6m NE-SW. This gully is not a perfect right-angle and both its butt-ends are sharp and clearly defined; that to the SW shows some evidence for once having held a post. It is not, however, convincing as a permanent building, and probably represents the remains of a temporary structure.

Relations/phasing: Both buildings are located outside the ditched Romano-British yards in areas of extensive Late Iron Age occupation. Structure 45 is probably somewhat earlier, but also in the Late Iron Age phase of the settlement.

Finds distribution (FIG 60): The finds from Structure 45 are too few for comment, but those from Structure 41 raise two points. First, the high but evenly spaced density of material in the back-filled gully F1053 suggests, perhaps, a common source (for example a rubbish or manure heap) for the material in it. Second, the comparative scarcity of material in the postholes F1061, F1063 and F1099 could indicate either that they filled in by weathering (or, alternatively, that they were filled-in with material that derived from a different source to that found in the gully).

Structure 42

Plan (FIG 61): 'Structure' 42 consists of two gullies (F72 and F74/85) and three pits (F76/80, F73 and F77), centred on Grid 370W/702N. The gullies are arranged north and south of two entranceways facing SE and NW (width 2.1 and 3.6m respectively). The northern gully (F72) is angular in plan and encloses three sides of a rectangle of 10.2m by 6.0m; the south-western butt-end shows signs of modification: originally the SW butt-end veered towards the SE, but this was abandoned, and the second, deeper, phase was terminated some 1.4m further north (indicated by the dashed line in FIG 61). The southern gully (F74) was originally straight, except at its eastern end where it turned north-west, as the gully F85. This gully was abandoned in the second phase where the pit F77 provided an eastern terminal for the main E-W gully.

Turning to the pits, these are all located at gully corners; F77 we have seen, belongs to the second phase of the southern gully. The pit F76 is either contemporary with, or represents a massive enlargement of, the second phase of the northern gully, F72; it appears to cut the large pit F80. Finally, the pit F73 is located in the north-eastern corner of the structure and appears to have been open at the same time as the gully (F72): gully and pit fillings merge into each other and are probably broadly contemporary. The location of the three large pits on the corners of the gully enclosure must indicate broad contemporaneity. The apparent relationships of the various pits and gullies most probably reflects the state of affairs when the structure,

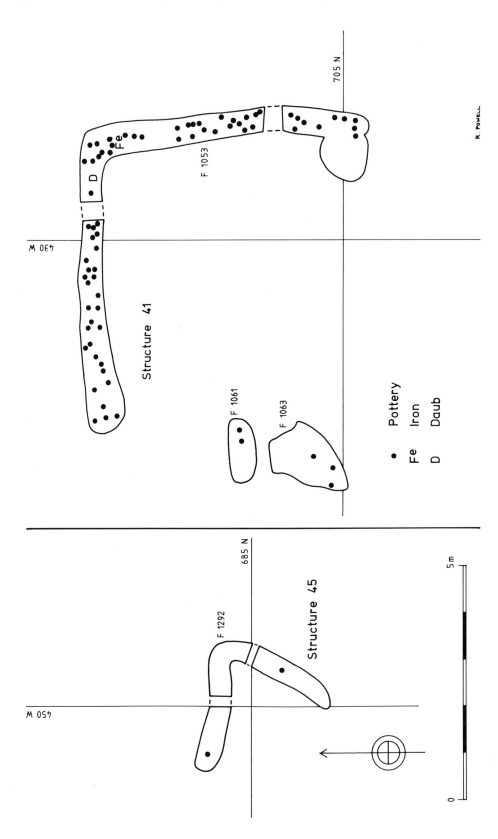

705 N

R. POWELL

430 W

Fe

D

Fe

F 1053

F 1061

F 1063

Structure 41

Pottery

Fe   Iron

D   Daub

685 N

450 W

F 1292

Structure 45

5 m

0

Fig. 60   Cat's Water subsite: Structures 41 (right) and 45 (left), finds distribution.

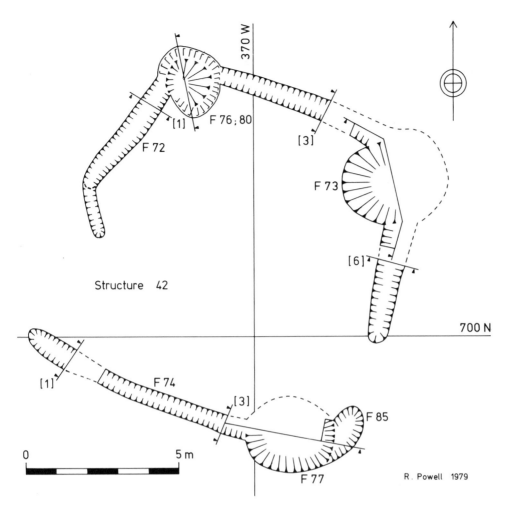

F 76 : 80

[1]

[3]

F 72

F 73

[6]

Structure 42

700 N

[1]

F 74

[3]

F 85

0   5 m

F 77

R. Powell 1979

Fig. 61   Cat's Water subsite: Structure 42.

as a whole, was cleaned out for the last time. The plan suggests that the structure was subject to modification and that the building, if such there was, was located within the area enclosed by the gullies and the corner pits. Certainly, the corner pits are too deep to be considered as structural features *sensu stricto* and are best seen as water-holes or soak-aways.

Relations/phasing: Its location on the extreme eastern edge of the settlement, together with the large quantities of scored ware found in the filling of its component features strongly suggest that Structure 42 is of Middle Iron Age date.

Finds distribution (FIG 62): The finds distribution is not very informative; the second phase of the northern gully's SW butt-end is well brought out by the distribution of pottery, but otherwise there is little of interest, except for the fact that the pottery and flint distribution are apparently unrelated. The tendency of flintwork to be concentrated towards the west may reflect the

presence of the second millennium ditch iii just 6.0m to the west.

Structure 43 — see Structure 9

Structure 44

Plan (FIGS 31 and 38): This structure, or, more probably, this enclosure, is defined by the curved gullies F1082 and F1200, centred on Grid 418W/698N. The area in question is much disturbed by Iron Age settlement activity, but it is probable that the two gullies originally joined together to form a continuous arc (approximate diameter 12.0m). The north and south butt-ends are, however, well defined; both show possible evidence for posts and that to the north has been recut at least once. Its irregular course is comparable, for instance, with that of the gully F491 (Structure 13, FIG 38), and its use as part of the building is possible. A more plausible explanation, however, is that it is

79

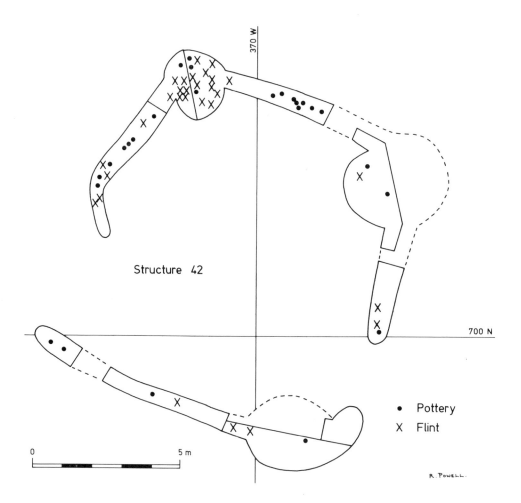

370 W

700 N

Structure 42

• Pottery

X Flint

0   5 m

R. POWELL.

Fig. 62 Cat's Water subsite: Structure 42, finds distribution.

associated in some way with an enclosure or corral — perhaps as a fence (or drain) bedding trench. Its course towards Structure 13 (FIG 38) might suggest a functional link, were it not for the fact that the latter building is securely dated to the Middle Iron Age phase of the settlement.

Relations/phasing: The gully of Structure 44 cuts that of Structure 6 (F1044) {Middle Iron Age) and the ditches F780 and F1089 (Late Iron Age). A Late Iron Age date is indicated.

Finds distribution (FIG 32 and 39): No significant pattern could be discerned.

Sections: None are drawn. The gully was shallow (depth 0.2m) and open u-shaped (width *c* 0.3m) with a filling of loam with clay lenses (10YR 3/2) and much charcoal, especially along the southern recut, immediately east of the north butt-end of F1082.

Structure 45 — see Structure 41

Structure 46
A post-built round building centred on Grid 500W/605N described at length in the Third Report (FNG 3, FIGS 94-96) and above (Part 2; see also FIGS 20 and M23). Probably of second millennium date.

Structure 47
Plan (FIG 63): Structure 47 was a round building defined by the '?' shaped gully F1552, centred on Grid 447W/556N. This structure was located on one of the lowest parts of the subsite where the natural gravel ('C' horizon) surface showed considerable signs of flood-disturbance. This often made the delineation and inter-pretation of features difficult. Much of the 'C' horizon was covered in a thin (*c* 0.05-0.1m) coating of gravel

80

pebbles in a clay matrix, which was probably the result of water-sorting (C A I French, pers comm); it is not improbable that many of the sand and gravel lenses that are frequently encountered in the fillings of these low-lying features are the results of flood-disturbance (eg FIG M58, bottom, F1553 layers 1, 2, 4, 5). The gully F1552 was approximately circular (diameter *c* 8.0m) and drained into the nearby main drain F1553 in the first of its two periods of use. Its northern terminal petered out and could not be traced further east, although its course along the dashed line was visible under favourable conditions; good conditions were also required to follow the westward course of the small gully 'A' which is best interpreted as a wall-slot; this feature ended in a small posthole (depth 0.30m) which probably formed the northern part of an eastwards-facing doorway. The southern part of the doorway was probably formed by the posthole F1567 (depth 0.10m); other post- or stake-holes may or may not be associated with the structure (F1550, F1554-5, F1564).

Relations/phasing: The curved gully F1552 shows clear evidence for two phases of use. The first phase is represented by layer 5 (FIG M58, F1552 [8]) which is represented in section 9 (FIG M58, bottom) by layer 7; this layer blends evenly into the main drain, F1553 layer 3 and, further east, into the smaller subsidiary ditches, F1556 and F1559. This phase would appear to be contemporary with a secondary phase of the main drain's period of use, ie subsequent to the deposition of F1553 layer 4 and 5, probably by flood action. F1553 is tentatively placed in the Early Iron Age on pottery evidence. The second phase of the gully is seen most clearly in section 7 (FIG M58, top right) where layer 1 is an off-centre, phase 2, recut of layer 2 (phase 1). The two phases can be seen in plan west of section 7; west of section 3, however, the two phases follow the same course (FIG 63). Nearer the main drain, in section 8, the second phase is represented by the southerly layers 1-4; these deposits produced large quantities of coarse shell-tempered (Fabric 1A) scored ware of characteristic Middle Iron type. The second phase recut is less clearly seen in plan at the intersection with the main drain, but F1552 layer 6 in section 9 is the equivalent of F1552 layer 3 in section 8; both layers are capped by thin gravel lenses (? flood-action). The main drain had gone out of use by the structure's second phase; consequently the gully ends in an expanded soak-away (indicated by shading in FIG 64). In sum, the available evidence suggests that the first phase is probably Early Iron Age (ie pre-scored ware), the second Middle Iron Age (scored wares).

Finds distribution (FIG 64): None of the suggested internal features yielded any finds. In the gully, the great majority of material derives from the deeper, eastern parts, especially those layers representing the second phase of use. Perhaps some of these finds were transported to their present positions by water. This gully is situated on the downhill side of the structure and

makes very obvious use of the land's slight slope; it also becomes progressively deeper from NE to SW, suggesting a deliberate drainage gradient (compare, for example, FIG M58, F1552 sections 1 and 8). The need to keep the gully clear might explain the apparent rarity of first phase finds (and deposits).

Structure 48

Plan (FIG 65): Structure 48 was a round building defined by the gully F1576, centred on Grid 454W/454N, approximate diameter 12.0m. Only the south-western part of this structure was revealed, the rest lay beneath spoil heaps or was obscured by flood disturbance. A clearly-defined entrance causeway (width 2.0m), facing west is an unusual feature, but there could be no doubt about the steep gully butt-ends on either side. No internal features could be defined, but this could be the result of flood disturbance.

Relations/phasing: Both segments of gully were cut by the Romano-British drainage ditches, F1530. Sherds of scored ware indicate a Middle Iron date for the building.

Finds distribution (FIG 66): There were too few finds for useful comment.

Structure 49

Plan (FIG 67): This round building was one of the most difficult to interpret, largely owing to its probable early date, pale filling and the considerable post-depositional flood disturbance, already alluded to (see Structure 47, Plan). This structure could be faintly discerned at the top of the 'B' horizon as a vague semi-circular stain clearly truncated to the west by the clay-filled upper layer of the Late Iron Age drain F1505. The gully, F1508, was roughly circular (diameter *c* 8.5-9.0m), shallow, open U-shaped and centred on Grid 435W/564N. A shallow depression (F1510) filled with gravel pebbles, but only a few artifacts (it was sieved through ½″ mesh) could possibly be seen as the remains of a floor, or perhaps more plausibly, as a localised flood disturbance (there were many similar examples in the neighbourhood). The gully's intersection with the main drain (F1505) to the north was obscured by a short arc of gully (F1509) which cut F1508, but was, in turn, cut by the main drain (see FIG M60 lower two sections).

Relations/phasing: The relationship of the gully to F1505 and F1509 has just been discussed and a pre-Roman date is indicated. The pottery was unusual and is probably of Early Iron Age type. The very pale filling of the gully would support such an attribution.

Finds distribution (FIG 68): There were too few finds for useful comment.

Structure 50

Plan (FIG 69): This structure was located in the most low-lying part of the settlement where the ground was considerably disturbed by flood action; this made the interpretation of features very difficult. Structure 50

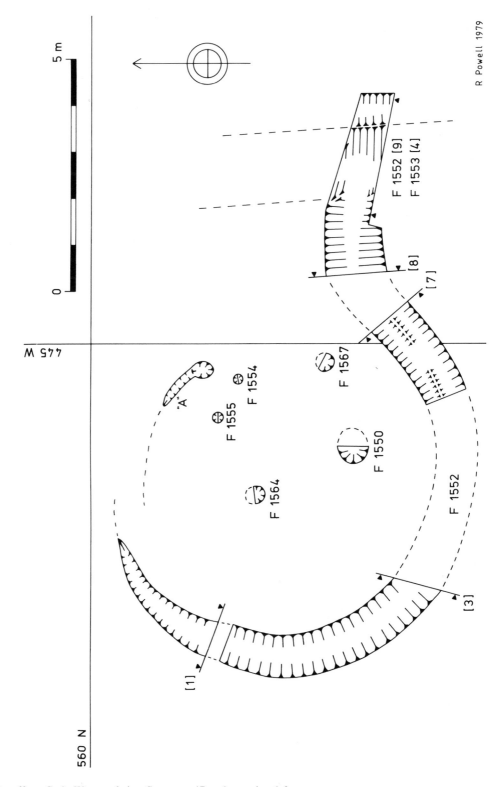

Fig. 63 Cat's Water subsite: Structure 47 and associated features.

82

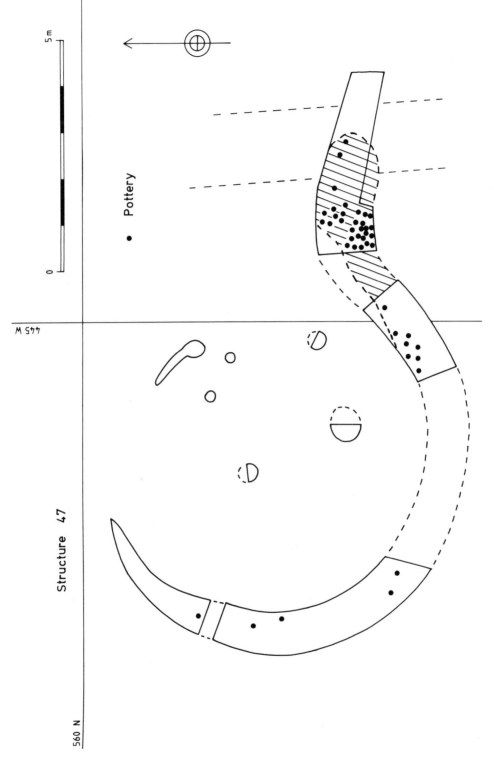

5 m

Pottery

●

M 577

Structure 47

560 N

Fig. 64 Cat's Water subsite: Structure 47, finds distribution (shading indicates the eastern extent of the second phase recut of the gully (F1552)).

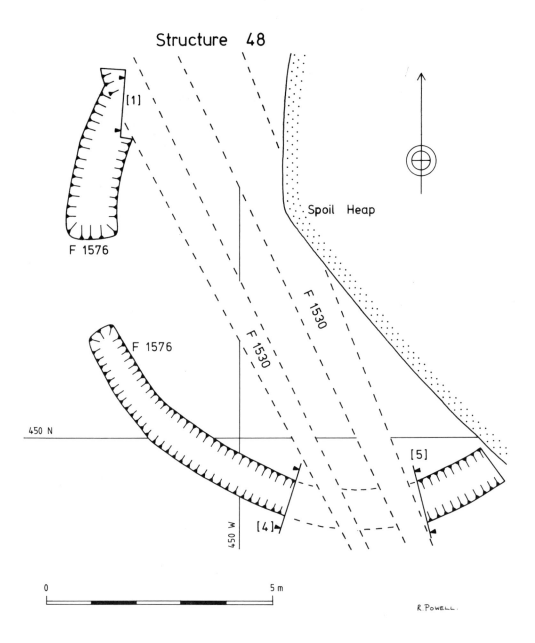

Structure 48

F 1576

[1]

Spoil Heap

F 1530

F 1576

F 1530

450 N

450 W

[4]

[5]

0   5 m

R. POWELL.

Fig. 65   Cat's Water subsite: Structure 48 (F1576).

Structure 48

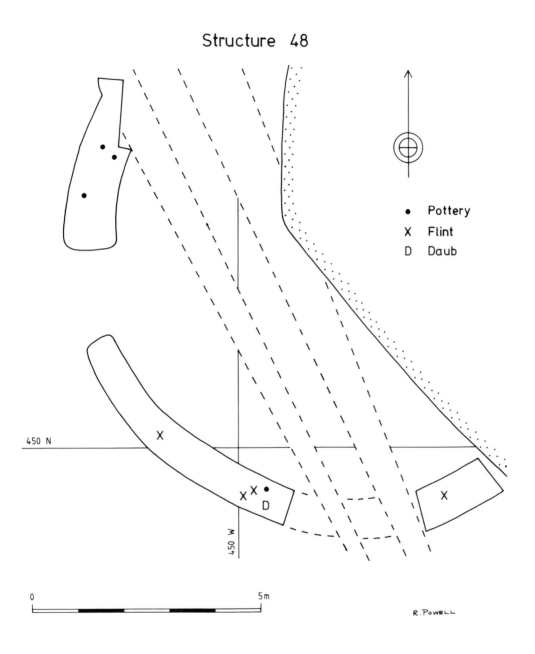

● Pottery
X Flint
D Daub

450 N

450 W

0   5 m

R. POWELL

Fig. 66   Cat's Water subsite: Structure 48, finds distribution.

Structure 49

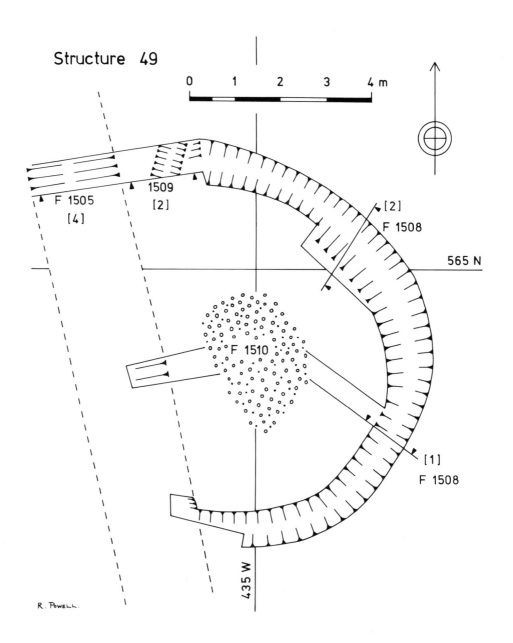

Fig. 67   Cat's Water subsite: Structure 49 and associated features.

86

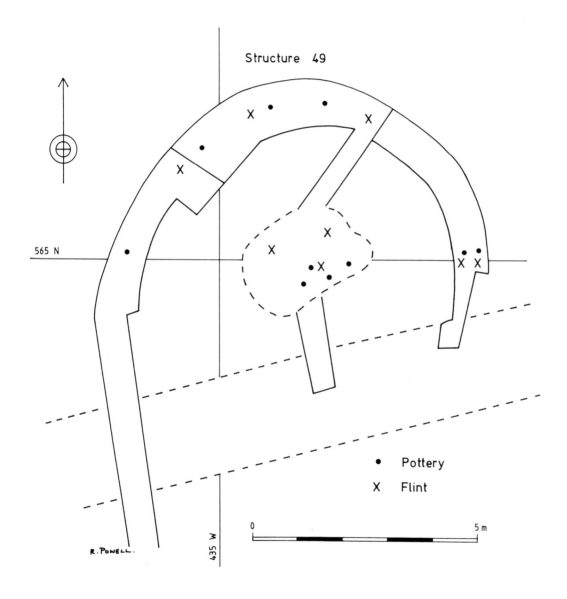

Structure 49

565 N

435 W

• Pottery

X Flint

0   5 m

R. POWELL.

Fig. 68   Cat's Water subsite: Structure 49, finds distribution.

87

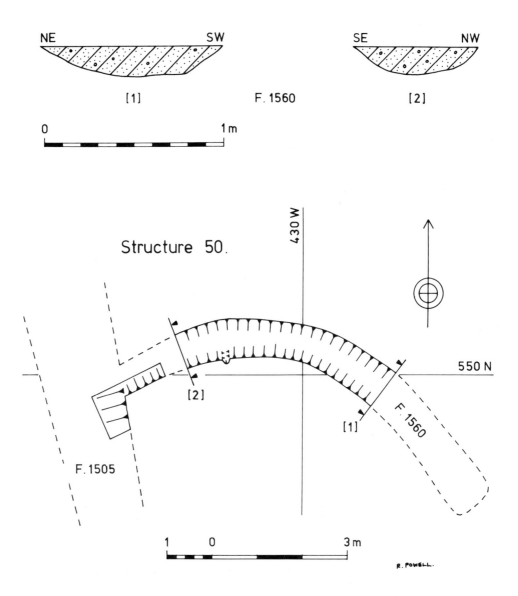

NE   SW   SE   NW

[1]   F. 1560   [2]

0   1 m

Structure 50.

430 W

550 N

[2]

[1]

F. 1560

F. 1505

1   0   3 m

R. POWELL.

Fig. 69   Cat's Water subsite: Structure 50 (F1560), plan and sections.

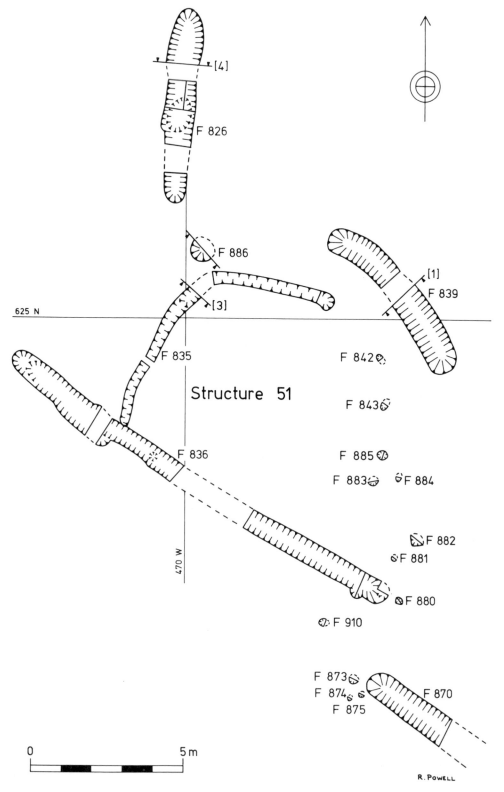

Fig. 70   Cat's Water subsite: Structure 51.

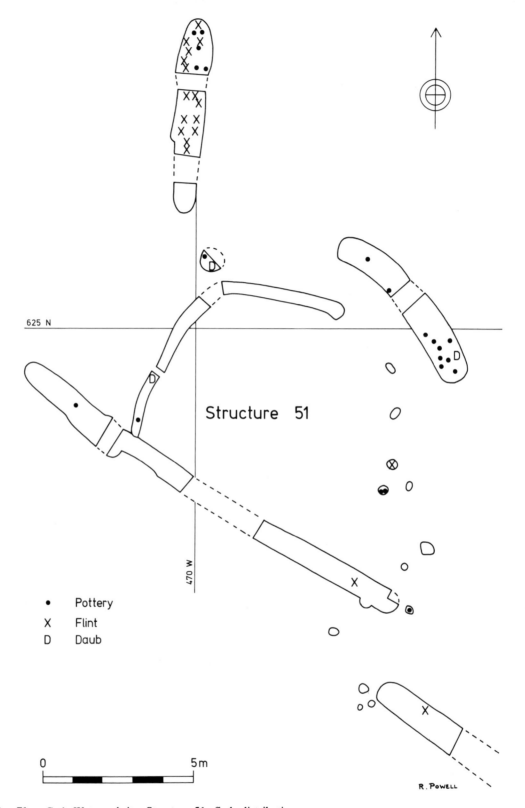

625 N

470 W

Structure 51

- • Pottery
- X Flint
- D Daub

0   5m

R. Powell

Fig. 71   Cat's Water subsite: Structure 51, finds distribution.

was a round building defined by an arc of ring-gully, F1560, of *c* 8.0m diameter, centred on Grid 431W/545N. Its course westwards was obscured by the main drain F1505 and the spoil heaps beyond. Surface patterns indicated a clear squared-off butt-end to the south-east, suggesting the presence of an eastwards-facing entranceway, but no southern extension of the gully could be seen — probably due to flood-action.

Relations/phasing: The gully was cut by the Late Iron Age drain F1505 and a Middle Iron Age date for the structure would seem reasonable — no Late Iron Age features are known from this very low-lying part of the subsite. There were no finds.

Sections (FIG 69): F1560 [1, 2] layer 1 (Structure 50 gully): Sand-silt with scattered gravel pebbles (no Munsell); charcoal common.

Structure 51

Plan (FIG 70): The features grouped here as a 'structure' are located immediately north of the second millennium BC ditch 4 at Grid 470W/625N. The features concerned are: an arc of gully, F839, *c* 5.8m long orientated approximately NW-SE (from Grid 465W/627N to 462W/622N); a longer (*c* 9.0m) curved L-shaped gully, F835, running approximately NE-SW (from Grid 465W/625N to 472W/621N); an irregular row of (?) eight postholes orientated NNW/SSE (features (N-S) 842, 843, 885, 884, 883, 882, 881, 880). The two gullies appear to respect each other and there is a narrow (1.2m) causeway between the two; the southerly gully, F835, has a slightly expanded easterly end, suggesting the presence of a (gateway?) posthole. The eight postholes to the south-east perhaps formed part of a fence or palisade. The south-western side appears to have been left open.

Relations/phasing: The gully F826 which bears a superficial resemblance to F839, produced many flints and a few sherds of second millennium type; its pale filling also indicates a second millennium date, but its alignment bears no resemblance to the orientation of the ditched enclosure system and its dating, although most probably pre Middle Iron Age, must remain obscure. The posthole, F886, produced similar pottery and is also probably pre-Middle Iron Age. The NE-SW ditches F836 and F870 are ditches 4 and 3 (respectively) of the second millennium system, and the small group of stakeholes, F873-5 are probably associated with them. Turning to the three elements of the Structure, the westerly gully, F835, produced a sherd of wheel-made Iron Age pottery, the north-easterly gully F839 produced sherds of scored and wheel-made pottery and the posthole F880 produced two sherds of scored ware. A date in the Late Iron Age for the structure as a whole would fit the evidence best.

Finds distribution (FIG 71): The finds distribution shows an even concentration of flint in the probable second millennium feature F826, to the north-west, and a concentration of pottery around the south-eastern butt-

end of the gully-arc, F839.

Structure 52

Plan (FIG 72, left): This 'structure' consisted of two gullies and a posthole, all centred on Grid 444W/705N. The two gullies were at right-angles: F57 ran NW-SE and was 5.0m long; F58/1323 ran NE/SW and was 3.0m long; the latter gully terminated some 0.05m short of F57 and showed evidence in plan for at least one recut and a possible stake- or post-hole. A vertical-sided posthole, F1324 was located immediately NW of the SW butt-end of F58/1323.

Relations/phasing: The gully F57 produced sherds of wheel-made Late Iron Age pottery.

Finds distribution (FIG 72, centre): There is a slight concentration of material in the NW end of F57.

Sections (FIG 72, right): F57 [1] layer 1 (Structure 52, NE gully): Loam with an even gravel mix (10YR 4/2); charcoal rare.
F58/1323 [1] layer 1: Sand-silt with clay lumps (small; *c* 0.05m) (no Munsell); charcoal rare.
F1324 profile (SW posthole of Structure 52)

Structure 53

Plan (FIG 73): Structure 53 was incorporated within the main easterly system of drainage ditches and was centred on Grid 400W/640N (note orientation of FIGS 73 and 74). It was defined by a multi-phased series of semi-circular ditches (features 569 with 584, 586, 621) of approximate diameter 11.5m. These ditches enclosed the south-eastern side of a semi-circular piece of land which also contained two postholes (features 590-1) and a shallow scoop (F565). The north-eastern butt-end of the inner semi-circular ditch (F569) was everted or expanded, perhaps to hold a large post, and the south-western butt-ends, although less pronounced, were sharp, steep-sided and clearly defined. The general plan (FIG 40) shows that the main drains north-east of Structure 53 either terminated just short of it, or else veered eastwards, apparently respecting it. Two large pits (F586 and F621) had been buried in the bottom of ditch F584, near its eastern edge.

Relations/phasing: Only one reliably dated Middle Iron Age feature (Structure 10) is known from the area, and that is cut by all Late Iron Age drains. The detailed phasing of Structure 53 is very difficult to establish, as recuts seem to cut and then be recut, apparently out of sequence; this probably reflects day-to-day patterns of farm management. In less detail, features 554 and 569 post-date the others, but whether this chronological difference signifies years, rather than decades, cannot be established. Feature 569, the most westerly of the structure ditches, is invariably the latest recut of the complex, and a Late Iron Age date for this ditch is confirmed by the abundant wheel-made pottery recovered.

Finds distribution (FIG 74): The even, widespread distribution of finds reflects the many phases of

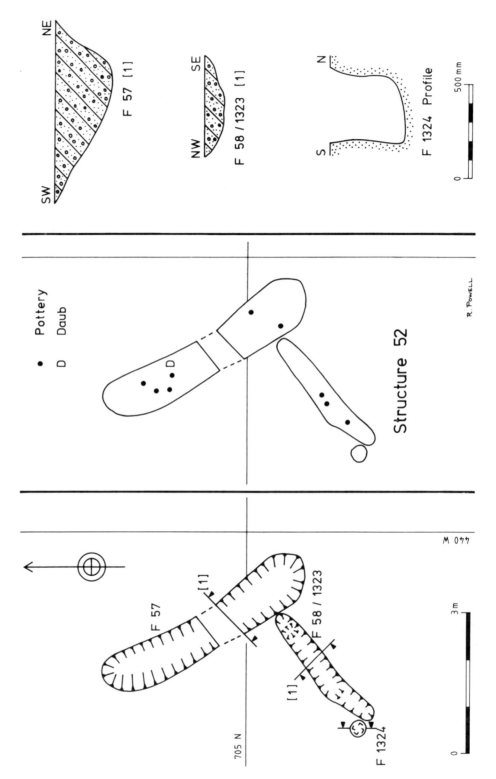

Fig. 72 Cat's Water subsite: Structure 52, plan, finds distribution and sections.

92

Structure 53

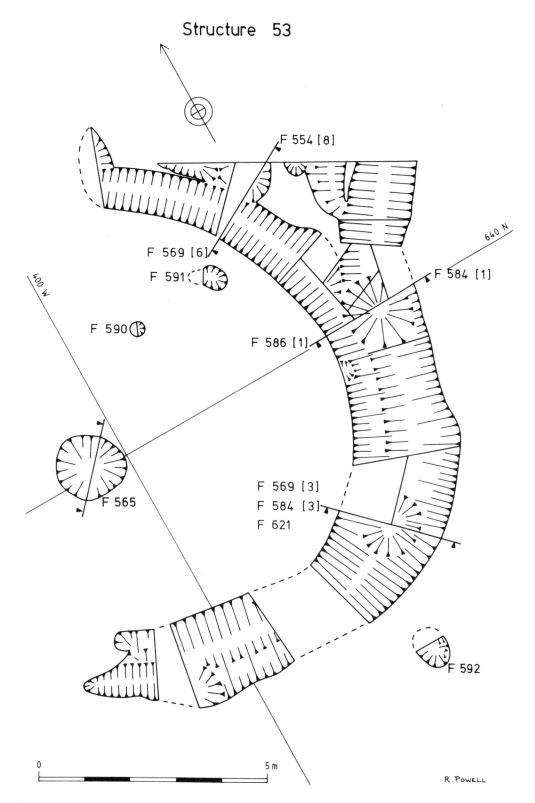

F 554 [8]

640 N

400 W

F 569 [6]

F 591

F 590

F 586 [1]

F 584 [1]

F 565

F 569 [3]
F 584 [3]
F 621

F 592

0   5 m

R. POWELL

Fig. 73   Cat's Water subsite: Structure 53, plan (note orientation).

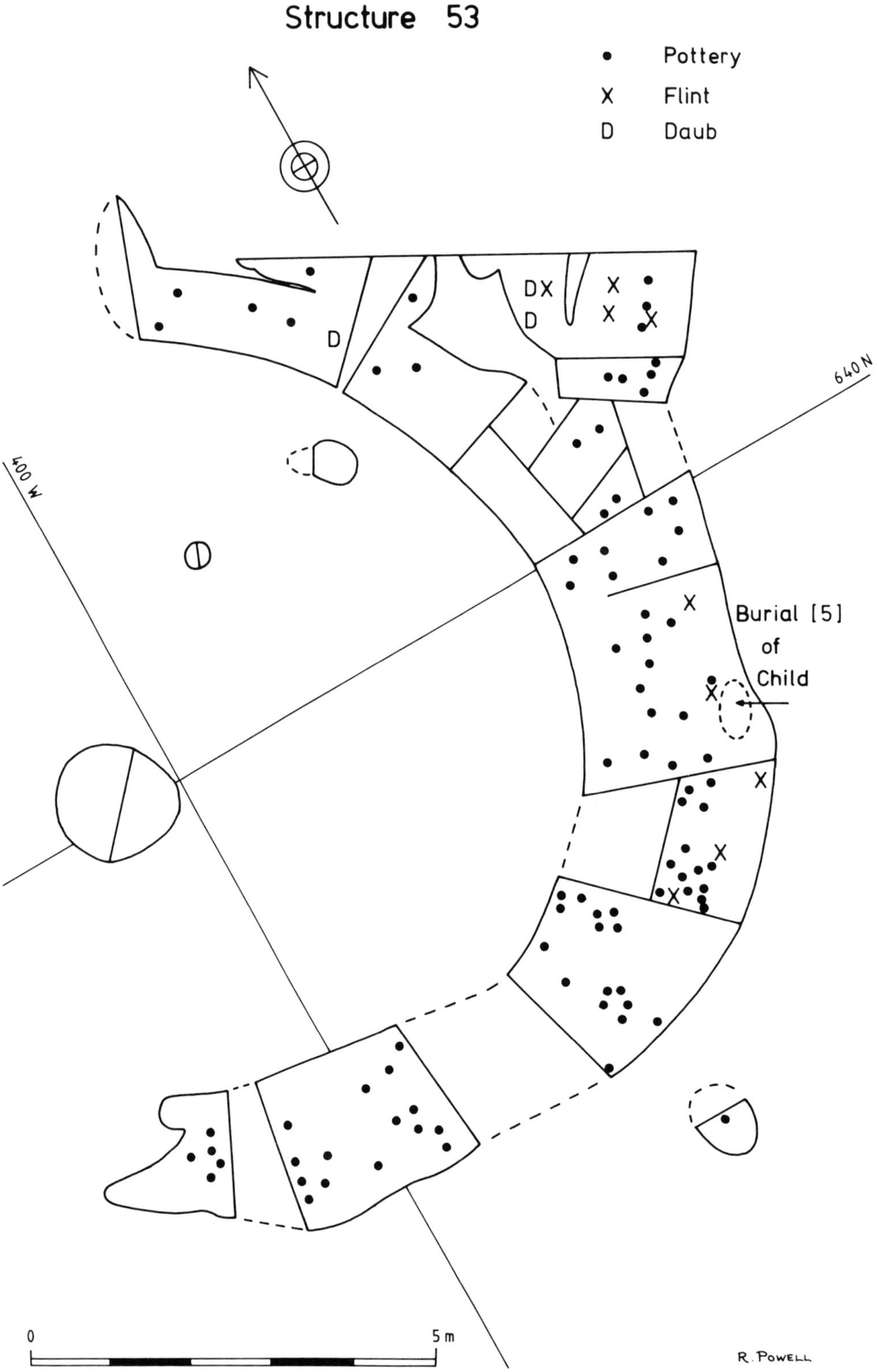

Structure 53

Fig. 74 Cat's Water subsite: Structure 53, finds distribution (note orientation).

recutting seen in the sections. The absence of material in the shallow scoop (F565), would be unusual if that feature had formed part of the Structure.

Structure 54

Introduction

Archaeological features in the southern parts of Area VI and most of Area X were preserved at a higher level — just below the top of the 'B' horizon — than other parts of the Cat's Water subsite. The reasons for this are not clear, but the greater thickness of clay on these lower-lying areas of the subsite may have aided preservation. These favourable conditions caused one building, Structure 54, to be particularly well-preserved and it was examined in greater detail than normal. This often tedious and time-consuming work was carried out by David Crowther and the late Mark Gregson; David Crowther also performed the post-excavation analysis, including the sieving experiments and the following is largely based on his notes.

Structure 54, in common with Structures 3 and 16 further north, was located in a ditched enclosure which appears to be contemporary with the building and abandonment of the structure itself. The following account will be in two parts: first, a discussion of the enclosure and its associated features; this will be followed by a more detailed consideration of the building. Finally there is a brief discussion and summary.

1. The Enclosure and Associated Features

Plan (FIG 75): The rectilinear enclosure around Structure 54 measured approximately 42m (E-W) by 23m (N-S). Its northern side was difficult to trace, owing to post-depositional disturbance; its eastern and western sides were continuous and not pierced by entranceways. Its southern side was laid out in the pattern of a very open V, with an entranceway at the point of the V (at Grid 440W/569N) and another some 7 metres to the east; the western entranceway was 6.4m wide, and the eastern was 5.0m. Both entranceways were characterised by round pits at or near their centres and it is probable that these pits are contemporary with the enclosure ditch (both were round, dia 0.8m, depth 0.20m and open U-shaped). A large pit or well, F1578 was located immediately inside the western entranceway at Grid 438W/572N. Finally, the butt-ends of the enclosure ditch on either side of both entranceways were steep, if shallow; NE, SE and SW corners were unusually sharp.

Relations/phasing: The phase plan (FIG 18) shows the general sequence well. The eastern and northern enclosure ditches cut the second millennium ditches 3 and 4, and the western ditch cuts the N-E second millennium drove ditches F856 and F862. The southern ditch, immediately west of the western entranceway clearly cut the possible Early Iron Age drain, F1553, in

both of its phases. The Late Iron Age main drain, F1505, cuts the enclosure ditch at its north-western corner before passing south-eastwards to cut Structure 54 itself; it then veers sharply south and west to cut the well, F1578 and the western tip of the short enclosure ditch between the two entrances. It cannot be positively proved, but there are strong indications that a part of the main drain F1505, which can be demonstrated to have been very frequently recut, was in use in Middle Iron Age times. The north-western enclosure ditch clearly swings westwards at its intersection with F1505, and equally clearly does not continue north of it. It is suggested that the main drain's south-western course, in Middle Iron Age times, was along the western and south-western ditches of the enclosure around Structure 54. Following the abandonment of the building, the well (F1578) and the enclosure ditches, the course of the main drain F1505 was extended eastwards — probably for reasons connected with the use of the main droveway that runs off the subsite to the south-west. The long extension SSW would have been required both to drain the new length of drove and to remove the extra water produced by a possible rise in the winter water table. A relative date for the enclosure is provided by the large quantities of Middle Iron Age scored wares from the well (F1578) and the building itself. Only a few sherds were recovered from the enclosure ditch.

2. The Building and Associated Features

Plan (FIG 76): Structure 54 consisted of two ring-gullies broached by an east-facing entranceway; a number of postholes were associated with the entrance-way and a large pit (F1501/1593) lay on the south-western side of the interior. The western part of the building was cut through by two phases of the main Late Iron Age drainage ditch F1505 and the northern half of the building had been damaged by ploughing and other post-depositional activity. Despite this, however, a large part of the building was preserved at an exception-ally high level in the soil.

The external gully was revealed in two segments (dia 10.5m): the northern (F1417) had a well-defined western butt-end in which lay the somewhat damaged bones of the crouched Burial 4 (FIG 94 and Appendix 9). There was no evidence that the external gully had been specially enlarged or recut to receive this inhumation. The southern segment was first defined immediately south of the disturbed area, where its greater width suggests at least one period of recutting, although the filling showed no evidence for this; the posthole F1600 was cut through the in-filled gully.

The internal gully (F1502) was only revealed in the undisturbed area where it followed an approximately semi-circular course 0.6-0.9m inside the outer gully. Its north-eastern butt-end was expanded, as if to receive a door-post, but the small stakehole, F1603, clearly post-dated the gully (cf F1600 0.2m to the SE). The course of the inner (?wall-foundation) gully was not smoothly

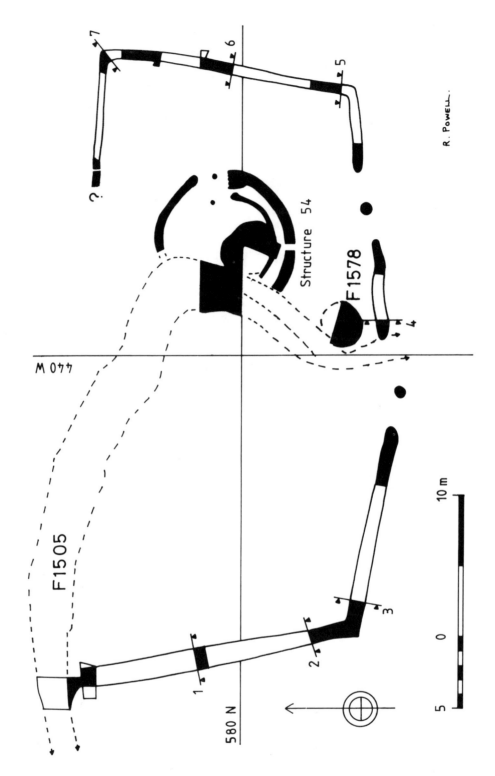

Fig. 75   Cat's Water subsite: Structure 54, general plan, including enclosure ditch; the section lines are for sections shown in FIG M63. Most Late Iron features are omitted, except part of the main drain F1505 which is shown by a dashed line.

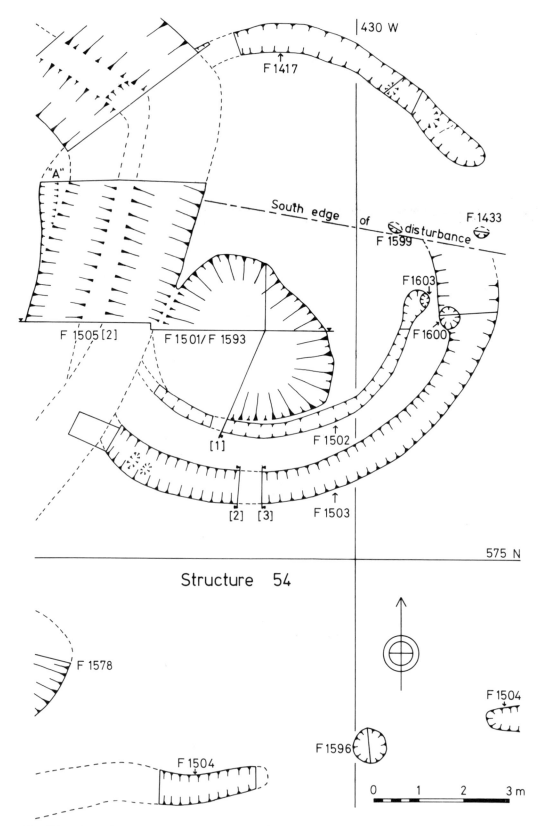

430 W

F 1417

"A"

South edge of disturbance   F 1433
F 1599

F 1603

F 1505 [2]   F 1501/ F 1593   F 1600

[1]

F 1502

[2] [3]   F 1503

575 N

Structure 54

F 1578

F 1504

F 1504

F 1596

0   1   2   3 m

Fig. 76   Cat's Water subsite: Structure 54, detailed plan (see also FIG 75).

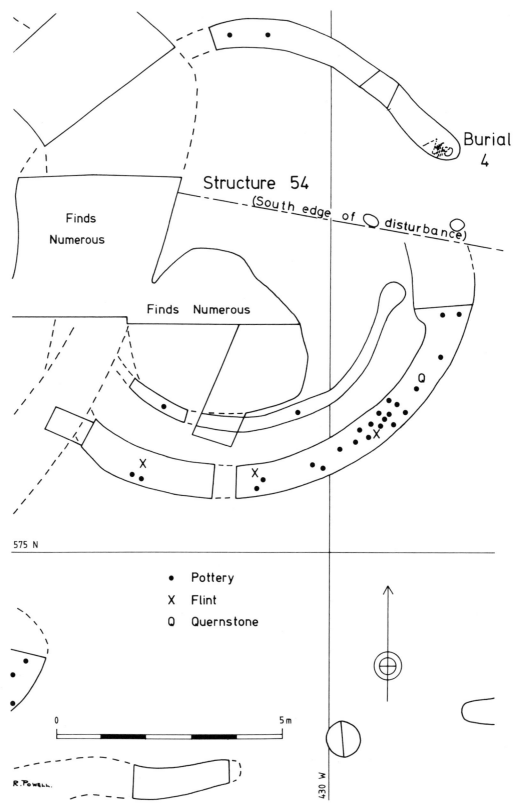

Fig. 77 Cat's Water subsite: Structure 54, finds distribution.

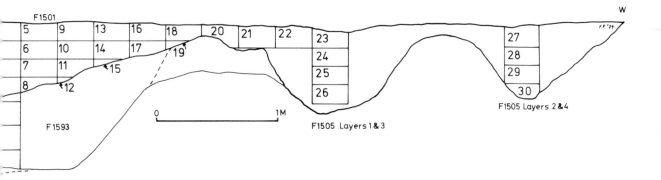

Fig. 78   Cat's Water subsite: Structure 54, location of sieved samples in the main section (see also FIGS M65 and M66).

circular and there was at least a hint of angularity, perhaps reminiscent of Structure 17 which may have employed wall-plate construction techniques. The small posthole F1599 lay just inside the disturbed area and may be the truncated remains of the northern door post, in which case the door width would have been 1.2m. The width of the eaves (taken from the centre of inner and outer gullies) was *c* 1.5m (*cf* Structures 7 and 14).

The large internal pit will be described in greater detail below, but its upper levels (F1501 layers 1-4) clearly respected the inner edge of the inner ring-gully and there can be no doubt as to their contemporaneity. The only anomalous feature is the posthole, F1433: it is located within the disturbed area and could, perhaps, have formed part of an external porch (although its position is too far south for this).

Relations/phasing: The general relations of the Structure have been considered in the discussion of the enclosure's phasing, above. Here we are principally concerned with the large internal pit F1501/1593 and the Late Iron Age drain, F1505 which cuts all gullies and the upper layers of the pit. The filling of the pit took place in two stages: the first is represented by F1593. This deposit is composed of dumped sand, gravel and clay loam and is clearly distinguished from F1501 above it (dashed line in FIG M65). The layers of F1501 represent rubbish that had accumulated while the building was in use. The pottery from both phases of the pit's life is identical: Fabric 1A (coarse shell-temper) and scored.

The main drain F1505 was clearly two-phased: the earlier phase was represented by layers 2 and 4 (FIG M66, where layer 4 is not present), the later by layers 1 and 3. The extreme western edge of the outer ring-gully can be seen to project beyond the early phase alignment of F1505 in FIG 76 at point 'A'.

Horizontal finds distribution (FIG 77): The rarity of finds in the disturbed area is of interest. First, both

gullies in the undisturbed area were dry-sieved through ¼″ mesh, so that the distributions shown are probably fairly free from gross distortion. Second, the scarcity of material in the inner, wall foundation, gully follows the pattern already observed in Structures 7, 14, 17. Third, the spread of material in the outer gully shows a concentration of material 2.0m to 2.5m back (south) from the entranceway — it should, however, be noted that this pattern may have been slightly distorted by the presence of an almost complete rotary quernstone (FIG 114) which occupied much of the area available for other finds! It should also be noted here that the many thousands of small potsherds found in F1501 (the internal pit) have been omitted for the finds plan.

Vertical finds distribution (FIG78; Table 2; PL14): A wet sieving experiment was carried out in the long section through the internal pit F1593/1501 and into the two phases of the later drain, F1505 (FIGS M65 and M66). This material was sieved through ¼″ mesh. Smaller meshes were tried (down to 0.5mm), but the quantity of material recovered was too large to work with; this was because much of the pottery was originally highly friable and was subsequently trampled in antiquity. The sample blocks measured 300 x 150 x 150mm; each 6750 cu cm block expanded when removed from the section to a volume of about 10,500 cu cm. The sample locations are given in the outline FIG 78 and the results of the analysis are presented in Table 2. The intention of the experiment was to investigate the nature of the apparently trampled 'floor' deposit of F1501 and to investigate to what extent this finely comminuted material found its way into the two-phased later drainage ditch, F1505.

The wet sieving showed that the greatest concentration of pottery was in samples 4, 8 and 11 (also 17) of F1501, ie at the very bottom of the suggested 'floor' deposit. There was also a sharp decline in the amount of pottery found in the back-filled

99

TABLE 2

CAT'S WATER SUBSITE, STRUCTURE 54: RESULTS OF WET SIEVING EXPERIMENT
(For location of samples see FIG 78)

Feature/layers	Sample No	Sherd count	Sherd weight (gm)	Sherd weight sample vol. (%)	Average sherd weight (gm)
F1501	1	—	—	—	—
layers 1 to 13	2	47	110	1.04	2.34
	3	92	120	1.14	1.30
	4	393	795	7.57	2.02
	5	5	20	0.19	4.00
	6	92	180	1.71	1.95
	7	205	290	2.76	1.41
	8	446	815	7.76	1.82
	9	10	40	0.38	4.00
	10	181	305	2.90	1.68
	11	459	670	6.38	1.45
	12	24	25	0.23	1.04
	13	25	40	0.38	1.60
	14	239	320	3.04	1.33
	15	70	95	0.90	1.35
	16	78	130	1.23	1.66
	17	207	270	2.57	1.30
	18	77	125	1.19	1.62
	19	12	30	0.28	2.50
	20	66	100	0.95	1.51
	21	31	60	0.57	1.93
	22	8	15	0.14	1.87
	23	6	30	0.28	5.00
	24	41	65	0.61	1.58
	25	12	40	0.38	3.33
	26	2	5	0.04	2.50
F1505	27	4	15	0.14	3.75
layers 2 to 4	28	5	15	0.14	3.00
	29	9	20	0.19	2.22
	30	5	20	0.19	4.00
F1593	1	57	165	1.57	2.89
layer 1	2	2	15	0.14	7.50
	3	—	—	—	—

feature F1593, when compared with F1501 above it. The upper layers of the second phase of the drainage ditch (samples 22-23) have less pottery than those below (nos 24-26); the same pattern is seen in the more distant, earlier, phase of the drainage ditch, but the quantities involved are markedly lower (samples 27-30). This confirms that it is spatial distance, rather than the length of time a deposit takes to accumulate, that is an important factor in the deposition of residual material.

Three additional samples of 10,500 cu cm each were wet sieved through ¼" mesh; one was from the outer (eaves-drip) gully F1503 and two were from the inner (wall) slot gully F1502; the former feature gave weight: volume percentage figures of 3.19%, the latter 0.09% and 0.02%. The figure for the eaves-drip is broadly comparable with the results obtained from upper levels of the 'floor' deposit; that from the wall slot, despite its proximity to the 'floor' is markedly lower and confirms the dry-sieved distribution of FIG 77.

The great disparity in sherd size between the deposits of the 'floor' and those of the back-filled pit beneath could not be properly demonstrated by the wet sieving experiment, as finds were so much rarer in the latter deposit and our resources were not sufficient to process the volume of filling required. The subjective impression gained in the field was that, on average, sherds from the back-filled deposit were five or ten times as large as those from the 'floor' (the contrast is, perhaps conservatively, illustrated by two 'grab' samples in PL 14). Some measure of objective support for the trampling in the 'floor' deposit is provided by an analysis of the charcoal found in the pit.

Structure 54 Charcoal — a note
by Maisie Taylor

Only layers 8 and 9 of F1501 produced identifiable charcoal. All other layers in Features 1501, 1502, 1503, and 1593 produced only occasional pieces of charcoal and these were all too small to identify.

F1501 layer 8: No oak (*Quercus sp*) but a considerable quantity of *Corlyus/Alnus* (hazel/alder) with a few pieces of *Populus/Salix* (poplar/willow). All material was from small (ie twiggy) wood.

F1501 layer 9: No oak and generally similar to layer 8. Layer 9 also contained one piece of carbonised bark from a twig (*c* 10mm diameter) of *Corlyus/Alnus* (hazel/alder).

Summary and Discussion

The discussion may be briefly summarised thus: a large pit or well was filled-in (F1593) immediately before, or as part of, the building of a round house. This structure was probably of one period and was composed of a wall-slot (F1502) and an outer eaves-drip gully (F1417/1503), with an eastwards-facing doorway. The filled-in well was replaced by another, F1578, to the SW of the house but within its small ditched enclosure. The soft, less compacted, filling of the original well

soon wore down, as the result of trample and other activities, and a 'floor' deposit accumulated (or was perhaps encouraged to accumulate) in the resulting, sinking, hollow. The building was abandoned, perhaps due to rising water levels, and a Late Iron Age drainage ditch was cut through it. The principal interest of this structure must lie in the differentation of its various deposits: the 'floor' contains rubbish that accumulated *in situ* and is, in Schiffer's (1976) terminology 'primary'. 'Secondary', redeposited, rubbish is found in the material that was dumped into the large internal pit at the time of the building's construction and in a recent paper (Pryor 1980c) it was suggested that the finds from the outer, eaves-drip, gully are examples of abandonment or *de facto* refuse. It is unnecessary to reiterate these arguments at length, but if it is accepted that the material found in the eaves-drip gully is correctly interpreted as being true *de facto* refuse, then items found there, which are not usually found in contemporary, associated, primary or secondary refuse, could be cherished, or curated items. It was also suggested that some pottery, only marginally of better quality than that found in primary or secondary rubbish, could have been curated; this is a matter of judgement and a qualitative decision can only be made by examining the actual pottery. It was mentioned merely to illustrate the dangers of assuming that modern definitions of 'fine' and 'coarse' wares necessarily reflect ancient usage. Apart from the pottery, the almost complete rotary quern (FIG 114) is a fine example of a curated item in an area where suitable stone is not readily available; the human body, too, can be seen as a 'curated' or cherished item: in wetlands where every ditch and gully must be kept open, it is senseless to block a drain, even with a body, unless it is no longer required for drainage. The explanation of the burial as an abondonment deposit, rather than a hypothetical 'foundation offering' would seem to fit the evidence best.

Structure 55

Plan (FIG 79): Structure 55 was centred on Grid 413W/747N. It consisted of two gullies at right-angles with a narrow gap (1.2m) between them; the northern gully (F220) was straight and ran NNE-SSW for 7.2m; its northern end terminated in a posthole, F347. The second gully, F376, ran WNW-ESE for 10.5m and terminated at its eastern end in a posthole, F377. Its central portion was disturbed by a later pit, F405.

Relations/phasing: This structure was too slight to produce reliable evidence from finds, but its layout suggests that it formed an enclosure fence or stockade for Structure 14, which is of Middle Iron Age date.

Finds distribution (FIG 80): Finds were too rare for useful comment.

Structure 56

Plan (FIG 81): Structure 56 consisted of two arcs of gully (F812 and F928) of approximate diameter 8.4m, centred on Grid 428W/595N. An entrance causeway

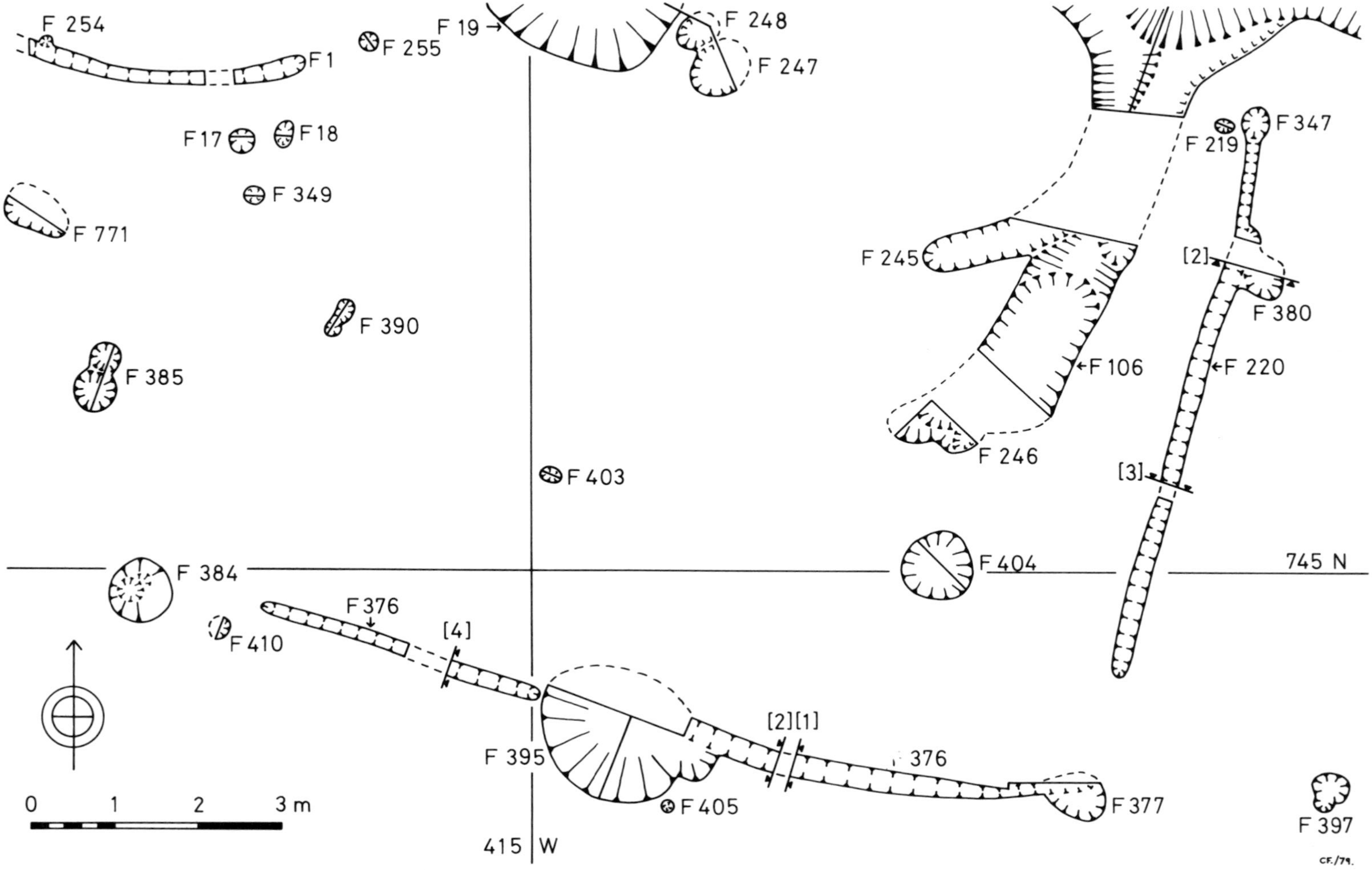

F 347
F 219
F 380
F 220
[2]
F 106
[3]
745 N
F 246
F 404
F 245
F 397
c.r./79.
F 377

F 248
F 247
376
F 19
F 403
F 255
[2][1]
F 405
F 395
415 W
F 390
[4]
F1
F 376
F17 F18
F 349
F 384
F 410
F 254
F 771
F 385
3 m
2
1
0

Fig. 79 Cat's Water subsite: Structure 55.

102

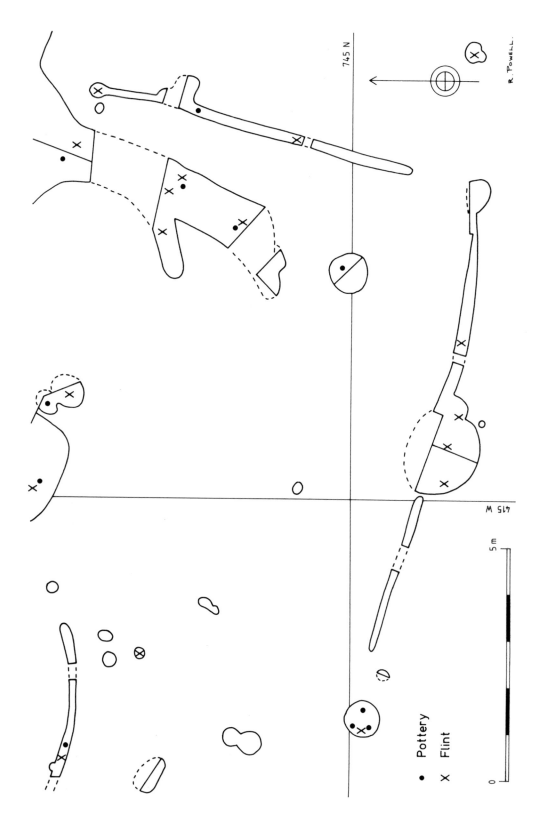

745 N

415 W

R. Powell.

5 m

• Pottery

X Flint

Fig. 80 Cat's Water subsite: Structure 55, finds distribution.

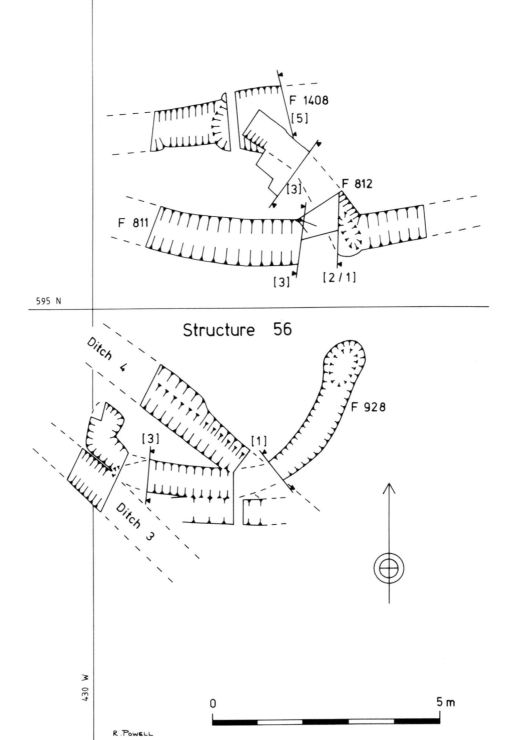

595 N

Structure 56

F 1408
[5]

F 812

F 811

[3]

[3]

[2/1]

Ditch 4

Ditch 3

F 928

[3]

[1]

430 W

0   5 m

R. POWELL

Fig. 81   Cat's Water subsite: Structure 56.

104

(width 1.8m) faced eastwards, but the situation further west was difficult to discern due to later activity and the silty sub-soil which provided little contrast with the feature fillings.

Relations/phasing: The southern gully, F928, was cut by second millennium ditches 3 and 4. The relationship of the northern gully, F812, to F811 and F1408 was not very clear, but F812 seemed to cut F811 in plan. No wheel-made pottery was found and a Middle Iron Age date is probable.

Finds distribution (FIG 82): The finds distribution shows that F812 cuts the northern ditch F1408 and that there is a concentration of pottery at this point, around the NW butt-end. In the southern gully, F928, material is mainly concentrated south of the entrance causeway at which point the ditch had been enlarged, as if to take a post (although there was no other evidence for this). The western butt-end of this gully also held a small group of finds. The distribution of flint was unrelated to that of the pottery.

Structure 57

Plan (FIG 83): A four-post structure centred on Grid 684W/630N, composed of postholes F831-4 (dimensions: N-S, 3.0m; E-W, 2.6m).

Relations/phasing: Probably Iron Age, on spatial grounds.

Finds distribution (FIG 83): Undiagnostic, but one posthole (F833) contained more finds than the rest.

Sections (FIG 83)

F831 layer 1: Sand-silt with scattered gravel pebbles (no Munsell); charcoal rare.
F832 layer 1: As above, but colour 10YR 5/4.
F833 layer 1: As above, but colour 10YR 5/2 and charcoal common.
F834 layer 1: As above, but colour 10YR 5/2.

2. LINEAR FEATURES
(SEE MICROFICHE PAGES 92-110)

Introduction

The linear features of the Iron Age and Romano-British settlement are of considerable importance, as they are the principal means of uniting such disparate elements as pits, postholes and the structures them-selves. Most of the main ditches provide evidence for frequent recutting, as shown by numerous, sometimes off-centre layers, and by undulating sides and bottoms. Most of the ditches were quite clearly of considerable importance as drains and would have held brushwood bundles to ease the flow of water (see the discussion of the 'brush drain', below). It should also be recalled that deep ditches, or, less effectively, wells, play an important role in locally lowering the water-table; they do not merely remove surface run-off (the principle is illustrated by P W Williams 1969, FIG 6 11 1). Thus some shallow ditches (see, for example section FIG M83 section 54) away from the main settlement area did not

have to penetrate the ground water table: they were only required to remove water from higher parts of the site and were accordingly dug shallow and wide. It should also be recalled that ditches dug into gravel below the permanent water table are inherently less stable than those cut into dry ground (this is illustrated by the necessity of lining wells with woven wattlework). Apart from the drainage functions and related use as soak-aways, the Cat's Water ditches were also used as yard and droveway boundary ditches. In general it is difficult to place the various ditches of the settlement into well-defined categories and this probably reflects their original multi-purpose role; the only possible exception to this, however, being the shallow sharp-cornered rectilinear enclosure ditch surrounding Structure 54. This ditch does not appear, at first glance, to have an obvious drainage function, although its western length may possibly be associated with an early phase of the main droveway's southern ditch.

Finally, evidence for banks accompanying the ditches is, on the whole rare. This, however, does not mean that they are not present; it merely implies that they were placed sufficiently far away from the sides to prevent material from slipping back into the ditch. Banks would probably have been low and wide and built of numerous layers of wet gravel mixed with organic mud removed from the ditch bottom during one of its regular recuts. Some of the modern dyke banks in the area are barely visible today, being perhaps three or four metres wide and half a metre high; low, wide banks were observed on either side of the Romano-British droveway ditches on the Storey's Bar subsite.

The 54 sections illustrated here are, in general, taken from undisturbed lengths of ditch and are chosen to give an impression of the variety of ditch sizes, profiles and fillings encountered. Only a very few examples of sections taken at ditch intersections are shown here; most relationships were as clear on the surface as in section and it was thought that a series of longitudinal sections through mainly naturally-accumulated ditch fillings would not give an impression of the variety of ditch types found at Cat's Water. Besides, many 'cut-lines' were only visible while the layers in question dried-out and drawings consequently must give a misleading impression of clarity. Very few relationships of dated main drains were in doubt; the only problems encountered concerned possible recutting of ditches of known date and phasing. The latter were, in general, minor problems which are discussed at length on the relevant layer cards of the archive.

Finally, it was noted in the Introduction to this chapter that section drawings and descriptions will be found on microfiche (and the reader is referred to FIG 6 for a list of the conventions used). Main ditch sections are shown in FIGS M68-M83, and the section line locations are shown in FIGS 84 and 85; details of archive information are also given in the fiche descriptions.

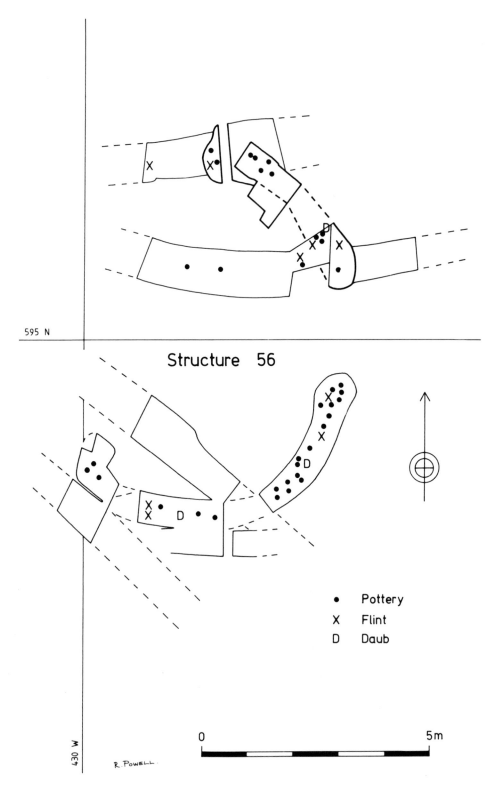

595 N

Structure 56

430 W

R. POWELL.

•   Pottery

X   Flint

D   Daub

0   5m

Fig. 82   Cat's Water subsite: Structure 56, finds distribution.

106

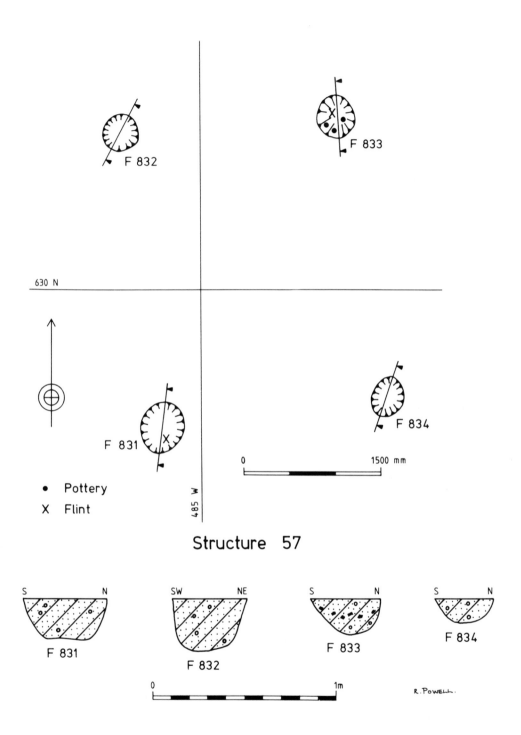

630 N

485 W

• Pottery
X Flint

Structure 57

S   N
F 831

SW   NE
F 832

S   N
F 833

S   N
F 834

0   1m

R. POWELL.

Fig. 83   Cat's Water subsite: Structure 57, plan, with finds distribution and sections.

107

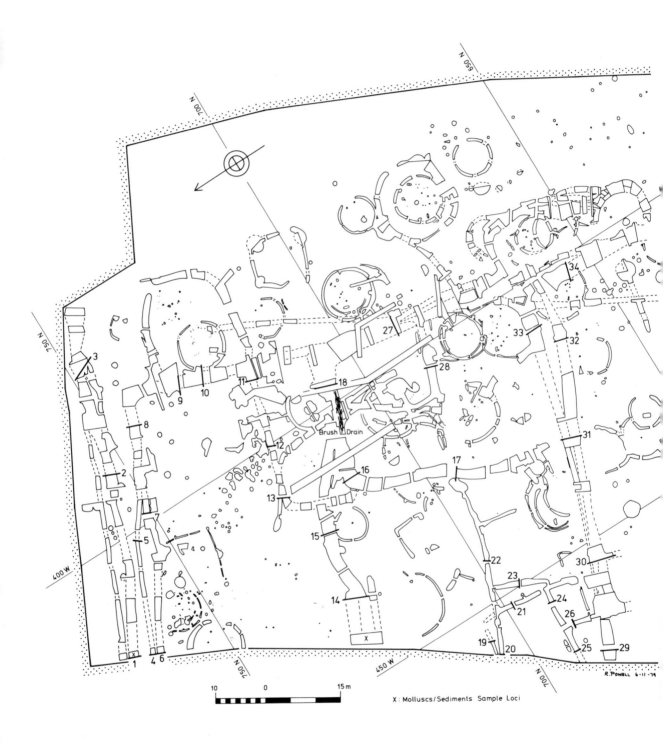

Fig. 84   Cat's Water subsite: location of main drainage ditch section lines — North (Sections 1-34).

108

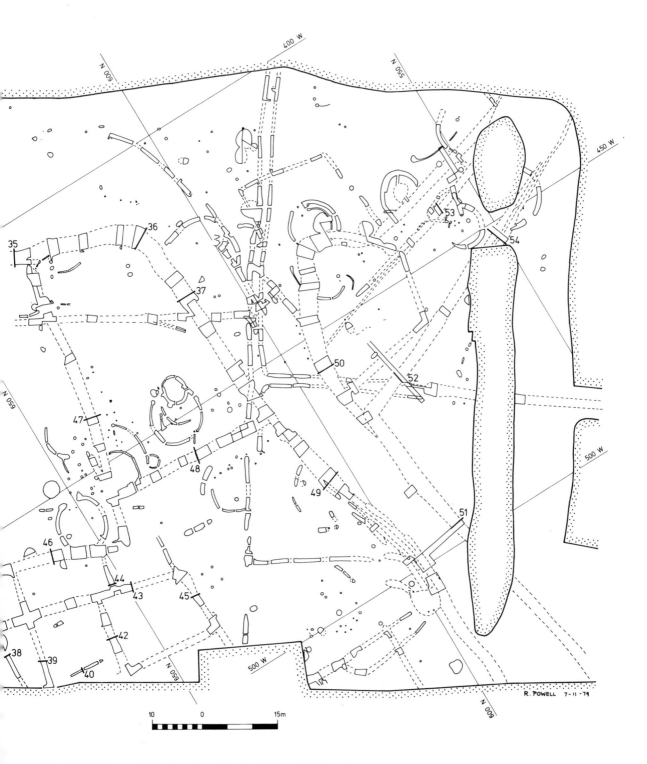

Fig. 85 Cat's Water subsite: location of main drainage ditch section lines — South (sections 35-54).

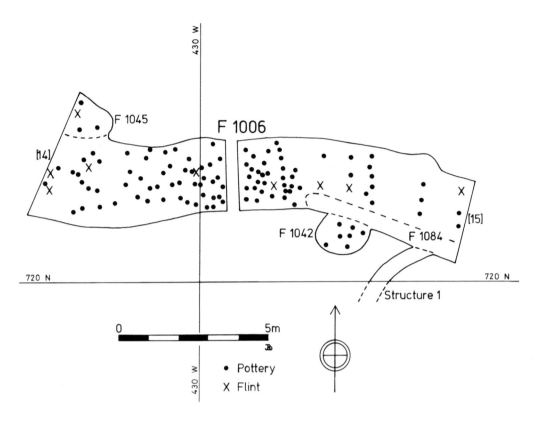

Fig. 86 Cat's Water subsite: finds distribution in the main drain F1006 and related features, between sections 14 and 15 (for location see FIG 84).

Distribution of finds within the linear ditches
(FIGS 86-87)

The distribution of finds within the linear ditches is more difficult to explain than that of the structures. The reason for this must lie in the different nature of the two deposits: in general, structural features were dug once and were then either maintained open — as, for example, eaves-drip gullies — or else were backfilled before building reconstruction. Alternatively they were abandoned, and *de facto* (abandonment) rubbish accumulated from the immediate vicinity (reflecting local activity areas). Natural erosion of these slight features would reduce most to shallow hollows after a few seasons.

Main drainage ditches, however, were different. First, they were more substantial and, once abandoned, would fill in slowly. This slow accumulation of material makes the distinguishing of local activity areas most hazardous. Second, being drains, they were recut according to immediate needs. Thus, if, for example, a collapsed tree blocked a ditch then appropriate action was taken, either to divert the stream, undercut the tree or remove it altogether; if, however, there was a

succession of wet winters then ditch modification, which might include large-scale deepening combined with local course modification, would have to be more elaborate. Day-to-day maintenance of prehistoric farm ditches is still very poorly understood, but in gravel soils regular thorough cleaning-out, at a conservative estimate perhaps every five years, would be necessary to keep the water flowing efficiently. For these reasons it is difficult to interpret ditch finds' distributions, except in those cases where the ditch can be shown to have had a short use-life (as, for example, on the Grooved Ware settlement, Storey's Bar Road subsite — FNG 2; FIG 14; a further example is the enclosure ditch around Structure 16, mentioned above — FIG 43).

It would appear from these considerations that the Cat's Water ditches, which in general show homogeneous or otherwise undiagnostic finds distributions, were maintained in use, and suitably modified, for a considerable period of time — perhaps indeed for several centuries. Thus, the ditches near Structures 21-23, 34, 35 (FIG 49); those near Structures 32 and 33 (FIG 58) and those near Structure 18 (FIG 29) do not show a pattern of finds distribution that can readily be

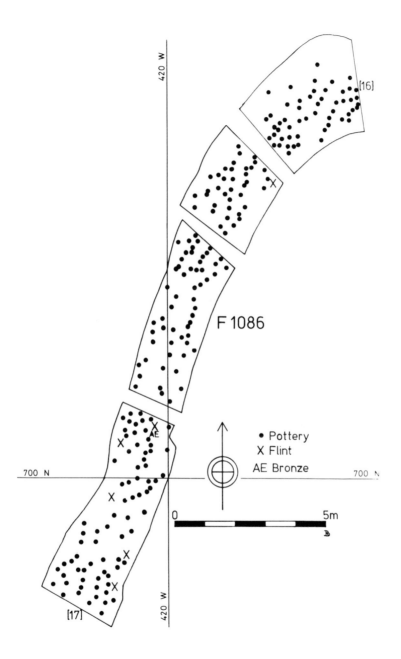

Fig. 87 Cat's Water subsite: finds distribution in the main drain F1086 between sections 16 and 17 (for location see FIG 84).

attributed to the presence of buildings. Finds' density and soil phosphate levels in large drainage ditches (for example FNG 3, FIG 112) can be affected by nearby settlement activity, as was quantitatively demonstrated in the Structure 54 wet sieve experiments described above, but these effects can also be removed or distorted by post-depositional processes, such as ditch cleaning. In short, apparently undiagnostic finds distributions from ditches on settlement sites could indicate that the settlement in question was long-lived and that the occupation was continuous, rather than intermittent. Intermittent occupation could result in ditches being recut appreciably off their original alignments; further the distribution of finds within the separate recuts would be patterned, perhaps relating to contemporary settlement areas and old rubbish heaps. This clearly was not the case at Cat's Water, as the examples cited above demonstrate. Two further examples of ditch finds distributions are also illustrated here.

The first example, FIG 86, shows the pattern of finds in the multi-period drain immediately north of Structure 1, between sections 14 and 15 (for location see FIG 84). Here the finds' density decreases as the building is approached; the ring-gully itself produced very few finds and it might be supposed that the increase in finds' density west of the building indicates that rubbish was being dumped three to five metres beyond it. This rubbish eventually found its way into the ditch to produce the pattern shown here. Such an explanation, however, disregards the presence of Structure 4 to the west (also Structure 41 to the south west) and assumes that the drain in question was evenly recut in the vicinity of the building, which clearly was not the case (see description of Structure 1, above). Had the large drain been smaller, evenly recut, and not multi-phased, then this explanation might hold good. The second example, FIG 87, shows a length of drain between sections 16 and 17 (FIG 84). The ditch in question, F1086, is of Late Iron Age date, at its final recutting, and passes close to two Late and two Middle Iron Age buildings (Structures 41/44 and 6/13 respectively). Unlike ditch F1006, considered above, ditch F1086 was, it would appear on stratigraphic grounds, evenly recut over most of its length; further, neither its plan nor profile showed evidence for short or discontinuous recuts. Ditch maintenance practice, therefore, rather than local structure distribution, or activity area patterning, may explain the extraordinarily homogenous spread of the many finds from this large ditch.

The Brush Drains

Description (FIG 88; PLS 15-17)

Two examples of 'brush drains' were found at Fengate, both from the Cat's Water Iron Age settlement, in large drainage ditches. The first, which was by far the better preserved of the two, was from the important Late Iron Age drainage ditch F1006. It lay along the sand and gravel bottom of the ditch and was centred on Grid 403W/708N (for location see FIG 84). The drain consisted of two bundles of osiers taken from a coppiced or pollarded willow tree, cut after 7-8 years of growth (see Appendix 5). The wood had been laid directly on the natural subsoil of the ditch bottom in two rough bundles, which were contemporary with each other, since osier A of bundle 2 passed between osiers B and C of bundle 1 (FIG 88). There was no indication that the bundles had even been tied and the wood still had its bark left intact. The total length of the drain, which could not be traced further east or west, was 6.2m; the length of both bundles was approximately 3m and the width varied from 0.15m to 0.60m. The thickness varied from one to four or five osiers (average thickness of osiers, as preserved: 20-30mm).

The second 'brush drain' was very poorly preserved. It consisted of very rotten twigs laid in close parallel rows along the bottom of the enclosure ditch around Structure 16 (F40) at Grid 371W/715N. Its original length could not be determined, but it survived for just under one metre and its breadth and thickness were comparable with the drain from F1006. Its state of preservation was too poor for a photograph or drawing, and it could certainly have been dismissed as insignificant, had not the better preserved drain been found in a previous season. The parallel twigs had almost vanished, leaving in their stead a series of small tubes in the clay, and short wisps of willow bark still adhered to the walls of these tubes.

Both drains were located on very low-lying parts of the subsite and the ditches in which they lay were covered by considerable thicknesses of flood-clay (c 0.5m). Although the ditches did not actually penetrate the modern water table they were nonetheless damp when first excavated; in addition, the fine clay-silts of the lower ditch fillings retained water well, and would have effectively excluded air, thus aiding preservation.

Discussion

At the time of writing the author has been unable to find archaeological parallels for the 'brush drain'. Its initial discovery was of particular interest, however: a short length of parallel osiers had been exposed (cf PL 17) and it was thought that these represented the collapsed remains of a wattle hurdle. A visiting party of Fenland farmers immediately suggested the 'brush drain' hypothesis and the excavation was accordingly extended until the whole surviving drain was exposed. Its Iron Age date cannot be doubted — despite the contrary views of the visiting farmers who were convinced of its recent age (a) because of its state of preservation and (b) because of its striking resemblance to modern 'brush drains', once it had been completely exposed. Apart from the fact that it was stratigraphically sealed beneath a great thickness of Iron Age ditch sediment, its Iron Age date is proven by the discovery of a nearly complete hand-made jar (in a very poorly-

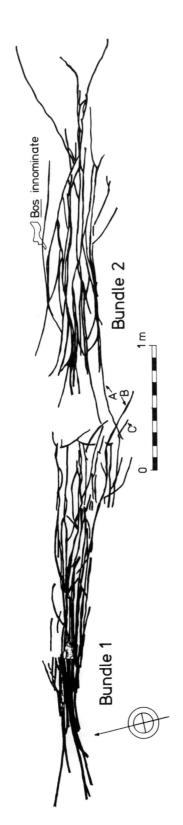

Fig. 88   Cat's Water subsite: Late Iron Age 'brush drain' in the main drain F1006 at Grid 403W/798N (for location see FIG 84; see also PLS 20-22).

fired shell-gritted fabric) which lay directly on top of bundle 1. Although largely replaced by the widespread introduction of earthenware pipes in the later nineteenth century, 'brush drains' of willow or blackthorn were still used locally until the 1920's and '30's (G E Evans 1969, 27-28, and G Tebbs pers comm). Sometimes the brushwood was placed in the bottom of drainage dykes, but more often it was used in spade-cut field drains.

Tebbs recalls that good brush drains could have a life of 10 or even 20 years and it is interesting to note that similar hand-cut field drains where 'the material used to channel the water was willow branches' have been recorded for the Isle of Man (Killip 1970, 63). Recent 'brush drains' are also commonly found in the peats of the Somerset Levels (S V E Heal, pers comm).

Finally, a striking example of continuity in farming methods is provided by a modern (?1940's) earthenware field drain which ran parallel to, but *c* 0.60m above, the Iron Age 'brush drain'. A pipe of this drain can be seen protruding from the baulk in PL 16.

3. NON-LINEAR FEATURES
(SEE MICROFICHE PAGES 111-114)

A. Isolated pits or wells

These features could not be shown to form part of any recognised structure and can be divided into four broad categories.

1. Large, steep-sided, round or oval pits

These form the most diagnostic group of non-linear features. They vary considerably in both size and depth, but are usually as steep as the natural sub-soil's angle of repose and are round or slightly oval in plan. They probably originally held woven wattle linings, but these have not survived on the Cat's Water subsite, with the exception, perhaps, of the stake from the bottom of F1551 (for wattle linings see FNG 1, FIGS 18 and 19). The best examples of prehistoric wells have already been described in this and previous reports. F1551 is the only well on Cat's Water that warrants discussion in the text (see below) and other wells and possible wells or water holes are described and illustrated, where appropriate, on fiche. Apart from F1551, the best examples, are: F415 (Section, FIG M84), F448 (Section, FIG M85), F1042 (Section, FIG M86; Plan, FIG 22, right) and F1561 (Section, FIG M87).

The Early Iron Age well, F1551 (FIG 89)

Grid 460W/564N; Dia *c* 2.0m; depth 1.05m. This feature lay beneath spoil heaps and only part (?half) could be excavated. All layers accumulated through natural weathering and the greater amounts of gravel in layer 1 may represent the collapse of sides or a bank/mound. The gravel spread in this layer is too even to have been dumped there. An oak stake was found driven into the natural gravel and sand had slipped against one side of it; the other side was embedded in sand-silt

which had accumulated after the stake had been driven in. An almost complete Late Bronze/Early Iron Age pot (78, 3155) lay in the sand-silt of layer 3, hard up against the stake which it touched at several points. The wooden stake is discussed below by Maisie Taylor. Layer 3 appears to have accumulated after the stake had been driven into the ground and also after the deposition of the vessel which was thrown in the well when it was still in use. Despite the excellent preservation of the oak stake the sand silt of layer 3 was free of other organic material (and was carefully searched by Mrs Gay Wilson on site).

2. Large Irregular pits

These features are less morphologically distinct than the wells just discussed. They were often incorporated in drainage or enclosure ditches and were also often deliberately filled with rubbish. The function of these large pits is not apparent from their plan or profile, which is usually steep-sided and flat-bottomed, but their frequent association with drainage ditches might suggest that they were used either to hold water, or as soak-aways, depending on season and height of the water table (Guy Beresford, pers comm). They are often irregular in plan, with numerous bays, indentations and bulges, indicating that they were enlarged piecemeal, according to immediate needs. Most of these large irregular pits are of Middle Iron date and are associated with Structures 3, 42 and 53 (the latter being Late Iron). A few examples will be considered in greater detail below:

Pits associated with Structure 3 (FIG 26): The relationship of these pits to the outer enclosure ditch has already been discussed at length and broad contemporaneity is beyond doubt. There are three main pits, all are steep-sided and show at least some evidence for recutting and multiple periods of use or enlargement: F87 is centred on Grid 377W/681N and measures 5m (E-W) by 4.2m (N-S); depth 0.80m. Feature 153 is centred on Grid 376W/667N, is approximately circular (dia 2m), with a slight expansion to the north (F154) and has an average depth of 0.75m. Pit F157 shows better evidence for multi-period activity than the two just mentioned; it is centred on 371W/666N and in plan appears to be three lobed, the northern lobe being an enlargement of the enclosure ditch, F79. The total length of the pit complex is 12m and the maximum width 3.5m; the greatest depth is 1.05m — just below the modern water table.

Pits associated with Structure 42 (FIGS 61, M56-M57): These pits have already been considered at some length in the discussion of Structure 42 and it should be sufficient here to point out that features 73 and 77 (FIG M57) are good examples of the class of pit under consideration. The third corner pit, F80 (FIG M56) is perhaps best seen as a well or water hole — although its location does not support this suggestion.

Pits associated with Structure 53 (FIGS 57 and M62):

114

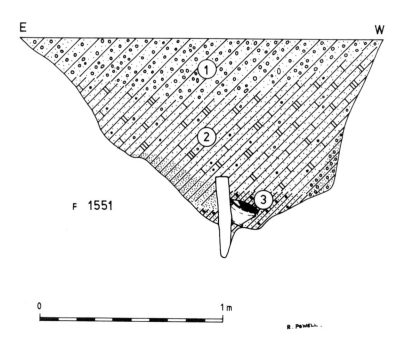

F 1551

0   1 m

R. POWELL.

Fig. 89   Cat's Water subsite: section through large Early Iron Age pit or well, F1551, at Grid 460W/564N.

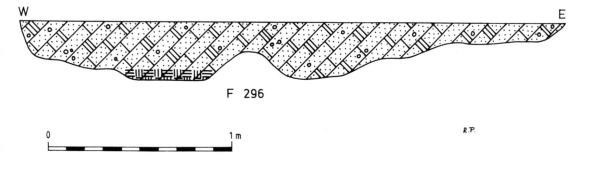

F 296

0   1 m   R.P.

Fig. 90   Cat's Water subsite: section through shallow pit or water-disturbed scoop, F269, at Grid 395W/725N.

115

Two pits of this class were found in the crescentic ditch east of the building. One (F586) was cut into a ditch, the other (F621) was cut by a ditch. Both were deep (F586: 0.80m; F621: 1.0m) and irregular in profile, if not in plan (which was hard to determine accurately owing to the disturbance caused by the ditch). The larger, and earlier, of the two pits, F621, held a human skull in its lower filling (FIG M62).

3. Irregular scoops and hollows (FIG 90)

These features were almost all confined to the areas which had been severely affected by flood-action. They were mainly distributed over the twenty metre square immediately north of Structure 5 (defined by the Grid points 410W/710N; 390W/710N; 390W/730N; 410W/730N), in an area deeply buried beneath Romano-British flood clays. Some of the features produced small amounts of mainly Middle Iron pottery, but most produced few, if any, finds. One of the larger pits of this class, F276 (Grid 392W/718N), clearly cut a large Middle Iron drainage ditch (between sections 11 and 12, FIG 84). A clue to the interpretation of these features lies on their spatial arrangement, for they can be seen to lie in a broad band running NW-SE. The NW end of this band is represented by the possible 'Structure' 26 which is composed of small pits, or large postholes; moving SE, however, the pits become progressively larger and more shapeless. It is suggested that we have here an example of severe post-depositional distortion, in this case by water. It is probable that small pits, represented for example by those of Structure 26, were substantially 'recut' and enlarged in an area of proven flooding by water turbulence (Turnbaugh's 1978, 595 'pothole erosion'; see also his FIG 2b — 'local turbulence'). One example of an enlarged pit is described below:

F296 (FIG 90): Grid 396W/725N; length 3.5m; breadth 2.0-3.5m; depth variable, but max. 0.4m. Filling of clay-silt with clay lenses and scattered gravel pebbles and redeposited limestone marl (10YR 3/2); charcoal rare; note the clay patch on the bottom. Archive: other features of this class (all FNG 77, Area IV) include F215; F224; F228; F270; F276; F277; F279; F284; F295; F323; F332; F337).

4. Small pits and postholes

A large number of smaller pits and postholes which cannot be assigned to any particular structure are distributed over the site (FIG 9). Postholes or pits of this type are well illustrated in the discussion of Structures 3, 14 and 26, above. Post moulds or 'ghosts' are, in general, rare — the main exception being the amorphous Structure 26 — and stone packing is also uncommon. The distribution of isolated small pits and postholes tends to follow the distribution of structures and other settlement features, and especially those of Middle Iron date, to the north and east. The scatter around Structure 2 is probably associated with that building and there is a thin spread of similar, but smaller features along the eastern margin of the settlement.

B. Burials and Cremations

1. Burials (FIGS 91-95)

The six burials described below are of characteristic Iron Age type, as exemplified in central and southern England (Whimster 1977). Grave goods are absent and bodies are all buried in the crouched or tightly crouched position; one could even be bound (FIG 91). Burials 1, 2 and 3 were in open graves which are orientated almost due N-S. All are described in detail by Faye Powell in Appendix 9, together with an account of loose human bones from other features of the settlement.

Dating of the graves, in the absence of grave goods, must depend on stratigraphic considerations. The closely comparable alignment of Burials 1-3 suggests a degree of contemporaneity; Burial 1 can be seen to respect Structures 14 and 15 which are both of Middle Iron date; similarly, Burial 2 seems to respect an almost contiguous Middle Iron ditch. Burial 3 would appear to have been located in the track of the wide Late Iron and Roman droveway and, again, a Middle Iron date would seem probable. Burial 5 was cut into a ditch filled with Late Iron deposits and a similar date would seem probable, but not certain (given the intensity of Middle Iron settlement in the area). Burial 4 was in the eaves-drip gully of a Middle Iron building and Burial 6, being located within the enclosure around the same building, could also be of that date. Finally, with the possible exception of Burials 3 and 6, the inhumations appear to have been made at the fringes of the Middle Iron settlement.

Burial 1 (FIG 91): The tightly crouched body of a young man, aged 17-25, was found in a small, shallow steep-sided grave located north of Structures 14 and 15 (FIG 40) at Grid 424W/758N. The grave is in apparent isolation, some 120m north of Burial 5.

Burial 2 (FIG 92): Like Burial 1, this consisted of the tightly crouched body of a man, aged about 25 years who was, however, buried in a slightly larger grave than Burial 1, at Grid 474W/604N. The grave was placed some 0.30m east of a Middle Iron ditch, which it seemed to respect — suggesting, perhaps, that the two were contemporary.

Burial 3 (FIG 93): The crouched body of another young man (aged 17-25 years) was buried in an isolated grave at Grid 442W/605N. This body lay on its right side (Burial 2 lay on the left), but, in common with the two other isolated grave burials (1 and 2), it lay with its head to the north.

Burial 4 (FIG 94): The crouched body of a male (aged 20-25 years) had been deposited in the eaves-drip gully of Structure 54 at Grid 427W/584N, immediately north of the entrance causeway (FIG 77). The body lay in the area of post-depositional disturbance (FIG 76) which

Burial 1

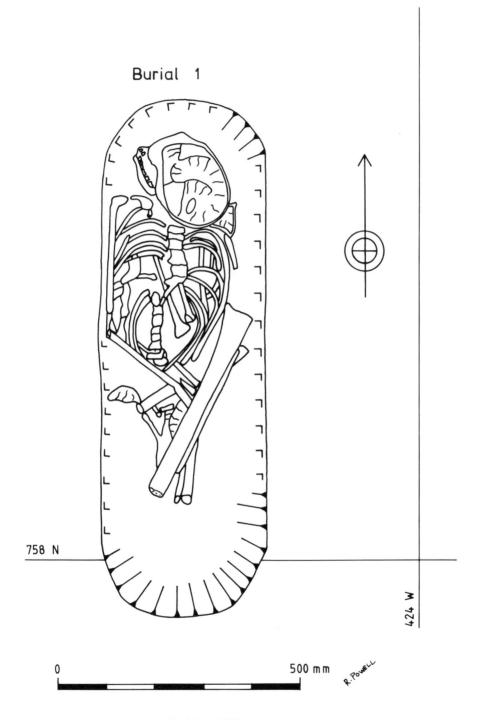

758 N

424 W

0   500 mm

R. POWELL

Fig. 91   Cat's Water subsite: Iron Age burial 1 (F773).

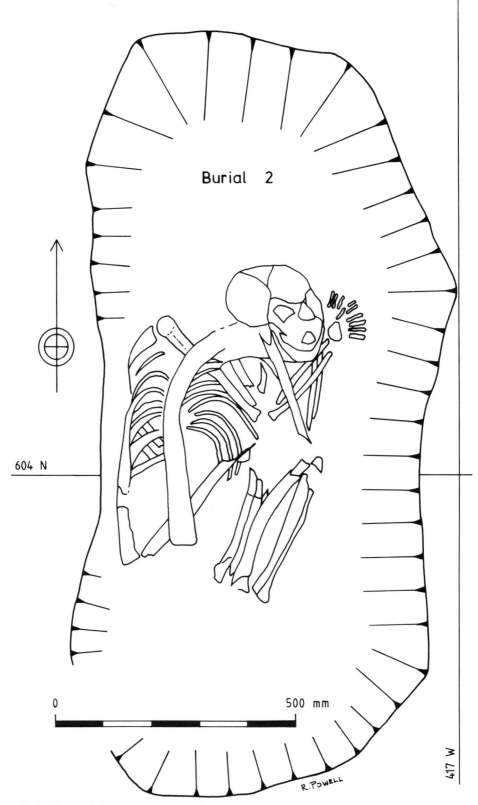

Burial 2

604 N

0   500 mm

417 W

Fig. 92   Cat's Water subsite: Iron Age burial 2 (F927).

Burial 3

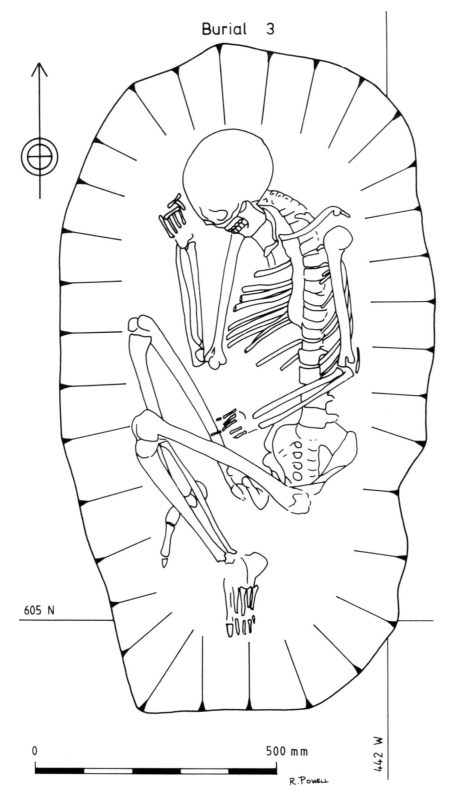

605 N

442 W

0   500 mm

R. POWELL

Fig. 93   Cat's Water subsite: Iron Age burial 3 (F1405).

119

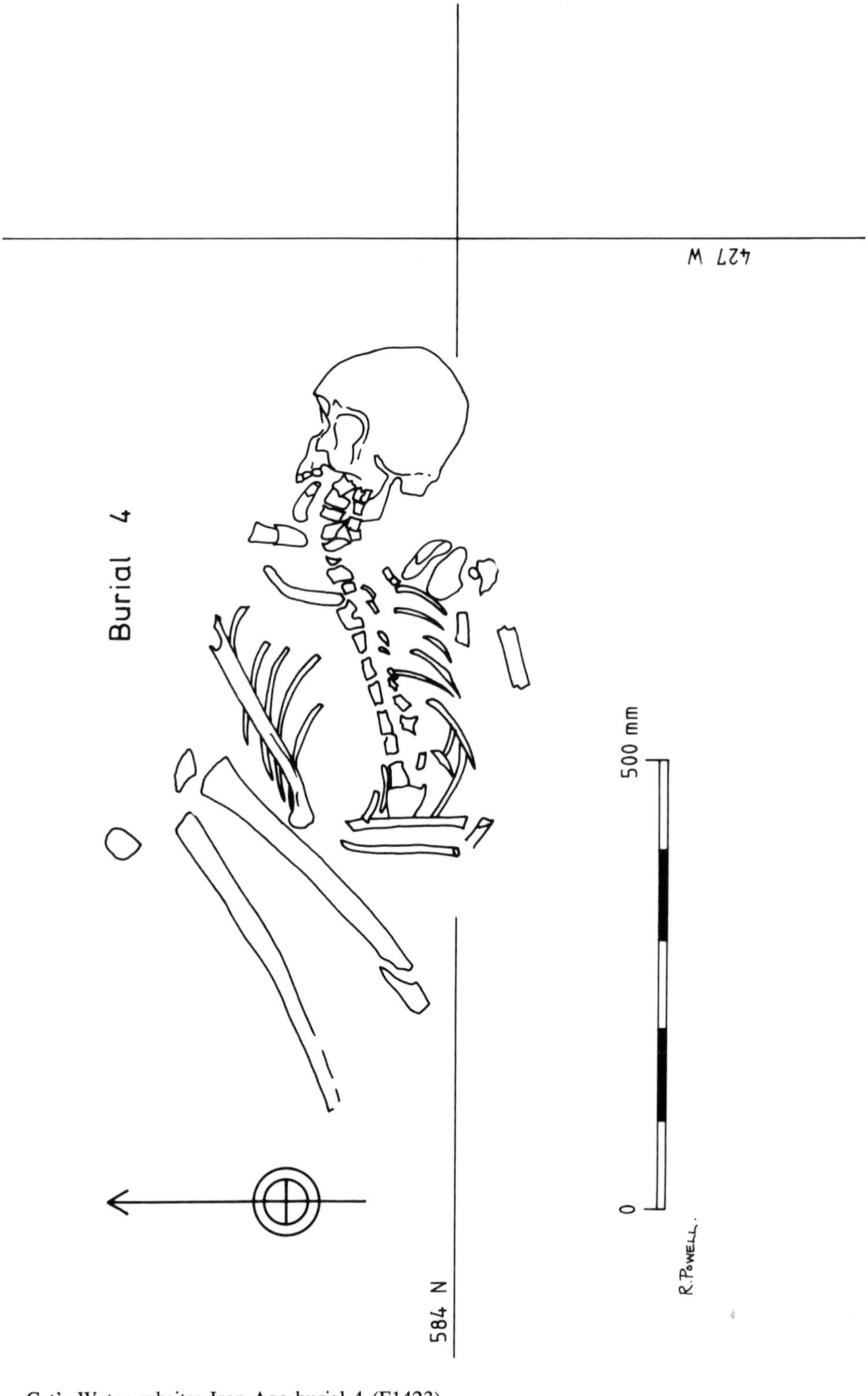

Fig. 94 Cat's Water subsite: Iron Age burial 4 (F1423).

120

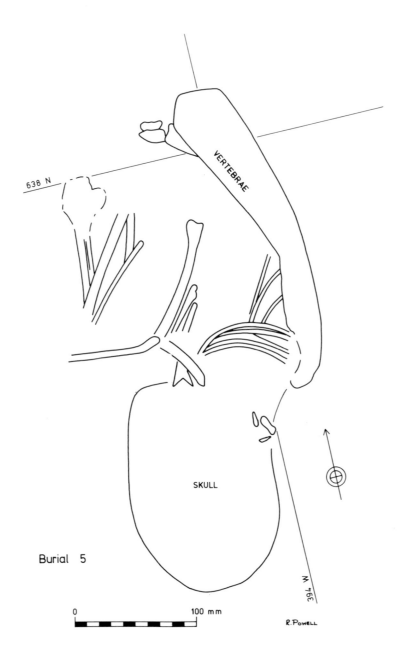

638 N

VERTEBRAE

SKULL

Burial 5

0   100 mm

394 W

R. POWELL

Fig. 95   Cat's Water subsite: Iron Age burial 5 (F584) — schematic drawing of a much decayed inhumation.

accounts for its poor state of preservation; its head was towards the entrance causeway.

Burial 5 (FIG 95): The crouched body of a child (aged 5-7 years) was found cut into the bottom and side of the Late Iron ditch F584 which forms part of Structure 53 (for exact location see FIG 74). The bones were poorly preserved — hence the schematic representation of FIG 95.

Burial 6 (not illustrated): This burial lay within the 'B' soil horizon at Grid 449W/589N within the enclosure of Structure 54. The bones had been severely disturbed by the plough and by subsequent earthmoving. Faye Powell considers the body, which stains in the soil showed was buried in the crouched position, to have been that of an adolescent — possibly male.

2. Unassociated Human Bones

Loose, unassociated human bones are a common feature of British Iron Age settlements and Cat's Water has produced what is probably a fairly typical collection. They are discussed in the second part of Appendix 9, but may be briefly summarised thus:

Middle Iron ditches: 2 acetabulum fragments; cranial vault fragments.

Middle Iron pit: frontal bone fragments.

Late Iron structure: clavicle and radius fragments.

Late Iron ditches: mandible fragment; child's femur; (?)child's frontal bone fragment; left femur fragment; left radius shaft; neo-natal right femur.

Late Iron pits: frontal bone fragments; right tibia fragments; complete male cranium (see FIG M62).

Romano-British ditch: left humerus fragment.

(Note three human bones from features of the Padholme Road (Iron Age) and Storey's Bar Road (Roman) subsites are described in Appendix 7.)

3. Cremations

One late Iron or Roman, and two possible Iron Age cremations were found. Fengate lies on the northern edge of the La Tène cremation distribution (Whimster 1977: FIG 2) and the occurrence of this rite in proven pre-third century contexts (each was sealed beneath the flood clay) is of interest. The cremations are indicated by the letter 'C' in FIG 16. The most southerly cremation (F1035 at Grid 412W/718N) was inserted into the top of a Late Iron drain (F1006) and may, therefore, be of early Roman date. Two small cremation pits (F26, dia 0.35m, depth 0.05m; F27, dia 0.30m, depth 0.13m) were located next to each other at Grid 392W/762N, just inside the northern limit of the excavation. Their dating is uncertain, but their location just outside the settlement suggests, perhaps, an Iron Age or early Roman date. Feature 27 produced a fired clay spool or pendant which has been deposited in the cremation pit after the body had been incinerated. The cremations are discussed in detail by Faye Powell in the third part of Appendix 9.

II DISCUSSION

Introduction

Part 3 of this chapter has been given over to a detailed consideration of the principal features that comprised the Cat's Water Iron Age and Romano-British settlement. The discussion that follows will be confined to those features only, and no attempt will be made to set the subsite in its local or regional context; to use the terminology of the Second Report (FNG 2, 6), we are concerned here with intra-community discussion and analysis. Wider comparisons must be sought in Chapter 8.

The discussion that follows will be in two parts: first, a brief summary of the relative chronology, with a more detailed consideration of the internal phasing of the settlement; second a general discussion of structures, linear features and non-linear features.

1. THE PHASING AND CHRONOLOGY OF THE SETTLEMENT
(FIGS 18 and 21)

The general plan of the main Cat's Water excavations (FIG 16) is intricate, and there can be little doubt that the palimpsest of features indicates settlement over a long period of time (FIG 21). We have seen above that certain features can be securely placed in the second millennium BC, or earlier, and their removal from the plan slightly simplifies matters. Nevertheless, the remaining features still present a complex problem of interpretation. First attempts at unravelling the network of features involved the use of a 'Harris Matrix' (Harris 1975, 1979). The construction of this matrix (the work of David Cranstone) soon showed that it would only be possible to attempt a very general phasing; the detailed development of the settlement, structure by structure and ditch by ditch, was for ever removed by the occupants themselves, who saw to it that drainage ditches were kept open and that buildings were maintained in good condition. Consequently it is the latest, and perhaps, the least informative, features which have survived the best; most earlier features are severely disturbed, but tantalising glimpses of the settlement's original layout are provided by peripheral features, such as Structures 3, 16, 54 and their associated enclosure ditches, which were 'left behind' as settlement shifted slightly north-west in the Late Iron Age. The discussion that follows is based in part on general spatial considerations (alignments, feature density, negative areas etc), on the Harris matrix, on pottery and other artefacts.

Iron Age pottery in Britian is a notoriously unreliable means of relative dating (Spratling 1974) and must be treated with the greatest caution. Considerable quantities were found at Cat's Water and these will be discussed in detail in Chapter 6. For present purposes, however, it will be sufficient to note that four periods of ceramics could be defined with some confidence. These periods are based on the introduction of significant new types, in an effort to combat the serious distorting effect of residual material. The periods are named, and not numbered, in order to avoid the impression of (spurious) accuracy inherent in such terms as 'Phase IIIc'. The absolute dating of the relative phases will be considered in Chapters 6 and 7. The phases (FIG 18) are as follows, and each will be considered in greater detail immediately below.

1-2. Pre-Iron Age
3. Early Iron Age (Chapter 6: Group 1)
4. Middle Iron Age (Chapter 6: Group 2)
5. Late Iron Age (Chapter 6: Group 3)
6. Roman (Chapter 7: late second century)

Early Iron Age

This period, broadly speaking the first half of the first millennium, is not well represented on Cat's Water. Only two features can be ascribed to it with any confidence, the wells F448 and F1551, but these are both features one might expect to associate with settlement. One N-S drainage ditch, F1553, at the extreme south-east of the settlement (see the discussion of Structure 47, above), one Structure (49), and two lengths of curved gully might be of this period, but the evidence (mainly pottery) is not very convincing. Pottery of this period is not well-fired, and although often thin, burnished and well-made, would probably not survive long, particularly in a drainage ditch subject to frequent recutting. Nevertheless, the almost complete absence of early pottery in the ditches of the later three periods is most striking and it can only be supposed that settlement on Cat's Water at this period was either intermittent or slight. Perhaps the two wells were originally dug considerably earlier, sometimes in the second millennium and went out of use later, in the early first millennium, when the material found in them was discarded.

Middle Iron Age

The absolute dating of Middle Iron Age 'scored wares' is still uncertain, but they seem to have been in use locally from the third or fourth to the first centuries (Cunliffe 1978, Appendix A22; Harding in Jackson 1975, 71). Features that produced pottery of this type at Cat's Water appear to be widespread across the area occupied, but with three main concentrations, one to the north (Structures 14 and 15), one to the east and north-east (Structures 47, 48, 50, 54 and 56, with possible outliers 21-23 and 34). The drainage ditches that served these buildings have mainly been obscured by later activity, but many of the ditches in use during the Late Iron Age period must also have been in use at this time. Hints of this are provided by short stretches of Middle Iron Age ditch due east of Structure 14, north of Structure 1, between and west of Structures 32 and 33 and south of Structures 40 and 45. Further, the west side of the enclosure around Structure 15 is apparently formed by a Late Iron Age ditch, but this feature shows

good evidence for frequent recutting, most probably from the Middle Iron Age period (see sections 9 and 10, FIG M70). If it is supposed that many of the Late Iron Age ditches follow paths laid out in Middle Iron Age times, then the available evidence would suggest that the northerly and easterly foci of Middle Iron Age settlement were linked by a common ditch system. This, of course, does not imply strict contemporaneity, since drainage ditches have longer use-lives than buildings. Certain structures in this enlarged group must, on strategic grounds, antedate the rest (Structures 6, 13 and 18). Perhaps these three buildings represent the beginnings of the settlement and as such they give an indication of the number of buildings that could have been in use at any other time; some show evidence for succession (Structure 8 cuts the enclosure ditch of (Structures 3), others for multi-phase rebuilding (Structures 3, 7, 42) and some cannot be contemporary on spatial grounds (Structures 32 and 33 would interlock). On available evidence, the maximum strictly contemporary size of this group of Middle Iron Age buildings would be about a dozen.

Turning to the south-easterly group, as defined above, the dating of the apparently outlying group of Structures 21-23 and 34, poses problems. These structures are probably of Middle Iron Age date as the few largely undiagnostic sherds which they yielded were all hand-made whereas Late Iron Age wheel-made pottery occurred abundantly in nearby drainage ditches. On the other hand, Structure 35 produced pottery of Late type and is somewhat similar in plan to those considered here. On present evidence, therefore, the question must remain unresolved. The main group of southerly features are situated on a low-lying part of the site which produced litle direct evidence for Late Iron Age occupation *in situ*. Indeed, the slight slope of the land south-eastwards seems to have been utilised in (?) Early Iron Age, Late Iron Age and Roman times to assist drainage, for it cannot be coincidence that ditches of each period run so precisely parallel to one another at this point.

The relationship of the southerly to the larger, northerly, group of structures is not at all clear, as any possible drainage ditches that might have linked them together have been completely recut and obliterated by the many phases of Late Iron Age and Roman activity that took place in the area between (see, for example Sections 35-37, FIG M78-M79). It was, however, suggested above that Structure 54 was abandoned, most probably due to rising water levels and this might indicate that Structures 47, 48 and 50 (which are even lower-lying) belong to a very early phase of the settlement's development. Finally, it should be noted that Middle Iron Age settlement could have extended south of Structure 50 for a short distance, although this is improbable, as water would have been a serious problem). We were unable to extend the area of excavation by hand, owing to the great thickness of clay (c 0.70m) involved, and machines were not permitted to work beneath the high voltage cables which crossed the subsite at that point.

Late Iron Age

Late Iron Age features are distinguished by the presence of wheel-made pottery in their fillings and a date in the later part of the first century BC, or first half of the first century AD is indicated. Late Iron Age features on Cat's Water may be broadly grouped into three elements, first, the northern edge of the settlement is defined by a ditched droveway, or, perhaps, a single linear ditch which runs E-W, directly south of the second millennium ditch 5. This northern Iron Age ditch cuts the second millennium ditch to the east where it shows evidence for multiple recutting. The apparent 'droveway' formed by the two northern Late Iron Age ditches cannot be proved and it may merely result from the enlargement or contraction of the main ditched enclosure system, but the two ditches do run very closely parallel to one another and the width of the trackway thus formed (3.5m) is similar to those of the earlier, second millennium, system — perhaps reflecting functional similarity. The second element of the Late Iron Age phase is represented by another droveway, this time to the south of the main excavated area. It can be seen on aerial photographs (PL 7) to traverse both Storey's Bar Road and Cat's Water subsites from WNW to ENE. Its ENE end, on Cat's Water, is clearly multi-phased. The southern droveway ditch passes through an almost semi-circular right-angled bend immediately north-west of Structure 54, which it cuts in both its phases. The first phase of this southerly ditch runs south-east, cutting Structures 49 and 50 en route, to leave the excavated area at Grid 429W/535N. The second phase of the southerly ditch ends in a large well or soakaway just inside the westerly entranceway of the enclosure around Middle Iron Age Structure 54. The width of the droveway is variable: at its easterly, Late Iron Age, end it is some 22m wide and at its narrowest point (opposite section 51, FIG 84) it measures 8m. The suggested droveway to the north of the main settlement area was probably intended to divert livestock (being driven down to the Fen pastures to the east) away from the settlement area, as there are no entranceways leading into the enclosures. The southerly drove can be interpreted in two ways, perhaps reflecting two or more different functions, or periods of use. First, the Romano-British double entranceway south-east of Structure 46 was not in use in the Late Iron Age and this could indicate that at some time in that period the southerly droveway served a function similar to that in the north, ie to divert beasts around the settlement area, towards pastures to the east. This hypothesis finds some support from the continuation, or earlier alignment of, the southerly drove ditch on either side of Structure 56. This small ditch appears to hook gently towards the north east at its extreme east end, as if it was making use

of the settlement's boundary ditch. The second interpretation of the droveway's function is suggested by the butt-end of a phase of the northern drove ditch immediately south-west of section 37 (FIG 84); this butt-end might mark the presence of an entranceway into the enclosed area of ditched yards immediately to the north.

The third, and most significant, element of the Late Iron Age period is the settlement within the ditched enclosures, between the two droveways. We have already noted that many of these ditches probably follow Middle Iron Age courses, but there is as yet no clear evidence that the southerly drove and enclosure ditches (ie those south and west of Structures 33 and 35) have such precursors. Indeed, with the exception of the dubiously-dated Structures 21-23 and 34, Middle Iron Age features are very rare south and west of Grid 450W. In general, the Late Iron Age period sees, as we have noted above, a slight shift towards the higher ground of the north-west, a move that may be a response to rising winter water levels. The ditched enclosures are difficult to interpret chronologically, for reasons given at length above, but the multi-period off-centre recutting of ditches east of Structures 10 and 53 (and with it, therefore, the rebuilding of the structures themselves) is stratigraphically early in the sequence. The eastern edge of the later phase is more 'cleanly' defined by a ditch which continues the alignment, southwards, of the ditch which passes close to the west side of Structures 16 and 7. Entranceways through this almost continuous late phase eastern boundary, or enclosure, ditch are hard to find; again, this is due to subsequent recutting and the associated problems of interpreting the homogeneous ditch fillings which characterised features from this part of the subsite. One possible contender, however, is the gap in the two ditches due south of Structures 9 and 12. Structures of the Late period appear to be quite evenly spread over the enclosed area, with the exception of two bands 30-40 metres wide to the north and south. (The only structures within these two bands are the two amorphous (?) buildings, 35 and 51). Buildings (as defined by true ring-gullies) are spread evenly over the area between the reserved bands to north and south.

Two general points of interest arise from this consideration of the Late Iron Age phase. First, despite the fact that, on ceramic grounds, the Late Iron Age period only lasted for about a century, the evidence for ditch recutting, realignment and construction is very substantial, and may reflect the communities' at times desperate response to rising ground water levels. Second, a glance at the phase plan (FIG 18) shows that Late Iron Age buildings exhibit a diversity of ground plan unmatched in Middle Iron Age times, where round houses were the almost invariable norm.

Roman

There appears to have been, on artefactual evidence, a gap of some 100 years between the Late Iron Age phase (which terminated shortly after the Roman

124

Conquest) and the full second century Roman phase of the settlement (as dated by the artifacts discussed in Chapter 7). This phase was short-lived, and with the possible exception of one building, Structure 28, and three wells or water holes, is represented archaeologically only by linear ditches or gullies. The absence of solid evidence for buildings is remarkable in view of (a) the quantity of pottery — mainly Nene Valley Grey Ware — recovered and (b) the discovery of many brick and tile fragments. There are two probable explanations for this; the first is that the Roman phase saw a continuation of the westward shift noted in the Late Iron Age phase. This westward shift saw the construction of buildings beneath the modern road which separated Cat's Water from the Padholme Road subsite. This suggestion, however, is not supported by the 1972 excavations on Padholme Road which revealed no Romano-British settlement features. The second hypothesis is that the pottery, brick and tile fragments were transported to the Cat's Water ditched yards, either as hard core or in manure. This hypothesis might explain the pottery found in an organic-rich deposit from the ditch F412, dicussed by Dr Hayes in Chapter 7 (see also Pryor and Cranstone 1978, 26); but it does not account for the quantities of fresh pottery, including sherds of an almost complete Samian bowl, recovered from the well F1561. This feature was filled-in with large amounts of domestic rubbish and there is no good reason to suppose that it had been transported for any great distance. It is therefore suggested that the scarcity of evidence for Romano-British settlement is due to post-depositional factors, and of these the most probable are flood-action and modern ploughing.

We have noted that the finds indicate a break in settlement of perhaps 100 years between the close of the Late Iron Age and the commencement of the Roman phases of the settlement. This is reflected on the Cat's Water subsite by the ease with which deposits of the two periods may be distinguished. Recuts are clear, continuous, and often off-centre and there is usually a considerable thickness of natural silting in those ditches which saw use in both periods. The only exception to this is the most south-easterly Roman enclosure ditch (it also forms the northern droveway ditch at this point) which follows the Late Iron Age alignment in an area where ditch fillings were difficult to interpret (but where undulations in profile provided means of correlating various phases of recutting — see Sections 36 and 37, FIG M79). Excavations on the Storey's Bar Road subsite showed that the Romano-British droveway closely followed the alignment of the Late Iron Age drove (an observation that was based in part on negative evidence, since the later ditches were deeper than their Iron Age counterparts). This also held true in the Cat's Water subsite. The southerly Romano-British drove ditch, however, swung south some twenty metres further west than its Iron Age precursor. The northern Romano-British drove ditch was pierced by a double entranceway

to the south-east of Structure 46, but this entranceway was not used in the earlier period; it probably provided access to the southerly ditched yards of the Romano-British enclosure system.

The northerly drove of the Late Iron Age settlement had gone out of use, and in its stead a length of NW-SE ditch was laid out, more or less along the centre of the earlier droveway. This ditch became difficult to follow once it joined the course of the earlier droveway's southern ditch. The role of this apparently isolated ditch in the interpretation of the Roman phase occupation is obscure, but it was not traced further west onto the Newark Road subsite.

The Roman enclosures were of two types, a group of 7-8 small sub-rectangular ditched yards, to the west, which passed out of the excavated area, and two large ditched enclosures to the east. Aerial photographs clearly show that these enclosures do not continue under the modern road, but the present excavations could not be extended further west due to recent sewer disturbance. The relationships of the various ditches of the small yards are shown in FIG 18, and are best interpreted as being of two phases, marked by the modification of entranceway arrangements and the extension, in the later phase, of the ditched enclosures northwards. Finally, it should be noted that all Roman phase features were capped with a deposit of flood clay. This clay is discussed in more detail by Charles French (Appendices 2 and 3). The latter study shows that it was of freshwater origin and that it can be correlated with the flooding known to have taken place, around the southern Fen-edge in the early-mid third century AD (Salway 1967; Bromwich 1970).

2. A FUNCTIONAL INTERPRETATION OF VARIOUS CAT'S WATER SETTLEMENT FEATURES

This section briefly reviews the variety of features found on the Cat's Water settlement and suggests ways in which they may be classified and interpreted.

Structures

The analysis of the 57 structures found follows the pattern of the Interim Report (Pryor and Cranstone 1978, 18-24). That paper, however, was written before the final season of excavation (1978) which produced a number of important new structures (Nos 46-51, 54 and 56). The new buildings fall generally within the scheme outlined in the interim report, but the proposed subdivision of round buildings, into types A, B and C now seems less clear-cut and will no longer be used.

1. Round buildings

The Cat's Water subsite produced evidence for 38 round buildings, which may be grouped into two distinct categories, buildings defined by continuous (annular or penannular) gullies, or buildings defined by a discontinuous ring-gully arc (or arcs).

Buildings with continuous ring-gullies

Buildings with continuous or annular or penannular gullies are the commonest type of structure found at Cat's Water. Well-preserved examples of this type are Structures 1-3; 6-9; 11-13; 16-20; 47-49 and 54; poorly preserved examples probably include Structures 14-15; 30-33. Structure 53 is a round building, but its classification is difficult. Buildings with continuous annular or penannular gullies that are poorly preserved are grouped in this class (a) if the gully survives for more than about a third of its circumference — as in Structures 6, 13, 18 etc and (b) if the gully peters out at one or both ends, as structures with discontinuous ring-gullies are marked by steep, well-defined butts at each end of the gully. Structures 15 and 48 are the only two which pass out of the excavated area and these have been classed as buildings with continuous gullies.

Round buildings with continuous gullies exhibit a wide range of size, from very large (Structures 6, 13, 18, 49, diameters 12.0m, 12.0m, 11.6m and 12.0m respectively) to very small (Structures 1, 2, 8, 19, diameters 7.0m, 8.0m, 7.5m and 7.0m respectively). These extreme sizes perhaps constitute the two most diagnostic classes of round buildings with continuous gullies (Pryor and Cranstone 1978, Types A and B). The larger buildings are stratigraphically early and the smaller buildings (with the exception of Structure 19 which is Late Iron Age) are also of Middle Iron Age date, but slightly more recent; they are more homogeneous morphologically, being characterised by well-defined east-facing entranceways.

The buildings exhibit a variety of constructional techniques. They are, however, easily distinguished from second millennium post-built structures, such as 46, by the comparative rarity of postholes within the area enclosed by the gully. This could be due to post-depositional factors, but the survival of sometimes quite substantial door postholes in a number of buildings (for example Structures 3, 7, 16, 20, 47, 54) argues against this. The change is better explained in terms of constructional technique, where the second millennium pattern of building (in which the weight of the roof was taken on posts set inside the building) was replaced by a load-bearing ring-beam set atop the walls. This technique would greatly increase the available space inside the house. An alternative explanation would require little change in building technique, but instead would suppose that rising ground water levels in the Iron Age would cause deeply sunk posts to rot. The simplest way of preventing this was to position each internal post above a stone or gravel pad, which would, of course, leave no archaeological trace after ploughing. Perhaps a combination of techniques was employed, wherein main load-bearing posts were either set in the ground to a shallow depth (for example, the central post of Structure 1) or else were placed on pads, while the remaining weight of the roof was taken on a ring-beam. There can, however, be little doubt that in nearly all Iron Age round buildings at Fengate the ring-gully served both to collect and soak-away water from the eaves and, in certain deep cases (such as Structure 54), to lower the high winter ground water table around the building's wall-footing. Evidence to support this hypothesis is provided by Structures 7, 14, 47 and 54 which all have smaller wall-slots running concentrically inside the outer and larger eaves-drip gully. The average eaves width was about one metre. The only building defined by a ring-gully which seems not to have had an eaves-drip gully was Structure 17; this building is also unique on Cat's Water in having been built using the wall plate construction technique.

Buildings with discontinuous ring-gullies

These buildings are defined by one or, in a few cases, by two arcs of ring-gully. These arcs are in general about one third of a complete ring-gullies' circumference. The building type is characterised by having two clearly-defined butt-ends to each gully arc. This characteristic distinguishes discontinuous ring-gully buildings from eroded or plough-damaged continuous ring-gully buildings. Buildings of this sort have not, however, been given sufficient attention in the literature where they may, for example, be dismissed as shelters or windbreaks. This is unfortunate, as in some cases the ring-gully arcs represent the remains of very substantial buildings indeed (for example Structure 4, diameter *c* 12m). Clues to the definition of the type were provided by finds' distributions which showed pronounced concentrations of artefacts around one or both butt-ends of gully arcs, and by three buildings (Structures 10, 19 and, perhaps 56) which used two gully arcs in their construction. Structure 10 was most interesting in that its southern arc of gully was considerably shallower than its northern gully. Different gully depths, therefore could account for the usual survival of just one gully at a time. Structure 5, for example, is composed of one gully arc to the north, but the nearby drainage ditch F1006, curves around its southern edge, in place of a second gully. This might also be the explanation of the curious Structure 53. Buildings represented by discontinuous gullies are Structures 4, 5, 19 (which was blocked at one end to convert it to a continuous ring-gully building), 29, 36, (?) 50 and 56; two others are also known from Storey's Bar Road subsite (see Chapter 3, Structures 1 and 2).

Discontinuous gully buildings are interpreted as having two entranceways or open sides, in the manner, for example, of Structure 10 or 19, the latter in its first phase of use. The function of these open-sided buildings is obscure, but is probably connected in some way with farming or livestock management; perhaps the two open walls would have provided a through-draft suitable, for example, for winnowing grain. The wider implications of this newly recognised type of building are considered in Chapter 8.

Finds distribution in round buildings

The study of finds' distributions in each building was particularly rewarding and cannot be properly summarised out of the context which each, separate, building provided. Flint and pottery distributions were, however, almost invariably independent, and finds frequently clustered around the entrance causeways in both continuous and discontinuous ring-gully buildings (for an example of the former see FIG 43 and of the latter see FIG 30). Most discontinuous ring-gully buildings showed finds concentrations around one butt-end only (for example), Storey's Bar Road Structures 1 and 2; Cat's Water Structures 4, 5, 36 and 56), but the first phase of Structure 19 showed a double finds concentration — around both sides of each entranceway. Finds were, in general, rare, or very rare, in the few surviving examples of wall-slots (Structures 7, 14, 17, 47 and 54). Only one building (Structure 54) provided an undisturbed floor deposit, although a shallow depression at the centre of Structure 49 could, possibly have been caused by trampling. Finally, although the precise role of the discontinuous gully arcs in the construction of the open-sided building must remain obscure until better-preserved examples of the building type come to light, the common occurrence of finds and their distinctive distribution around at least one entranceway strongly recalls the pattern observed in eaves-drip gullies of continuous ring-gully buildings. The ring-gully arcs, in common with the eaves-drip gullies of the continuous ring-gully building, were of open U-shaped profile and showed no evidence whatsoever for postholes, stake-holes or for post packing.

2. Rectilinear structures

Three possible structures could have been rectilinear in plan. The two parallel slots of Structure 40 could possibly be the remains of a rectangular structure, which would, perhaps, have fulfilled the same function as its circular antecedent (Structure 24). Structure 41, however, is more substantial and is best seen as a building with two open sides. Structure 45, a small L-shaped gully, is only doubtfully classed as a building.

3. Four-post building

Structure 57 is the only four-post building (there were no convincing two-post 'drying-racks') found on the subsite.

4. Miscellaneous structures

The remaining Structures are probably best interpreted as farm buildings. Three very small ring-gullies (Structures 22, 24, 25) could have been dug either to receive the run-off from circular hay or straw stacks (Bradley in FNG 2, 223, with refs), or, less probably, to provide footings for circular walls (an explanation that is more acceptable for Structure 22). The complex of Structures 21-23, 34 (and ? 35) finds good parallels

at Hod Hill (see description above) and at Abingdon, Ashville (Parrington 1978, FIG 12) and, perhaps, at Stanwick, Yorks. (Wheeler 1954, FIG 3). The interpretation of these structures and their 'annexes' must remain speculative, but an association with livestock seems probable. This view is supported by recent research at Farmoor, Oxon. (Lambrick and Robinson 1979, FIG 11). The association of Structures 37-39 with the small ring-gully Structure 24 and its succeeding (?) rectilinear building, Structure 40 vaguely recalls the small ring-gully, Structure 22 and its curved 'annexes', and, again, a farming connection seems probable.

'Structure' 26 received much attention in the interim report (Pryor and Cranstone 1978, 22), but it is now best seen as, perhaps, a morphologically indistinct group of postholes which has been given false prominence by subsequent water action.

Structure 28, of possible Roman date, is, in plan, a cross between a round and a rectilinear building; it has one open side — and in this recalls Structure 41 — and a smaller side entranceway marked by a pronounced increase in finds density. Structure 42 is similarly unusual in plan and the three large pits located at the corners suggest that the gully frequently held water (or manure) and was not, therefore a constructional feature, despite its regular profile and steep sides. Perhaps the building, if such there was, stood within the small enclosure defined by the gullies which are pierced by two entranceways, to east and west. Structures 43, 44, 51 and 55 are most probably not roofed buildings and could have been used as specialised shelters or enclosures for livestock during, perhaps, the months of winter.

Linear features

The ditches have been discussed at some length above, so only a few points deserve further mention. First, the discovery of two lengths of 'brush drain', one from Middle and one from Late Iron contexts serves to emphasise the importance of drainage. Second, many of the ditches show massive evidence for recutting and there is, on the whole, little evidence for seriously off-centre recutting. The cleaning out of ditches must, therefore, have been a regular part of the annual work cycle. Ditches frequently became progressively enlarged over the years, however, thus obliterating substantial lengths of Middle Iron drains and rendering a detailed reconstruction of the Middle Iron settlement impossible. This regular maintenance of ditches and the evidence of westward settlement drift from Middle to Late Iron times suggests that occupation was probably continuous and not intermittent. The only demonstrable gap, that between the last Late Iron settlement and the Roman occupation of the second century AD, is marked by the laying out of many new ditched yards and the digging of new enclosure ditches, substantially off the alignment of their Late Iron precursors. Only the main southern droveway ditch alignments seem to have been followed with any care and this may simply be a result of their straight and easily followed course; more probably, however, it could suggest that the drove itself continued in use throughout the early Roman period. In this regard, the two rectilinear enclosures north of the droveway on the Storey's Bar Road subsite may well be directly associated with the Late Iron settlement on Cat's Water. Similar links with the Middle Iron pits on the Padholme Road subsite are, however, less convincing and a second settlement of this period, west of Cat's Water, could be indicated.

Non-linear features

Most of the non-linear features on Cat's Water are associated with structures. Clay-lined pits or water holes occur within buildings (for example Structure 3) and the numerous small pits or postholes which are distributed in and around structures help to define areas of intensive occupation. We have seen above how the water table must always have been a problem at Fengate, before the recent widespread draining of the Fens, and there are very few prehistoric features which can confidently be interpreted as storage pits (*contra* N H Field *et al* 1964,

378). Grain and livestock feed must have been stored above ground perhaps over the rafters of the buildings, as two and four post structures are so rare. Most of the substantial non-linear features on Cat's Water are associated with water in some way, either as wells or as larger soakaways or reservoirs. It is also important to recall that many of the smaller pits (and ditches too) on low-lying parts of the subsite have probably been seriously distorted by post-depositional flood-action.

Finally, the remains of six burials, most of Middle Iron date, were located. In general they were poorly preserved and many had been damaged by post-depositional agencies, including later settlement and modern ploughing. None contained grave goods and all but one lay around the south-east perimeter of the settlement. Many loose human bones were also found in non-funerary, settlement, features (such as pits and ditches) and three cremations, all sealed beneath the third century flood clay were located in the northern half of the subsite and two were (?carefully) positioned beyond the Late Iron and Roman northern boundary ditches.

INTRODUCTION

This chapter considers pre-first millennium artifacts from subsites discussed in this report. Neolithic or earlier Bronze Age pottery was found in two features of the Cat's Water subsite and from a small pit from Vicarage Farm. Bronze Age flintwork was found in linear ditches of the second millennium enclosure system of the Storey's Bar Road and Cat's Water subsite. The pottery will be considered first (all dimensions are in mm).

POTTERY

CATALOGUE OF ILLUSTRATED POTTERY (FIG 96)

1. Rim sherd. Reddish yellow (7.5YR 6/6) ext and int; core black. Sandy fabric with (?) crushed shell.
Decoration: lightly incised herringbone in hollow of neck and upper shoulder. Single lightly incised line on rim top suggests additional decoration, but sherd very abraded.
Vicarage Farm Area II, F5 layer 1. 72:394
2. Wall sherds. Three sherds of *c* ten are illustrated. Int and core are black; ext: light brown (7.5YR 6/4). Coarse fabric with crushed shell and (?) vegetable temper.
Decoration: pinched rustication of two types. Vertical pinched-up rough (?) cordons above/below random, spaced, pinching and finger stabbing.
Cat's Water Area IV, F420 layer 1; Grid 420W/759N. 77:1422
3. Three rim sherds (illustrated) and numerous wallsherds (not illustrated). All sherds are much abraded and appear to come from an open U-shaped bowl.
Fabric: light grey int and core; ext: greyish brown (10YR 5/2) crumbly fabric with (?) vegetable temper (vacuoles) and grog; some fine sand.
Decoration: opposed uneven diagonal lines on rim top; ext of thickened T-shaped rim marked with rough V-impressions (? chevron) made with tool *c* 4.5mm in length.
Cat's Water Area VI, F816 layer 1; Grid 434W/604N. 78:562
4. Rim sherd very dark brown (10YR 2.5/2) int, ext and core; mainly sand temper with some (?) crushed shell; fabric generally hard, well-fired. Dia 170.
Decoration: Rim top, impressed herringbone; ext: three unequal bands of impressed herringbone; int: irregular, lightly scored, concentric pendant semi-circular motif directly below the internal rim bevel.
Cat's Water Area VI, F816 layer 1; Grid 434W/604N. 78:555

DISCUSSION

The single example of sherds with fingertip and pinched-up rustication (FIG 96, no 2) is essentially a Late Neolithic or earlier Bronze Age type and it would be inadvisable to attempt a more precise dating. Its fabric, however, is unlike that of Grooved Ware, as represented at Fengate and is also very dissimilar from local rusticated Beaker pottery (FNG 3, Appendix 10).

The sherds representing the three remaining vessels are, however, of considerable interest as they are the only examples of Peterborough pottery found in the present series of excavations. Moreover, of the three sherds found, none is in the eponymous style for which Fengate is well-known.

One sherd, although much weathered, is probably of Ebbsfleet Ware (FIG 96, no 1). The angle of this sherd is uncertain and it could, possibly, be slightly flared; it is generally thinner and of higher quality than most of the Fengate and Mortlake Wares from the site and is in a characteristic slightly sandy fabric. The remaining two sherds (FIG 96: nos 3 and 4) belong to the Peterborough tradition of Late Neolithic pottery but cannot be attributed directly to any of its recognised sub-styles, as currently defined. The decorative motifs, and to some extent the fabrics too, recall Mortlake usage, but the internal semi-circular design of No 3 finds parallels in a sherd of Fengate Ware from the site (I F Smith 1956, FIG 66). The unusual shape of No 4 is represented locally by a sherd from Ecton, Northants (Bamford in Moore and Williams 1975, FIG 8, no 22).

FLINT

CATALOGUE OF ILLUSTRATED FLINTS (FIG 97)

1. Projectile point with single barb and broken tip. Fine, bifacial 'nibble' retouch. Light brown flint, no cortex.
Cat's Water, Area IV, F115 layer 1 (second millennium ditch) Grid 388W/757N. 77:233
2. Projectile point with single pronounced barb and sharp tip. Fine, invasive bifacial retouch. Black flint, no cortex.
Cat's Water Area V, F600 layer 1 (undated pit) Grid 402W/642N. 77:3530
3. Single barb or transverse projectile point with sharp tip. Invasive retouch is mainly confined to the dorsal face of the flake. Dark grey flint with gravel pebble cortex present.
Cat's Water Area V, F598 layer 1 (undated pit) Grid 402W/640N. 77:3513
4. Leaf-shaped arrowhead with two notches (for hafting). Very fine invasive bifacial retouch. Dark brown flint, no cortex.
Cat's Water Area X, top of stripped surface at Grid 405W/565N. 78:2201

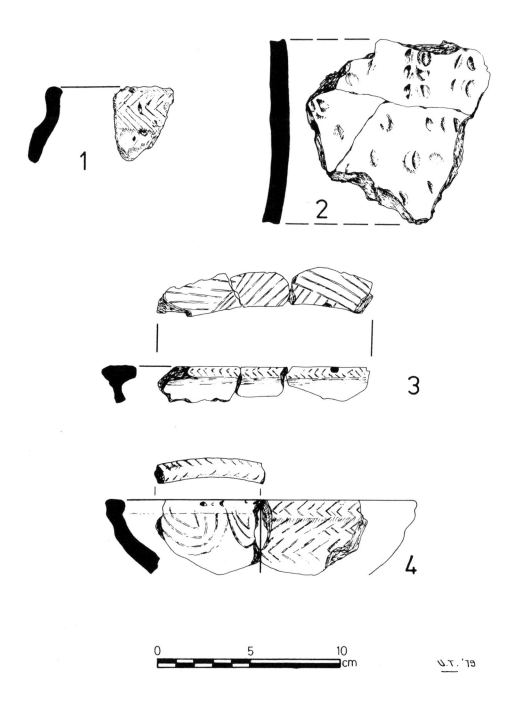

Fig. 96   Neolithic and Bronze Age pottery from the Vicarage Farm (no 1) and Cat's Water (nos 2-4)subsites.

130

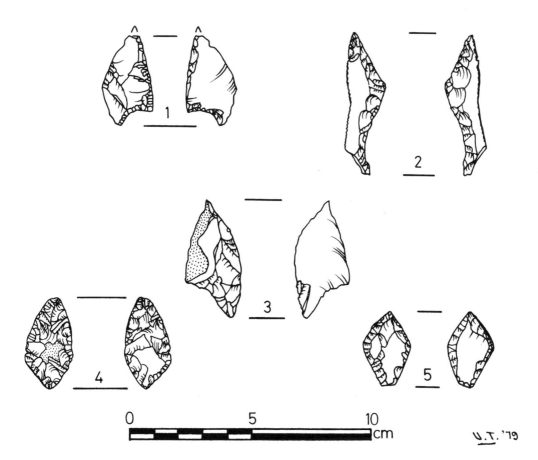

Fig. 97   Cat's Water subsite: flints.

5. Angular leaf-shaped arrowhead. Fine, bifacial 'nibble' retouch. Pale grey flint, no cortex. Cat's Water Area V, F320 layer 2 (undated pit) Grid 400W/724N. 77:1205

DISCUSSION

Storey's Bar Road Subsite (See microfiche Table M1)
The following 115 flints were found in the filling of the probable second millennium ditch P18 (Chapter 3 and FIG 10):

Implements (41% of total)		(%)
Scrapers	3	6.4
Transverse arrowhead, type D	1	2.1
Utilised flakes (whole)	19	40.4
Utilised flakes (broken)	11	23.4
Serrated flake	1	2.1
Awl	1	2.1
Unifacially retouched flake	1	2.1
Utilised irregular workshop waste	5	10.6
Denticulated tools	5	10.6
Total	47	

The implements are generally of Bronze Age type, as described at length in the Third Report (FNG 3, chapter 2, Finds); particularly characteristic are the five denticulated tools, but the transverse arrowhead is less typical and could derive from the Grooved Ware settlement to the south. Dimensions of the 19 unbroken utilised flakes are given in Table M1; although the numbers are small, the pattern recalls that observed on Newark Road (FNG 3, FIG 73).

By-products (59% of total)		(%)
Waste flakes (whole)	35	51.5
Waste flakes (broken)	13	19.1
Cores (A2 and B2)	2	2.9
Irregular workshop waste	18	26.5
Total	68	

The by-products are entirely typical of the Bronze Age, with many short, squat flakes (Table M1) which frequently are side struck or exhibit hinge fracture. In some cases it was difficult to distinguish between true flakes and irregular workshop waste.

Bronze Age (Cat's Water Subsite)
Breadth : Length Ratios
Waste Flakes (32)   Utilized Flakes (44)

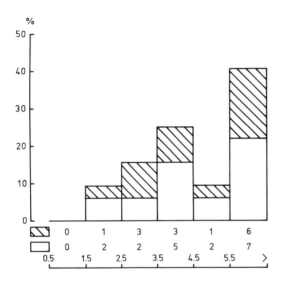
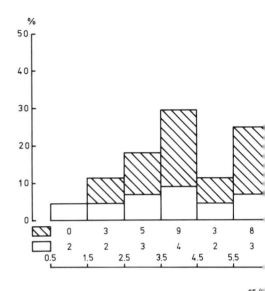

Fig. 98   Cat's Water subsite: histograms of Bronze Age flint dimensions.

Cat's Water Subsite (Table M1; FIG 98)

The 166 flints described below were found in the fillings of second millennium ditches (see phase plan, FIG 18 for location):

Implements (56.6% of total)

		(%)
Scrapers	6	6.4
Single barb projectile point	1	1.1
Awl	1	1.1
Piercer	1	1.1
Retouched flakes	4	4.2
Retouched irregular workshop waste	2	2.1
Utilised irregular workshop waste	7	7.4
Utilised flakes (whole)	44	46.8
Utilised flakes (broken)	17	18.1
Denticulated flakes	10	10.6
Serrated flake (broken)	1	1.1
Total	94	

The six scrapers are composed of three short-end scrapers (type A(ii)); one on a broken flake (type E); one disc (type C) and one on a piece of irregular workshop waste. The high proportion of denticulated flakes is consistent with Bronze Age practice as recognised at Fengate (Newark Road subsite). The only arrowhead or projectile point found in the Cat's Water second millennium ditches is of Late Neolithic type and could, perhaps, be residual. The other four arrowheads/ projectile points found on Cat's Water are from undated contexts, but Nos 2 and 4 (FIG 97) are of interest: No 2 is remarkable for the extreme length of its single barb and recalls examples from the Grooved Ware settlement on Storey's Bar Road (FNG 2, FIG 43); no 4 has two distinct notches for hafting. Attention should also be drawn here to Stephen Green's discussion of the (?) earlier Neolithic leaf arrowhead found lodged in the ribs of a crouched burial.

The breadth:length histogram (FIG 98) shows the same bimodal tendency seen at Newark Road (FNG 3, FIG 73) and a similar preference for shorter squatter flakes. The unusually high proportion of implements to by-products is also of interest.

By-products (43.4% of total)

		(%)
Waste flakes (whole)	32	44.4
Waste flakes (broken)	19	26.4
Cores	2	2.7
(1 on irregular workshop waste: one type B3)		
Irregular workshop waste	19	26.4
Total	72	

The smaller collection of waste flakes shows the same bimodal pattern seen in the utilised flakes (FIG 98), and is also broadly comparable with the Bronze Age collection from Newark Road.

INTRODUCTION

The greatest part of this chapter is given over to a description and discussion of the pottery. It should, however, be noted that the use of the term 'Iron Age' is for convenience only. The Roman conquest of 43/4 AD, while of great long-term significance, did not appear, on archaeological evidence, to affect the Cat's Water settlement in the mid-first century AD. Consequently, finds of pottery and metalwork that may immediately post-date the conquest are treated here as 'Iron Age' (see, in particular, the report by Dr Reece, below). Chapter 7 will be given over to a discussion of finds of the 'full' Roman period, after *c* AD 60/70.

Part I considers pottery. It is divided into four sections: first, a description of the Type Series (which includes a fabric analysis by Dr D Williams): second, a selection of complete or near-complete vessels; third a selection of pottery from structures and, fourth, a discussion of the assemblage. The pottery collection is large and the vast majority of material derives from ditches that had been open and recut in many periods. These contexts are stratigraphically very unreliable and pose significant problems of intrusion and residuality. Pit groups are also very rare. Further, being derived from disturbed contexts, most of the pottery occurred as very small sherds. For these reasons it was found impractible to group the sherds by complete vessel form (eg carinated bowls etc); and the Type Series is therefore arranged by Rim/Form, Body/Form and Base/Form (further discussed in the Introduction to Part I, below). Many of the sherds illustrated in the Series are too small for the standard reduction of Iron Age pottery (¼ scale); illustrations are thus reproduced at ½ scale. For these three reasons it was decided to place the Iron Age pottery Type Series catalogue and illustrations on microfiche. Restorable complete and near-complete profiles and sherds from more reliable, closed, contexts are described and illustrated in the text (FIGS 99-104).

Part II discusses miscellaneous finds. This section includes reports by J P Wild (on clay loomweights), Martin Henig (a silver finger-ring), Richard Reece (coins), Paul Craddock (slags and refractories), D F Mackreth (brooches), and Maisie Taylor (worked wood).

PART I: POTTERY
(SEE MICROFICHE PAGES 119-183)

INTRODUCTION

The unusual post-depositional history of the Cat's Water subsite, which yielded the great majority of Iron Age vessels, is discussed in the Introduction to the

discussion of Group 2 pottery below. In essence, the subsite has produced very few pit groups (because the high water table precludes the digging of pits) and the vast bulk of the pottery has been found in drainage ditches. These drains were frequently renewed and the artifacts in them became mixed together and broken up (see the even spread of material in FIG 87).

The site has produced a large quantity (*c* 11,600 sherds) of pottery, most of it, in effect, poorly stratified. It was therefore thought desirable to attempt an assessment of the ceramic material using a sherd-based Type Series. At the same time, we have been at considerable pains to reconstruct complete, or near-complete profiles from sherds; results of this work may be seen in the Type Series illustration and in FIGS 99-101. It should also be noted from the outset that the Type Series is purely 'archaeological' in the sense of Hardin (1979).

Pottery illustrated in the Type Series is derived, wherever possible, from what are believed to be true contexts; thus, the large quantities of Middle Iron Age material from Late Iron drains does not appear as illustrations in the Type Series, but in cases where we have had to depart from this rule the illustrated sherd is labelled as residual. The Type Series is based on rims, bodies and bases. Rims are defined by their angle, and treatment of exterior, interior and, where applicable, top. Many of the sherds chosen to illustrate rim forms, for example, include parts of the shoulder and belly, but these should be ignored for purposes of classifying Rim Forms alone. Base sherds are defined by their angle, their exterior treatment, and their interior and underside profiles. Body or wall sherds comprise the remainder. In many respects, body sherds have proved the least amenable to this treatment: it was often difficult to decide whether a sherd belonged to a belly or shoulder, hence the inclusion of types such as Group 2 Body Form 8, or Group 3 Body Form 4. Each category of sherd — rim, body and base — is followed by a Type Series of appropriate Decorations.

The Type Series is divided into three parts:
Group 1
This group contains hand-made pottery of pre-'scored ware' type of the Early Iron Age, and is found in deposits which are stratigraphically and spatially quite distinct from Groups 2 and 3.
Group 2
This group contains all hand-made Iron Age pottery not included within Group 1. It is not, therefore, a period division.
Group 3
This contains all wheel-made Iron Age (as defined in the Introduction to the chapter) wares. In certain cases it proved difficult to distinguish between wheel- and hand-

fashioned wares and in cases of doubt sherds were assigned to Group 2.

Surface treatment (abbreviated to ST) and fabric types, which are both common to all Groups, are considered first. This section is followed by a detailed description of each Type Series Group, starting with Group 1. It should be noted that details of fabric, surface treatment and provenance apply to the example sherd only, and not to other sherds exhibiting the same formal or decorative features.

Surface Treatment

The following abbreviations will be used in the text and microfiche catalogues:

0 — Surface absent (weathering or heat damage)
1 — Burnished surface
2 — Smooth surface (this includes coarse sandy wheel-made fabrics).
3 — Medium smooth (a category for the many sherds that were neither smooth nor rough)
4 — Rough (mainly applies to large coarse ware vessels and does not include surface rustication, for example scoring, which is treated, for purposes of analysis, as decoration).
A — 'Corky' texture resulting from the burning-out or dissolving of shell, or, more rarely, of vegetable temper.

These surface treatment (ST) types apply to the exterior of each sherd only. Thus, the exterior surface of a medium smooth vessel with a 'corky' texture would be abbreviated as: ST 3+A.

Fabrics

A selection of 57 possible fabric types was made from Iron Age features of the Cat's Water subsite. Pottery from features of many types was examined, but special attention was paid to features such as main drainage ditches which were located in the heart of settlement areas. The selection of pottery for submission to Dr Williams was by Calum Rollo, whose assistance is gratefully acknowledged. The selection process was exhaustive, and involved the examination of many hundreds of sherds; it is reasonable to assume, therefore, that most significant fabric types have been included. It should also be noted here that Dr Williams' report agrees well with the previous analysis of Iron Age pottery from the Padholme Road subsite published in the First Report (FNG 1, 26, 'Ware I' is Williams' Fabric 1A; 'Ware II' includes Williams' Fabrics 1B and 1C). The present chapter discusses pottery from all subsites that have produced Iron Age material and only uses the surface treatment and fabric types discussed here.

A FABRIC ANALYSIS OF SOME IRON AGE
POTTERY FROM FENGATE
by Dr D F Williams

A representative selection of Iron Age sherds from Fengate was submitted for fabric analysis. All the sherds were studied macroscopically with the aid of a binocular microscope, and many were thin sectioned and examined under the petrological microscope. This allowed a number of fabric groupings to be made on the basis of the type of inclusions present in each sherd.

The vast majority of Iron Age pottery examined contains inclusions of shell, with a small amount of limestone. Like the Bronze Age pottery (Williams in FNG 3, 87) the shell appears to be fossiliferous and local materials, for example the Oxford Clay may well have been used. However, as there is nothing particularly distinctive about the nature of the inclusions, and as the Jurassic outcrops over a large area in this part of the country, a non-local source for some of the pottery cannot be ruled out.

It may be useful at this stage to divide the samples into three sub-groups based on the size of shell and quartz inclusions present.

Fabric 1A

This group is characterized by numerous large (up to 6mm across) fragments of shell normally scattered throughout the fabric. In some cases the shell has been dissolved out and has left the surfaces pitted with voids. The colour of the sherds varies, but tends to be towards dark brown to grey, and all have a soapy feel about them.

Fabric 1B

The composition of this group is very similar to that of Fabric 1A, except that the size of the shell is usually much smaller (average size 2mm across).

Fabric 1C

These sherds contain lesser quantities of shell than the two groups above, and in addition have a fair amount of subangular quartz grains present, with a scatter of small sandstone. Hard fabric, light to dark grey and noticeably sandy.

Fabric 2

All the sherds in this group appear to be heavily charged with quartz sand grains. There is, however, a considerable degree of difference in texture between many of the samples. For example, two samples (Archive samples 52 and 49) are quite finely textured, while at the other end of the scale one (Archive 59) is much more granular in texture. Due to the non-distinctive nature of the quartz inclusions it is difficult at this stage to offer useful comments on the possible origins of these sherds, other than to say that a local source is quite possible for all of them.

Fabric 3

Fairly hard fabric, tending towards reddish-yellow surfaces, dark grey core. All these sherds appear to contain a small quantity of grog, together with subangular quartz grains and a little shell. Grog tempering is not a common feature in the Iron Age, it has previously been noted by the writer at Little Waltham, Essex and Hascombe Camp and Holmbury, Surrey.

1. THE IRON AGE TYPE SERIES CATALOGUE
(SEE MICROFICHE PAGES 119-183;
FIGS M88-M135)

2. CATALOGUE OF POTTERY WITH COMPLETE
OR NEAR-COMPLETE PROFILES (FIGS 99-101)

Note

Most of the vessels described below are reconstructed
from a number of different sherds, each one of which
has its own finds number; to avoid repetition only the
number of the largest sherd is quoted below. Complete
or near-complete sherds already illustrated in the Type
Series are not illustrated again, but reference will be
made to them in the Discussion, below. Complete or
near complete vessels of Group 1 are either illustrated
in the First Report (FNG 1: FIG 14) or in the Type
Series.

Group 2 (FIGS 99 and 100)

1. Large, slightly flared, bucket-shaped jar with crudely
beaded rim. Fabric 1A. Dia 320; ht 320; base dia 200.
From Late Iron main drain, CW Area II, F1210, layer
1; Grid 405W/669N; depth 0.40. *Cf* Rim Form 56.
75:3172

2. High, slack-shouldered jar with smooth ext. finish
and simple rim. Fabric 1B. Dia 190; ht 135; base dia 9.
From filled-in pit of 'pit complex', Middle Iron,
Padholme Road, Area XII, F2, layer 1. *Cf* FNG 1: FIG
21, No 1. See also Base Form 2. 72:23

3. Slightly flared, bucket-shaped jar with regularly
beaded rim. Fabric 1A. Dia 180; ht 180; base dia 92.
From Late Iron main drain, CW Area I, F1006, layer
2; Grid 419W/720N; (no depth given). *Cf* Rim Form
56. 75:1324

4. Jar with slightly rounded walls and simple rim.
Fabric 1A. Dia 143; ht 110; base dia 80. From
Middle/Late Iron posthole, CW Area VI, F916, layer 1;
Grid 415W/589N; depth 0.30. *Cf* Body Form 38; see
also No 15 below (associated with it). 78:1413

5. Straight-sided jar with upright, simple rim. Fabric
1A. Dia 105; ht 112; base dia 97. From Late Iron main
drain, CW Area I, F1086 layer 2; Grid 318W/706N;
(no depth given). 75:3151

6. Barrel-shaped jar with simple, slightly thickened
everted rim. Fabric 1A. Dia 175; ht 195; base dia 112.
From Middle Iron ditch, CW Area I, F1038, layer 2;
Grid 406W/699N; (no depth given). 75:1174

7. Small jar or cup with slightly flared sides and simple
rim. Fabric 1B. Dia 100; ht 76; base dia 70. From
Middle Iron main drain, CW Area II, F1277, layer 1;
Grid 414W/679N; depth 0.28. 75:3789

8. Convex-sided jar with slightly thickened closed rim.
Fabric 1A. Dia 124; ht 127; base dia 102. From Late
Iron main drain, CW Area I, F1086, layer 2; Grid
398W/706N; depth 0.40. 75:3151

9. High-shouldered jar with finger-grooved neck,
abraded ext of base. Fabric 1B. Dia 140; ht 138; base

dia *c* 80. From Late Iron main drain, CW Area II,
F1006, layer 1; Grid 396W/672N; depth *c* 0.30.
75:3203

10. Small jar with everted rim and bulbous profile.
Fabric 1A. Dia not possible to measure; ht 88; base dia
not possible to measure. From Late Iron main drain,
CW Area II, F1006, layer 1; Grid 397W/675N; depth
0.15. *Cf* Base Dec 3. 75:2976

11. High-shouldered jar with flared sides and ext
thickened rim. Fabric 1B. Dia 182; ht 160; base dia 90.
From isolated Late Iron pit, CW Area II, F1263, layer
1; Grid 417W/675N; depth 0.10. *Cf* (?) Rim Form 3.
75:3431

12. Large globular jar with ext thickened rim of angular
profile; this vessel may have been finished on a slow-
wheel or turntable. Fabric 1A. Dia 295; ht 280; base dia
250. From Late Iron main drain, CW Area II, F1260,
layer 1; Grid 389/655N; depth 0.08. 75:3605

13. Globular jar with simple everted rim. Fabric 1A.
Dia 145; ht 186; base dia 87. From a shallow pit or
scoop, Late Iron, Storey's Bar Road, Area I, Feature
P33, layer 1; Grid 97W/145N; depth 0.30. 74:289

14. High, slack-shouldered jar with short everted rim.
Fabric 1A. Dia 140; ht 150; base dia 100. From a Late
Iron main drain, CW Area II, F1260, layer 1; Grid
389W/655N; depth 0.08. *Cf* Rim Form 47. 75:3600

15. Large globular jar with scored ext. Fabric 1A. Dia
210. From a Middle/Late Iron posthole, CW VI, F916
layer 1; Grid 415W/589N; depth 0.15. See also No 4
above (associated with it). 78:1409

Group 3 (FIG 101)

1. Carinated bowl with concave wall, groove above
carination, U-shaped cordon at the point of greatest
constriction and ext thickened rim. Fabric 4. Dia 120;
ht 95; base dia 60. From the gully of Late Iron Structure
28, CW Area V, F427, layer 1; Grid 434W/661N;
depth *c* 0.20. *Cf* Body Form 11. 77:2056

2. As 1, above, but cordon defined by two shallow
grooves. Fabric 4. Dia 130; ht 93; base dia 60. From
Late Iron ditch associated with Structure 32 (?), CW
Area V, F505, layer 2; Grid 418W/647N; (depth not
recorded). *Cf* Body Form 11. 77:2937

3. Carinated bowl with concave wall, groove above
shoulder and two grooves at the point of maximum
constriction. Fabric 1C. Dia 145; ht 83; base dia 70.
From gully of Late Iron Structure 40, CW Area II,
F1274, layer 2; Grid 429W/682N; depth 0.58. *Cf* Body
Form 13. 75:3719

4. Jar with angled shoulder (and corrugation), flared
neck and ext. thickened rim. Fabric 3. Dia 180; ht 125;
base dia 90. From Late Iron enclosure ditch, Storey's
Bar, Area I, P28, layer 1; Grid 90W/152N; depth 0.10.
Cf Body Form 19. 74:864

5. As No 4, but with higher shoulder. Fabric 3. Dia
190; ht 142; base dia 90. Single hole (dia 15mm) bored
after firing. From Phase 6 (R-B) ditch cut into Phase 5
(Late Iron) ditch; residual. CW Area V, F412, layer 2;

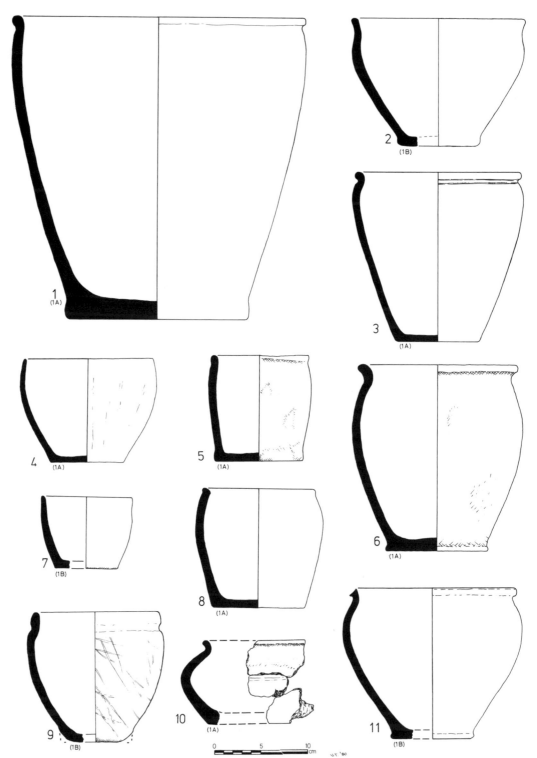

Fig. 99   Iron Age pottery: Group 2 (hand-made) Iron Age pottery: complete and near-complete profiles. 1 (CW F1210); 2 (Padholme Road, XII, F2); 3 (CW F1006); 4 (CW F916); 5 (CW F1086); 6 (CW F1038); 7 (CW F1277); 8 (CW F1086); 9 (CW F1006); 10 (CW F1006); 11 (CW F1263). Scale 1:4 (continued on FIG 100).

136

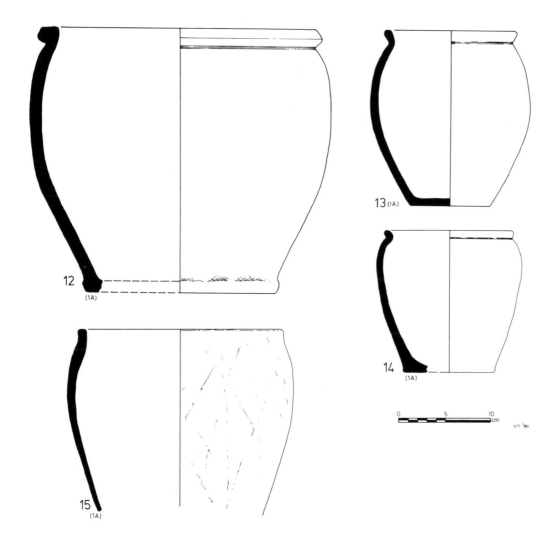

Fig. 100 Group 2 (hand made) Iron Age pottery: complete and near complete profiles. 12 (CW F1260); 13 (Storey's Bar Road, I, P33); 14 (CW F1260); 15 (CW F916). Scale 1:4 (continued from Fig 99).

137

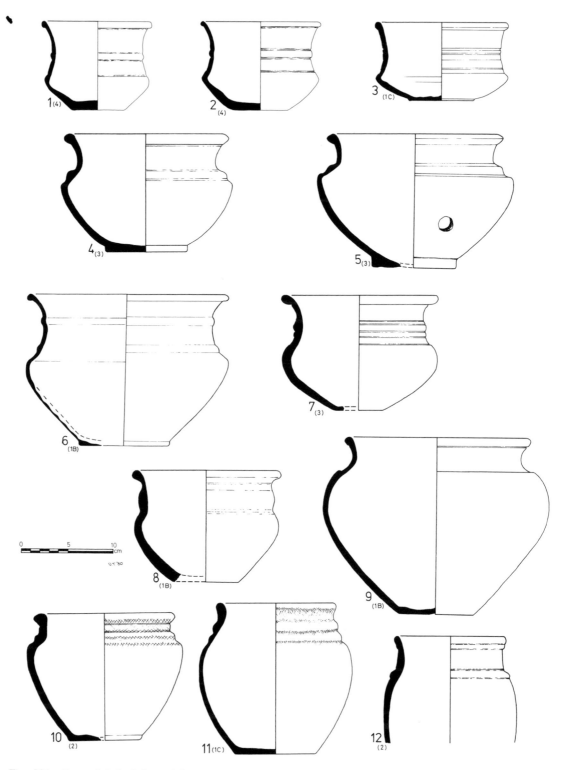

Fig. 101   Group 3 (wheel-thrown) Iron Age pottery: complete and near-complete profiles. 1 (CW F427); 2 (CW F505); 3 (CW F1274); 4 (Storey's Bar Road, I, F28); 5 (CW F412); 6 (CW F1267); 7 (CW F1287); 8 (CW F1006); 9 (CW F1267); 10 (CW F1199); 11 (CW F1059/1086); 12 (CW F1287). Scale 1:4.

Grid 462W/680N; depth 0.25. *Cf* Body Form 19. 77:1814

6. Globular jar with rounded shoulder and hollow neck with two cordons, beaded rim. Fabric 1B. Dia 220; ht 160; base dia 100. From Late Iron main drain, CW Area II, F1267, layer 1; Grid 438W/677N; (depth not recorded). 75:3469

7. Globular bowl or jar with rounded belly/shoulder and concave neck decorated with grooves and cordons. Fabric 3. Dia 170; ht 122; base dia 55. From Late Iron main drain, CW Area II, F1287, layer 1; Grid 454W/694N; depth 0.30. *Cf* Body Form 16. 75:4042

8. High-necked jar, with low cordon on neck and rounded belly/shoulder. Fabric 1B. Dia 160; ht 120; base dia 70. From Late Iron main drain, CW Area I, F1006, layer 2; Grid 393W/689N; depth 0.10. 75:2602

9. High shouldered jar with cavetto neck defined by grooves at rim and shoulder. Fabric 1B. Dia 200; ht 187; base dia 80. From Late Iron main drain, CW Area II, F1267, layer 1; Grid 445W/699N; (no depth recorded). *Cf* Body Form 18. 75:3500B

10. High-shouldered globular bowl or jar with rounded cordon on shoulder and short neck defined by two grooves; ext thickened rim. Fabric 2. Dia 155; ht 135; base dia 80. From Middle/Late gully (cut by main drain F1086), CW Area I, F1199, layer 1; Grid 410W/699N; depth 0.20. *Cf* Rim Form 24. 75:2437

11. Bipartite jar with rounded weak shoulder and corrugated neck; thickened, slightly everted rim. Fabric 1C. Dia 130; ht 158; base dia 85. From Late Iron main drain intersection, CW Area I, F1059/1086, layer 1; Grid 412W/711N; depth 0.10 *Cf* Group 2, Body Form 89 (FIG M108: no 1) for a hand-made imitation of the general form. 75:1600

12. Butt beaker, locally made in Fabric 2; the only near-complete example from Fengate. Possible butt beaker copies are discussed with other material from Group 3, below. See also Body Dec 3. Dia 120. From Late Iron ditch (cut by Phase 6 ditch F 1288), CW Area II, F1287, layer 1; Grid 453W/693N; depth 0.25. 75:4100

3. POTTERY FROM SELECTED STRUCTURES
(FIGS 102-104)

Structure 7 (Middle Iron Age) (see FIGS 102 and 103)
Note Nos 1-8 are all from CW Area I, F1020 layer 1. All are of Group 2.
1. Fabric 1A; dia 260. Grid 379W/691N. 75:568
2. Fabric 1A; dia 340. Grid 378W/697N. 75:204A
3. Fabric 1A; dia 130. Grid 379W/690N. 75:577
4. Fabric 1A. Grid 387W/691N. 75:587
5. Fabric 1A. Grid 379W/690N. 75:583/1
6. Fabric 1A. Grid 379W/691N. 75:572
7. Fabric 1A; base dia 92. Grid 379W/690N. 75:583/2
8. Fabric 1B; base dia 100. Grid 379W/691N. 75:575

Structure 4 (Late Iron Age) (see FIG 104)
Note Nos 1-7 are all from CW Area I, F1101 layer 1.

1. Fabric 2; dia *c* 205; Group 3. Grid 437W/710N. 75:1614A
2. As no 2, but dia *c* 245. 75:1614B
3. Fabric 2: dia 205; Group 3. Grid 438W/709N. 75:1617A
4. Fabric 1A; dia 185; Group 2. Grid 438W/709N. 75:1617C
5. Fabric 1B; dia 200; Group 2. Grid 439W/709N. 75:1620
6. Fabric 1C; dia 160; Group 3. Grid 441W/709N. 75:1625
7. Fabric 1C; dia of belly 180; Group 3. Grid 436W/710N. 75:1612

4. DISCUSSION OF THE IRON AGE POTTERY

This discussion is largely based on data presented in the preceding three sections. The pottery will be considered under the three Group categories used above.

Group 1

Introduction
Pottery of Early Iron or, perhaps, of Late Bronze Age type was found in the Vicarage Farm, Newark Road, Fourth Drove and Cat's Water subsites. With few exceptions, deposits from which it derived were pit infillings and the pits were never associated with other, contemporary, occupation features, such as posthole scatters, drainage ditches or structural gullies. In this respect the depositional history of Group 1 pottery contrasts with that of Groups 2 and 3, nearly all of which derived from well-defined settlements.

Newark Road and Fourth Drove
This material bears close comparison with that from the nearby Cat's Water subsite. Newark Road pottery essentially derived from two sources. First, and most significant, was the four-post structure in Area II. This structure post-dated the natural infilling of the second millennium ditch 9, which seems most probably to have taken place around 1000 bc. One structural posthole (F17) had been filled-in with occupational debris which included potsherds and charcoal. It is probable that the charcoal and pottery are contemporary, as the potsherds were not weathered and the ancient breaks mended together well (FNG 3, FIG 61, no 39). The reconstructed vessel finds no immediate parallel with the Group 1 material considered here, but its fabric and distinctively smooth finish were closely similar. It was rather unevenly finished at the rim, so the angle may not be reconstructed with certainty, but there is, perhaps, a passing similarity with, for example, the vessel illustrated as Rim Form 1 (FIG M88), which came from the large Cat's Water pit F448. The radiocarbon date is of great interest: (HAR-773) 790±80 bc. This may be calibrated, using R M Clark's (1975) method and curve,

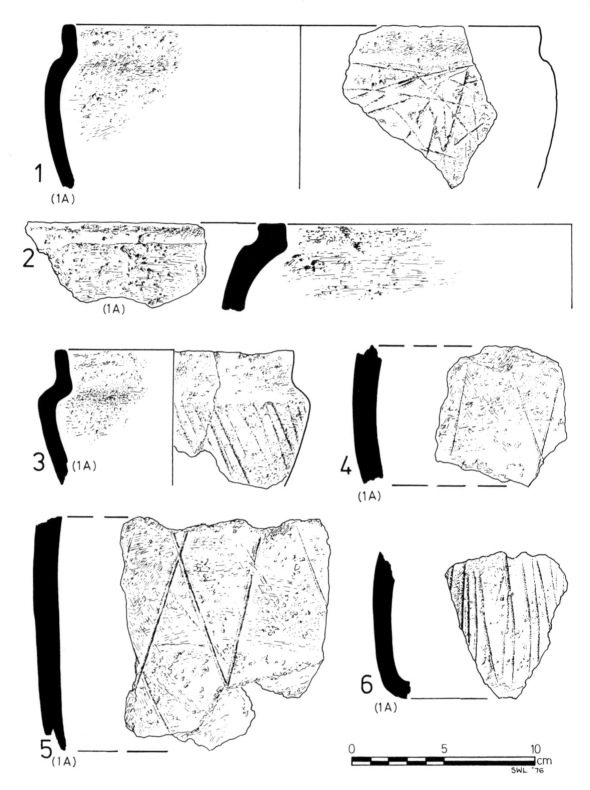

Fig. 102   Group 2 pottery from Middle Iron Structure 7 ring-gully, Cat's water, Area I, F1020. Scale 1:2 (continued on FIG 103).

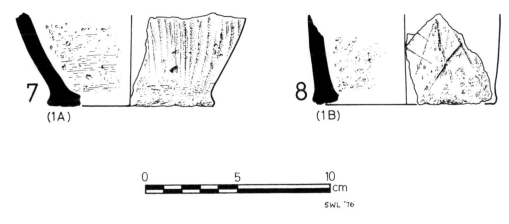

7
(1A)

8
(1B)

0   5   10
                    cm
              SWL '76

Fig. 103   Group 2 pottery from Structure 7 (continued from FIG 102). Scale 1:2.

to a span of 1225 to 775 BC, at two standard deviations, or from 1075 to 875 BC, at the more conventional single standard deviation. Bearing in mind the dangers inherent in using just one determination, a date for the pottery within the Late Bronze Age is indicated. This date, as we will see, is markedly earlier than others obtained for pottery of Group 1.

The second group of pottery from Newark Road came from isolated pits north of the second millennium ditch 10. This material (FNG 3, FIG 61, nos 40-44) bears close comparison with that illustrated in this report, particularly the sherds of 41, 42 and 44 which, in manufacture and style, closely resemble the sherds illustrating Rim Forms 1, 8 and Body Decoration 10, respectively (FIGS M88 and M92).

The three sherds from the Fourth Drove subsite (FNG 3, FIG 89, nos 4-7) were found in features just north of the Cat's Water subsite and closely resemble vessels in the Type Series, in fabric, finish and style (*cf* Rim Forms 1, 8 and Body Decoration 1 — FIGS M88, M89 and M92).

Finally, it should be noted that the nine sherds just described were omitted from the Group 1 tables.

Vicarage Farm

All drawable sherds of Group 1 from this subsite are illustrated in the First Report (FNG 1, FIG 14 all sherds, except feature 10 — nos 23-25 — and FIG 15, all sherds except feature 22 — nos 1-8). The important, near-complete bowl shown in the First Report (FNG 1, FIG 14, no 3) is here photographed (PL 1), as is the wrapped wooden handle which is shown in close-up in PL 2. Some of the sherds shown in the much-reduced figure of the First Report have been reproduced at a larger scale in the Type Series, above.

The Vicarage Farm group derives from back-filled pits cut into solid limestone. They are closely grouped together in one corner of Area I (FNG 1, FIG 12; this

report FIG 5). The tightly-packed distribution suggests contemporaneity, but, as noted above, there are no other settlement features present other than substantial pits. The most important deposit of pottery was layer 4 of the (back-filled?) pit F6 which penetrated below the permanent water table. Well-preserved twigs from this layer gave a radiocarbon date (UB-822) of 340±125 bc (reported in FNG 2, 227). This date may be calibrated (R M Clark 1975) to 800-50 BC, at two standard deviations, or 520-200 BC, at one standard deviation. Again, one must note the dangers of using just one determination, but, as in the case of the Newark Road date just discussed, the sampled material is reliable and well associated with the pottery dated from it.

Cat's Water

Group 1 pottery from this subsite came from three sources, the first, and perhaps least reliable deposit was the infilling of ditch 1553 in Area X — in the south-eastern part of the main excavated area. This ditch was stratigraphically early and only produced one diagnostic potsherd which is illustrated in the Type Series as Rim Form 5 (FIG M88). The body form (5) is not common among vessels of Group 1 (the nearest equivalent being Body Form 11 — FIG M91), but the surface finish — very smooth ('soapy') — and soft/hard firing in fabric 1B were entirely typical of Group 1 fine ware practice. This sherd was found at Grid 441W/559N, not far from the well F1551 (Grid 460W/564N), which produced just one Group 1 vessel (Rim Form 9, FIG M89); the pot — a rounded, high-shouldered jar — was in the fine ware just described and was well finished. It actually touched (see section, FIG 89) the oak stake discussed below, which gave a radiocarbon date of (HAR-3199) 360±60bc. The pot was quite soft and in one piece and probably owes its survival to the water which filled the bottom of the well; its condition, which is fresh and unweathered, and the fact that it actually was touching

141

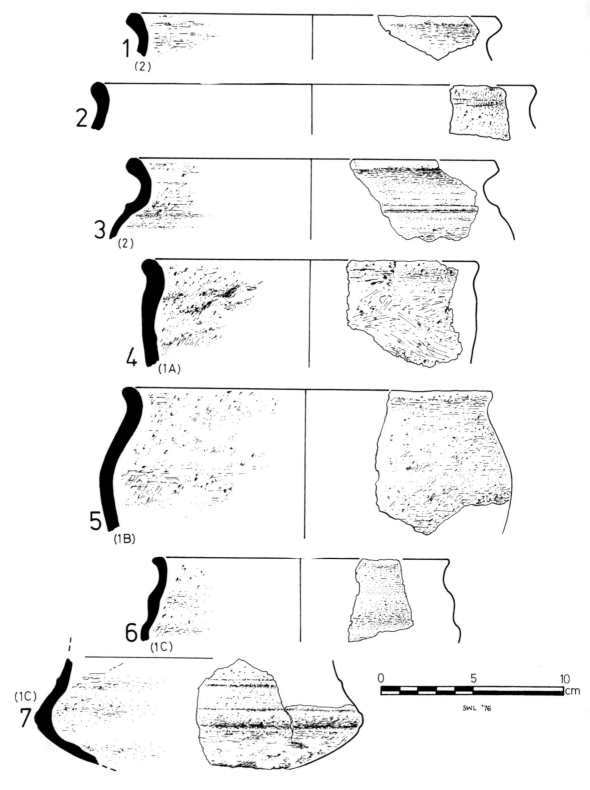

Fig. 104 Groups 2 and 3 pottery from Late Iron Structure 4 gully, Cat's Water subsite, Area I, F1101. Scale 1:2.

142

the wood which provided the radiocarbon sample (and lay directly on the gravel subsoil of the well-bottom), leaves little room to doubt the association of dated material and pottery. When calibrated (after R M Clark 1975) the date ranges, at two standard deviations, is from 700 BC to 200 BC, and at one standard deviation is from 480 BC to 400 BC. A date within the early Iron Age is indicated.

The largest deposit of Group 1 material from Cat's Water was found in the large well in Area V, F448 (Grid 449W/652N). The fine wares from this feature closely resemble that from F1551, but no material suitable for radiocarbon dating could be obtained. Table M6 lists the pottery from F448 and Table M5 that from the principal Vicarage Farm deposit, F6. The range of wares and surface treatment (excepting the burnished sherds from F6) is essentially the same, but the pottery from F6 is more frequently decorated than that from F448. Diagnostic pottery from F448 is illustrated in the Type Series under Rim Forms 1-3; Decoration 1; Body Form 2; Body Decoration 1; and Base Form 1.

Finally, it should be noted that the occurrence of Group 1 pottery within Middle or Late Iron Age features was surprisingly rare, indeed, only one sherd (illustrated as Body Decoration 6) from a later feature could be reliably ascribed to Group 1. This absence could be attributed to a number of factors: the relatively poor firing of Group 1 wares; the possibility that the settlement represented by finds of Group 1 was only slight or intermittent in nature or, perhaps most probably, that there was a gap of many years between the deposition of Groups 1 and 2, during which time features of the early phase could infill naturally and turf could form over surface rubbish, thus preventing it from finding its way into later features.

General considerations

We must first consider the grounds on which the pottery from Vicarage Farm and Cat's Water has been treated in the same Type Series (this is not, however, an irrecoverable concatenation as all diagnostic pottery from the two subsites is illustrated separately in this report and FNG 1; moreover, a complete listing of the two principal deposits is provided in Tables M5 and M6). There are, first and foremost, close similarities in fabric and finish between fine and coarse wares of the two subsites; these similarities, it should be added, are also reflected in the Wyman Abbott pre-War Fengate pit groups now housed in Peterborough Museum. Indeed, the 'smooth' surface treatment accorded to, for example, the vessel from Cat's Water illustrated as Rim Form 3 (FIG M88) is only marginally rougher than a true burnish — as seen on the well-preserved bowl from Vicarage Farm (FNG 1, FIG 14, no 3; this report FIG M114 Body Form 10). In general the coarse wares are also similar, but the Cat's Water material is slightly more sandy. This also holds good for Group 2 and may reflect the sandier subsoil of the latter subsite, where it

often proved hard to distinguish between wares in Dr Williams' Fabrics 1B and 1C.

Absolute dating for pottery of Group 1 is provided by three radiocarbon dates discussed at length above. That from Newark Road (HAR-773: 790±80bc) is clearly significantly older than those from Vicarage Farm and Cat's Water (UB-822: 340±125bc and HAR-3196: 360±60bc respectively), but the pottery itself would not be seriously out of place in either of the latter two assemblages. One cannot ignore three well-associated, apparently reliable absolute dates which, when calibrated, indicate a minimum lifespan for Group 1 pottery roughly occupying the first three quarters of the first millennium BC.

The Fengate dates agree well with those quoted by Jeffrey May from Washingborough Fen and Brigg Lincs. The Washingborough sample appears to be well associated with pottery, similar in many respects to that from Fengate, and it also produced an antler cheekpiece which finds a good parallel from Late Bronze Age contexts at Runnymede Bridge, Egham (Coles *et al* 1979, FIG 4; Longley 1976, FIG 2, a). The Washingborough Fen date (Q-1163: 303±70bc) when calibrated (R M Clark 1975) spreads from 600-130BC, at two standard deviations, and from 440-220 BC at one standard deviation. The Brigg date (Q-77: 602±120bc), when calibrated, spreads from 1050-430 BC and from 920-570 BC, at two and one standard deviations, respectively. Statistically, there is 95% probability that the range of the two standard deviation dates is correct; similarly the single standard deviation range offers about 68% probability of being correct. It must be recalled, however, that the standard deviation is merely a measure of dispersion on either side of the mean (Moroney 1956, 112). In the case of radiocarbon dates, the greater the standard deviation, the flatter the normal curve of points which represent years on both sides of the mean — the date quoted by the laboratory. Calculations of date ranges, whether calibrated or not, must bear this in mind and any attempts to 'stretch' radiocarbon dates to fit one's theories must be avoided. It is therefore misleading to interpret the important Washingborough Fen date as 'being a century later than would be expected on the calibrated date at two standard deviations' (May, in Coles *et al* 1979, 9). It would be less misleading to say that the date was about 270 years later than the expected date (the standard deviation, as listed, is recalculated to 86 years using R M Clark's (1975) formula). It is , however, even more misleading to quote the calibrated date (based on the earlier tables of Ralph, Michael and Han (1973) at 640-170 BC, and then to state that the likeliest date for the site falls 'towards the end of the seventh or the sixth centuries BC' (May 1976, 112). Statistically, a date in the first or second centuries would be just as probable!

This rather prolonged discussion is required to demonstrate the dangers of necessarily placing all apparently Late Bronze/Early Iron Age domestic pottery in the earlier centuries of the millennium. It is true that the Washingborough Fen cheekpiece finds a close parallel at Runnymede Bridge in sound Late Bronze contexts, but that does not exclude the possibility, perhaps even the probability, that such utilitarian objects could continue in use, more or less unmodified for perhaps two or four hundred years in north-west Lincolnshire, or elsewhere. It is admittedly dangerous to place too much reliance on calibrated radiocarbon dates of the first millennium bc, but there is no good reason to suppose that they are necessarily less reliable than conventional, mainly art-historical, means of dating a notoriously illusory period. As we will see, the picture that is slowly emerging for eastern England is of a ceramic tradition, which is apparently firmly tied to later Bronze Age antecedents and seems, in certain areas, to last until the third quarter of the first millennium BC. It is appropriate now to consider the later years of the tradition. The evidence from Fengate shows a clean separation between Group 1 and Group 2 vessels as represented by scored and globular coarse wares and slack-shouldered bowls in local variants of Harding's 'smooth dark ware' (1972, 101 cf FNG 1, FIG 21, no 1; this report FIG 99, no 2). The Washing-borough material includes a small (and perhaps dubiously) scored rim sherd within an early assemblage, but in general the two traditions seem to be distinct; it would, moreover, be a mistake to treat scoring as a necessary 'type' trait for Middle Iron Age pottery in East England and the East Midlands, particularly as its function — decoration or otherwise — is as yet poorly understood. Having said this, it should be remembered that scored wares were found in an infilled well, (at Padholme Road), the wattle lining of which gave a radiocarbon date (see FNG 1, 38) of 350±46bc (GaK-4198). When calibrated after R M Clark (1975), the range is from 600-200 BC, at two standard deviations, and from 480-400 BC, at one. This range is indistinguishable from the later two Group 1 dates and even indicates a degree of overlap. It will be remembered that this sample came from the Padholme Road subsite and is not at variance with the suggestion made above that there was a gap in the Cat's Water sequence between the Early and Middle Iron Age phases 3 and 4.

Great care is necessary when considering the Wyman Abbott Fengate material (Hawkes and Fell 1945). The material was collected by Mr Abbott on periodic visits to the site (Abbott, pers comm) and it is possible that pit groups were not kept strictly apart by the workmen involved. Certainly, it would now be impossible to accurately relocate the various findspots within the general area occupied by the pre-War gravel workings (the general area is shown in FNG 2, FIG 3). Turning to the material recovered, there are many stylistic similarities between the earlier finds and pottery from the recent excavations. The closest similarities are with pottery of Hawkes and Fell's 'Middle Phase', which Dr

Champion would now place before the 'Early Phase' (Champion 1975, 136; FIG 3). Champion sees close parallels between Fengate 'Middle Phase' pits and late Urnfield material, HaB/HaC, from Holland; if Champion's parallels be accepted — and the resemblance is striking — then 'Middle Phase' material from Fengate could have been in use 'as early as the ninth or eighth century' (ibid, 136). Champion further argues that the well-known find of a fifth century swan's neck sunflower pin from pit A would place the contents of that pit relatively late in the sequence.

Champion sees a resemblance between the Fengate furrowed bowl, K1, and the Wessex series of furrowed bowls, (for distribution see Harding 1974, FIG 43) for which a starting date in the seventh century at least would seem assured (Cunliffe 1978, 35). This vessel is of interest, as it quite closely resembles the well-preserved vessel from Vicarage Farm F6 (FNG 1, FIG 14, no 3). A closely similar vessel is recorded from Woodston, on the west side of Peterborough (Fox, Burkitt and Abbott 1926, FIG 6) and the two vessels from Cromer, although larger, are stylistically very similar (R R Clarke 1960, PL 20). On the question of size, it should be noted that the vessel Q2, figured by Hawkes and Fell (1945, FIG 6) is reproduced at ⅛ and not ¼ of original size, as indicated in the figure caption.

The carefully executed incised decoration seen on vessels from Vicarage Farm F6 finds parallels among the Wyman Abbott collection (vessels from pits C, P, and M), as does the use of finger-tip and fingernail on the outer edge of rims. The three rows of fingernail decoration on the vessel illustrating Rim Form 6 (FIG M88) find close parallels in pit 1 (Hawkes and Fell 1945, FIG 4), and the high shouldered jar from Cat's Water F448 (FIG M88, no 3) is closely matched by a vessel from pit E (ibid FIG 3).

Pottery of this very early Iron Age type occurs rarely on excavations in the area. One recent discovery was made at Werrington, just north of Peterborough. This material came from an isolated pit that predated the main Middle/Late Iron Age settlement, which is discussed in greater detail in Chapter 8. The pottery features fingertip decoration on rim top and shoulder (Mackreth and O'Neill 1980, FIG 14); in general, the forms are undiagnostic, but the many points in common with, for example, Padholme Road (FNG 1, FIGS 20-22) make the proposed fifth or sixth century date seem somewhat early.

Moving further afield, the site at Washingborough Fen produced a small and fragmentary assemblage characterised, like Group 1, by simple, unthickened rims. Of the stratified sherds, two may be compared with Fengate material (compare Coles et al 1979, FIG 3, nos 2 and 5 with sherds illustrating Rim Form 1 and Rim Decoration 1 — FIGS M88 and M90). Further south, Peter Chowne's excavation at Billingborough Fen have produced, in (his) Phase 3, vessels comparable with Fengate Group 1 and Washingborough; one vessel is of

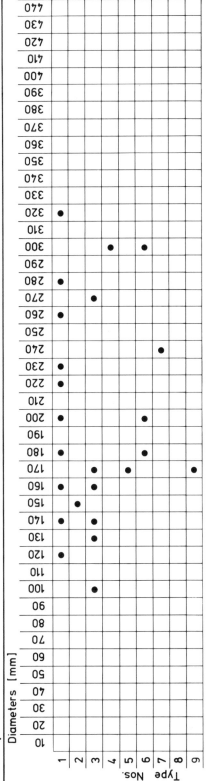

Group 1   Rims

Diameters [mm]

Fig. 105   Range of Group 1 rim diameters.

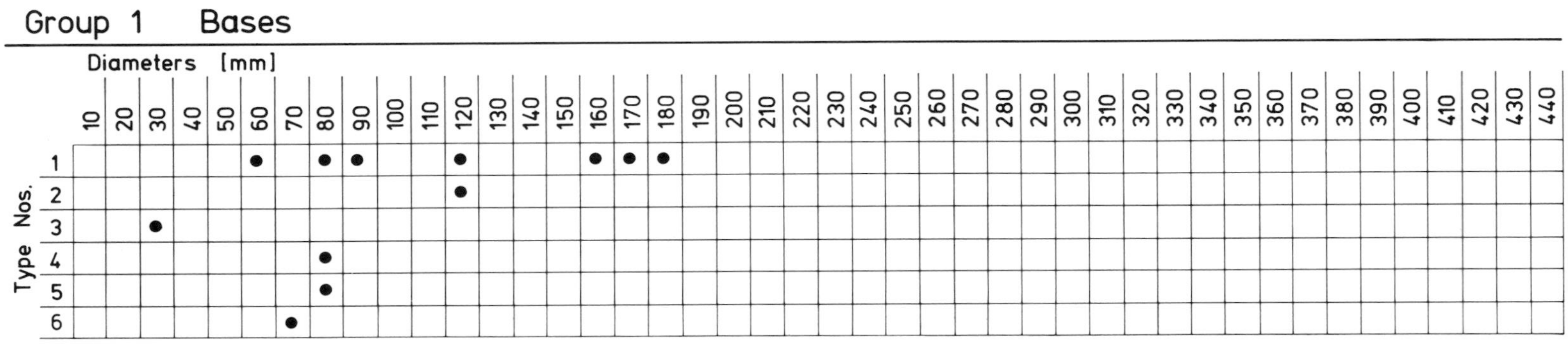

Group 1   Bases

Diameters [mm]

Fig. 106   Range of Group 1 base diameters.

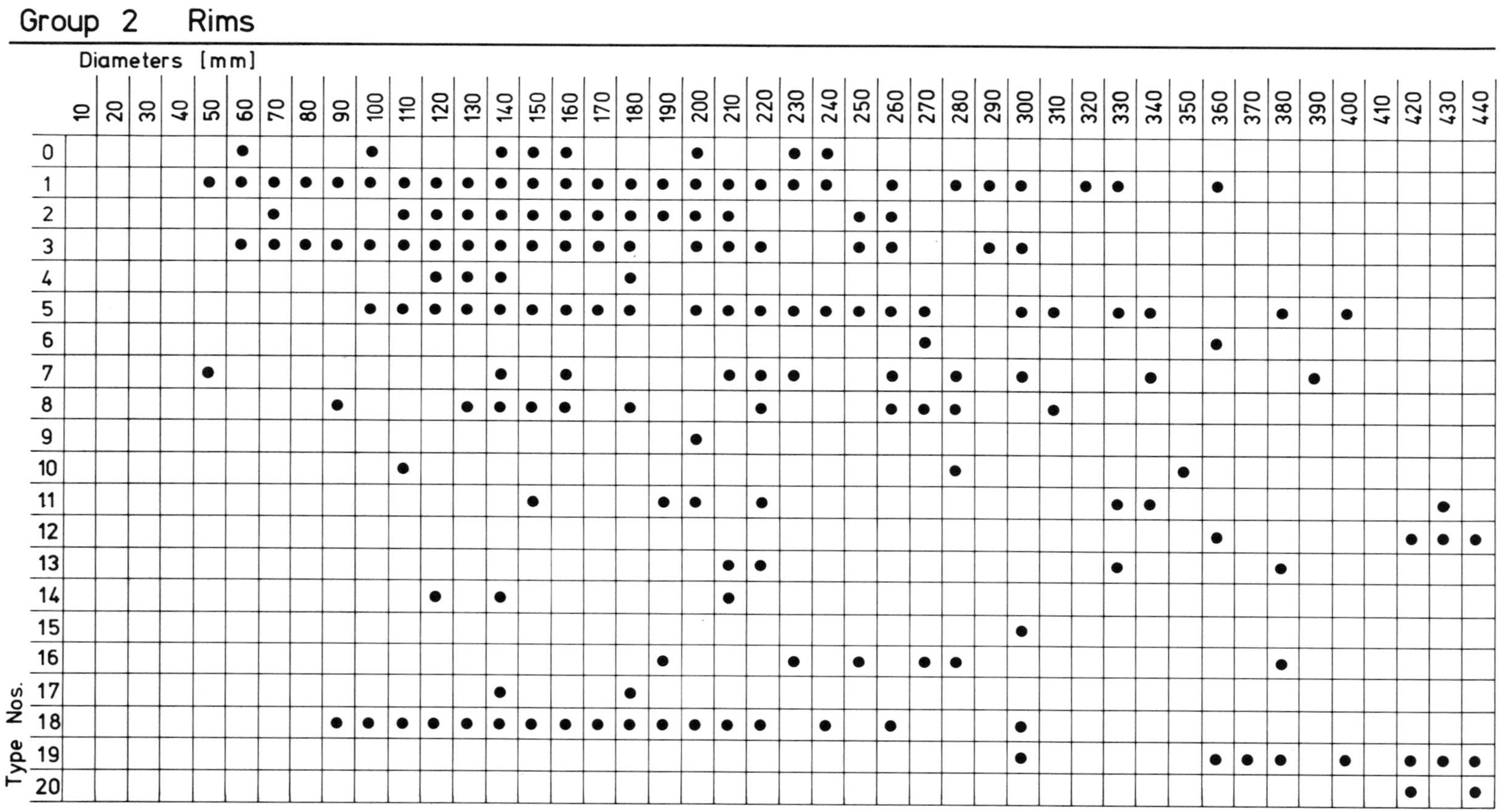

Group 2 Rims

Diameters [mm]

440, 430, 420, 410, 400, 390, 380, 370, 360, 350, 340, 330, 320, 310, 300, 290, 280, 270, 260, 250, 240, 230, 220, 210, 200, 190, 180, 170, 160, 150, 140, 130, 120, 110, 100, 90, 80, 70, 60, 50, 40, 30, 20, 10

Type Nos. 0, 1, 2, 3, 4, 5, 6, 7, 8, 9, 10, 11, 12, 13, 14, 15, 16, 17, 18, 19, 20

Fig. 107 Range of Group 2 rim diameters (continued on FIGS 108 and 109).

146

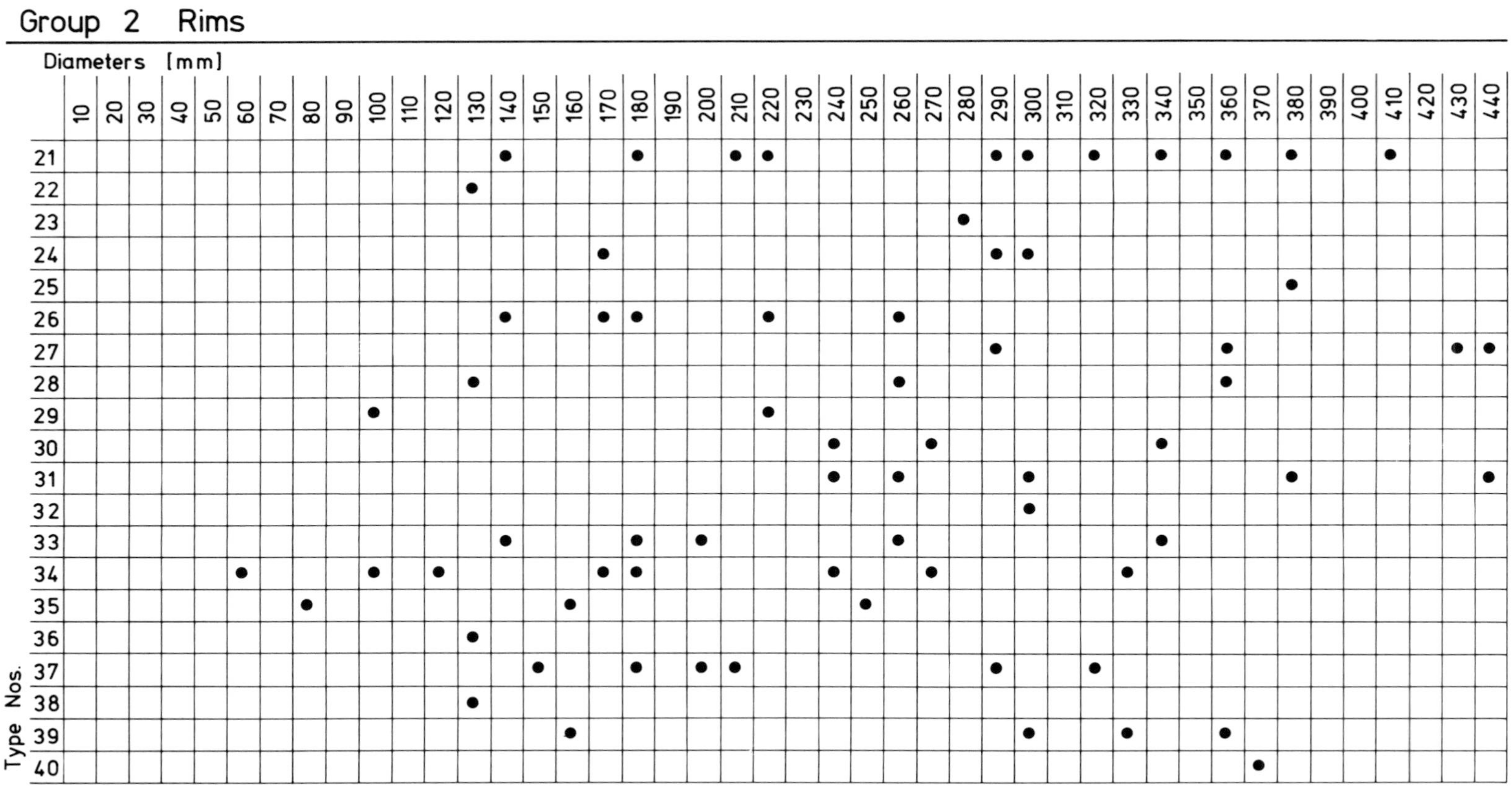

Group 2 Rims

Diameters [mm]

Type Nos.

Fig. 108 Range of Group 2 rim diameters (see also FIGS 107 and 109).

147

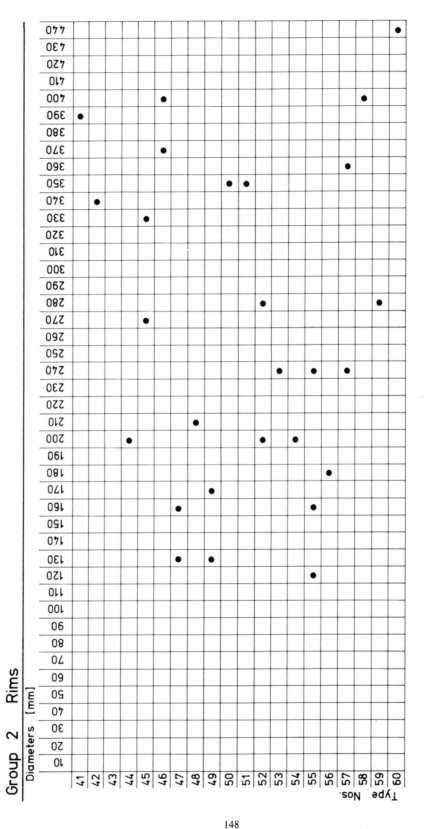

Fig. 109   Range of Group 2 rim diameters (continued from FIGS 107 and 108).

Group 2   Bases

Diameters [mm]

Fig. 110   Range of Group 2 base diameters

Type Nos.

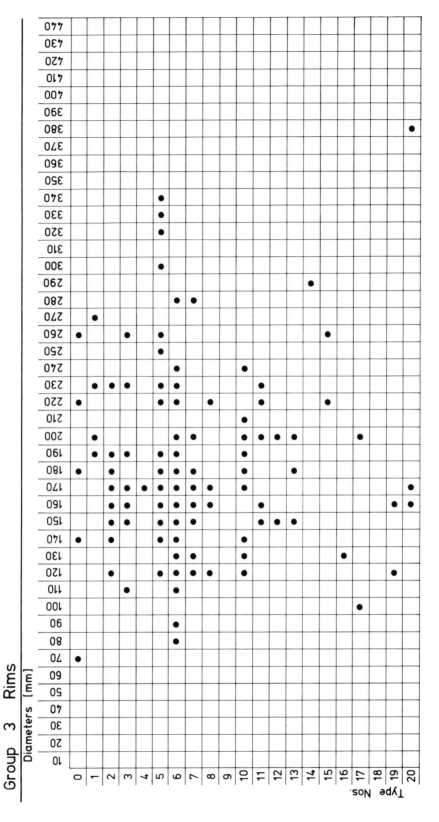

Fig. 111   Range of Group 3 rim diameters (continued on FIG 112).

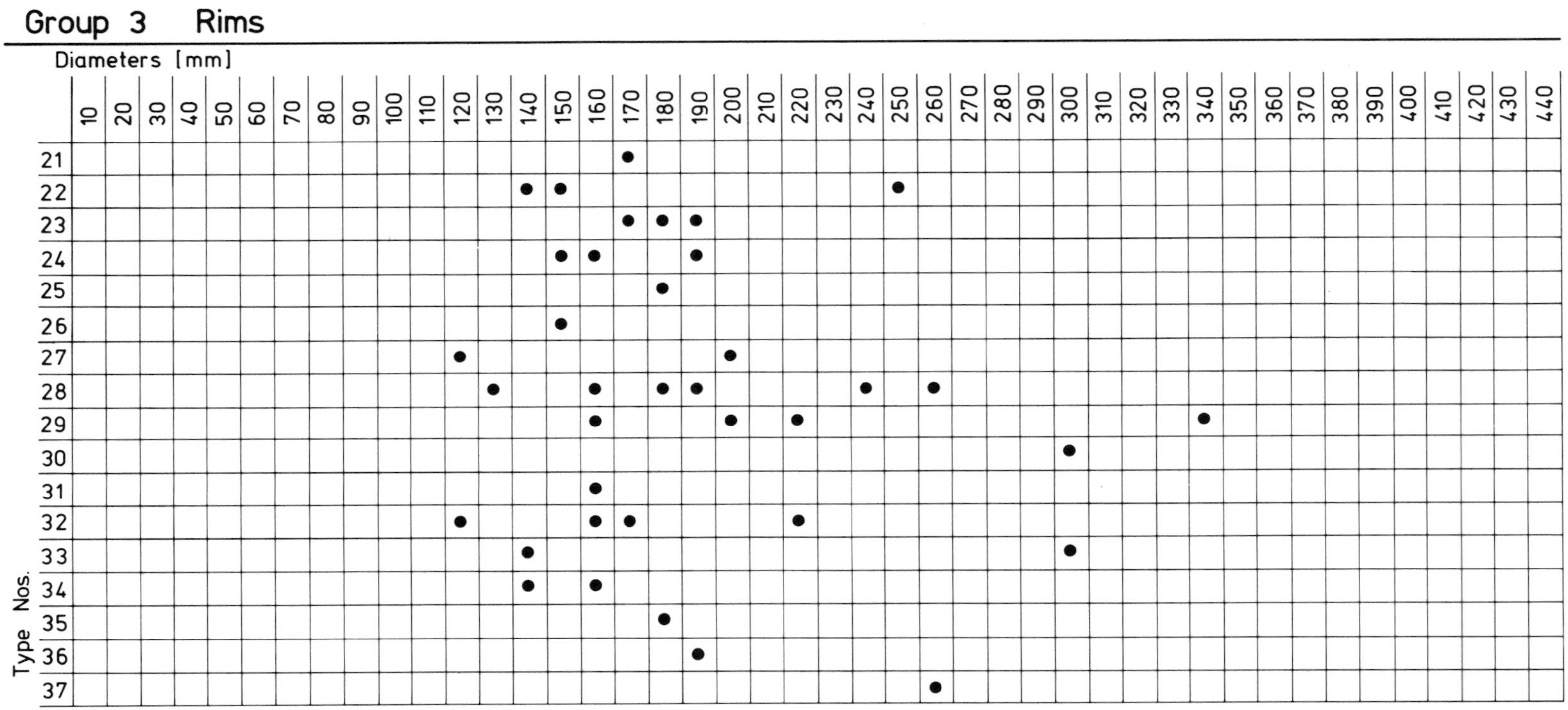

Group 3   Rims

Diameters [mm]

470 430 420 410 400 390 380 370 360 350 340 330 320 310 300 290 280 270 260 250 240 230 220 210 200 190 180 170 160 150 140 130 120 110 100 90 80 70 60 50 40 30 20 10

Type Nos. 21 22 23 24 25 26 27 28 29 30 31 32 33 34 35 36 37

Fig. 112   Range of Group 3 rim diameters (continued from FIG 111).

151

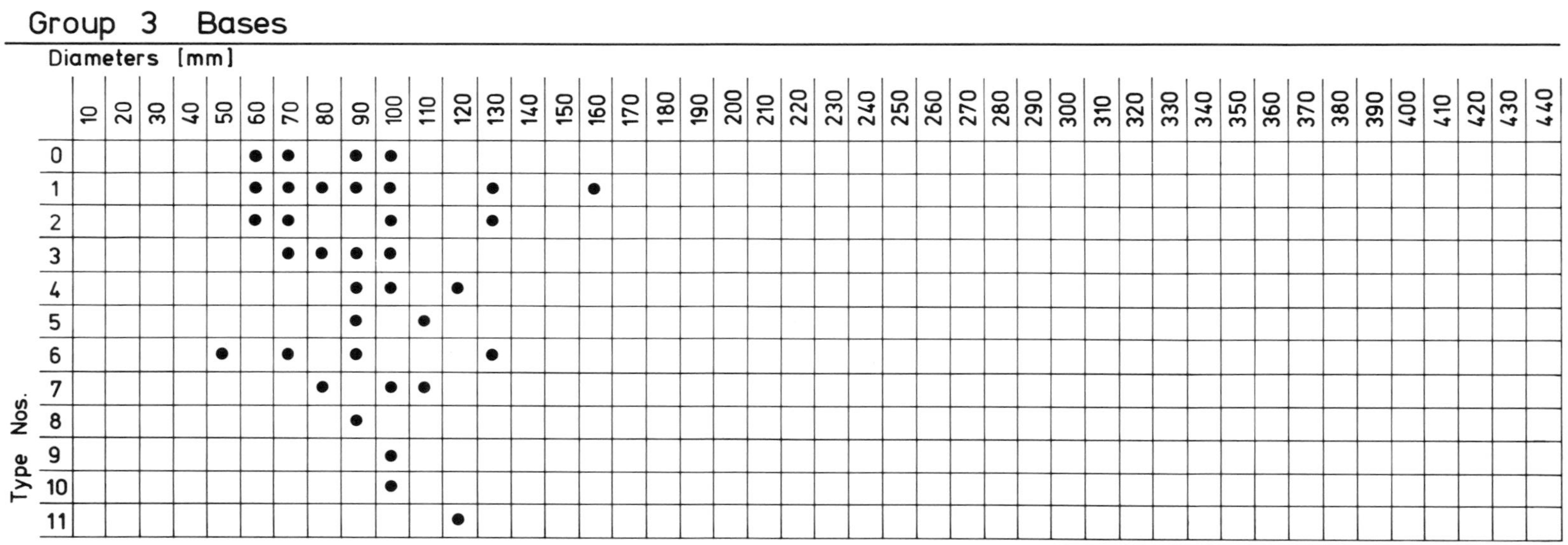

Group 3 Bases

Diameters [mm]

Type Nos.

Fig. 113 Range of Group 3 base diameters.

152

special interest (Chowne 1978, 18 and FIG 7, no 22), in that its incised decoration is filled with white inlay (*cf* Body Dec 3, FIG M92). Chowne dates Phase 2 at Billingborough to the sixth and seventh centuries, on the basis of parallels with Washingborough. North of this group of essentially Fenland sites well-known examples of Late Bronze/Early Iron Age pottery have been recovered from pits at Scarborough (R A Smith 1927, FIGS 24-56) and from the small hillfort at Staple Howe (Brewster 1963, FIG 37 for comparanda for the vessel illustrating Rim Form 5 — FIG M88 — which is hard to parallel locally).

Turning to East Anglia, we have already noted the bowls from Cromer, but close parallels for Group 1 material have also been found at Darmsden, Suffolk (Cunliffe 1968). This pottery was found in two episodes, one in 1938 and one in 1945. The 1938 sherds (Cunliffe 1968, FIG 4) cannot be regarded as a closed group unlike those recovered in 1945 (*ibid,* FIGS 2 and 3); the latter vessels have many points in common with Fengate Group 1, including high shouldered bowls with simple everted rims and the use of grooved decoration, in the fine wares. The fingertip-decorated coarse wares are also very similar to those from Fengate. It is of particular interest to note, however, that recent research (Balkwill 1979, 208) has shown that a finely finished, haematitite-coated vessel, believed by Cunliffe to have derived from the 1938 collection, did in fact come from the excavations of 1946 and must, therefore, be associated with the bowls of the closed group. The haematite- coated vessel may be closely compared with vessels of Cunliffe's Early All Cannings Cross Group which he dates to the eighth to seventh centuries (1978, FIG A2). This new evidence accords well with Champion's suggestion of an early date for Scarborough, Fengate and Darmsden (Champion 1975, 131).

Another recently published Suffolk collection, was from Kettleburgh on the River Deben (O'Connor 1975); as published, this group consisted of undecorated fine wares (*ibid* FIG 2, no 2) associated with fingertip-decorated coarse wares. The fine ware, with simple tapered rim, flaring neck and high shoulder compares closely with, for example, Group 1 Rim Forms 3 and 9 (FIGS M88 and M89). The association, however, between coarse and fine wares in O'Connor's Group 2 has now been shown to be false (Balkwill 1979, 209). Perhaps the most important published Early Iron age excavation in East Anglia is still that at West Harling (Clark and Fell 1953), and the pottery, particularly the fine wares of Class VI (*ibid,* FIG 15) and the fingertip-decorated coarse wares of Class II, has many points in common with Fengate Group 1. Professor Cunliffe dates the West Harling-Staple Howe group to the sixth century (Cunliffe 1978, FIG A4).

Further south, Fengate Group 1 pottery finds similiarities with Cunliffe's (1978, FIG A5) Ivinghoe-Sandy group of the sixth century, and Longley and

Needham's recent excavations on the Thames waterfront at Runnymede Bridge, Egham, Surrey have produced fine wares from undoubted Late Bronze Age contexts which find surprisingly close parallels at Fengate. In particular the fine, high-shouldered jars with thin walls, concave necks and tapered rims of Runnymede Bridge (Longley 1976, FIG 4, nos 2 and 5; Needham and Longley 1979, 264, nos 2-4) recall vessels illustrating Group 1 Rim Forms 1, 3, 8 and 9 (FIGS M88 and M89).

In conclusion, most of the published parallels for Fengate Group 1 pottery can be dated, typologically, to the sixth, seventh or even eighth centuries BC. The calibrated radiocarbon dates from Fengate, on the other hand, indicate a fourth or fifth century date. A similar radiocarbon date was also obtained from Washingborough Fen, Lincs. The dates in question are all from well associated material of known origin and it is no longer possible simply to disregard them as anomalous. In view of the above, it seems reasonable to suppose that an ultimately Late Urnfield-inspired ceramic tradition continued to flourish on the western Fen-edge (if not elsewhere) until about the third quarter of the first millennium BC.

Group 2

Introduction

A few words are necessary here on the depositional and post-depositional history of deposits which contained pottery of Groups 2 and 3. It will be apparent from preceeding chapters that the first millennium water table at Fengate was rarely more than a metre below the ground surface. Consequently storage pits are virtually absent; the few large pits that were discovered, moreover, appear to have been dug as shallow 'sock wells', just a few centimetres into the permanent ground water table. For obvious reasons, once a well was dug it was rarely filled-in again, so unless there are good reasons to the contrary, we must assume that most well deposits accumulated through natural means once the feature had been abandoned. 'Pit groups', as such, are, therefore, extremely rare at Fengate (this should be borne in mind when considering the Group 1 material published by Hawkes and Fell (1945)).

We know from molluscan analysis and the discovery of two 'brush drains', that the Iron Age ditches at Cat's Water were used as drains. The subsite is virtually flat and, with a few exceptions to the south-east, most drainage ditches do not follow the ground's contours, insofar as these may be discerned beneath the third century AD flood deposits that form the bulk of the modern topsoil. The purpose of most drainage ditches, therefore, must have been the provision of a linear soakaway and for this arrangement to work effectively, clean gravel must be exposed along the ditch bottom, and at least on part of its sides.

Ditches must have been subjected to constant recutting, perhaps on an annual basis, and this process must inevitably mix together deposits of all periods. This frequent recutting finds material expression in the generally small size of sherds from the Cat's Water sub-site, where only two or three vessels were recovered at all complete. Most complete or near-complete vessels in this report have been reconstructed from sherds. Despite the fact that the vast majority of Iron Age pottery was found in ditches or main drains, every effort has been made to select vessels which illustrate the Type Series from less unreliable contexts. Unfortunately, structural ring-gullies seem to have served a drainage function, and in most cases were left to fill-in naturally after their abandonment. This presents the archaeologist with serious problems of interpretation: traditionally, small, battered and crushed sherds would be regarded as 'residual' whereas fresh, larger sherds are seen as 'primary' i.e. contemporary with the feature in question. If, however, rubbish was being disposed of away from current habitation, it would be reasonable to expect it to be dumped in redundant ditches that are not linked with the linear soakaway system currently in use. Ring-gullies of abandoned buildings would be obvious candidates for such dumped rubbish; thus the small, crushed sherds could be regarded as 'primary' material, resulting from trample when the structure was inhabited, and the larger fresh sherds now become 'intrusive'. This paradox is made worse on a settlement such as Cat's Water where occupation was apparently quite prolonged, and was, moreover, confined, probably as a result of high winter water levels, to a comparatively small area. It is inevitable, given the above constraints, that the large ceramic assemblage from Cat's Water is only of limited use in furthering the typological study of Middle and Late Iron Age pottery in the region. It provides a picture of the *range* of pottery types in use over a long period of time, but is generally uninformative on the evolution of individual pottery styles. Despite these caveats, it has proved possible to isolate a few closed deposits which are probably representative of the beginning, middle and end of the period represented by vessels of Groups 2 and 3.

Padholme Road

Area XI of this subsite (see Chapter 2) contained two large Middle Iron Age pits. The smaller of the two pits, F3, was a wattle-lined well which had been backfilled with rubbish including large pieces of hand-made pottery. This pit group was fully illustrated in the First Report (FNG 1, FIGS 21 and 22) and all sherds, including those not drawn are listed in this report, Table M7. Some of the sherds joined with others from a large quarry pit, also apparently backfilled, into which the well had been cut. The pottery from both pits was stylistically and technically indistinguishable and it is probable that both assemblages derived from the same ultimate source. Material from the larger, stratigraphically earlier, pit is listed in Table M8. The pottery from

both pits will, therefore, be considered together.

All sherds were shell-gritted and most sherds were in the coarser ware 1A. The range of Rim Forms was considerable: 1-3, 5, 8, 10, 11, 13, 15, 16, 21 and 52, as was the range of Rim Decorations (1-4, 6, 9, 11), but the repertoire of Body Forms was restricted to vessels with slack, high shoulders or rounded, globular bodies (Forms 1-6). Body decoration was scored and nearly the whole repertoire of Fengate scored motifs was employed (Body Decs 1-8, 10, 11 and the undiagnostic scored motif 33). Base Forms (1-4) were severely limited and Base Decoration was not encountered. A radiocarbon date (GaK-4198) was obtained from wattle-work lining the later well, F3, which, when calibrated (R M Clark 1975) at one standard deviation gives a spread of 480-400 BC (FNG 1, 38). The wattlework dates the last lining of the well that was subsequently filled with material which probably derived from the same source as that which filled the larger pit into which it (the well) was cut! In other words, the C-14 date gives a *terminus ante quem* for the material thrown into it. Parallels for the assemblage are discussed at length in the First Report (FNG 1, 1, 37) and need not be reiterated; it is sufficient to note, however, that the best parallels for Padholme Road are to the south, in Northamptonshire. The Twywell report (Jackson 1975) has now been published and the correspondence between the two sites may be clearly appreciated. If Harding's view (in Jackson 1975, 70) that the finger-tip impessed decoration on shoulders preceeds finger-tipping on rims, then there is no material of this earlier phase in Group 2; Harding would see this apparently important switch in the location of decoration as happening 'from around the 4th century BC onwards'. The single C-14 date from Padholme Road would push this estimate back somewhat. It is most interesting to note that Professor Harding is inclined (*ibid* 72) to look for the closest parallels for Twywell 'in the eastern coastal sites of Cambridgeshire and Suffolk'. These views tend to support ideas tentatively put forward in the First Report (FNG 1, 37-8) and could point to the existence of a southern Fen-edge style-zone which may reach up the Nene valley, to the south-west, and also, perhaps, up the lower reaches on the Welland ('scored wares' from the author's current excavation at Maxey, Cambs, are strikingly similar to those from Fengate). It is hoped that the gradual emergence of a new style-zone will help explain the distribution of at least some of the ill-defined 'bowls and coarse ware', which currently typify the region's later Iron Age pottery in Professor Cunliffe's synthesis (1978, FIG A, 22); certainly the distinction between undecorated elements of the Hunsbury-Draughton style (*ibid* FIG A, 21; J H Williams 1974, FIGS 13 and 14) and the eastern 'bowls and coarse wares', especially those from Cambs and Hunts (*ibid* FIG A, 22 nos 2, 7-9), is difficult to maintain, in the light of recent research in the region.

The current understanding of Nene and, latterly, of

Welland valley Iron Age pottery owes much to the published excavations of Dennis Jackson. Since Twywell (Jackson 1975), a number of reports have appeared which are relevant to Fengate, but as these are in general somewhat later than Twywell (and Padholme Road), they will be considered with other local parallels at the conclusion of this section.

The backfilled pits from Padholme Road produced 42.8% (by weight) scored wares (36.1% from the back-filled quarry pit; 50.5% from the well, F3). This ratio of scored to non-scored decorated pottery may be compared with three pit groups from Middle Iron contexts on Cat's Water (Tables M9-M11). These three pits were selected for more detailed study because (a) they contained an unusually large amount of pottery and (b) because they had been backfilled and abandoned before the introduction of Late, wheel-made, wares. Two pits associated with the enclosure ditch around Structure 3 (Tables M10 and M11) contained, by weight, 38.7% and 59.6% scored wares; the percentage figure for both pits was 53.2%. The third pit was cut by a Late Iron main drain; it was located near Structure 53 (at Grid 403W/640N), but was stratigraphically earlier. It produced 50.4% scored wares. The scored to non-scored ratio of Middle Iron features on both subsites is broadly similar — given the different sample sizes involved.

Cat's Water

Turning now to the composition of the Cat's Water pit groups, the two pits associated with Structure 3 (Tables M10 and M11) exhibited less stylistic variation than did the assemblage from Padholme Road; this, however, is probably an expression of sample size (Padholme Road weighed 13.9 kg, whereas the two Cat's Water pits produced just 1.0 kg). Rim Forms 1, 5 and 50 were encountered, but only one sherd carried decoration on the rim (Rim Dec 7). The repertoire of scored motifs was limited to Body Decs 2, 3, 5, 22 and 33; there was no other body or base decoration and Base Form 1 was the only base type encountered. Body Forms, too, were restricted to simple, straight, or weak, high-shouldered forms (1-2). The third Cat's Water pit (Table M9) produced 0.86 kg of pottery; Rim Forms encountered were 1, 5 and 18, there was no rim decoration and Body Forms (2 and 3) were generally similar to those from the two other Cat's Water pits. The repertoire of body decoration was largely scored (3 and 22) but two small sherds carrying a scratched herringbone pattern were also found (Body Dec 16). Fabrics were entirely shell-gritted, with fabric 1A predominating. Late Group 2 material at Cat's Water is represented by two larger assemblages, both of which contained wheel-made pottery which will be discussed in greater detail below. These deposits have been chosen (a) because they are in contrasting positions *vis a vis* the area of Middle Iron occupation and (b) because it is probable that they were both backfilled with comparatively fresh, unabraded domestic refuse. The Late Iron Age pit F1058 probably

originally served as a well. It cut all features in the area, and must be one of the latest Iron Age features on the subsite. It produced a considerable quantity of Group 2 pottery (6.4 kg) which included 7.3%, by weight, comb-decorated coarse wares (Body Decs 13 and 14) and a surprisingly high figure (52.3%) for scored wares. The latter sherds were, on the whole, fresh and despite the proximity of Middle Iron Structure 6 (which in turn produced very few finds), it is reasonable to suppose that a proportion at least of these scored wares are contemporary with the wheel-made and comb-decorated vessels (scored motifs encountered were Body Decs 1-5, and 33; motif 20 was also found). All Group 2 pottery was in wares 1A-C. Rim Forms were simple and, on the whole undiagnostic (nos 1, 5, 7, 10, 18 and 21). Rim Decoration was confined to three sherds (weight 108gm) which carried motif 5. The range of body forms was restricted to slack-shouldered vessels of various sizes (Body Form 2). The repertoire of Base Forms was similarly restricted (Forms 1-2), but four sherds (weight 7gm) of Base Form 10 — a foot-ring form — were also recovered.

The second assemblage came from the filled-in gully of the Late Iron rectangular building, Structure 41 (Table M12). This feature lay outside the main area of Middle Iron occupation and the composition of its Group 2 pottery is instructive. First, the assemblage is of adequate size (2.2kg) and the percentage, by weight, of comb-decorated pottery is high: 77.2%. The concentration of scored wares is considerably lower (3.1%). Combed motifs are Body Decs 13-15 and scoring is confined to Body Dec 33 — the category allotted to sherds with undiagnostic scored decoration. Rim Forms are limited to nos 1, 5, 18 and 47, but none are decorated. Base Forms are limited to nos 1, 3 and the foot-ring form 7, but none are decorated.

These two features are probably contemporary; this being the case, it is interesting to compare the material from their infillings. The structural feature contains large amounts of comb-decorated hand-made pottery, but only a minimal number of scored sherds, all of which are too poorly preserved to classify further. The pit group, on the other hand, is an assemblage which, if 'conventional wisdom' be accepted should provide the most reliable group of pottery. It contains a very large proportion of scored wares, most of which are indistinguishable from known Middle Iron types. The condition of these sherds is fresh, and many join together, so it is possible that some may be contemporary with the Late Iron wares associated with them. On the other hand it is most surprising not to find coarse scored wares, which presumably had a domestic function, in the back-filled ditch of a building unless, of course, they had been replaced by comb-decorated equivalents. Finally, it should be noted that both deposits are well removed from the known area of second century Romano-British activity, so that later interference can be ruled out.

Certain vessels (Body Form 89, FIG M108) are hand-made copies of wheel-made forms; certain others may be copies, for instance, the sherds illustrating Rim Form 49, (?) 59 and Body Decoration 13a and 35. In the case of Rim Forms 26 and 28 (total weight of 11 sherds, 372gm) it was difficult to determine whether or not the sherds were in fact hand-made, but all examples of the two forms derived from Late Iron contexts.

Decorated rims are most probably a feature of the Middle Iron Age at Cat's Water and the examples from Late Iron contexts are probably residual; similarly, combed decoration is not found in features of Middle Iron date.

Pottery from the filling of the ring-gully around Structure 7 is of Middle Iron type (FIGS 102 and 103). The building in question was cut by a ditch of Late Iron date, and yet no wheel-made pottery was found in the earlier ring-gully which had probably accumulated its filling by the time the later feature was cut through it. All diagnostic pottery is illustrated and this is dominated by a preponderance of scored sherds, one of which (FIG 102, no 5) is finished in diagonal lattice scoring (Body Dec 9). The pinched-out exterior — in effect a protruding foot — of FIG 103, no 7, is a feature largely confined to Middle Iron wares. The assemblage may be usefully compared with that from the Late Iron Age Structure 4. This structure was located west of Sructure 41, discussed above, and is thus removed from the Middle Iron occupation area; wheel-made forms predominate and scoring is absent. It should, however, be recalled that this is a very small assemblage and need not be typical of Late features in general.

We may posit, largely on the basis of the Padholme Road assemblage, a starting date for Group 2 pottery perhaps as early as the fifth century. It is probable that the Cat's Water Middle Iron Age settlement began shortly after that date, perhaps in the fourth century. The spatial arrangement of features on Cat's Water, and most particularly the maintenance of ditch systems, indicates that there was no break in occupation between the Middle and Late Iron ages, the latter being defined simply by the introduction of wheel-made pottery, and with it the technique of comb-brushed body decoration. Many Late Iron ditches follow the alignment of earlier Middle Iron ditches, usually completely disturbing the latter deposits; it would therefore be misleading to attempt a quantitative analysis of material from the ditch fillings, on a period basis. Gross figures for Group 2 formal and decorative types are given in Tables M14-M16; an analysis of Fabric types and Surface Treatment (see Introduction to this chapter for ST coding) is given in Table 25. Finally, Tables M20 and M21 list Type Series formal and decorative attributes of Middle (Table M20) and Late Iron (Table M21) date. The problems posed by the residual survival of pottery inevitably mean that the Late Iron lists are the least reliable of the two; this particularly applies to the commonly encountered scored body decorations (Table M21 Body Decs 1-4, 9). The simplest rim forms and the least diagnostic body

forms (for example simple upright or everted rims, gently curved body sherds, sometimes exhibiting a slack shoulder, or the plain sherds of globular jars) are found in very large numbers in both Middle and Late contexts. No attempt has been made to sort these sherds chronologically, but efforts have been made to quantify the material recovered. The size range of all sherds is illustrated diagrammatically in FIGS 107-110 and principal associations of Rim Body and Base Forms are listed in Tables M14-M16.

The Late Iron component of Group 2 is contemporary with Group 3 and it would appear that there was no break between the Middle and Late Iron Ages on Cat's Water. Consequently, local and regional parallels for the assemblages are best considered together, directly after the discussion of Group 3, below.

Group 3

The vast majority of Group 3 wares derived, like those of Group 2, from drainage ditches. There were, however, three apparently closed deposits, two of which have been partially considered above (F1053 — Table M12 — and F1058 — Table M13). The third was from ring-gully surrounding Structure 20 (centred on Grid 457W/651N). This apparently backfilled deposit has been used extensively in the formation of the Group 3 Type Series. Vessels from Structure 20 illustrate Rim Forms 1-9, Body Forms 4, 7, Body Dec 1 and Base Forms 1,2. Apart from sherds of a hand-made storage jar (Group 2, Rim Form 20), the wares are wheel-made and include globular jars (Rim Forms 3, 5 and 9) and necked jars with cordons or corrugation on shoulder (Rim Form 2; Body Form 4) and neck (Rim Form 1); carinated bowls with concave walls are also represented (Rim Forms 4, 6, (?) and 7). The stratigraphic relationship of this structure to the main Late Iron drain immediately west of it was obscured by an R-B ditch, but there are strong grounds to believe that the two are contemporary (see Structure 20, Chapter 4).

Turning to the two backfilled Late Iron features F1058 and 1053, these most probably date to a very late phase in the sequence. The well, F1058, is stratigraphically later than all features in the area, and most probably post-dates the two important Late Iron drains F1086 and F1006. The alignment of the rectangular structure 41 (F1053) suggests contemporaneity with the N-S ditch F1008 which cuts F1006, the principal Late Iron main drain in the area. F1008, moreover, curves, as if to respect the well (F1058) and terminates immediately alongside it. We may therefore regard non-residual material from the well and Structure 41 as providing a *terminus ante quem,* ceramically speaking, for an important element of the Late Iron drain system. We have seen above that much of the material from the well is most probably residual, but the necked jar with flattened cordons and rouletted decoration on the shoulder is a form not encountered elsewhere on the subsite, and although the fabric is local, the shape, especially the rim treatment may recall local Romano-British usage (Frere and St Joseph 1974, FIG 53; Jackson and Ambrose 1978, FIG 41 nos 9, 10, 15, 17). Similar flattened cordons and running (finger nail) impressed exterior decorations are found on a slack-shouldered necked jar from the Late Iron main drain F1006 (Body Form 15).

Wheel-made pottery from the well, F1058 was mostly from the vessel mentioned above, which was in Fabric 1C (96.7% by weight). Remaining wheel-made sherds were in Fabrics 1A (Rim Form 15) and 3. The total weight of pottery from the well was 9.2kg, of which about 30.0% was wheel-made.

The gully of Structure 41 produced 2.9kg, of which 22.4% was wheel-made. Large vessels in Fabric 1 were less common among the wheel-made wares of F1053 (51.2% by weight), where Fabrics 2 and 3 were more frequently encountered. We have noted above that despite their apparent contemporaneity, Group 2 material from the two enclosed assemblages was remarkably dissimilar; it can be seen that this also applies to the wheel-made wares of Group 3. The material upon which the above comparison is based is listed in Tables M12 and M13.

Typologically, the latest vessels represented on the subsite are the copies of Gallo-Belgic imported wares, of which numerically the most important are butt beakers. The subsite produced just one sherd of rouletted butt beaker in hard, sandy fabric, probably of Hertfordshire manufacture (Body Dec 3). This sherd was found at a depth of 15cm in the Late Iron main drain, F1006. A more complete, but locally-made butt beaker was found in another Late Iron main drain, F1287 (see FIG 101). Other sherds that might also be imitations of butt beakers are represented by Rim Forms 11, 25, 27 and possibly 23. The date when these forms were introduced into the area is still far from certain, but it was most probably in the early decades of the first century AD and J H William's estimate of AD 10±20 years for a similar assemblage from Moulton Park, Northampton, would probably suit Fengate (Cunliffe 1978, 93; J H Williams 1974, 20). One rim sherd of a platter, made in a local fabric, was found in the gully of Structure 5. The form has no published local parallels, but can best be matched with some of the 'Sub-Belgic' vessels from Camulodunum (Hawkes and Hull 1947, PL 50, forms 27 and 28). Another unusual sherd, that of a neckless globular jar was also found in the gully of Structure 5 (Rim Form 26). The globular jar, like the platter was made in a local, but very soft shell-gritted fabric (cf Birchall 1965, FIG 4, 30).

Typologically late forms, such as those just discussed, are, on the whole rare: only one near-complete locally-made butt beaker was found (FIG 101, 12) and the few probable butt beaker sherds represented in the Type Series amount to about 2.3%, by weight, of the total Group 3 material recovered. Apart from coarse ware vessels (Fabric 1) of globular form, which recall Late

Group 2 practice (see, for example, Group 3 Body Form 9 or Body Dec 5), the majority of vessels are either necked jars, with or without cordons or corrugations, or carinated bowls/jars, generally decorated with grooves or cordons at or near the wall's point of maximum constriction.

It is not known precisely when wheel-made pottery was first introduced into the area, but a date in the second half of the first century BC would seem reasonable (Cunliffe 1978, 95; May 1976, 186). The few late pottery forms, taken with the coin (R Reece, below) and brooch (D F Mackreth, below) evidence would suggest that the last years of Cat's Water Late Iron Age settlement were post-Conquest in date.

Cat's Water pottery of Groups 2 and 3:
General Considerations

Dr William's analysis of the pottery, above, indicates that there were three main, probably locally made, Iron Age fabric types. The first group of fabrics could be further subdivided, depending on the size of shell in the clay and the presence or absence of sand. Fabric 1A was in general used for the coarsest wares, in all three Iron Age Groups. Its impression of coarseness was often enhanced by the fact the local soil conditions (high humic acid concentration, clays etc) caused surface shell inclusions to dissolve out, giving rise to 'corky' surface treatment. When attempting the reconstruction of vessels, however, it was frequently observed that 'corky' sherds would join smooth-surfaced sherds. Often sherds of very dissimilar surface appearance could be shown to have derived from the same two or three-metre length of ditch and it is therefore probable that the local soil pH was extremely variable. Only rarely could the loss of shell temper be reliably attributed to fire or heat. This perhaps accounts for the fact that finely-finished burnished wares (ST 1) were sometimes found with a 'corky' surface finish. Such wares would probably not normally have been used for cooking.

The harder, sandier Fabrics 2 and 3 were almost exclusively reserved for vessels of Group 3. Wheel-made coarser wares made greater use of finely-crushed shell temper (Fabric 1B) and sand-with-shell temper (Fabric 1C). Very rough surface treatment (ST 4) was rarely found in wares of Group 3.

The search for local parellels for pottery of Groups 2 and 3 must start in Peterborough itself. The pre-War researches of Mr Wyman Abbott at Fengate produced very little material of Middle or Late Iron date. A few sherds from the G W A collection in Peterborough Museum, labelled 'Fengate', however, are in Fabric 1C, are wheel-made and probably come from cordoned necked jars. A fine cordoned necked jar from Woodston, Peterborough is illustrated by Fox, Burkitt, and Abbott (1926, FIG 9) who also figure a carinated bowl closely similar to examples from Cat's Water (*ibid,* FIG 10); vessels from Woodston and Fletton, of probably Middle Iron date are, again, closely similar to examples from Cat's Water (*ibid*, FIGS 11 and 12). The strong resemblance between the illustrated pottery from Fletton, Woodston and Fengate is most striking and there can be little doubt that the three locations are probably subsites within a larger spread or continuum of sites which may originally have spread through Peterborough, westwards, via Longthorpe, to the Middle Nene valley. Peterborough has seen a large increase in archaeological activity since 1973 when the Nene Valley Research Committee's full-time archaeological Unit began work in earnest. Some of the sites excavated have been of Middle and Late Iron date; none are yet published in final form, but useful interim statements may be found in the NVRC's house journal *Durobrivae*. These interim reports tend to illustrate plans or sections rather than finds, but it is understood that wheel-made Iron Age pottery from Orton Longueville (Dallas 1975) and Werrington (Mackreth and O'Neill 1980) did not contain significant numbers of imported or locally-made butt beakers (R Perrin pers comm). The rarity of butt beaker copies at Fengate may indicate local preference for alternative vessel shapes and not, necessarily, that the site was thinly settled in the final years of the Iron Age. Butt beakers were similarly rare at Moulton Park, Northampton, but in this case a chronological explanation is at least possible (Williams 1974, 25).

Recent research into the Late Iron Age of Lincolnshire has been well summarised by Jeffrey May in an important recent publication (1976, chapters 6 and 7). We have already discussed implications of recent work in Lincolnshire in the discussion of Group 1 pottery, above, but later material is also plentifully available, in interim if not in final published form. Most of our knowledge of the Iron Age of Lincolnshire has been gained since 1960 and, perhaps inevitably, publications are few. It has been decided, therefore, not to quote unpublished material, especially as the sites often involve long periods of occupation and complex stratigraphy.

The Ancaster Quarry site (May 1976, 133-141) produced numerous hand-made jar forms, many of which carried scored body 'decoration'; other decoration was confined to rim tops and consisted of fingertip impressions or incisions. Only one non-jar form — a foot-ring bowl — was found. The assemblage was dated to about the third century BC on the basis of associated metalwork (*ibid*, 140). This material finds its closest parallels at Fengate in the Padholme Road pit groups, both in the form of jars, their scored surface treatment and rim top decoration. The rounded shoulders of the jar cannot be exactly paralleled on Padholme Road or Cat's Water, but foot-ring bases have been found in secure Middle Iron contexts (*cf* the type sherds for Group 2 Base Forms 7 and 14).

The Ancaster Gap Late Iron Age settlement is thought by May (*ibid*, 176) to have been occupied 'at least during the later first century BC, and the early first century AD'. It succeeds the neighbouring Ancaster Quarry site, after a probable break in settlement during the second century BC. Similar pottery to that from Ancaster Gap was also found at Old Sleaford. Both sites produced wheel-made wares which included plain and cordoned necked jars, sometimes with foot-ring bases (*ibid*, FIG 87). On the whole, the Fengate Group 3 pottery was not given the same, burnished 'lustrous' finish nor the carefully executed groove and rouletted decoration. The three vessels illustrating Group 2 Body Form 89 (FIG M113) are burnished, as are nos 4, 5 and 11 of FIG 101, all of which bear some resemblance to the Old Sleaford and Ancaster Gap fine wares. Finely executed grooved decoration on the upper shoulders and neck of burnished necked jars is only found on two vessels at Fengate, the near-complete vessel illustrating Group 3 Rim Form 21 and that illustrating Group 2 Body Dec 35 (FIGS M124 and M114). Square-toothed rouletted decoration was extremely rare at Fengate and will be discussed further below.

The assemblage from Dragonby in the north west part of the county does not find close parallels at Fengate, especially in its somewhat ususual, high quality, ware of Phase 1 (May 1970, FIGS 7 and 8; 1976, FIG 92). Phases I and II at Dragonby succeeded each other without an apparent break. Phase II pottery includes wheel-made forms of 'Early' Aylesford-Swarling type not generally found at Fengate, where cordons and corrugations are markedly less pronounced and frequently encountered than at Dragonby. Fengate Group 3 pottery with fewer cordons, S-profiled necked jars and carinated bowls, recalls Phase III at Dragonby which includes imported and copied Gallo-Belgic forms. May (1976, 188) would see Dragonby Phase III starting in the earliest years of the first century AD. The scarcity of 'Early' Aylesford-Swarling forms from Fengate is of considerable interest, as there is no reason to suppose that settlement was anything but continuous at Cat's Water from about the third, or even fourth centuries BC. It is, of course, unwise to attribute too much to typological similiarities when one is considering a site about a hundred miles north of the Thames estuary, but of the 'early' forms listed by Birchall (1965, 248), the biconical jar (Group 2 Body Dec 13(?); see also FIG 101, no 11) is the only type represented in any quantity on Cat's Water. Corrugated or cordoned pedestalled 'urns' are most notably absent. More recently Dr W Rodwell (1976) has published groups of coarse ware jars with combed or grooved exterior finish, beaded or upright rims and, often, corrugated or cordoned shoulders. The material (*ibid*, FIGS 15-17) mainly derives from northern Kent, Essex, parts of Beds, Herts and Cambs. This wider selection of early wheel-made wares does, however, include some of the forms found at Cat's Water (see also, Group 3 Rim Forms 2, 24; FIG 101, 10), and may serve to bridge the gap between 'Early' and 'Middle' or 'Late' forms, as defined by Birchall (1965).

Stylistically it is often hard to compare Fengate

Groups 2 and 3 with other sites, as the repertoire of forms and decorations is, in general, very restrained. We have briefly compared Cat's Water with the fine assemblages from Dragonby and sites in south Lincolnshire and it remains now to consider the range of body decorations encountered at Fengate. The vast majority of sherds bore either scored (in which bundles of twigs, or something similar, were dragged across the wet clay before firing) or combed 'decoration'. It is doubtful whether this form of surface treatment was necessarily decorative and the various types of 'scoring' and combing are illustrated in the Type Series (for scoring see Group 3 Body Decorations 1-10; 22; 23(?); 26 and 33; for combing see Group 2 Body Decorations 13-15; 21; 24; 27; 34; 36 and 38; Group Body[3] Decoration 1 and 5). The discussion of Lincolnshire decorated wares leads to a brief discussion of stamped and rouletted decoration, which has recently been reviewed by Elsdon (1975).

Despite the fact that Sleaford and other south Lincolnshire sites are only about 35 miles north of Fengate, the latter has produced only very few sherds decorated with a square-toothed roulette wheel. Indeed, bearing in mind the large numbers of sherds found, the quantities of non-scored or combed decorated sherds of any sort is minute (perhaps 30 sherds in total). The sherd illustrating Group 2 Body Dec 12 is small and its surface very 'corky', but the paired punctate impressions are probably rouletted. A very similar decorated sherd in which punctate impressions are used to imitate a toothed roulette is illustrated as Body Dec 30. Roulette imitations may also perhaps be seen in Body Decs 30a and 28. The only sherd with undoubted roulette decoration is that illustrating Body Dec 19; the surface of this sherd is covered with vertically-arranged shallow grooves separating one, and part of another, zone of paired roulette impressions. Stamped designs are even less commonly found than rouletting, excepting, of course, the early Group 2 stamped and impressed rim tops and exteriors of the Padholme Road subsite, discussed at length above. Sherds with *bona fide* stamped impressions include Group 2 Body Dec 99, no 2 (FIG M114) and, possibly Group 2 Rim Dec 99 (FIG M105). The latter sherd is decorated with a row of small (5.0mm/max) irregular stamped circular impressions just above the shoulder, and parallel to the rim. The former is decorated with a frieze of incised chevrons bounded by two parallel lines; the point of each chevron encloses a small (6.0mm) stamped circular impression. This pattern recalls Elsdon's (1975, FIG 8) Lincolnshire patterns 15 and 17. The sherd illustrating Group 2 Body Dec 99 - 3 carries an overlapping chevron design based on paired scratched lines. This much impoverished repertoire of stamped and rouletted motifs is probably broadly contemporary with Dragonby Phase I.

Large assemblages of later Iron Age pottery, but often exhibiting quite a restricted repertoire of forms and decorations, seem to be a feature of rural sites in the Peterborough area (see discussion above). The same may also be said for sites in which Middle Iron scored wares play a principal role and this discussion will not be repeated here. Recent published research has, however, thrown much light on sites in the region which have their roots in Middle Iron times, but where occupation seems to extend up to, and sometimes into, the Roman period.

Hall and Nickerson's (1968) salvage excavations at Irchester, near Wellingborough, Northants revealed a reduced Middle Iron presence, followed by substantial Late Iron features, including lengths of ditch with multi-period fillings. The Late Iron phase at Irchester could be divided into three periods Ci (characterised by thick, black wheel-made pottery, often burnished); Cii (mid-Belgic: carinated vessels and necked jars); Ciii (Late Belgic: butt beakers and Romanised native forms). The Iron 'B' material from Irchester slightly resembles that from Fengate, particularly in the decorative treatment of rim tops (Hall and Nickerson 1968, FIG 9, nos 14, 15 and 22). The first phase of wheel-made pottery (Ci) is represented by a few vessels at Fengate (Group 2 Body Dec 89; Group 3 Rim Forms 2, 21, 24; FIG 101, no 11). The second (Cii) is well represented at Fengate, but the third (Ciii), Late Belgic, phase is again poorly represented. All 'Belgic' pottery from Irchester is strikingly more elaborate and 'adventurous' in decoration and form than that from Fengate; this is even true for phase Cii, but particularly true for the Late phase Ciii. It is of interest to note that Hall and Nickerson consider that occupation during Cii phase at Irchester may have been off-site but it is probable that the pottery of phase Ciii comprises the domestic rubbish and cinerary ware of the latest Iron Age inhabitants of a settlement that later was to become a small Romano-British town. Cat's Water, on the other hand, was not destined to achieve such status and its relatively simple material culture — as exemplified by the metalwork and pottery — may reflect its status as a long-lived farmstead, rather than, perhaps, a village or rural regional centre. It is probable that some of the ceramic stylistic dissimilarities observed between Fengate and Dragonby, Ancaster Gap or Old Sleaford may be due to the same causes.

Recent research in Northamptonshire has also revealed a number of contemporary later Iron Age farmsteads or small settlements, more directly comparable with Fengate than Irchester. Two enclosures at Moulton Park revealed an important assemblage of pottery which may be divided into two groups: Group 1 includes hand-made pottery of essentially Middle Iron type; Group 2 mainly consisted of wheel-made wares. Group 1 material largely comprises globular jars in Cunliffe's Hunsbury-Draughton style (1978, FIG A, 21) and does not find many good formal parallels at Fengate, where jars tend to be more elongated and less squat; exceptions, however, should be noted, especially the vessel illustrating Group 2 Base Dec 3 (FIG M120) which carries a compass-drawn design very slightly reminiscent of certain vessels from Hunsbury iteself (Fell 1936, FIG 6); the concave-sided bowl illustrated in FIG 99 no 10 recalls Hunsbury-Draughton, but, in general the coarse ware bowls and jars from Fengate tend to have straighter, less rounded sides, and more pronounced upright or everted necks. Moulton Park Group 2 pottery, however, is strikingly similar to wheel-made forms from Fengate, both in form, finish and where present, in decoration. In particular, the Moulton Park carinated bowls have a simplicity of design and consistency of form which is most similar to Cat's Water and constrasts with 'the more elaborate and multi-cordoned forms from Camulodunum and Prae Wood' (J H Williams 1974, 49; see also Snailwell-Leth-ridge 1953, FIG 3 nos 5, 3, 18). We have already noted that the material from Irchester provides a similar contrast. All of Williams' seven classes of Group 2 vessels are represented at Cat's Water, with the exception of corrugated necked bowls — of which only three examples were found at Moulton Park (J H Williams 1974, FIG 19 nos 146, 147(?) and 148).

Salvage excavations at Rushton, near Kettering (Jackson 1976) produced an assemblage of pottery from three settlement ditches; the sherds themselves were too small to allow comparisons with Fengate to be drawn, but it would appear that the site was occupied from the last years of the Middle Iron Age until some time in the 'Belgic' period. The gravel quarry site at Aldwincle, near Thrapston, contained two Iron Age ditched enclosures, one of which (Jackson 1977, FIG 4 — Enclosure E) appears to have been occupied for at least a hundred years, from the first century BC until the introduction of Romanised wares (ibid, 33). Pottery found could be classed into three groups: Group 1 was contemporary with later phases at Aldwincle (it included scored wares and the principal form was the globular jar); Group 2 was slightly later than Group 1 and included little or no scored ware and rims tended to be beaded; Group 3 was of 'Belgic' date, but not all wheel-made. Vessels from Aldwincle Groups 1 and 2 find parallels with Late material from Cat's Water Group 2 (see Table M21).

Decorated sherds of Group 2 (Jackson 1977, FIG 13) find close parallels at Cat's Water, especially in the common use of punctate impressions, perhaps imitating a toothed roulette wheel. The wheel-made pottery of Aldwincle Group 3 (ibid, FIGS 14 and 15) resembles Fengate Group 3 in many respects: the beaded and everted rims of shell-gritted coarse ware jars are very similar, as are the generally slack-profiled body forms; of finer wares, simple necked jars and, to a lesser extent, carinated bowls seem to predominate. Imported butt beakers appear to be absent, but one or two illust-rated sherds could, perhaps, be locally-made copies (ibid, FIG 15, nos 89 and 96; no 88 is a girth beaker).

A long term watching brief combined with limited salvage excavation led to the remarkable discoveries at Hardwick Park, Wellingborough (Foster et al 1977). A series of ditched enclosures dating between 100 BC and AD 250 was discovered during building operations; these were associated with an early Romano-British lime kiln, but no actual structures were recovered, almost certainly because of the adverse conditions under which the site was recorded. The function of the enclosures is seen as stockyards 'since none of the ditches could claim to be defensive' (ibid, 58); but it might perhaps be better to interpret Hardwick Park with Fengate, Twywell, Aldwincle, Wakerley etc as another example of an enclosed settlement (in which the ditches served both to drain the perimeter and to retain or exclude livestock). Such an interpretation would certainly accord with the quantities of domestic refuse found within the enclosure ditches. Evidence for a Middle Iron presence comes from the ditch around enclosure 7 (ibid, FIG 12, nos 39-41). Enclosure 5, however, produced sherds of carinated, cordoned jars and necked jars which find many close parallels at Fengate; the majority of the site is somewhat later, perhaps contemporary with the Vicarage Farm Romano-British episode (see J P Wild, chapter 7).

Dennis Jackson's recent excavation at Wakerley in the Welland valley, 28km due west of Fengate is a major contribution to local Iron Age settlement studies (Jackson and Ambrose 1978). The site was situated near the river and was also adjacent to ironstone outcrops, which were probably worked in later Iron Age and Roman times. A series of ditched enclosures were constructed and up to three circular buildings were in use at any one time. Phase I (?second century BC) is not directly associated with settlement, but is represented instead by a post-built fence and discontinuous ditch which traversed the south-westerly part of the site from NW to SE. The discontinuous ditch (ditch C) produced iron slag and pottery of Middle Iron type in which high-shouldered jars predominate and spaced vertical scoring is frequently found (Jackson and Ambrose 1978, FIG 36, nos 1-10; Fengate Group 2 Body Dec 5; see also vessel illustrating Group 2 Base Form 3). Spaced vertical scoring at Fengate is largely confined to the Padholme Road subsite and is early in the sequence (see discussion above). Phase II (early first century BC) produced globular hand-made wares (ibid, FIG 36, nos 11-25) similar to Moulton Park, Group 1 (see discussion above) which are currently thought to immediately pre-date wheel-made ('Belgic') pottery over most of Northamptonshire. Vessels of this type are generally rare at Fengate, where taller, thinner variants, also with beaded rims, are found (eg sherds illustrating Group 2 Body Decs 26, 28, 30, 30a, 31, 32 — FIG M113). The top layer of the Phase II enclosure ditch contained wheel-made and associated hand-made pottery (ibid FIGS 37-39, nos 28-82). The coarse hand-made vessels are mainly simple-rim barrel-jars of a type also found at Fengate (Group 2 Rim Form 47; FIG 99 nos 5, 7 and 8); wheel-made pottery is strikingly like that from Cat's Water, both in the limited range of forms and restrained decoration. Necked jars with corrugated shoulders (eg *ibid, FIG* 38, no 51), S-profile necked jars (eg *ibid, FIG* 39, no 83) and carinated bowls (*ibid, FIG* 38 nos 53-57; FIG 39 nos 85 and 87), are particularly similar to examples from Fengate. In Wakerley Phase III (first century AD) the finer wares remain the same, but coarse shell-gritted vessels are harder and better fired.

In conclusion it must be recalled that most of the pottery here came from open ditch deposits. Despite this, it was possible to distinguish three main Iron Age phases. The first is represented by pottery of Group 1, which is discussed at length above. Group 1 pottery probably went out of use in the fifth century BC, at which point the first Middle Iron Age (mainly scored) wares were introduced. Two large back-filled pits on the Padholme Road subsite (the well and quarry of Area XI, and the 'pit complex', of Area XII) provided a sealed group of early Group 2 pottery which was most probably in use, largely unaltered, from the third or fourth centuries BC until the mid-first century. A group of globular jars, frequently decorated with impressed or incised geometric motifs, most probably immediately ante-dates the introduction of the earliest wheel-made pottery. This globular pottery cannot be distinguished stratigraphically, as it occurs with equal frequency in Middle and Late ditches. Its form is, however, sufficiently diagnostic and its occurrence in neighbouring parts of Northamptonshire is frequent enough to allow its selection on typology alone. These bowls are placed with Middle Iron Group 2 formal and decorative types in Table M20, but are distinguished by the letter 'L'. The bowl illustrated in FIG 99: no 10 should also be placed in this group. Typologically, all other vessels illustrated in FIGS 99-101 derive from true contexts and are not considered to be residual. Hand-made Late Iron vessels in Group 2 are listed in Table M21.

Most of the wheel-made pottery consists of the earliest such forms commonly found in the region — these include examples of Birchall's (1965) 'Early' and 'Middle' types. Only a few 'Late' forms are found, and these, together with the brooches and (unstratified) coins suggest a mid-first century date for the last Late Iron features. The size of the assemblage only reflects the scale and extent of the excavation. The pottery is, in general, simple in form and decoration and cannot readily be compared with the major urban sites of Hertfordshire and Essex; it even seems restrained alongside assemblages from proto-urban sites such as Irchester, Old Sleaford or Dragonby. It should be seen for what it is: the domestic refuse of a small farmstead or rural hamlet.

PART II MISCELLANEOUS FINDS

1. STONE (FIG 114)

The nearly complete top half of a rotary quern was found in the eaves-drip gully of Structure 54, in Cat's Water Area X (F1503, layer 1; Grid 427W/578N; depth below 0.20m; finds no 78:2813). The handle socket is very irregular in section, but is about 20mm wide; the central perforation is slightly funnel-shaped in section, the diameter ranging from 27-53mm. The stone is very soft and the grinding surface (dia 65mm) apparently well worn. Ths stone used is Lincolnshire Limestone, of the Jurassic Inferior Oolite Series (kindly identified by Dr Peter Crowther, Assistant Curator, Peterborough Museum; drawing by David Crowther).

2. MISCELLANEOUS FINDS OF SHALE, FIRED CLAY, METAL AND BONE (FIGS 115 to 118)

1. Fragment of shale bracelet, ext diameter 40mm. Oval section, width 6.5mm; ht 10.00mm. CW Area II, F1210 layer 1; Grid 405W/665N; depth 0.47. 75:3180 (From LIA main drain; for local parallel see Williams (1974, FIG 25, no 227)).
2. Ceramic object, in shape of a flanged spool. Soft, sand-tempered fabric, light brown ext, black core. Ext dia 32mm; int dia 12mm; thickness 16mm. From cremation, CW Area IV, F27 layer 1; Grid 392W/762N. 76:9000
3. This bronze finger-ring is the subject of the brief report by Dr Martin Henig, below: Bronze finger ring. Hoop of D-shaped section with central beading. Width somewhat uneven 5-8mm; external diameter 24mm (internal 20mm). It is a product of Late La Tène tradition, rather than that of Rome; though similar specimens have certainly been recorded from early Roman sites in Germany. See Henkel 1913, pp 68 ff.; 217f. and PL XXVI, Nos 601 (Mainz), 602 (Kreuznach), 605 (Augustan period grave at Coblenz), 613 (Ober-Winterthur) and from 'free Germany', Beckmann 1969, p 27, Group 1, form 2.

These are dated to the reign of Augustus and to the early Empire. Wheeler (1943, 275 and FIG 90, 9) shows what appears to be a similar ring from a 'Belgic level' at Maiden Castle *c* AD 25-50.

From Late Iron main drain, CW Area II, F1210 layer 1; Grid 405W/667N; depth 0.30. 75:3195
4. Bronze finger-ring; ext dia 25mm; thickness 1.5mm; width 3mm. From Late Iron main drain, CW Area I, F1086 layer 1; Grid 422W/700N; depth 0.22. 75:2531
5. Fragments of a bronze finger-ring; ext dia 23mm; thickness and width similar to 4, above, but too corroded to measure. CW Area II, F1156 layer 1; Grid 400W/670N; depth 0.20. 75:1986
6. Corroded bronze needle, length 62mm; max width 1mm; round section (?). From Late Iron main drain, CW Area II, F1260 layer 1; Grid 389W/656N; depth 0.08. 75:3298
7. Fragments of bone point; tip worn; length 66mm; width 10mm; thickness 2mm. From Late Iron pit, CW Area IV, F1105 layer 1; Grid 407W/752N; depth 0.15. 76:2318
8. Fragment of bone point or tapered dowel; length

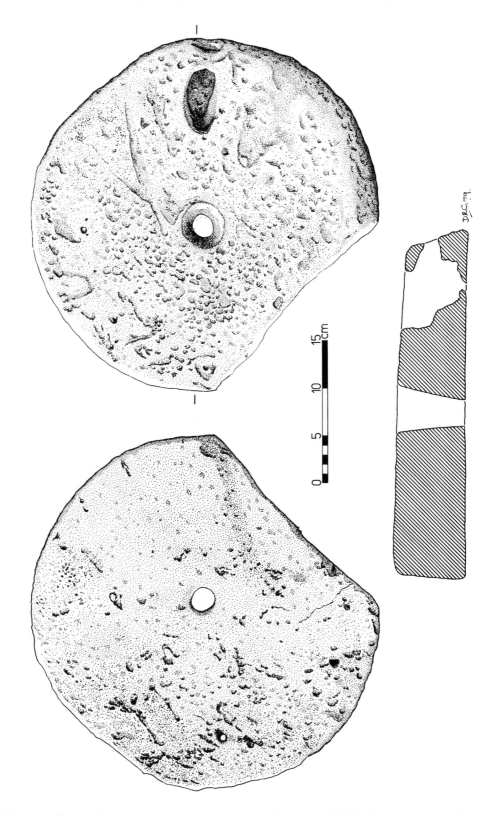

Fig. 114 Cat's Water subsite: rotary quern from Structure 54 (Area X, F1503, layer 1). Scale 1:4.

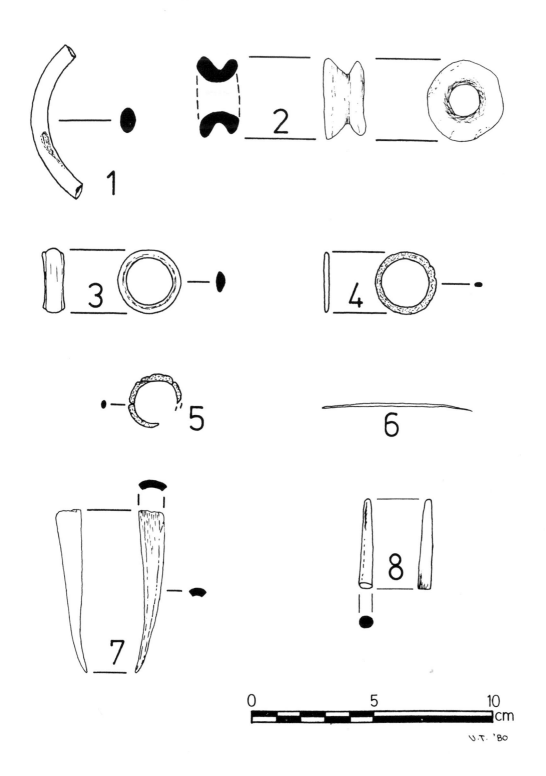

Fig. 115 Miscellaneous finds from Iron Age features, Cat's Water subsite. 1, 3 (Area II, F1210); 2 (Area IV, F27); 4 (Area I, F1086); 5 (Area II, F1156); 6 (Area II, F1260); 7 (Area IV, F105); 8 (Area V, F467). Scale 2:3 (continued on FIG 116).

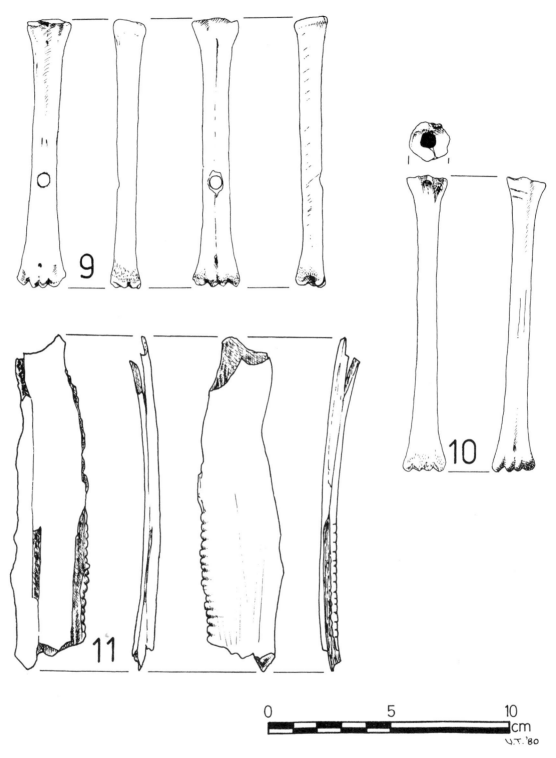

Fig. 116 Miscellaneous finds from Iron Age features, Cat's Water subsite. 9, 10 (Area VI, F903); 11 (Area I, F1086). Scale 2:3 (continued from FIG 115).

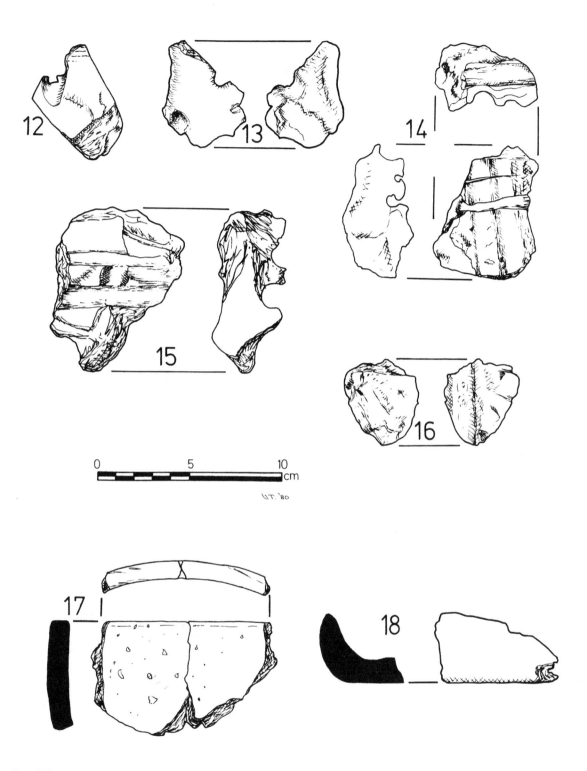

Fig. 117 Miscellaneous fired and burnt clay finds from the Cat's Water (12-17) and Storey's Bar road (18) subsites. Scale 1:2.

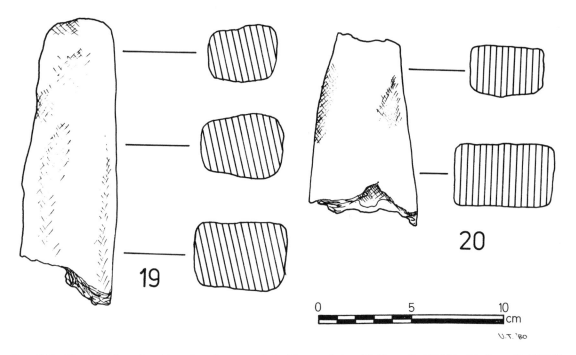

Fig. 118   Fire-bars from Late Iron Age features, Cat's Water subsite. 19 (Area II, F1287); 20 (Area II, F1086). Scale 1:2.

36mm width (max) 6mm (min) 3mm. From gully of Late Iron Structure 36, CW Area V, F467 layer 2; Grid 439W/648N; depth 0.40. 77:2517

9. Ovicaprid metacarpal with perforated shaft; immature specimen with unfused distal epiphysis. Cleanly-cut perforation, dia 5mm. From undated pit, CW Area VI, F903 layer 1; Grid 413W/584N; depth. 78:1357/1

10. Ovicaprid metatarsal with perforated proximal epiphysis and unfused distal epiphysis. Provenance as no 9. The function of these objects is not known, but quite close parallels are recorded from Late Iron contexts at Elstow and Odell, Beds (Woodward 1977, 48-51; fn 22; see also Gray and Cotton 1966, 310). 78:1357/2

11. Much damaged short-toothed comb on horse/cattle rib. Surface scratched; tooth length *c* 2-3mm. From Late Iron main drain CW Area I, F1086, B horizon baulk; Grid 421W/693N. 75:2524

12-16. Fragments of burnt 'daub' with wattle impressions; average dia of wattle-impressions *c* 10-15mm. All pieces have been unevenly tempered with (chopped?) vegetable material. Provenances:

    12. CW Area VI, F855 layer 1 (Middle Iron Structure 21 gully)

    13. CW Area V, F479 layer 1 (Late Iron main drain)

    14. CW Area II, F1251 layer 1 (Middle/Late Iron slot — Structure 10)

    15. CW Area II, F1260 layer 1 (Late Iron main drain)

    16. CW Area VI, F839 layer 1 (Late Iron ditch — Structure 51)

17. Soft, shell-gritted (Fabric 1A) vessel with straight sides, dia 260mm. The 'rim' has been sawn through, at right-angles. Possibly a salt mould (*cf* FNG 3, FIG 13, no 1). From Middle Iron pit, CW Area IV, F90 layer 2. 76:3247

18. Very soft shell-gritted (Fabric 1A) shallow bowl/dish of large dia (300mm+). Tapered rim. Possibly a salt evaporation vessel, but fabric lacks the coarse vegetable temper often associated with saltern material. From Late Iron enclosure ditch, Storey's Bar Road, Area I, P28 layer 1; Grid 89W/151N; depth 0.20. 74:871

19. Fire-bar, broken at lower end (as illustrated). Vegetable temper, hard and well-fired; rounded rectangular section. Surviving length 155mm; max width 52mm; thickness 36mm. From Late Iron ditch, CW Area II, F1287 layer 1. 75:4115

20. Fire-bar, broken at both ends. Temper material uncertain, but includes crushed stone. Softer than no 19; rectangular section. Surviving length 92mm; max width 58mm; thickness 33mm. From Late Iron ditch, CW Area II, F1086 layer 1; Grid 428W/687N; depth 0.20. 75:3751

Oven Fragments

Fragments of vegetable-tempered fired clay, often, but not always, finger-smoothed on one or more

166

TABLE 3

TRIANGULAR CLAY WEIGHTS FROM STOREY'S BAR ROAD AND CAT'S WATER SUBSITES
(For illustrated examples see FIG 120)

Provenance	Surviving length (mm)	Maximum thickness (mm)	Diameter of holes (mm)	Weight (mm)	Organic temper
1. SBR I, P48, layer 1 74:977	140 x 110	55	8	600	present
2. SBR I, P48, layer 1 74:993	115 x 70	55	17	450	absent
3. CW I, F1101, layer 1 75:1621	90 x 70	48	10	340	absent
4. CW I, F1086, layer 3 75:1836	150 x 140	c. 70	12, 13 & 15	1250	present
5. CW II, F1086, layer 1 75:2070	90 x 70	75	18	510	v little
6. CW I, F1039, layer 1 75:2360	50 x 50	60	15	140	present
7. CW II, F1274, layer 1 75:4240	90	50	9	280	v little

surfaces, were found in most of the larger drainage ditches. One pit, however, was packed with pieces of fired clay oven. These are illustrated in FIG 119 and PL 18. They had not been burnt *in situ,* but could be substantially reconstructed: the pieces form the floor of a pierced clay oven with a central opening *c* 120mm dia. A series of 6 smaller (25mm) holes are arranged, irregularly, around the circumference of the central opening, *c* 50mm from it. Many parallels from Iron Age contexts see, for example, Gussage All Saints (Wainwright 1979 FIG 78, 4040, 4057); Little Woodbury (Brailsford 1949; 159, FIG 2); Maiden Castle (Wheeler 1943, PL 37, nos 2, 3); Harrold, Beds. (Evison 1970, FIG 4). The feature containing the fragments was undated, but was stratigraphically later than the second millennium ditch iii. CW Area II, F1137 layer 1; Grid 402W/669N; depth 0-0.40.

The Triangular Loom Weights from the Cat's Water and Storey's Bar Road subsites, Fengate
by John Peter Wild

1. *Form and Composition* (FIG 120; Table 3)

The best preserved triangular weight (no 4) measures 150 by 140 by 135mm and is *c* 70mm thick. Its present weight is 1250gm, but some of its outer surface (perhaps 100gm) has been lost. The other material from the site consists of corner fragments from weights of much the same dimensions, or possibly slightly smaller. Weight no 5, however, at 750mm thick may represent a larger, heavier type. The transverse holes through the corners of each weight vary from 8mm to 18mm in minimum diameter. Most weights have rounded corners; but weight no 3 has a shallow external groove round the angle in the same plane as the hole.

Two types of fabric are present; the one contains a considerable admixture of grass, hay or straw (nos 1, 4, 6) while the other has few traces of organic inclusions (nos 2, 3, 5, 7). There was evidently little attempt to prepare the raw clay, apart from the addition of grass temper, and the weights show a laminated structure in the break like puffed pastry. There is a hint that sticks to make the holes were introduced into the clay mass while the weights were still being kneaded into shape. They may have been left to burn out during the subsequent bonfire-firing. External surfaces of the weights are mostly oxidised, the interior reduced. Weights nos 2 and 7 seem to have been oxidised throughout.

2. *Function*

The triangular coarse clay weights of the European Iron Age have been traditionally regarded as warp-weights for use on the warp-weighted vertical loom (Wild 1970, 62ff; Harding 1974, 85ff). However, neither the character of the weights themselves nor the contexts in which they have been found offer any precise evidence for function (Wilhelmi 1977, 180ff; *cf*

Champion 1975, 133ff, 142ff.)(1). Interpretation is not made easier by the great diversity of forms of 'loom-weight' which existed at different times and places in Europe. Forms and functions were not intimately related.

Annular clay loomweights have often been found in quantity in Anglo-Saxon *Grubenhäuser* (2); in some cases groups of them seem to have been threaded on ropes or sticks for storage (Wilson 1976, 271, PL XV). There is supporting documentary evidence that *Grubenhäuser* were used for weaving, and so the identification of the purpose of the annular weights seems secure (Dolling 1958, 12, 61ff). Given that the warp-weighted loom was the standard weaving implement of Iron Age Europe (Hoffmann 1964, 151ff; Schlabow 1976, 40ff), it would seem reasonable to claim that the triangular weights are the only artefacts in the late Iron Age cultural assemblages of Britain comparable with the annular Anglo-Saxon loomweights.

The triangular weights are heavier than either the cylindrical clay weights of the Bronze Age (3), the pyramidal weights of the Mediterranean (Small 1977, 203ff; Davidson 1952, 147) or the annular weights of the migrating Germans. Nevertheless, they are lighter than some of the stones used by modern traditional weavers on the warp-weighted loom (Hoffmann 1964, 20ff, 339 note 14). The latter take special care to match the weights attached to front and rear warp-systems and sometimes use heavier weights at the selvedges (Hoffmann 1964, 42, 65). It is not clear how they were fastened to the warp; for they would probably have disintegrated if they had been suspended from a single corner. String passing through at least two of the three holes then attached to a bundle of front or rear warp-threads, may be assumed (4). The external groove often encountered on the triangular weights may have been a string-guide.

Notes

(1) Wilhelmi cites a hoard of 15 triangular weights from the Iron Age pit at Bad Lippspringe (Kr Paderborn).

(2) *Cf Medieval Archaeol,* 21, 1977, 214 (Swindon Old Town); *Sussex Archaeol Collect,* 114, 1976, 306ff (Shoreham); *Medieval Archaeol,* 13, 1969, 5 (West Stow); 15, 1971, 124ff (Mucking).

(3) A complete specimen from Fengate (Area IV, Feature 112(1) 76:112) weighs *c* 730gm.

(4) I cannot accept G Loewe's suggestion that the warp was threaded through two of the holes: *Germania,* 55, 1977, 182 Abb 2.

A Report on the Bronze Brooches from Fengate, Cat's Water Subsite
by D F Mackreth

Note the brooches are illustrated in FIGS 121 and 122.

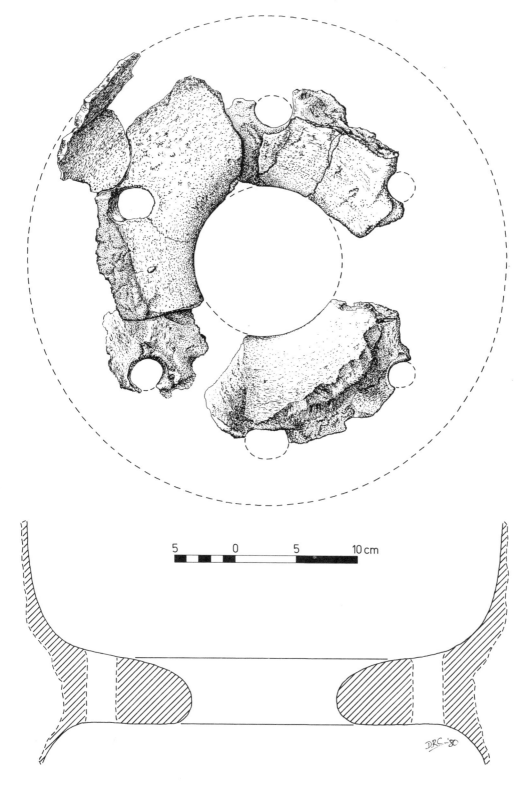

5   0   5   10 cm

Fig. 119 Cat's Water subsite, Area II, clay oven fragments from F1137, layer 1, Grid 402W/669N. The transverse section is partly reconstructed. Scale 1:3.

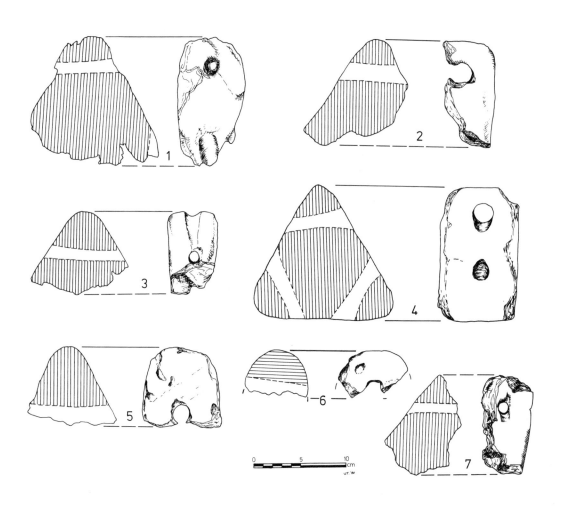

Fig. 120 Clay weights (see report by J P Wild). 1, 2 (Storey's Bar Road, Area I, P48); 3 (CW Area I, F1101); 4, 5 (CW Areas I and II, F1086); 6 (CW Area I, F1039); 7 (CW Area II, F1274). Scale 1:4.

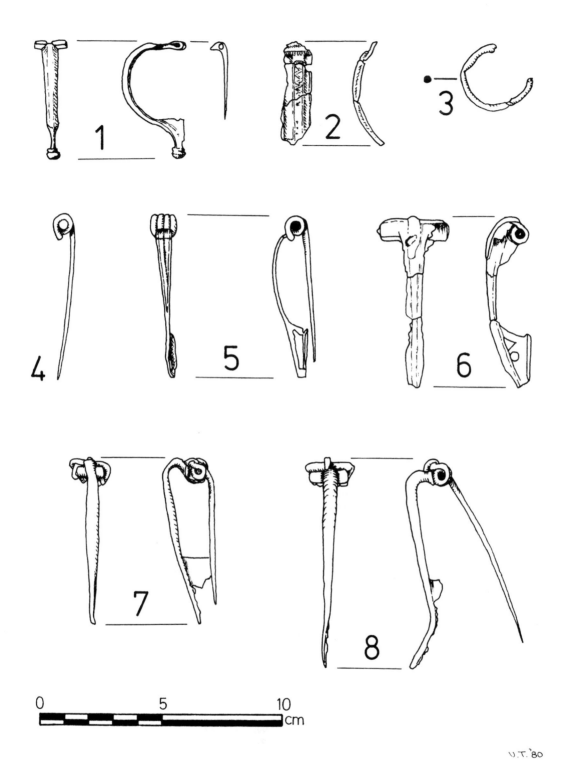

Fig. 121 Cat's Water subsite, copper alloy brooches (see report by D F Mackreth). Scale 2:3 (continued on FIG 122).

Aucissa

1. 75:1, B surface find, bow: (Grid 398W/407N), pin: (Grid 398W/401N). Uninscribed, ? of standard type; corrosion has taken away a lot of detail. Head showing? devolution towards Hod Hill type. Date *c* AD 40-60 in Britain.

Hod Hill

2. 75:854, Area I, F1060, layer 1, (Grid 402W/711N), depth 0.05. Probably Hod Hill. Date in Britain *c* AD 40-65 in use.

Penannular

3. 75:2108, Area I, F1006, surface, (Grid 396W/708N). No terminals or other diagnostic features, therefore no date.

Nauheim Derivative

4. 77:883, Area IV, F207/242, layer 1, (Grid 387W/714N), depth 0.05. Pin and half spring only, from a large brooch which might therefore be first half of the first century.

5. 77:872 and 487, Area IV, F207/242, layer 1, (Grid 388W/714N and 387W/714N), depth 0.15 and 0.01 respectively. Two joining fragments forming complete brooch. Probably first half of the first century.

Colchester Derivative

6. 75:2601, Area I F1006, layer 1, (Grid 394W/688N), depth 0.12. The only type known so far which had probably developed completely by the Roman Conquest. Suggested date range AD 30-50.

Colchesters

Rough sequence is as follows: 75:1202, 75:40, 75:41, 77:2919, 75:378, 77:3422.

7. 75:1202, Area I, F1089, layer 1, (Grid 413W/697N), depth 0.06. Flat-sectioned bow, sharp re-curve at top, ?Augusto-Tiberian.

8. 75:40, Area I, surface, (Grid 398W/708N). Straight, facetted bow, sharp re-curve at top, large size. Probably pre-Conquest.

9. 75:41, Area II, surface, (Grid 446W/701N). Large size, ? late pre-Conquest.

10. 77:2919, Area IV, F53, layer 2, (Grid 467W/685N), depth 0.22. Smaller, just before Conquest/Conquest Period.

11. 75:378, Area III, B, surface (Grid 422W/656N). Large size, combination of zig-zag down bow plus decorated wings. Conquest period. (See also report by Maisie Taylor, below).

12. 77:3422, Area V, F624, layer 1, (Grid 413W/634N), depth 0.30. Smaller, squat broad bow not unlike form of Colchester Derivative. Decorated foot, late Colchester, Conquest Period /+.

The progression given is secure for first and last and impressionistic for the intermediates.

Birdlip

13. 75:328, Area I, B, surface, (Grid 423W/728N). Safest date is pre-Conquest.

14. 75:1283, Area I, F1055, layer 1, (Grid 405W/695N). Pin fragment, probably from a brooch.

Roman Coins from the Cat's Water subsite, Fengate
by Richard Reece

Two Roman coins were found on the B horizon surface, Area II, during the 1975 season. They are both copies of the Emperor Claudius I and can be described as follows:

75:38. Claudius I reverse showing Libertas standing left with a cap of liberty. Parts of the legends on both obverse and reverse are legible, but it seems unlikely that the full legends were engraved on the dies. All features correspond to the regular coin described in *Roman Imperial Coinage,* Claudius I, no 69, but the size, weight, portrait, and poor lettering leave no doubt that it is a copy of a regular coin.

75:39. Claudius I reverse showing Minerva walking left holding a shield and brandishing a javelin. Some lettering is visible on the obverse but much of the legend would have been struck off the flan. This is a moderate copy of the regular coin in *Roman Imperial Coinage,* Claudius I, no 66.

Two further points are worth mentioning; the likely date of these coins, and their significance on the site. Their date range is reasonably well known; paradoxically the fact that they are not regular coins, but copies, makes the date of their striking less certain than for regular coins, but their likely date of circulation more certain. Claudius I came to the throne in AD 41 and died in 54; his regular coins were therefore struck between those two dates. But his successor, Nero, did not strike any bronze coin from 54 to 64, the first ten years of his reign, and, just as the copies were probably struck to alleviate the shortage of bronze during the reign of Claudius, so they were even more needed in the next ten years. The likely date range in which they were struck is therefore 43 to 64. Regular coins, once struck remained legitimate coin for a considerable time, and though their striking date is often known to within six months, their date of loss may properly be given as at least a century. A regular coin of Vespasian, for instance, may well have been lost anything up to 130 years after it was first struck (69-79). Irregular coins were struck apparently only as coins of convenience, and, once regular coinage was available, it was used in preference to the rather obvious copies, which, it must be assumed, would no longer have enjoyed the official toleration once accorded to them. The flood of Nero's new coin of AD 64 to 68 therefore pushed the irregular coins from circulation, and, so far as I can see, the continued good supply of bronze under Vespasian and Domitian (69 to 96) effectively ended their useful life. It is often suggested that Claudian copies found in levels

172

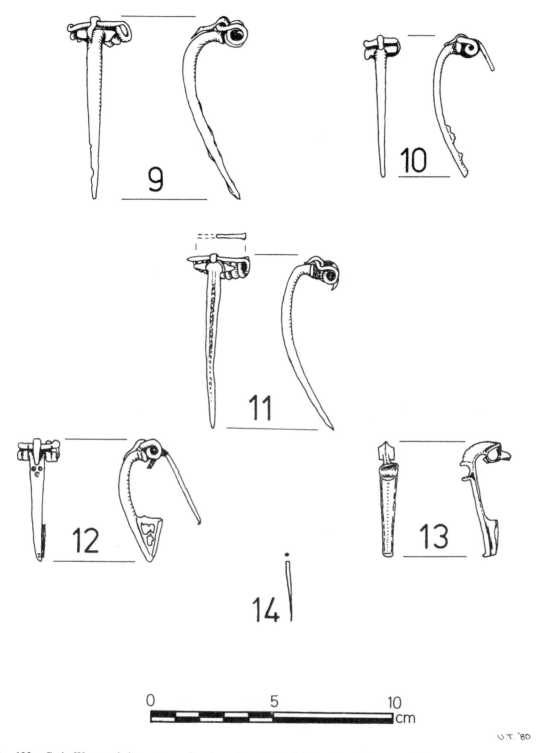

Fig. 122   Cat's Water subsite, copper alloy brooches. Scale 2:3 (continued from FIG 121).

173

of the second and even third century show that they had a much longer life than I have suggested. The point needs to be made that such evidence is only admissible when the levels are on sites which have no occupation before about AD 85. When levels on sites with a continuous history from the Claudian invasion onwards produce Claudian copies in later levels I suspect that this is much better evidence for the disturbance of early levels, than for the continued circulation of such coins. I therefore suggest that the presence of these coins at Fengate demands a date of, roughly, AD 50 to 75.

These coins therefore belong to the Late Iron Age, rather than the Roman period. The absence of Iron Age coins on the site, the presence of a later Roman phase, and the absence of coins from that phase, all give some reason for considering the implications of these two early Roman coins in a Late Iron Age context.

Firstly it is perverse, but interesting, to try to date the later Roman phase by its non-existent coin evidence. While coins of the early empire are reasonably common on British sites there seems to be a gap in supply of coin to the province from about AD 180 to 250. Some coin of these dates comes into Britain, and hoards are quite well known, but the average site has very few coins of this period. If a site were newly re-occupied from, say, 180 to 220, with no residual coin on the site, and no official supply easily obtainable, it is perfectly possible that a full and flourishing occupation could leave no numismatic traces. This is of course possible for any type of rural occupation which is below the coin-using threshold on the economic and social hierarchy. But it does leave open the interesting speculation that a site apparently otherwise flourishing, and dated by pottery towards the end of the second century, may be more accurately dated by *lack* of coins to the period 180 to 250.

The absence of Iron Age coins and the presence of a non-coin losing later Roman phase points up the presence of the two Roman coins at the end of the Iron Age. They are not on the site as part of an Iron Age coin use, and they must presumably be there because of immediate contacts with a coin using community, which at that period must be the army based at Longthorpe. The two coins therefore represent the meeting of the monetized Roman army and the non-monetized economy of the local Iron Age.

A Report on the Scientific Examination of the Refractory and Slag Fragments from Iron Age Contexts at Fengate. by Dr P T Craddock

Introduction

Six examples of refractory clay or slag, together with a possible crucible, were submitted to the British Museum Research Laboratory for identification. They were examined visually and by X-Ray Fluorescence to determine their composition.

Results of Analyses

Sample 1 (Storey's Bar Road Area I, P48, layer 1, Grid 73W/191N; depth 0.02m; 74:1366 — the gully of Middle Iron Structure 1).

This is a fragment of crucible with part of the rim surviving (FIG 123:1). It is partially vitrified around the rim edge showing that it was heated from above, as is usual with early crucibles (Tylecote 1976, 18; FIG 9). The white material on the inside of the crucible is tin oxide with a little copper and lead. Tin melts at only 232°C and thus a temperature sufficient to vitrify the ceramic would not be necessary. It is, therefore, more probable that the crucible had previously been used for melting leaded bronze for which a high temperature would have been required, and that it was subsequently used to melt tin.

Sample 2 (Cat's Water Area IV, F31, layer 1; Grid 446W/720N; depth 0.10m; 76;2525 — a Late Iron Main Drain).

This is a small vessel tentatively identified as a crucible (FIG 123, 2). However there is no evidence of vitrification of the clay. Furthermore the clay of the vessel contains shells, and would be most unsuitable for use as a refractory. The surface of the interior was analysed by x-ray fluorescence but there was no trace of non-ferrous metals. The vessel lacks any lip for pouring, and although of typical dimensions would thus be unsuitable as a crucible. It is therefore very unlikely that the vessel was made or used as a crucible.

Sample 3 (Cat's Water Area V, F445, layer 2; Grid 461W/655N; depth 0.15m; 77:1920 — Late Iron Age ditch near Structure 20).

This is a fragment of bloated partially vitrified clay with some evidence of glazing. The glazing was caused by the Potassium from wood ash (Potassium was detected in the glazing but not in the clay by x-ray fluorescence). Thus the clay had been subjected to an intensely hot wood fire. This rules out most processes; metal *smelting* requires charcoal not wood, and obviously pottery would not be fired to a temperature which would vitrify the clay. This leaves a crucible *melting* furnace for which a wood fire could produce a sufficiently high temperature as the most likely source of the fragment. Very similar fragments have been observed on other Iron Age sites, Highstead, Kent for example (Tatton-Brown 1977).

Sample 4 (Cat's Water Area V, F547, layer 1; Grid 400W/649N; depth 0.10m; 77:2744 — Middle Iron Main Drain).

This sample is described as daub. It has the vestiges of a circular hole in one edge, which would have suggested a tuyere hole in a furnace lining. There is no evidence of the intense burning that one would expect on a furnace wall fragment. Furthermore, the diameter of the hole is only 15mm which is far too small to accommodate a tuyere. This piece is therefore almost certainly a fragment of burnt daub from a hut.

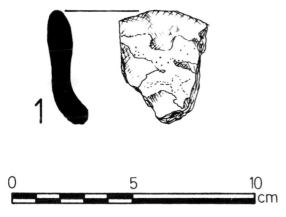
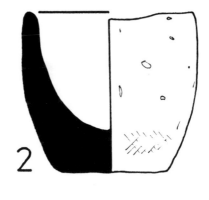

U.T.'80

Fig. 123 Illustrations to report by P T Craddock. I, crucible fragment (Storey's Bar Road, Area I, P48); 2, small pottery vessel, not a crucible (CW, Area IV, F31). Scale 2:3.

Sample 5 (Vicarage Farm, Area II, F14, layer 1 — Late Iron Pit).

This is a piece of slagged refractory. The piece is too large and thick to be part of a crucible, and this must be part of a furnace lining. The slag as a typical fayalite structure with only iron present, and thus the piece is presumably a fragment of a bloomery furnace for smelting iron.

Sample 6 (Padholme Road Area XI, F10, layer 4; 72:677 — large Middle Iron backfilled pit).

Sample 7 (Cat's Water Area IV, F569, layer 1; Grid 397W/635N; depth 0.24m; 77:3045 — ring-gully of Late Iron Structure 53).

Two samples of fayalite iron slag, both the product of iron smelting in a bloomery furnace. No trace of other metals present.

Conclusion

Recent excavations at a number of Iron Age sites (Gussage-All-Saints, for example — Wainwright 1979) has shown that iron *smelting* and bronze *casting* were regularly practised on quite small settlements. The finds of iron slag, furnace fragments and a crucible fragment, dispersed around Storey's Bar Road, Cat's Water and Vicarage Farm subsites, show that iron smelting and possible bronze casting were practised here also.

The tin stained crucible (Sample 1) fragment is an unusual and important find. Presumably the tin was separated in the crucible to be used alone, rather than to be mixed to form an alloy. The tin could have been cast into an artifact or used for tinning; although rare, tin artifacts are known (Glastonbury Lake Village), as are tinned bronze and iron objects (for example, a dagger from Spain in the British Museum — reg no 1922, 7-5,6).

Early Iron Age stake with dovetail housing joint from F1551, Cat's Water subsite, Fengate (FIG 124)
by Maisie Taylor

This stake (78:3521) was originally slightly longer than the piece that survived. Part of it originally extended above the water table and remained as a shadow in the section of the pit (FIG 89). The wood is a piece of oak, radially split from a log with a dovetail housing joint cut into it. The stake itself is a reused piece of wood and the housing joint was originally cut for some purpose which is now lost. There were no traces of any other wood in the pit. The joint still carries traces of the method of cutting in the form of a number of chisel marks across its face. There are one or two inferences that can be drawn from these marks. First, the chisel that was used must have been flat and quite narrow. Second, there is no evidence for sawing of the joint and, third, all other cuts appear to have been made either with a larger chisel or an adze. The stake was knocked into the gravel very firmly near the bottom of the pit with the joint facing the side. Presumably the stake, which was much longer, was associated with some structure or revetment higher up in the pit.

The antiquity of dovetail joints has been discussed elsewhere (Keepax and Robson 1978, 39) and they were certainly known in the classical world, but examples have survived only rarely. At the time of writing no other example has been found of a true dovetail from such an early period. McGrail (1978, FIG 82 and FIG 162) illustrates two double dovetail clamps but they do not have the true dovetail shape and are closer to the box joints which were known from very early times in the classical world.

The single radiocarbon sample (HAR 3196: 360±90 bc — see Appendix 12), although on its own, probably provides a secure date for the stake and the pot which was associated with it, and would place the finds in a period at which woodworking techniques were well advanced and sophisticated tools were available. This find should remind us of how much information is lost and how much the picture is distorted by the limited survival of organic material, even on sites such as Fengate.

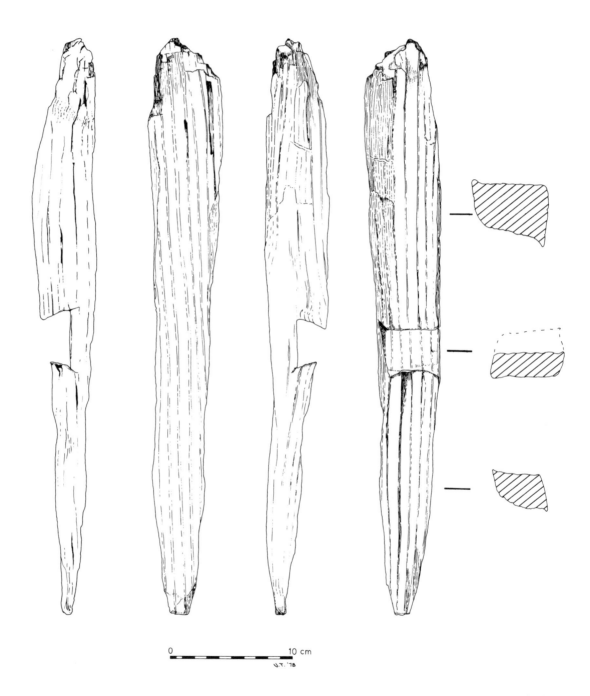

0   10 cm

Fig. 124   Oak stake from Early Iron Age pit or well, Cat's Water subsite, Area I, F1551 (see report by M Taylor). Scale 1:3.

CHAPTER 7: ROMAN FINDS

INTRODUCTION

This chapter is devoted to finds from deposits of Roman date from the Vicarage Farm and Cat's Water subsites. The report on pottery from Vicarage Farm was first drafted by Dr Wild in 1974, prior to the discovery of the large Cat's Water ditched settlement and livestock management complex. The quantities of pottery recovered from Cat's Water were too large to be managed by Dr Wild, who already had substantial commitments in the Nene valley, and so Dr Hayes, of the Greek and Roman Department of the Royal Ontario Museum, was approached; he kindly undertook the considerable task of preparing the Cat's Water pottery report, working in close co-operation with Dr Wild and Mr R Perrin of the Nene Valley Research Committee. It is hoped, therefore, that the Fengate Roman pottery reports will provide useful comparanda with the definitive final publications of the many sites in the Nene valley excavated by staff and members of the Nene Valley Research Committee.

Although to the east of Peterborough, Fengate does nevertheless lie in the Nene valley. It is traversed by a Roman Road — the Fen Causeway (FNG 3, chapter 3) — which is thought to link the Fenland to Durobrivae, the principal town in the region. Trade, or exchange with centres further up the valley, as evidenced by locally made grey and colour-coated wares, must have been considerable. There is abundant material evidence for habitation at Fengate during Roman times and although it was not urban or even suburban in character, it is nonetheless important, as there are some hints that the economy showed some signs of specialisation. If livestock were indeed important, as the evidence suggests, then neighbouring communities must of necessity have become closely involved, either as buyers and/or suppliers to the industry. In short, the relationship of the site to the region is a matter of considerable interest, but further speculation must await the publication of the many excavations that have lately taken place. In the meantime the reader is referred to Dr Wild's important recent publication which provides an excellent introduction to Nene valley Roman archaeology (Wild 1974).

Finally it remains to say a few words on the chronological relationships of the various Fengate Romano-British settlements. The earliest must be that represented by Period 5 at Cat's Water. For the purpose of this report this occupation is considered to be Late Iron Age, but chronologically it may well have lasted into the 50s or even 70s AD (see Dr Reece, Chapter 6). The next occupation is that at Vicarage Farm which, on pottery evidence alone, is thought by Dr Wild to belong

to the second half of the first century, but no later (features of the subsite are discussed in Chapter 1, above). The third occupation takes place on the Cat's Water subsite, for a rather short time, say, 40 years, centred on the third quarter of the second century. The fourth occupation is represented by pottery in Peterborough Museum and is discussed by Dr Hayes in Appendix 10. Much of the pottery is contemporary with the later (Period 6) Cat's Water settlement and a functional association seems probable. Some pottery is, however, later and this might represent renewed settlement or, just as probably, continuity. The finds in the Museum were made by Mr Wyman Abbott under salvage conditions and provenances must therefore be treated with caution; consequently we are never likely to know whether (a) the Abbott material really was associated with the Cat's Water Period 6 or (b) whether the later material represents continuity of occupation or resettlement. Taking a broad view, it would appear that Roman settlement at Fengate was a shifting phenomenon of short-lived episodes; we do not seem to have evidence for continuous occupation and, with it, 'settlement drift' (for example, Cat's Water Periods 4 and 5; see also Vicarage Farm — FNG 1, 17) that appears to characterise what we know of local Iron Age groups.

This chapter is largely composed of contributed reports. First, Dr Wild considers pottery from Vicarage Farm; this is followed by Dr Hayes on coarse pottery, Mrs Wild on samian ware, and Mrs K F Hartley on mortaria all from Cat's Water. The chapter concludes with a brief description of shale and copper alloy objects. The reader's attention is also drawn to Dr Hayes' Appendix (10) the significance of which is briefly considered above, and to the reports in the previous chapter by Dr R Reece and Mr D F Mackreth (on coins and brooches, respectively). A concordance list of Roman pottery numbers, is published on microfiche (Table M24).

REPORT ON A GROUP OF ROMANO-BRITISH POTTERY FROM THE VICARAGE FARM SUBSITE

by J P WILD

The following vessels were found in features 37 and 83 of the Vicarage Farm subsite, Area I (FIG 125):

1. Wide-mouthed jar with pronounced shoulder and wide cordon above it. The fabric has a medium-hard grey core with a few grits, and a smooth orange-buff surface inside and out. The vessel may be dated to the mid first century AD. It is derived from the Belgic

pedestal urn (*Swarling,* FIG XI, 6). Compare *Hardingstone* no 88. The type may have lost its cordon by the late Flavian period (see *Brixworth* no 132).

2. Jar in medium-hard grey fabric (Munsell *c* 2.5Y N5 'grey'). Internal and external surfaces are sandy, but there are few grits in the clay. The shoulder is decorated with grooves and the foot is well finished. The vessel can be paralled in a pre- or early Flavian context at Great Casterton (*Great Casterton* III, FIG 14, 4), but close parallels could only be claimed on the basis of fabric-correspondence.

3. Jar in medium-hard sandy fabric with fine grits. It has an organge core and internal surface, but a brown-black reduced exterior.

4. Jar in medium-hard fabric containing fine grits and some sand. Its surfaces are grey, but there is a darker grey core.

5. Jar in medium-hard light brown fabric (Munsell 2.5Y 5/4) with grey core. It has a weathered 'corky' surface showing vacuoles from which vegetable temper had been burnt out. The shoulder is decorated with grooves.

6. Jar with flared everted rim in medium-hard buff fabric (Munsell 10YR 5/4) with a light grey core. Its smooth surface is marked by a few small dark grits.

7. Waisted (carinated) bowl in buff fabric with grey core containing dark grits. Compare *Weston Favell,* FIG 2, 11 (mid first century AD), *Camulodunum* nos 211A, 212A (mid first century) and *Hardingstone* no 69.

8. Jar in medium-hard sandy fabric with ground limestone temper. It has a black-grey core and dark-grey surfaces. Form and fabric are reminiscent of *Hardingstone* no 99.

9. Jar in medium-hard fabric, grey to dark grey in colour with a lighter grey core. The temper includes a few large pieces of calcined flint, small dark grits and much coarse sand.

10. Bowl with sharp shoulder or carination in a medium-hard grey-brown fabric (Munsell 2.5Y 4/2) with a grey core. The fabric includes some ground limestone and large amounts of coarse sand. For a parallel see *Camulodunum* no 227, a form of which is found in the Neronian period, but continues into the second century.

11. Base of a calcite-gritted storage jar with a soft to medium-hard fabric, brown in colour.

12. Base of a small jar in a medium-hard dark grey fabric with a light grey to buff core. The fabric is tempered with fine sand.

13. Wide-mouthed jar in medium-hard dark grey fabric with a darker grey core and coarse sand temper.

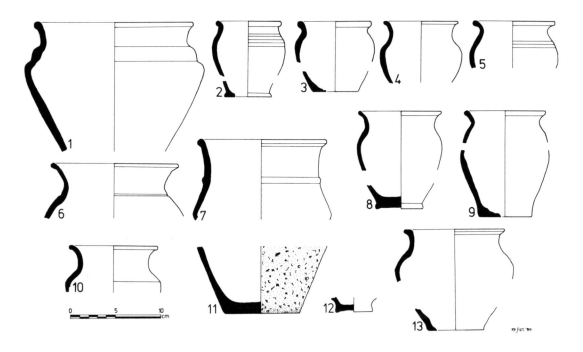

Fig. 125   Roman pottery from Vicarage Farm, Area I, F37 and 38 (see report by J P Wild). Scale 1:4.

Discussion

A date within the third quarter of the first century AD may be tentatively proposed for the deposition of this pit group. The cordoned jar (no 1) and the carinated bowl (no 7) may be paralleled in other pre- or early Flavian groups of pottery in south-eastern Britain. The forms and fabrics of the rest of the vessels from the pit are consistent with this dating. All of them, except perhaps the storage jar (no 11), are wheel-turned. The forms stem from the repertoire of the Belgic potter.

The composition of the group is interesting; for all, except no 7, are jars, probably kitchen ware. Dishes and platters of Gallo-Belgic type are absent, nor is there any early samian ware. On the other hand there is surprisingly little calcite-gritted ware. One would perhaps not expect the products of the Claudio-Neronian military potters at Longthorpe or the imported fine wares and amphorae used by the local garrisons to be represented at a native site on the Fen edge. The absence of grey-ware jars with slashed-cordon decoration and bowls with compass-drawn ornament copying Dragendorff Form 37 which were being made in the Nene Valley by the end of the first century suggests a *terminus ante quem* for the Fengate pit group.

I am grateful to Mr F M M Pryor for the fabric descriptions quoted above.

ABBREVIATIONS

Brixworth	Woods 1971
Camuludunum	Hawkes and Hull 1947
Great Casterton	Corder *et al* 1961
Hardingstone	Woods 1969
Swarling	Bushe-Fox 1925
Weston Favell	Bunch and Corder 1954

THE ROMAN POTTERY FROM THE CAT'S WATER SUBSITE, FENGATE

by J W HAYES

About 60kg of Roman pottery, along with some 20kg of brick and tile fragments, were recovered from the Cat's Water site. Almost all of this is of second-century date, and associated with the complex of rectilinear farm ditches. This material was mostly sealed by the flood deposit, in which occasional scraps of later Roman colour-coated ware and the like were observed; scarcely any sherds of Roman date occurred in the surface levels. Given the 'sealed' nature of the site, which offered the possibility of recovery of virtually all the pottery used and discarded on the site during the final farm occupation, plans were made for detailed location analysis of the sherds found, in the hope of isolating areas of specialized activity and illustrating the scattering of fragments of individual vessels through activities such as manuring. This could not, however, be pursued, since too small a sample of the ditches was in fact excavated to give a clear picture. However, the recording system was such as to permit such an analysis to be carried out in the future should wholesale excavation of the ditch-system be undertaken. Admittedly, the quantity of pottery found is already such as to make the identification of the scatter pattern of individual vessels (except for the less common wares) almost impossible to reconstruct.

The finds so far come mostly from a dozen or so concentrated dumps within the ditch-system, which in general were fully excavated. The pots include a good number of restorable vessels. No particular concentrations of specialized functional types were noted in any one spot; the normal jars and cooking-pots, in plain grey and calcite-gritted fabrics, everywhere predominate. Presumably this pattern is representative of the site as a whole. The quantity of organic material present along with the pottery in some of the deposits (eg Area IV F412) points to the dumping of general household refuse.

Roman brick and tile fragments were also found in several of the deposits, though nowhere in very large amounts, suggesting that the structures from which they came were not in the immediate vicinity. Since no remains of the foundations of brick-built buildings were encountered anywhere on the Cat's Water subsite, and the sealed nature of the Roman levels was such as to preclude the possibility of their total removal if such had existed, one is forced to conclude that the finds represent dumped debris from a farm complex situated on the higher ground towards the west, perhaps at the western end of the droveway visible on the air photographs. A number of old finds (mostly complete pots) from the western parts of the Fengate area, now in the Peterborough Museum (see Appendix 10) may tentatively be assigned to this presumed farmstead; several look similar in date to those from the present site. Thus the brick debris may have been carted down to the low-lying Cat's Water subsite to provide hard-core for temporary structures or areas of animal movement (*cf* the similar concentrations in modern farm gateways) in what must, in the later stages at least, have been a rather damp and soggy area.

Almost all of the Roman pottery can be assigned to a rather brief period in the second century AD, spanning the introduction of the local colour-coated ('Castor') wares(1); a date-bracket of *c* AD 140-170/80 may be suggested. The large deposits from F412 (partly published in *Durobrivae*, 6, 1978, 12-13; here republished in full) and from the pit F1561 (Grid 518W/600N), along with the finds from the main drain, F535, should belong to the end of this period, while those from another drain, F65 (which is cut into by F412), and a ditch, F460, should be appreciably earlier. The contents of ditches F55, 62 and 65, all rather similar, may (at least in part) go with the earlier groups. In all of these deposits, if we exclude the various calcite-gritted fabrics (partly Iron Age survival material), the classic smooth-bodied local grey ware (see below, Ware 1: 'Nene Valley Grey Ware') predominates, thus placing the assemblage later than the large deposit from Monument 97 at Orton Longueville(2). Various parallels occur with the published kiln-group from Sulehay(3), though this was probably not a major source of the present material. The 'early' groups are characterized by examples of the local grey-black 'imitation samian' ware (Ware 5), while the 'late' ones include early colour-coated wares. The decoration of the 'imitation samian' shows some peculiarities which set it apart from the general range of early second-century 'London Ware' types(4); diagonal strips of rouletting and patterns of small barbotine dots more appropriate to the 'poppyhead' beakers (here absent) may be noted, while compass-incised circle patterns seem to be lacking. The colour-coated sherds are rather variable in fabric, most commonly beige rather than white, and thicker and softer than the classic 'Castor' ware; only one or two scraps bear barbotine decoration. They should belong to an early experimental phase of the ware, before regular exportation had started. One colour-coated beaker from an 'early' group (F65, FIG 130, 64) may be from a non-local source. Samian ware is rather scarce, underlining the rural nature of the site; other demonstrably non-local wares are very rare. The few samian fragments seem consistent with the mid-second-century date here proposed; they include some East Gaulish pieces(5). Each of the two large 'late' deposits (F412, F1561) includes one near-complete samian vessel, in each case mended in antiquity — though this need not betoken a particularly long period of use.

Among the numerous grey-ware jars and cooking pots are some which retain marked Belgic features of form (eg FIG 129, 47; FIG 130, 66). Flagons (in off-white and buff wares) are poorly represented; most of these seem also to be in local wares. The few mortaria, though possibly all made locally, show a variety of grit treatments, in contrast to the uniform black ironstone gritting on later Nene Valley mortaria. Some fragmentary stamps occur on them(6). Among the calcite-gritted wares, the most distinctive is a class of hard thin-walled grey-black or brownish-black cooking-pots (with some related dishes and lids), of which several restorable examples occur: see Ware 6B below. This ware, presumably rather short-lived, seems not to have been noted before, and contrasts with the normal Nene Valley red products; it is perhaps an attempt by the makers of calcite-gritted ware, whose usual products were large storage-jars, to break into the market for cooking wares. Thicker calcite-gritted sherds, mostly red-bodied (see Ware 6A), are commoner than these at Cat's Water, but provide few useful forms — most should come from large jars, but a couple of large flat-bottomed tubs occur in F412 (no 36) and F62. These red-bodied wares include an indeterminate — but no doubt appreciable — proportion of Iron Age survivals, which, given the rough and friable nature of the ware, cannot be neatly distinguished from the products of Roman date. The evenly fired shell-gritted red wares with a layered texture and satiny surfaces found on other Nene Valley sites are here rare.

One mendable pot, found in isolation, seems earlier, and may possibly relate to the construction of the Fen Causeway. Material of the post-Conquest period is totally lacking, though finds of this period have been noted from the Vicarage Farm subsite (see report by J P Wild).

CLASSIFICATION OF WARES

1. 'Nene Valley grey ware' (here designated NVGW). Made from the same Jurassic clays as the later colour-coated 'Castor' wares, with reduced or part-reduced firing. Hard, slightly granular (or smooth) body, with few visible inclusions; core fired off-white to light grey (Neutral 7-9)(7), surfaces mostly steel-grey (Neutral 4-6), smoothed, with horizontal polished lines and sometimes shallow burnished patterns; some flaking at surface.

2. Smooth light grey ware with satiny surface texture. A variant of the preceding: body Neutral 7-8, with darker core and somewhat darker surface (ranging to Neutral 4). Uncommon: see 77 F412, no 6.

3. White ware: creamy-white, with some fine sand. Not common, mostly used for jars, while a buff-white variant is used for flagons, etc. The same ware (sometimes slightly more sandy) is used for the early Nene Valley mortaria.

4. Colour-coated ware (early variety). Body as 3 above (ie rather sandy); rare red inclusions. Slip mostly thin. Some sherds in smoother light brick-red fabric (approx Yellow/Brown A6) may represent a variant: see 77 F412, nos 21-22.

5. Dark grey-black ware, used mainly for imitation samian forms. The local version of 'London Ware'. Fairly smooth-bodied, with some fine sand and mica; near-black polished surface, and sometimes a near-black core. Varied decoration: combed, rouletted, stamped (sometimes in combination).

6. Calcite-gritted wares. Rather rough-textured, vesicular, with wet-smoothed surfaces; angular calcite grits, with some shell. Two main varieties:

6A. Reddish, fired irregularly to brown and grey; used for large thickish vessels. Similar to Iron Age wares, but wheel-made.

6b. Dark grey-black, hard and thin, with drab brownish patches on exterior; used mainly for cooking-pots.

In addition to these listed wares, small quantities of more or less sandy grey wares and a few scraps of oxidised fabrics, not readily classifiable (but probably mainly from local sources), are present. One or two pieces of the former (eg FIG 130, no 67) may match the Sulehay products. Imports are represented by small amounts of Central and East Gaulish samian, a few fragments of Spanish(?) amphorae, and perhaps the colour-coated beaker from F65, FIG 130, no 1. These are all briefly noted in the Tables which follow.

FREQUENCIES (BY WARES)

Tables 4 and 5 indicate the quantities of each ware in the main pottery-producing features, expressed by weight and by sherd count. Weights are to be regarded as approximate only (within a few percentage points); figures under 5g represent estimates. However, the degree of error should be roughly uniform. The isolated finds from other parts of the site add only 5% or so to the totals listed.

CATALOGUE OF DEPOSITS

The two large late deposits are listed first.

F412 (FIGS 126-128)

Already partly published in *Durobrivae*, 6, 1978, 12-13; the numbering adopted there is retained, with the addition of further material. Note: nos *4* and *11* were omitted in the preliminary publication (the reference there to no *4* in fact applies to *5*).

Almost all the pottery listed here comes from a concentrated dump (with brick fragments and organic material) in the lower filling of the ditch: site co-ordinates 457-465W/679-681N. Total weight of pottery from this location: *c* 24.67kg.

1. Samian dish. See report by Felicity Wild, below, F412 *A*.
2-5, 9-10. Jars in NVGW (=Ware 1). Steel-grey (core off-white), with horizontal polishing marks (indicated on *2*) and burnished patterns. *5* is misfired buff to brownish-grey. *2: cf* P J Woods, *Britannia*, 9, 1978, 199, FIG 48 nos 131-132, from Wakerley.
6. Jar in smooth light grey ware with darker core (Ware 2). Half-preserved; rivet holes. A second similar (same pattern): see half-profile at left.
7. Dish, NVGW (Ware 1). Chamfer at base. Horizontal spatula marks on inside of wall, transverse on floor.
8. Dish, Ware 5, imitating samian form 36. 'Sandwich' firing; parts accidentally burnt. Fine rouletting on floor.
11. Upper part (rim missing) of narrow-necked jar. undecorated ? *Cf* Sulehay (note 3 above) no 11.
12-13. Jar fragments in creamy-white ware (Ware 3); carbon remains on outsides.
14. Lid, Ware 5, fired light red (grey tint at core); carbon round edge.
15. Sherds of an early Nene Valley mortarium. Ware 3 (as *12*, but more sandy); red-brown grits.
16. Flagon neck in soft yellow-buff version of Ware 3.
17. Jar(?) rim, Ware 6A (rough, reddish, unevenly fired, with brown and grey patches.
18. Cooking pot, Ware 6B (brownish areas on exterior). One side preserved.
19-20. Lid and casserole, fragmentary, Ware 6B.
21-22. Sherds of colour-coated beakers. Light red clay,

reddish slip (Ware 4, variant). No slip on base of *22*.
23-26. Dishes (*24-25* are sherds) in early colour-coated ware (Ware 4). Dark slips. For rouletting on *23*, *cf* Sulehay no 13 (with plain rim and chamfer). Slip on *26* (brown) almost vanished.
(Not previously published:)
27. Jar fragment (one side restored), NVGW.
28. Jar fragment. NVGW, with speckled surface (black spots).
29. jar rim (one side restored). NVGW, fired white.
30. Dish (half), as *7* NVGW. Slight four-way spatula-marks on floor.
31. Jar rim (one side restored). Creamy-white ware (Ware 3, rather clean). One only; perhaps a survival.
32. Jar fragments. Ware 3: gritty creamy-white ware (Ware 3, rather clean). One only-perhaps a survival.
33. Dish rim (one side restored), colour-coated. Off-white, hard; dull sepia to black slip.
34. Bowl fragment (one side restored), Ware 5. Decoration: diagonal rouletted strips and stamped circles. See PL 19. (Perrin 1980, no 12). *Cf* a bowl from Grandford, March (T W Potter, forthcoming report, no 186).
35. Cooking-pot, fragmentary. Calcite-gritted ware (6A): reddish to buff at surfaces, greyish at core (rim blackened). Pitted surface, flaking. Shell(?) grits.
36. (Drawing by D A Gurney.) Large tub, Ware 6A (calcite-gritted, red). In many fragments; preserved weight *c* 3010g. Wall-profile partly restored, height approximate. Finger impressions below rim. Illustrated at ⅛ scale in FIG 131.
Also:
Nine other samian fragments, see report by Felicity Wild, below.
The following sherds come from a low level at 458W/680N and may belong to an earlier phase (*cf* 1977 F65). FIG 128.
37. Bowl rim (one side restored), Ware 5, imitating samian form Drag 37.
38. Neck of narrow-necked jar. NVGW.
39. Lid fragment. Hard grey-black calcite-gritted ware (Ware 6B).
A well preserved Belgic jar came from another part of the same ditch (at 462W/680N), indicating that at least some sections of the ditch are of Iron Age origin (FIG 101, no 5).

F1561 (FIG 129)

Small pit; filling more or less contemporary with 1977 F412. Weight of pottery recovered *c* 5750g. *47* and *51-53* come from the upper levels.
40. Samian cup, see report by Felicity Wild, below, F1561, *C*.
41-50. are in NVGW:
41. Jar, fragmentary. A second example, similar, from the same layer.
42. Base of slender jar/beaker (*cf 46*). Whitish variant ware.

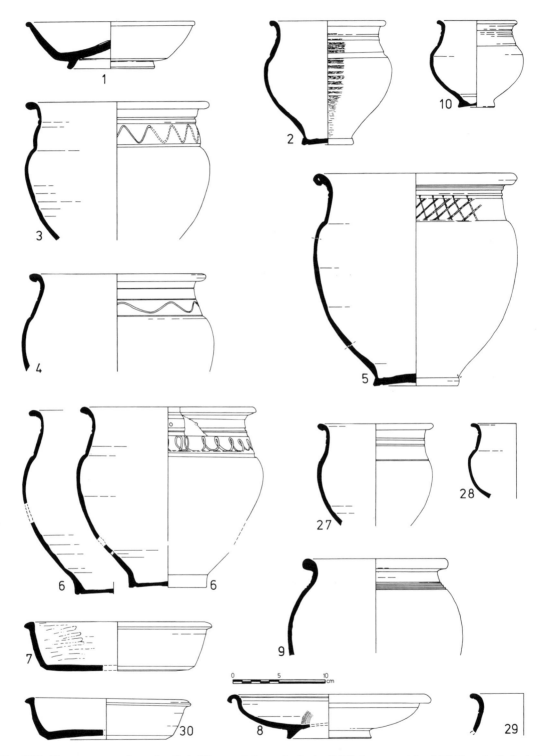

Fig. 126 Roman pottery from the Cat's Water subsite main drain, F412 (see report by J W Hayes). Scale 1:4.

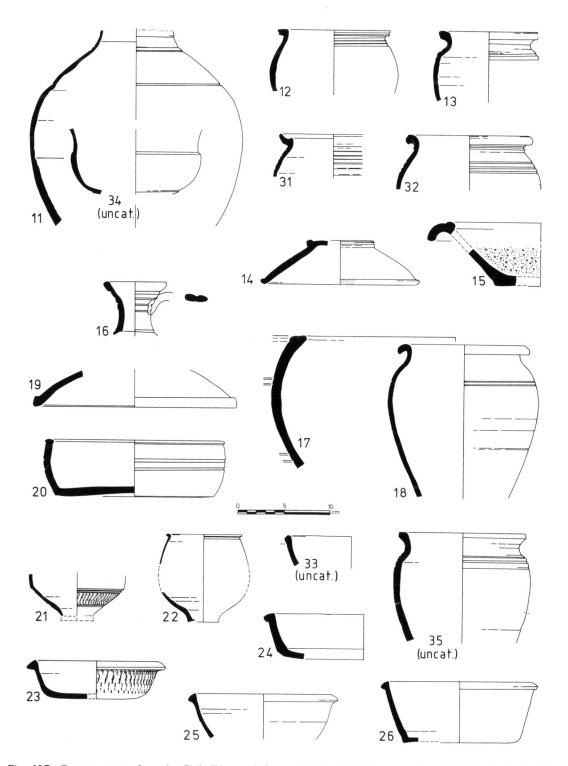

Fig. 127 Roman pottery from the Cat's Water subsite main drain, F412 (see report by J W Hayes). Scale 1:4.

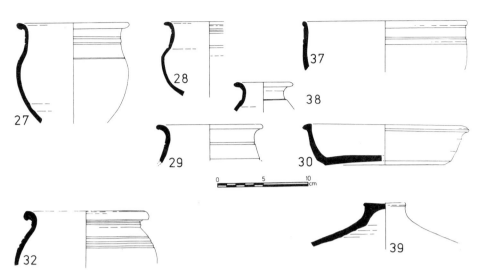

Fig. 128 Roman pottery from the Cat's Water subsite main drain, F412 (see report by J W Hayes). Scale 1:4.

43. Jar, near-complete (only one piece mended). Polished in horizontal stripes. Weight: *c* 283g.

44. Jar, near-complete (mended up). Polished surface as on *43*. 156g.

45. Lower part of jar. Similar, larger: one base.

46. Slender jar (lower parts).

47. Jar with bulging shoulders: two-thirds, in pieces. Variant ware: white core, dark grey inner surface, grey-beige exterior; not highly polished. Some carbon stains on outside of rim, etc. (Weight extant: *c* 270g).

48. Jar rim (one side restored). Soot on exterior.

49. Bowl rim (two sherds).

50. Dish (half). Some polishing-lines.

51. Jar rim, unclassified ware: light grey, soft, rather sandy (beige layer under surface).

52. Dish: fragments of wall and rim. Sandy light yellowish ware, blackened on outside. Shallow chamfer at base. Abraded.

53. Five sherds of a colour-coated indented beaker (or possibly a jug, drawn upside-down). Ware 4: cream, soft, with dull black slip. One side restored. About five indentations.

54. Base fragment of jug. Ware 4: as *53*, with dull black slip on outside only. Three loose sherds of rounded body. Similar ware: three sherds of beakers.

Other colour-coated sherds: dish fragment (red slip), chamfered base of dish (orange-red slip).

F535 (FIG 130)

Top layer of ditch fill at 465W/645N (layer 2 is Belgic). Late in sequence (*cf* 1977 F412).

55. Mortarium rim. (Est D at rim 24-25cm) Short hanging flange. Light orange to light grey, fairly sandy. (Layer 1 and surface.) For a base, see *59* below.

56. Small jar with frilled neck: four sherds. Ware 3 (off-white).

57. Fragments of narrow-necked jar. Soft grey, rather sandy. Layers 1 and ?2; possibly residual.

Also: a number of colour-coated sherds, including dish fragments with chamfered bases, and sherds of a small jar(?) with small barbotine blobs.

F818 (FIG 130)

Related to the preceding? Ditch fill finds from layers 2 and 3.

58. NVGW dish rim. Similar(?): one base sherd with chamfer.

59. Mortarium rim. Cream clay, tiny angular black (ironstone) grits. Loose base in F535 probably belongs.

60. Mortarium base. Cream clay with some black specks; very close-set angular red grits. Join from F649, layer 2.

61. Bowl, fragmentary (one side part-restored). Ware 4: cream, traces of black colour-coating on rim and flange.

62, 63. Dish fragments, Ware 4. Fugitive orange-red slip.

Also: one samian scrap, Drag 18 or 31.

F65 (FIG 130)

Fill of ditch cut by F412. Early phase.

64. Small bag-beaker, fragmentary. Light orange-buff clay (Brown/Yellow A6-7, tending to Yellow/Brown A6), with traces of lime and red specks; speckly matt red-brown to dark brown slip (Yellow/Brown A3-4 to Red/Brown B4). Probably not local ware (possibly Colchester?).

65. Various sherds of a deep dish in Ware 4 (profile reconstructed, one side restored). Rouletted (*cf* F412,

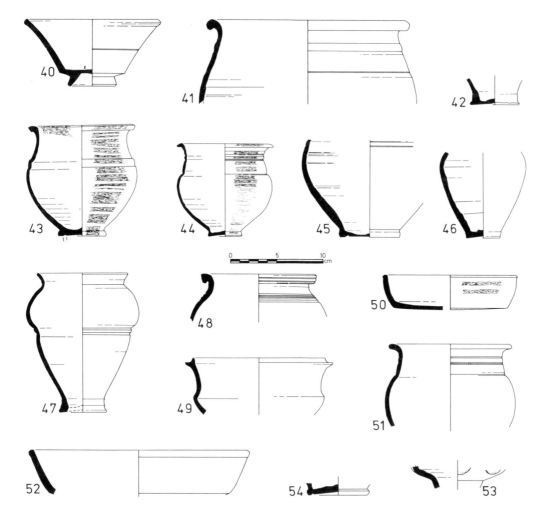

Fig. 129   Roman pottery from the Cat's Water subsite pit or well, F1561 (see report by J W Hayes). Scale 1:4.

23). Flaky brown slip.

66. Jar, fragmentary, Ware 5. Rough 'rouletting'.

67. Jar fragments in off-white ware. Slashes on bulge. *Cf* Sulehay no 9 (with more flaring rim).

68. Cooking-pot, Ware 6B. Near-complete (weight extant *c* 972g; possibly two vessels).

69. (Not drawn.) Bowl sherds, Ware 5. Strip of multiple rouletting on wall.

F460 (FIG 131)

All items from layer 2, in location 471-472W/654-655N. Early phase.

70. Rim sherds and base of bowl as Drag 37, NVGW; steel-grey surfaces. Five-line vertical combing. Two sherds from F459 may belong.

71. Jar: unbroken apart from parts of rim. NVGW. Weight 412g.

72. Fragmentary jar (rim lost). Ware 3.

73. Jar, near-complete (mended). Thin grey ware (unclassified), rather sandy, with a few large flinty grits; reddish tint at core, surfaces dark grey; wet-smoothed. Weight 353g.

74. Cooking-pot fragments. Light brownish to grey, calcite-gritted, rather soft (variant of Ware 6B).

F62 (FIG 131)

Ditch fill (Grid 453W/691N — 470W/692N). Material mainly early in character, but some links with the late groups.

75. Samian fragment, Drag 33. Lezoux ware?

76. Bowl, Ware 5, imitating Drag 37. Repeating impressed patterns. Near-complete; weight 252g.

77. Rim and wall sherds of dish, Ware 5, as Curle 15. Grey, smooth.

185

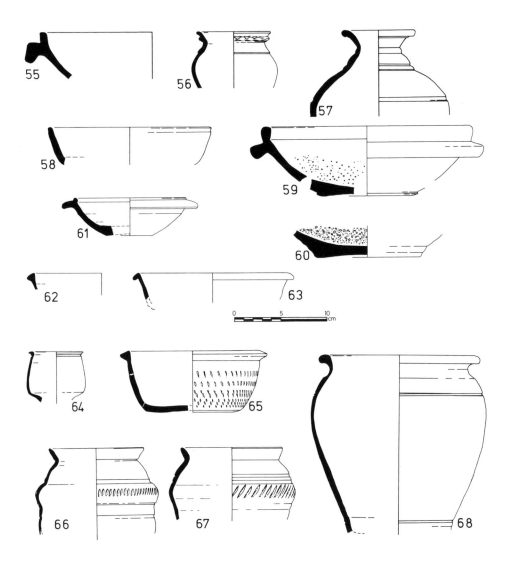

Fig. 130   Roman pottery from the Cat's Water subsite, various ditches: F535 (nos 55-57); F818 (nos 58-63); F65 (nos 64-68) (see report by J W Hayes). Scale 1:4.

78. Dish base, Ware 5.

79. Small bag-beaker, Ware 4: rim and wall sherds. Black slip.

80. Base of baggy rough-cast beaker, Ware 4. Good black slip, dark reddish to bronze in places.

81. Mortarium, Ware 3. One-third extant (single fragment), in fresh condition. Cream, some black specks; close-set angular grey and black grits. Weight 690g.

82. 'Cheese press', mended from two pieces. Perhaps Ware 5: orange to grey, slightly micaceous. Four small holes in inner hollow, one suspension-hole near rim.

Weight 215g.

83. Jar base, Ware 1 (NVGW). Groove on bottom.

84. Jar, partly restored (base lost). Oxidized version of Ware 6B: light red, burnt light grey on outside, rather soft, vesicular. Weight preserved 615 (+110?)g.

85. Lid sherds, Ware 6B.

86. Fragmentary tub(?) with squarish rim (*cf 36* above). Ware 6A. Weight preserved *c* 1545g. (Not illustrated). Also: a few possible sherds of vessels in F412 (including *7*), body fragments of a colour-coated jug/flagon (rouletted), fragments of a colour-coated 'Castor Box'(?) with rouletting.

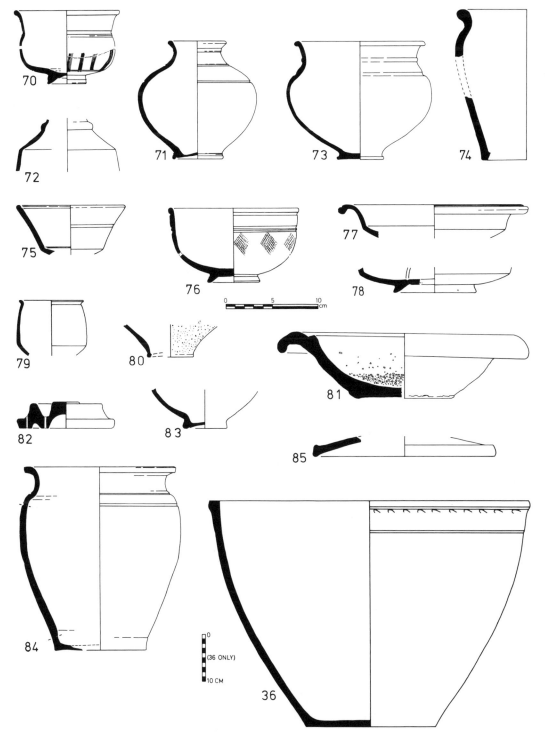

Fig. 131 Roman pottery from the Cat's Water subsite, various ditches: F412 (no 36 — note scale): F462 (nos 70-74); F62 (nos 75-85) (see report by J W Hayes). Note no 36 is a tentative reconstruction and partly stylised. Scale 1:4, except no 36.

F55 (FIG 132)

Ditch fill. 462W/686N (*94, 100* from 448W/714N; perhaps not main group). Contemporary with F62? *95* a surface find, rest from layer 1.

87. Bowl sherds, Ware 5, imitating Drag 37. Repeating impressed patterns.

88. Cup rim, Ware 5, imitating Drag 33.

89. Dish, reconstructed, imitating samian form Curle 15. Ware 5: smooth grey, polished. Traces of rouletting between grooves on floor, pattern stamp at centre. Iron staining on outside.

90. Rim sherd of small rough-cast beaker, Ware 4. Also: three sherds of similar beakers.

91. Jar fragment, NVGW (Ware 1).

92-93. Jar rims, NVGW. Burnished horizontal lines on *92*. Also: fragment of NVGW jar with double-bulge shoulder and row of slashes (*cf* Sulehay no 9).

94. Dish rim, NVGW.

95. Ring-necked flagon: rim sherd: White ware, slightly blackened, rather loose-textured (variant of NVGW?).

96. Flagon: body and neck, mended up. Ware 3; exterior fired grey to yellowish, with some soot patches. Stumps of a single handle. Weight 805g.

97. Jar fragment. Calcite-gritted ware, grey with reddish exterior.

98. Jar: rim and shoulder sherds. Ware as *97*.

99. Jar rim as *13* above. Ware 3.

100. Jar (or dish?) rim, Ware 6A.

1977 F443 (FIG 132)

Ditch (467W/670N-471W/654N). Fragments only.

101. Samian bowl, Drag 38 (early). East Gaulish? Layer 2 (possibly = F67). 464W/669N.

102. Flanged bowl rim, NVGW. Layer 1 (470W/656N)

103. Dish rim, NVGW. Layer 2 (location as *102*).

104. (Not drawn) Jar base, as *6* above; Ware 2. Layers 1 and 2 (468W/667N).

105. Rim of large jar. Sandy grey ware, reddish at surface, with small angular calcite grits. Layer 2 (469W/661N).

F649 (FIG 132)

Ditch fill. Rather scrappy.

106. Mortarium base fragment (one side restored). Cream, slightly sandy (Ware 3). Angular grits: grey, some brown ironstone (a few similar in clay of body). 429W/637N, Layer 1.

107. Rim, in clean white ware. 446W/640N, Layer 2.

108. Large jar: rim and shoulder fragments, in fresh condition. Light brown to grey (slight 'sandwich' firing), sandy. 446W/640N, Layer 2; loose rim and body sherds of same from F422, Layer 2, at 460W/657N.

Selected individual finds (FIG 133)

Samian:

109. Wall fragments, see report by Felicity Wild, F814, 2.

110. Rim sherd, Drag 32. Probably East Gaulish; ware similar to *101*. 1977 F422, 460W/657N, Layer 2. (Not drawn).

Colour-coated:

111. Dish: rim and base sherds. Thin orange-brown slip. Chamfered base. Rouletted. 1977 F457, 462W/650N, Layer 1 (rim), and 469W/652N, Layer 1 (base).

112. Rim of bowl/'Castor Box'. Ware 4, with black slip. 1978 F814, Layer 1 (CW Area VI, at 448W/610N).

Mortaria:

113. Rim and base fragments. Soft whitish ware with fine specks. Sparse small rounded grey and red grits. On rim, end of stamp: ...]ΛF F461-457, layer 1 (at 472W/652N).

Perhaps the same vessel: rim sherd (buff, sparse brown specks), with edge of stamp: C:Λ[... F65, layer 2.

NVGW Ware:

114. Dish rim, imitating Curle 15(?). 1976 F67 Layer 2 (480W/674N), and F459 layer 2 (475W/655N).

115. Rim of large jar. F67 layer 1 (480W/673N).

116. Base fragment of jar. F67, layer 2 (480W/673N).

Other coarse wares:

117. Jar (many fragments; profile partly restored). Thin, light grey, very sandy. Rivet-holes. Late 1st century type? 1977, Area VI, surface of B horizon.

118. Jar, fragmentary. Calcite-gritted ware, tan-brown, vesicular. Some blackening on outside. F457, layer 1 (469W/652N).

119. Cooking-dish, Ware 6B. Fragmentary. F461 layer 1 (472W/649N).

Amphora (FIG 133):

120. Rim of globular amphora (Dressel 20), Spanish. Sandy ware. F450, layer 1 435W/656N.

Fragments of similar amphora (body, stump of handle) in F814 (CW Area VI) 449W/609N level 3, and 461W/607N layer 1.

Toronto, Royal Ontario Museum, February 1980

NOTES

1. For the basic survey of Nene Valley wares, see B R Hartley, *Notes on the Roman pottery industry in the Nene Valley* (Peterborough Museum Society, Occasional Papers, No 2, 1960). Reassessment of finds from the Antonine Wall and elsewhere has led to the redating of the beginnings of the colour-coated wares; an initial date around AD 130-140 is now accepted.

2. Briefly noted by C Dallas, *Durobrivae*, 3, 1975, 26 (also *Britannia*, 6, 1975, 252); final report forthcoming.

3. J. Hadman and S Upex, 'A Roman pottery kiln at Sulehay near Yarwell', *Durobrivae*, 3, 1975, 16-18 with FIG 7. Pottery report by J P Wild.

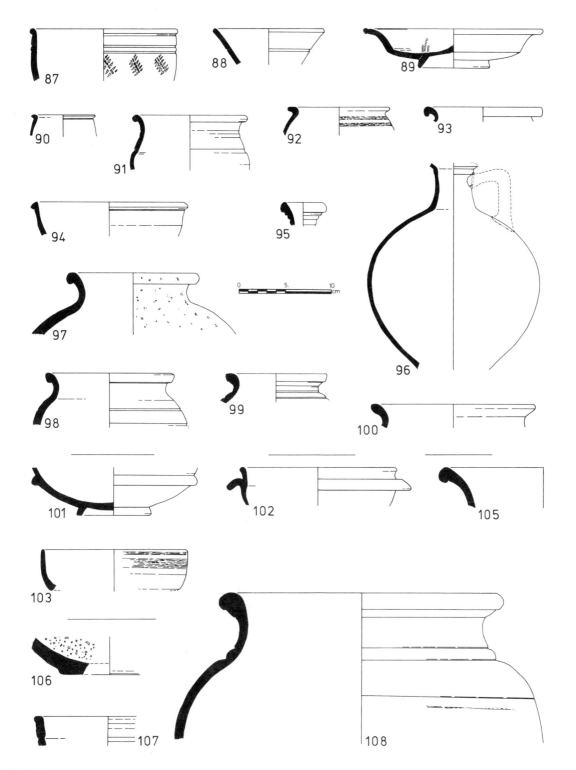

Fig. 132 Roman pottery from the Cat's Water subsite, various ditches: F55 (nos 87-100); F443 (nos 101-105); F649 (nos 106-108) (See report by J W Hayes). Scale 1:4.

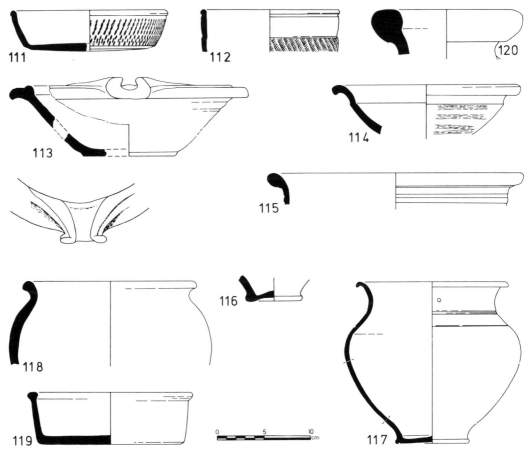

Fig. 133 Cat's Water, selected Roman pottery from various deposits — for explanation see text (see report by J W Hayes). Scale 1:4.

4. For these, see W Rodwell, in (ed P Arthur and G Marsh) *Early fine wares in Roman Britain* (*BAR* 57; Oxford, 1978) 225-92 *passim* (also G Marsh, in *ibid* 123-29).

5. I am indebted to Mrs Felicity Wild for these observations. Mrs Wild has provided comments on the individual pieces (see report below).

6. See comments below by Mrs K F Hartley.

7. Colour references here and in the Catalogue follow the Pottery Colour Chart compiled by the Study Group for Romano-British Coarse Pottery.

REPORT ON SAMIAN WARE FROM THE CAT'S WATER SUBSITE, FENGATE

by FELICITY WILD

Most of the samian from the site was recovered from the drainage ditches. With the exception of one small sherd, from the pit F1531, it was all of Central Gaulish manufacture and mid- to late-second-century date.

From the drainage ditches:
Area IV, F67
1. Form 37, Central Gaulish. Eight fragments, some joining, of a bowl in very worn and friable fabric. The decoration, barely distinguishable, shows the Actaeon (0.124) and tail of the sea-monster (0.54) (FIG 134, 1). Both types occur on work in the style of Doeccus. The Actaeon and a pedestal, possibly also occurring next to the type here, appear on a signed bowl (S and S, PL 149, 31). The ovolo and beaded border are in too poor a state to be certain of the detail, but are similar to those used by Doeccus. *c* AD 160-190. (76:2948)
Area V, F412
A group probably dating to the second half of the second century, comprising fragments from five examples of form 31 and possibly two of form 38, together with the following stamped bowls:
A. Form 31, Central Gaulish (FIG 126, 1). An almost complete bowl, rivetted together in antiquity with five lead rivets, and stamped PINNΛEΛ (FIG 135, 1). The die is die 1a of Pinna, who probably worked at Lezoux.

TABLE 4

CAT'S WATER SUBSITE; ROMAN DEPOSITS: POTTERY WEIGHTS (IN GRAMS)

	Feature	Samian	Colour-coated	Ware 5	Mortaria	Amphorae	Total pottery	Tile/brick
	Main ditch systems:							
'76	F 62	3	35	500+	690	—	7045	1960
	F 67	33	—	—	—	—	310	445
'77	F 65	—	41	150	—	138	3644+	—
	F 412	640	791	358 +250e	c.100	—	24675	7575
	F 422 (2)	3	—	—	—	320	603	270
	F 423 (3)	—	—	—	—	—	55	—
	F 457	—	53	—	—	—	2454	140
	F 459	—	—	5	—	—	381	400
	F 461	—	10	—	296	—	3045	590
	F 535 (0-1)	—	154	—	156	—	2363+a	805
	F 649b	—	—	—	215	—	779+b	—
'78	F 818 (1-2)	5	126	—	259	—	653	—
	(3)						32	
	Pit:							
'78	F 1561	164	102	—	—	—	5752	4710
	Various:							
'76	F 55	2	23	205	—	—	2226	5
'77	F 415 (1)	—	—	—	—	292	343+c	—
	F 428	—	1	—	—	—	14	—
	F 443	120	—	—	—	—	561	1455
	F 460						1307	—
	F 463	—	—	—	—	—	25	
	Totals	970	1336	1218 (1468)e	c.1700	750	56367+	18355

PERCENTAGES OF TOTAL POTTERY, BY WEIGHT

	F412	Other deposits	All deposits
Samian	2.59%	1.04%	1.72%
Colour-coated	3.21%	1.72%	2.37%
Ware 5 (imit samian)	1.45% (2.46%)d	2.7%	2.16% (2.6%)d
Mortaria	c. 0.4%	5.10%	c.3.02%
Amphorae	—	2.37%	1.33%
NVGW (Ware 1)	35.125%		
Ware 2	2.45%		
Ware 3 (all)	5.47%		
Ware 6A, 6 misc	31.07%		
Ware 6B	10.95%		

NOTES (to Table 4)

a) Plus c.500 g, probably pre-Roman
b) Plus a quantity of pre-Roman material (not weighed)
c) Plus 51g, probably Iron Age survivals
d) Second figure = oxidised lid 14 (presumably this ware)
e) Second figure includes no.14

Ditch deposits not weighed (generally small groups only):
76 F 69, 77 F433, 441, 522, 548/633, 78 F814, F 1530/1532

Individual vessels of interest:
- F 62 cheese-press 215g. (= no *82*)
- F 433 jar base, Ware 2 (as no *6*) 145g.
- F 450 amphora rim 378g. (= *120*)
- F 67 + 459 imit samian form in NVGW (no 114) 100+g
- 77 trench 8, jar (*117*) 506g preserved
- F 814 samian (*109*): 34g + 33g from F 67

TABLE 5

CAT'S WATER ROMAN DEPOSITS: SHERD QUANTITIES
Note: sherds of a single vessel are counted as one.
Accompanying figures in brackets indicate the number of individual sherds.

Deposit:	76-55	62	65	67	77-65(2)	412	443	457	459
Ware:									
Samian	1	2	—	1(8)	—	11 (19)	—	—	—
Colour-coated	7	5 (9)	—	—	8 (16)	25 (53)	—	1 (3)	—
Mortaria	—	—	1	—	—	3 (4)	—	—	—
Amphorae	—	—	—	—	1	—	—	—	—
NVGW closed shapes	53(59)	37(47)	2(3)	4(5)	22(23)	404(586)[e]	2	9(17)	2
NVGW open shapes	3	3	—	1	1?	18 (44)	2(7)	1 (8)	1
NVGW sandy variant	—	—	—	—	—	5	2	—	—
Ware 2	—	2(10)	—	—	—	2 (46)	1(7)	—	—
Buff/white (Ware 3) closed	4	6	1	—	12[c]	69 (98)[f]	—	2	2
Buff/white (Ware 3) open	—	—	—	—	—	2	—	—	—
Misc grey closed	2	8(20+)	3	1	7 (14)[d]	78(115)	8	17(73)	2
Misc grey open	—	—	2(3)	—	—	—	—	—	1
Misc sandy orange/red	8(11)	1 (2)[a]	—	—	—	4	—	—	—
Ware 5	3(16+)	7(32)	1	—	4 (9)	11 (34)[g]	—	—	1(2)
Ware 6(A)	31(32)	30(42+)	—	—	20 (28)	190(243)[h]	—	—	1
Ware 6B	10	18 (?)[b]	—	1	4(109)	121(226)[i]	1	4	1
Brick/tile present (*)	*	*	—	*	—	*	*	*	*
Totals (pottery)						943+ (1479+)			

a)   Cheese-press, no *82*
b)   Many fragments (not counted)
c)   Includes one light pink-buff sherd, in fairly clean fabric
d)   Includes Sulehay(?) jar, *67* (8 sherds)
e)   Number of individual sherds approximate only. Includes 18 sherds (none joining) fired white
f)   Number of individual sherds approximate only
g)   Includes red lid, *14* (6 sherds)
h)   Number of sherds approximate. Includes the 'tub', *36* (*c* 50 sherds)
i)   Includes lid and casserole, *19-20* (23 sherds)
j)   Includes one dish (9 sherds)
k)   Some may be Iron Age survivals

| | | | | 78- | | | Totals | |
460	461/457	461	535	814	818	1561	mended	unmended
—	—	—	—	1	1	2 (3)	19	35
—	—	1	22	1	2	5 (14)	77	128
—	1(7)	1	3 (6)	—	2	—	11	21
—	—	—	—	2+	—	—	3+	3+
2 (3)	4(?)ᵇ	31(37+)	31	2	6	59(148)	670	975+
—	—	—	1	3	2(3)	2 (4)	38	79
—	—	—	—	—	—	9	16	16
—	—	—	—	—	—	4	9	67
1 (6+)	—	—	16(19)	1	—	12 (13)	130	168+
—	—	—	—	—	1(3)	1 (7)	4	12
2 (?)	—	c.17(20)	9(18)	1	—	15	170	294+
—	—	—	—	—	—	—	3	4
—	—	—	—	—	—	5	18	22
1(12)	—	—	—	—	—	—	28	106+
2 (3?)	—	?ᵇ	40+ᵏ	—	4	7	326+	400+ᶠ
2 (?)ᵇ	—	c.24(45)ʲ	13+?9	—	4	41(44)	c.253	c.487
—	—	*	*	*	—	*		
							1775+	2817+

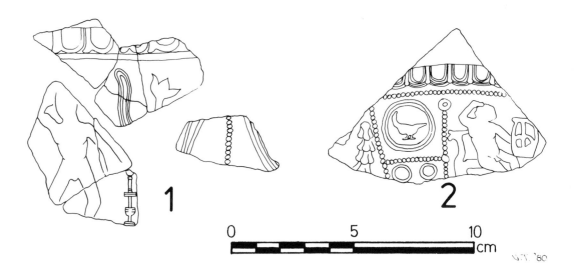

Fig. 134 Decorated Samian ware from the Cat's Water subsite: 1 (F67, layer 2); 2 (F814, B horizon surface). Scale 2:3.

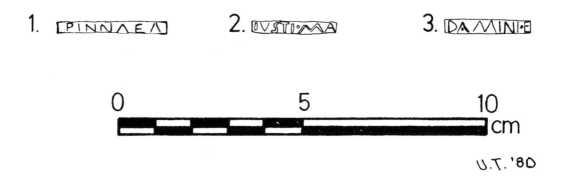

Fig. 135 Potters' stamps on Samian ware from the Cat's Water subsite: 1 (F412; reg no 77:1840); 2 (F412; reg no 77:1832); 3 (F1561; reg no 78:3103). Scale 1:1.

PINNΛEM may have been intended, but there is no room on the die for the second half of a symmetrical letter. This stamp was used only on forms 18/31, 18/31R, 31 and 33. Pinna's repertoire also includes forms 27, 38, 79 and 80. One of his other stamps occurs in a pit-group of the 140s at Castor. *c* AD 140-170. (77:1840)

B. Form 33, Central Gaulish, stamped IVSTI.MA, die 2d of Iustus ii of Lezoux (FIG 135, 2). This is one of Iustus's less common stamps, also recorded on form 31R. His decorative style and his plain forms (such as 79 and 80) put him in the range *c* AD 160-190. (77:1832)

CWV F65 and CWV1 F818 both produced one fragment of form 31, Central Gaulish, and of Antonine date.

Area VI, F814
2. Form 37, Central Gaulish. Two fragments, not joining, but showing the same ovolo and probably from the same bowl. The decoration is in panels, with the festoon (Rogers 1974, F16); bird (0.2298) in medallion over circles, and Apollo (0.84) (FIG 134, 2). The style is that of Criciro, who used the ovolo, the tongue of which is often stamped over the edge of the preceding impression (S and S, FIG 33, 2), and bird. The festoon occurs on pieces in his style, as well as on those of his slightly earlier associates, the Sacer-Attianus group, who used both types. *c* AD 135-170.

Area VI, F961
Two fragments, probably from the same dish of form 18/31, Central Gaulish, Hadrianic or Antonine.

Area X, F1574
Form 18/31R, Central Gaulish. Hadrianic or early Antonine.

From the pit F1531 (Grid 500W/600N)
Form 27, South Gaulish. Flavian or Trajanic.

From the back-filled well, F1561 (Grid 518W/600N)
C. Form 33, Central Gaulish, showing rivet-hole and stamped DΛMINI.F (FIG 135, 3). The die is die 4a of Daminus, who worked at Lezoux, although this particular stamp has not been found there. This is only the third example of this stamp to be recorded, all on form 33. No site dating for Daminus has appeared yet, but he regularly made forms 79 and 80. A mid- to late-Antonine date is therefore fairly certain. (78:3103)

ACKNOWLEDGEMENT

I wish to thank Miss Brenda Dickinson of Leeds University for providing the notes on the potters' stamps. The potter and die numbers are those due to appear in Mr B R Hartley's forthcoming *Index of potters' stamps on samian ware*.

ABBREVIATIONS

O — F Oswald, *Index of figure types on Terra Sigillata*, 1936-7

S and S — J A Stanfield and G Simpson, *Central Gaulish potters*, 1958

Rogers 1974 — G B Rogers, *Poteries sigillées de la Gaule Centrale* I, Gallia Supplement XXVIII

A REPORT ON MORTARIA FROM THE CAT'S WATER SUBSITE, FENGATE, PETERBOROUGH

by K F HARTLEY

CW Area IV, F62
(R-B main drain, same as F1288)
Almost half of a well-worn mortarium in hard, white, fine-textured fabric with a very little quartz tempering; abundant, dark-brown to black trituration grit. The fabric is typical of mortaria made in the Mancetter-Hartshill potteries of Warwickshire. Manufacture can be attributed to *c* AD 130-165. Layer 1; 76:2720

CW Area IV, F65
(R-B main drain)
A flange fragment in hard, white fine-textured fabric. The fragmentary stamp preserves part of SA[, from one of the dies of Sarrius who worked in the potteries at Mancetter and Hartshill in Warwickshire. His stamps are common on the Antonine Wall and a closely dated example, *c* AD 155/160, is recorded from Verulamium (Frere 1972, 378, no 35 and FIG 146, no 35, for a stamp from the same die as the Fengate one). A date of AD 135-170 will certainly cover his activity. Layer 2, depth 0.02m; Grid 462W/689N; 76:3151

CW Area V, F412
(R-B main or yard drain)
A body fragment in off-white fabric with bluish grey core, possibly burnt. Made in the Midlands, perhaps in Warwickshire. Later than *c* AD 120. Layer 2; 77:5472

Similar fabric to 77:5472, immediately above, also possibly burnt. A fragment from a mortarium made in the Midlands with the period AD 120-170. Layer 2; 77:AA

CW Area V, F535
(R-B main drain, same as F649, below)
Pink fabric with blackish grey core, probably intended to be cream. Insufficient survives of this unusual mortarium for it to be attributed to a specific workshop with any confidence, but its origin is likely to have been in the Oxford region, or Northants, probably in the fourth century (but note, if this is a Verulamium product it would be AD 160-200). Layer 1; 77:2599

CW Area V, F649/818
(same as F535, above)
Two body fragments burnt while still joined, but after the vessel was broken. Probably made in the Mancetter-Hartshill potteries in Warwickshire after AD 120. F649 layer 2, depth 0.20m; Grid 452W/641N; 77:3828 joins F818 layer 2, depth 0.34; Grid 689W/639N; 77:3828

CW Area V, F649
(same as F535, above)
A burnt body fragment in cream fabric with mixed

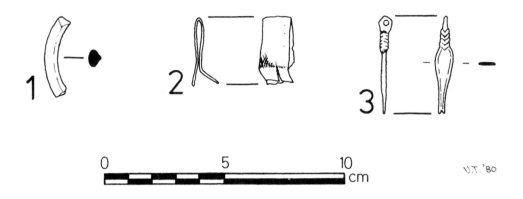

Fig. 136 Cat's Water subsite miscellaneous Roman finds: 1 (F1172); 2 (F649); 3 (F53). Scale 2:3.

red-brown and brownish black trituration grit. Made in the Midlands. Undateable. Layer 1, depth 0.02m; Grid 429W/637N; 77:3802
CW Area VI, F818/535
(R-B main drain)

A burnt mortarium in slightly sandy cream fabric, probably made in the Oxford potteries in the fourth century. F818 layer 2, depth 0.35m; Grid 489W/639N; 78:421

Body fragment, possibly from the same vessel. Burnt (unfortunately all the trituration grit has fallen from both these fragments). F535, layer 1; 77:2600

MISCELLANEOUS FINDS (FIG 136)

SHALE/LIGNITE
1. Fragments of lathe-turned shale or lignite bracelet, dia (ext) 50mm; smooth finish with rounded ext section and two slightly concave int facets. Compare Verulamium (Frere 1972, FIG 57 no 222); Maiden Castle (Wheeler 1943, type 21). Cat's Water Area II,

F1172, layer 2; Grid 423W/667N; depth 0.38m. 75:2256

COPPER ALLOY
2. Narrow (120mm) strip of bronze sheet folded double at centre. Very slight trace of shallow punctate impressions parallel to edge. Strap end? Cat's Water Area V, F649, layer 2; Grid 457W/645N. 77:3248
3. 'Nail cleaner', *L* 39mm; *B* 7mm. Extensively corroded. Many parallels from Roman contexts (eg Hall and Nickerson 1968, FIG 16, no 8; Frere and St Joseph 1974, FIG 32 no 75; Hawkes and Hull 1947, PL C, nos 34 and 36; Wheeler 1936, FIG 45 no 49). An especially fine local example from Lynch Farm, Orton Waterville has been published recently (S C Hawkes 1976). The Cat's Water nail cleaner was found high in the filling of an undoubted Period 5 ditch. The layer in which it was found had a high clay content and was subject to cracking in dry weather; it is most probably, therefore, intrusive. Cat's Water Area V, F53, layer 1; Grid 460W/682N; depth 0.25. 77:1866

INTRODUCTION

This chapter will summarise the principal results of the Fengate project and will set them in their wider contexts. It is divided into six parts. Part I considers the environmental and depositional background to the site and Part II assesses the original aims and objectives of the project and the way these have been subsequently modified. Part III is a synthesis of the main results, in chronological order, in which emphasis is accorded to the Iron Age and Roman periods that have formed the main topic of this report. Part IV attempts to set the results of the excavations in their regional, national and wider contexts; this is followed by Part V which considers practical lessons learned from the project and suggestions for future research. Finally, Part VI is a descriptive index to the major topics of this and previous reports; it is organised chronologically and makes particular reference to specialists' contributions.

PART I, THE ENVIRONMENTAL AND DEPOSITIONAL HISTORY OF THE REGION

INTRODUCTION

Any attempt to summarise the current state of research into the archaeology of the Fen-edge must inevitably be incomplete as, happily, much important work is still in progress. The intention here is not to provide a brief history of Fenland research (for which the reader is referred to Phillips 1970, iii-viii; 1980; Godwin 1978, chapter 5; Salway 1970), but rather discuss work which has tried to relate Fenland to its surroundings, marine, upland and 'island'.

Attempts to understand the archaeology of Fenland have always relied heavily on the succession of geological and vegetational deposits that fill the Fen basin. This sequence gives both an absolute chronology and, at the same time, a picture of contemporary environments, which often varied sharply over quite short distances.

SEDIMENTS OF THE FENLAND BASIN, THEIR FORMATION AND CHRONOLOGY

The formation of Fenland deposits has already been briefly discussed in the Second and Third Reports. The review that follows is more comprehensive in its treatment, but does not claim to be complete; little attempt, for example, has been made to discuss the minutiae of sea level changes, as Fengate is located well inland from the present Wash shoreline and does not seem to have been directly affected by many of the numerous marine transgression and regression episodes that dictated the location of prehistoric settlement nearer the coast. The discussion will be limited to the southern Fenland of the North, Middle and South Bedford Levels; the Lincolnshire Fens are, as yet, less intensively studied than those to the south and it is still inadvisable to attempt a correlation of the archaeological and sedimentary sequences in the two areas. It should nonetheless be recalled that the Lincolnshire Fenland is approximately as large as that of Cambridgeshire, Norfolk and Suffolk put together (for a discussion of Iron Age coastlines in south Lincs see Simmons 1977; 1980).

The Post-Glacial, or Flandrian, deposits with which we are concerned formed in a natural depression in the underlying Jurassic and Cretaceous strata; these, in turn, were considerably affected by glacial action, both by deposition of boulder clays and by the scouring out of sometimes substantial channels (for the general solid and glacial geology see Chatwin 1961; Haines and Horton 1969; for smaller specific areas see the introductory chapters of Seal 1975 and Hodge and Seal 1966). The western edge of Fenland, between Sleaford to the north and Huntingdon to the south, is marked by a series of glacially-filled valleys which cut the underlying surface Jurassic deposits (usually clays and mudstones). These valleys 'appear to drain towards a major valley which formerly carried the combined waters of the present rivers Ouse, Nene, Welland and their tributaries, together with parts of the drainage of the Trent' (Gallois 1979, 3). The formation of these valleys has been the subject of considerable discussion; Sparks and West (1965, 38) considered the buried Cam valley to have formed during the Gipping (Wolstonian) glacial; more recently Gallois (1979, 22, with refs) has postulated a pre-Glacial, fluvial, origin for the glacially-filled valleys of Fenland. The Fenland basin, then, at the close of the Pleistocene period was traversed from west to east by the filled-in valleys of a dendritic river system, and its naturally undulating floor was further corrugated by the action of ice and water combined with the deposition of gravels and boulder clay. It is the gently undulating Pleistocene gravels and boulder clays, together with more erosion-resistant outcrops of underlying Mesozoic deposits, that form the low 'islands' and 'peninsulas' that protrude through the Flandrian peats that surround them. These areas of flood-free dry land within the Fen were an important focus for the activities of ancient communities.

Turning to the river valleys of the Peterborough area which drain into the Fen, that of the river Nene has recently been studied by Horton *et al* (1974, 53ff). Three terraces were distinguished, the results of successive down-cutting and aggradation, of which the oldest is the Third; Fengate is located on the First Terrace. These terraces are of probable Pleistocene origin, the Third overlying the undated but interglacial deposits of the Woodston beds (*ibid,* 53). A *terminus ante quem* for the most recent (First) terrace is provided by two radiocarbon dates from overlying alluvium, the oldest of which is mid-third millennium bc (*ibid,* 57). The earliest Fengate C-14 dates are, of course, of approximately similar age. Cryoturbation structures in the Third Terrace beds at Woodston suggest glacial conditions (*ibid,* FIG 13).

North of Peterborough the Fen-edge is marked by deposits of Fen Gravel. The origin of these deposits is not entirely clear, but they 'may have formed as alluvial fan deposits largely dating from the Second Terrace (Nene and Welland) times...' (*ibid,* 58). A braided river channel within the (?) First Terrace Welland gravels at Maxey yielded pollen spectra of Ipswichian I and II type and a molluscan fauna of similar age (R G West and C A I French, pers comm). The river channel was overlain and cut by fluvial deposits of Devensian age.

The Flandrian or Recent deposits of the southern Fenland were first analysed and described in a comprehensive manner by Skertchly (1877), who distinguished (*ibid,* 3) three categories of land: Gravel-land (discussed above), Peat-land and Silt-land. This monograph, and his later collaborative work with the antiquarian S H Miller (1878), laid the foundation for all later research into the Recent deposits of the Fens. Organic and inorganic deposits in the Fenland basin depend for their formation on the height of the contemporary sea-

level: the mean high water level (MHL) will dictate the location of both human settlement and tidal deposits; the mean sea level (MSL) will have an important bearing on the outfall of rivers draining into the Wash. Thus, a constricted or inadequate outfall will lead to a backing-up of fresh water in the Fen rivers and, frequently, to flooding inland. Fengate is situated on the landward margin of the modern Fenland and would consequently have been sheltered from the immediate effects of minor episodes of marine transgression or regression. The discussion of sea levels that follows will, therefore, confine itself to major episodes only.

The retreating Devensian ice caused locked-up water to be released and sea levels to rise. This, eustatic, rise in MSL was such that ten thousand years ago the North Sea was approximately 40-50m below modern Ordnance Datum. The initial rise in MSL was strong, but it gradually levelled-off after about 4000 BC (Jelgersma 1966, 64-6) In very approximate terms, the MSL at 3000 BC would have been about -5m OD; by AD 0 it would have been about 2m below the modern level (*ibid,* FIG 7). The continuous eustatic rise in North Sea MSL was, in general, smooth and without sudden sharp fluctuations (*ibid,* 60ff). Variations in sea level — transgression and regression episodes — are, however, visible over periods of shorter duration than the whole of the Post-Glacial considered by Jelgersma. A more recent curve of MHL in the Netherlands (Louwe Kooijmans 1974, FIG 14, curve E) showed a continuous rise, but one subject to short-term fluctuations or changes in rate. All the reasons for the fluctuations are still not properly understood, but long-term factors, such as the epirogenetic subsidence of land-masses, glacio-isostatic upheaval (in marginal areas) or hydro-isostatic subsidence (in flooded areas) must contribute to the overall picture (ibid, 65-7; Willis 1961, FIG 1). Recent research into English sea level changes shows a similar, continuous, rise to that observed in the Low Countries, but the detailed pattern of transgression and regression is still not altogether clear (Akeroyd 1976).

Current evidence suggests that peats had begun to form in stream beds, and other low-lying parts of the Fenland in Boreal times; samples from the well-known peat-filled stream channel at Shippea Hill gave radiocarbon samples (Q-587 and Q-588) of 5650±150bc and 6660±160bc; the second sample was taken 0.3m below the first (Clark and

Godwin 1962). These lower peats — which are separated from the Upper Peats by the Fen or 'Buttery' clay — began to form somewhat later nearer the western Fen-edge. Samples from the outer rings of oaks growing in the basal forest layer (probably inundated by rising ground water), from Wicken Fen (Q-129 and Q-130) and Queen Adelaide Bridge, Ely (Q-589) gave dates of 2430±140bc, 2655±110bc and 2545±120bc, respectively (Godwin and Willis 1961). Nearer Fengate, a sample of wood grown *in situ* in a *Cladium* fen (which overlay muds above the basal clay), gave a radiocarbon date (Q-406) of 3008±130bc. This sample was taken from Site E at Holme Fen, some six miles south of Fengate (Godwin and Vishnu-Mittre 1975, 575). The Lower Peat at Holme Fen shows a transition from alder fen woods to a wet *Cladium* (sedge) — *Phragmites* (reed) fen which in turn gives way to a bog flora, particularly in deeper parts of the Holme Fen basin and beneath the shell marls of Whittlesey Mere, in which *Sphagna* predominate. Holme Fen sits in a protected 'bay' on the extreme western Fen margin, and the stratigraphic succession observed there is probably not altogether typical of the open Fen or Fen-edge; the Fen Clay, for example, was unable to spread over the area due to the presence of a substantial raised bog *(ibid,* FIG 22).

The Lower Peat is separated from the Upper Peat by Fen Clay (Godwin 1978, chapter 7). The latter deposit was the result of a substantial marine incursion. This episode, or series of episodes, was widespread over most of the southern Fenland and is particularly thickly deposited in creeks and river channels that would originally have drained into the Fen Clay lagoon (the extent of the Fen Clay is shown in R Evans (1979) FIG 4, 'limit of Fen Clay creeks'). The silt-filled watercourses show-up clearly in wintertime against the more quickly eroded dark peat soils; these 'roddons' were studied by the late Col Gordon Fowler before the last war (see G Fowler 1933; 1934). Today, aerial photography of winter bare earth can reveal the full extent and complexity of the creek network (see, for example, Phillips 1970, PL ix; Seale 1975, maps 1-4). In this regard it is of special interest to note that the absence of Fen Clay on aerial photographs of the Cat's Water south of Eye strongly suggests that the stream is not following a natural course (R Evans (1979) suggests that its canalised course is probably Saxon in date). Further, the absence of a substantial roddon north

of Whittlesey indicates that the original course of the Nene lay south of that 'island' (R Evans 1979; this contrasts with earlier opinions of Fowler and Godwin — see Godwin and Clifford 1938, 375-7; but recent work (1982) by D N Hall (pers comm) again throws the matter open for discussion).

Foraminiferal analysis of the Fen Clay shows it to have been laid down in semi-salt estuarine conditions above most of the then existing peats of the southern Fenland (Macfayden in G D Clark 1933, 289-92; Godwin and Clifford 1938, 387). At Shippea Hill, the foraminifera from the Fen Clay deposited in lagoons outside the river channel were less marine in character than those from the tidal silts of the roddon proper (Macfayden, *ibid,* 291-2). The Fen Clay tends to thin out and disappear towards the Fen-edge, but towards the sea the deposits become much thicker, and are interlaminated with silts, subtidal, tidal and creek deposits (see, for example, Gallois 1979, FIG 19 and note that 'Barroway Drove Beds' = Fen Clay).

The date of the Fen Clay has been established by radiocarbon; these dates indicate that it is contemporary with the Calais IV transgression of the Western Netherands (Louwe Kooijmans 1974, 75). Willis (1961) has dated the top of the Lower Peat beneath the Fen Clay at St Germans, near the sea — where the Clay is 'about 12 feet thick' — to 2740±120bc (Q-31). Wood peat from a deposit which immediately post-dates the Fen Clay at Wood Fen, just beyond the maximum landward extent of the marine incursion, gave a date of 2245±110bc (Q-544) (Godwin and Willis 1961). The transgression reached its maximum extent about 2500bc and subsequent regression was rapid; peat growth resumed about 2200bc, inland, and about 2000bc nearer the sea (Willis 1961, 373). As with the Lower Peat, deposition of the Fen Clay appears to have started earlier in low-lying river channels, such as that at Shippea Hill where brackish water spread up the valley at about 2700bc (Godwin and Willis 1961, 72; Clark and Godwin 1962, 21).

Turning to the Upper Peat (Godwin 1978, chapter 8), we have seen that the Fen Clay was unable to penetrate the Holme Fen basin because of the presence there of a raised bog. During the first half of the second millennium conditions were sufficiently dry to allow access onto the growing peats on a seasonal, or even, perhaps on a year-round basis (Godwin 1941, 262, 300). Fen woods could develop in these drier conditions, and Sir

Cyril Fox's well-known distribution maps show Late Neolithic and Bronze Age artifacts to be widely spread over the peatlands (Fox 1923, map III; Fox, Burkitt and Abbott 1926, 'prehistoric map'). It should be borne in mind, however, that the contexts of these stray finds are seldom adequately understood or recorded, and there are strong reasons to suppose that the peats in which they lie are not contemporary with the objects themselves (D N Hall, pers comm; Pryor 1980c). Towards the end of the millennium the climate became wetter and there is evidence that natural Fen drainage could not cope with the additional rainfall, with the result that freshwater flooding took place (FNG 3, FIG 86; for general discussion of climatic deterioration see Chapter 5, pt 6). It is of interest to note that there is evidence beyond Holme Fen for the formation of *Sphagnum* dominated oligotrophic plant communities, probably as part of a raised bog (Godwin 1978, 68). As conditions became wetter it is probable that acid peats spread over wider areas. Although Upper Peat soils have been seriously eroded through wastage there is increasing evidence for acidity in the Cambridgeshire Fenland (D N Hall, pers comm) and it would appear probable that previous studies may well have underestimated the part played by acid bog species, even in a region, such as the southern Fenland, where groundwater is base-rich (Walker 1970, 135-7). Indeed, the Upper Peats immediately abutting the tidal silts and clays of the Silt Fen 'Marshland' soils around the Wash are highly acidic (R Evans and D N Hall, pers comm), and it is remarkable that these later tidal deposits did not cover an area as extensive as that penetrated by the earlier Fen Clay incursion. The answer probably lies in the presence of a continuously growing raised bog which prevented significant marine penetration inland. Robert Evans (1979, 10) notes that 'by the end of the Roman period it is likely the tidal marshes and creeks had silted up about 1.8 to 2.4m OD, with the adjacent peats at a similar level'. The earliest date is provided by Q-547 (1355±120bc) which came from the top of the Upper Peat immediately below the overlying silt, with shells of *Cardium edule* still *in situ;* this would suggest that there was no erosion between the growth of the peat and the deposition of the silt (Churchill 1970, 134). It is probable that this phase of sedimentation is the same as Dunkirk 1 in the Western Netherlands (Louwe Kooijmans 1974, 9, 75). Louwe Kooijmans (*ibid,* 75) accounts for the absence of

Dunkirk 0 (which follows Calais IV — our Fen Clay — and precedes Dunkirk 1a in the Dutch sequence) deposits in the Fenland, by suggesting that thick accumulations of Fen Clay prevented their spread further inland (for recent work on sea level changes see F H Thompson (1980)). This may indeed be the case, but recent evidence would now suggest the additional possibility of an intervening raised bog. David Hall (1982, pers comm) has recently suggested that large areas of apparently 'Iron Age' marine soils were actually deposited in the Bronze Age. These newly recognised soils (for example around Thorney) provide a good East Anglian contender for the illusive Dunkirk 0 transgression phase (Louwe Kooijmans in F H Thompson 1980).

The gradually forming silt Fen and the extremely wet peat were uninhabited throughout most of the first millennium BC. A glance at Fox's (1923) map of Bronze and Iron Age finds from Cambridgeshire should illustrate this point well; there can be little doubt that the increasing ground wetness of the first millennium BC did not favour settlement in such low-lying areas (Godwin 1968, 11; Lamb *et al* 1968; Pryor 1976a; FNG 3, Chapter 5, with refs.). We will see, in Part IV below, that increasing ground wetness during the first millennium had significant effects on the organisation and layout of many river valley Iron Age settlements in Britain. This is not the place to discuss the causes of this increased ground wetness, but climate (rainfall and storm tides), sea level, alluviation (perhaps reflecting agricultural intensification and latterly the introduction of winter cereals) must have played a part.

The peat Fens were never permanently settled in antiquity, although it is highly probable that they were extensively exploited for hay, grazing and winter protein. Roman settlement of the southern Fenland around the Wash was confined to the tidal silts and clays of the later (Iron Age) marine transgressions. Most Roman settlement is confined to land between 7 and 25 feet above OD. The earliest Roman settlement on the silts can be dated to the latter part of the first century AD, and as Iron Age finds are absent on these soils, the earliest Romano-British occupation must provide a *terminus ante quem* for their deposition. Salway (1970, 8-9) sees the newly deposited silts 'ripe for settlement' after AD 50 (for a recent sumary of the Roman Fenland see Wilkes and Elrington 1978, 47-56).

Returning to the Peat Fens, there is good

evidence from the extreme Fen-edge, and now from Fengate (Cat's Water subsite), for freshwater flooding in the third century AD. Conditions on Cat's Water were extremely wet, both in very late Iron Age times and during the brief Romano-British re-occupation of the subsite in the latter part of the second century AD (see Appendix 2). Thick clay deposits are found in all upper fillings of ditches belonging to the full Romano-British phase of the Cat's Water settlement. A *terminus post quem* for these clay deposits is provided by pottery which is dated by Dr Hayes (Chapter 7) to AD 140- 170/80. This dating is supported by coin and other evidence. The ditches had accumulated perhaps 50% of their filling before the flood clay deposition began, and this would accord well with the picture along the southern Fen-edge, where ceramic evidence again suggests that flooding took place between about AD 230 and 270 (Bromwich 1970, 122). Similar floods are known from Somerset and other parts of southern Britain, although it is now doubtful whether they need necessarily be attributed to a 10 to 20 ft rise in MSL (Cunliffe 1966, 72).

The Fen-edge at Fengate does not appear to have been settled at all extensively in Saxon and Medieval times, and this may well be partly due to environmental factors. There is evidence for a transgression between about the fifth and seventh centuries which caused partial, if not nearly complete, abandonment of the 'Marshland' settlements around the Wash (Hallam 1970, 47-8). This transgression phase may be correlated with Dunkirk II in the western Low Countries (Louwe Kooijmans 1974, table 1). Settlement was able to resume on the silts and lower-lying lands of the Fen-edge (but not apparently at Fengate) from the seventh/ eight centuries until the onset of wetter conditions in the late thirteenth, fourteenth and fifteenth centuries (Hallam 1961, 155; Darby 1940, 155ff; Ravensdale 1974, 156). These later Medieval wet episodes probably correspond with Dunkirk III on neighbouring parts of the Continent. It should however be emphasised that these marine episodes were mainly confined to the Wash littoral; there are no marine deposits later than the Iron Age in Cambridgeshire (D N Hall, pers comm). Finally, the cutting of the canalised parts of the river Nene, by Bishop Morton of Peterborough *c* 1478 marks the beginning of the modern, drained, Fenland landscape in our area (Darby 1956; Hills 1967; L E Harris 1952).

PART II, AIMS AND OBJECTIVES

INTRODUCTION

The first season of excavation at Fengate was in the summer of 1971, but most of the project planning took place in the preceeding winter. The years 1969 to 1972 were important to the development of archaeology in the Peterborough area: 1969 saw the publication of the RCHM survey of the antiquities in the area threatened by the development of the New Town (C C Taylor 1969) and the Nene Valley Research Committee's full-time archaeological Unit was set up in 1972. Despite its name, Fengate was initially seen more as a complex of sites within the Nene valley — an eastwards extension of such important sites as Lynch Farm, Orton Longueville, Ferry Meadows, Orton Waterville and Woodston (all of which are discussed more fully below and in Chapter 6). The site's role within the Fen-edge was only properly appreciated after the discovery in the winter of 1972/3 of the main second millennium BC enclosure system. The tendency to view the site more in terms of its Nene valley than Fen-edge context is still apparent in the Discussion of the First Report (FNG 1, 29-38). Subsequent reports, including this, place far greater emphasis on the Fenland.

RESEARCH PRIORITIES

Our understanding of Fenland archaeology is growing rapidly, largely thanks to the work of David Hall and the revived Fenland Research Committee. The straightforward depositional succession of Lower Peat, Fen Clay, Upper Peat, Upper Silts is now seen to be more complex than had hitherto been believed and, in particular, local variation and modification of the general succession (as witnessed by, for example, Holme Fen (Godwin and Vishnu-Mittre 1975)) is seen to be of great significance. Thus the tendency to understand the site more in terms of the Fenland than the Nene valley is given emphasis by the direction of current local research. Attempts were made in Chapter 6 to correlate the Cat's Water Iron Age pottery assemblage with material from similar sites in the middle and upper Nene; it is hoped that these tentative efforts will acquire greater credibility when the material from the intervening lower Nene valley is published. The same also holds true for those important sites in the lower Welland valley which, when published, will help link Fengate to its important (and also unpublished!) Lincolnshire counterparts. In the meantime, the reader must make allowances for the Fen-bias which is so evident in this and previous Fengate reports.

Richard Bradley has provided a characteristically lucid discussion of the Fen/Fen-edge transhumance cycle within its British context (Bradley 1978, chapter 4). Other papers which have mentioned Fenland transhumance patterns include Coles' summary of Cambridgeshire prehistory (Coles 1975). Discussing Fen-edge sites (*ibid,* 121) Professor Coles notes that 'The settlements perhaps represent summer occupation, where water springing from the chalk was available and where the Fens provided grazing for cattle before the rains made them unsuitable'. A more colourful account of Fen transhumance was provided by Lethbridge (in Leaf 1935, 126-8); his discussion of C S Leaf's detailed field survey of Beaker and Early Bronze Age material near Mildenhall concluded that 'the settlement sites show that the solid ground on the Fen margin was the place usually chosen...in order that the firm "horse fen" could be grazed in summer'. He concludes that there is evidence for 'some kind of seasonal migration of cannibal communities, which included herdsmen and hunters. Possibly they lived in a state of war with similar bands. We may imagine clusters of skin tents, savage bowmen, and shaggy cattle, and perhaps preserved heads hanging from the tent poles.'

Chapter 5 of the Third Report considers transhumance in detail and there seems little point in reiterating that discussion here. Suffice it to say that prehistoric transhumance in the context of the Fenland is not a new idea, but it remains a concept of fundamental importance to any explanation of the various prehistoric Fen economies.

Many discussions of the prehistoric Fenland have arisen from Fen 'island' or rodden excavations, of which the best known are those by Professor Clark at Shippea Hill. 'Island' sites were particularly well suited to the excavation techniques of the '30s, '40s and '50s: they were of manageable proportions, were of strictly limited extent and, above all, provided ideal vehicles for the multi-disciplinary projects involving archaeologists, palynologists and quaternary geologists that were then being organised at Cambridge. The 1960s, however, saw the widespread use of the 'open-area' excavation techniques that were first employed extensively on wartime and post-war gravel sites (for example Grimes 1960a; Atkinson *et al* 1951). Initially the open areas were cleared by gravel companies or contractors, and the archaeologists then had to extract what they could from these often unsatisfactory surfaces. Techniques, however, improved and the stripping of large areas soon became possible (see, for example, Wainwright and Longworth 1971; Wainwright 1979; M U Jones 1974).

The original focus of the Fengate project was, as we have seen, towards the Nene valley; it was supposed to use techniques of open-area excavation to find areas of prehistoric occupation, in order to tie the site into its regional setting and to provide cultural and palaeoenvironmental contexts for the original, pre-War Wyman Abbott Fengate finds. The actual techniques of open-area stripping at Fengate took two seasons to evolve; this was due (a) to the soft and variable nature of the subsoil which gave rise to mechanical problems and (b) to the great thickness of the overburden — the results of freshwater flooding and recent nightsoil deposition. By the time that these techniques had been evolved, the significance of the site's Fen-edge location was more fully appreciated. A result of these developments was the season of 1973, in which techniques associated with small-scale Fen 'island' sites (techniques such as the three dimensional plotting of all artifacts) were combined with large scale open-area excavation.

The season of 1974 was the first to combine the two approaches with any success: a *pro forma* recording system was introduced (see Appendix 1) and greater emphasis was given to the study of waterlogged material and ditch sedimentation. The study of the relationship of Fen to Fen-edge in the various later prehistoric and early Roman periods was now a possibility; but the dispersed settlement pattern was such that excavation had to be carried out on a large scale.

The justification for this cost-intensive approach lies in the nature of the site: Fen 'islands' concentrate within certain limits, generally defined today by the distribution of peats. The Fen-edge, on the other hand, is a ribbon of land where occupation is known to have been intense at various times and in various places. The location of Fen-edge settlement must depend on a number of factors of which the size and condition of local human and animal communities, and the state of the neighbouring upland or Fen are among the most important. Given these constraints, it is not surprising to discover that Fengate, although intensively occupied at various times, does also have large areas that were apparently unsettled. These 'negative' or 'off-site' areas are of great significance to the understanding of ancient settlement patterns and provide the single most important justification for the open area approach.

Finally, although more research on the topic is required, it is probable that most prehistoric settlement of the smaller Fen 'islands' was intermittent. The available evidence suggests that they were mainly occupied in the drier months of summer perhaps during hunting forays, or as part of seasonal cattle drives etc. The Fen-edge, on the other hand, may be occupied seasonally or all-year round; it may also be exploited for grazing or agriculture, either intensively or extensively. Although the Fen-edge lacks the finite physical boundaries of the 'island', and although it is often less readily tied into the known Fen depositional sequence, it does provide an important, contrasting, comparison with the deeper Fen sites. Put succinctly, the aim of the Fengate project, from 1973 onwards, was to explain the observed sequence of prehistoric and Romano-British culture in terms of contrasting archaeological and depositional succession of the Fenland; direct comparisons with the hinterland were made difficult by the interpolation of modern Peterborough.

PART III: SYNTHESIS OF RESULTS

INTRODUCTION

This section is an attempt to draw the excavations together. it must be emphasised, however, that this is not the final word on the site: explanations offered here are bound to alter significantly in the light of future research.

Absolute dates for the site are provided by 36 C-14 dates which are shown schematically in FIG 137. The plus/minus figures given by the issuing laboratory have been used, without the increases suggested by R M Clark (1975). 'Approximate Calendar Dates' are intended as a rough guide only: precise date ranges in years BC should not be extrapolated from this diagram without following the procedures, and using the curves provided by Clark.

It has been found convenient to describe the

succession of prehistoric culture at Fengate in broad, essentially economic, phases, these phases are not absolute, and there was probably much overlap between them.

FIRST PHASE: CONSOLIDATION (LATE 4th/EARLY 3rd MILLENNIA BC)

This is the earliest phase for which we have good evidence at Fengate. Unlike Ballynagilly, for example, where there is abundant palaeo-environmental and archaeological data from earliest Neolithic times (ApSimon 1976), Fengate does not have features that could antedate the Middle Neolithic (compare, for example, ApSimon 1976, 15). The excavated sample of the site currently lacks any archaeologically recognizable 'pioneering or adaptive phase', to use Whittle's (1977, 15) terminology. Presumably such a phase of Clearance and Consolidation (Bradley 1978) would have taken place in the millennium or so preceding c 2445 bc when the Padholme Road house was in use. Certainly, this is the sequence at Shippea Hill (Clark and Godwin 1962), and there seems no good reason to doubt a broadly similar series of events at Fengate. The solution to this problem lies in the lower peats of the neighbouring Fen, especially in those areas (such as the buried soils beneath the banks alongside Morton's Leam) where the earliest peats have been protected from wastage by accumulations of alluvium or made-ground.

Absolute dating evidence is sparse. The Padholme Road house gave two C-14 dates of which the earlier (GaK 4196) is most probably residual. The younger date (GaK 4197) is more reliable, but unfortunately is on its own, and consequently must be of limited value. Artifacts are, however, of some use in obtaining at least a relative date: the re-used collared jet bead, Group VI axe-fragment, blade-based flint industry and Grimston/Lyles Hill pottery indicate an earlier Neolithic date, but any greater precision is impossible (I F Smith 1974, FIG 13; H S Green, above, Chapter 4; Whittle 1977, 219).

The first phase of occupation that is archaeologically attestable represents the consolidation of the earliest Neolithic presence. Direct evidence for the economy is sparse and speculation has already been considerable (for example Pryor 1976a; FNG 3, 178-80), but small-scale settlement involving nuclear family units spaced around the developing Fen is indicated. These groups probably subsisted

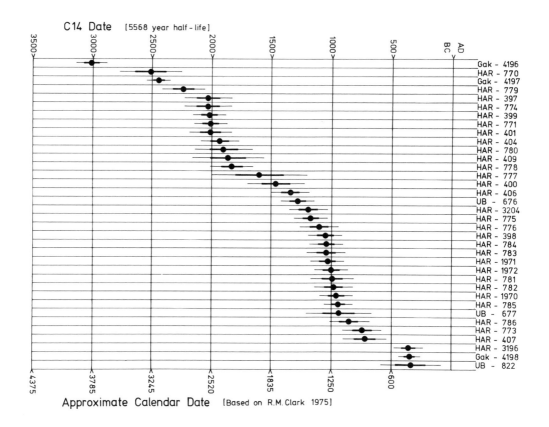

FIG 137 Radiocarbon dates from Fengate. These are plotted at one (thick line) and two (thin line) standard deviations on either side of the mean (filled circle). A brief key to the various sample numbers is given below; HAR nos 3196 and 3204 are described in Appendix 12, below, and the remaining samples are listed in Appendix 12 of the Third Report (with refs to FNG 1 and FNG 2). Dates below are listed from left to right in the figure.

Lab. No.	Date bc	Provenance	Notes
GaK-4196	3010 ± 64	E Neo house, Padholme Road	Probably residual
HAR-770	2510 ± 130	Grooved Ware pit outside main settlement	Small sample
GaK-4197	2445 ± 50	E Neo house, Padholme Road	Dates the house
HAR-779	2240 ± 90	2nd mill ditches f and i, Newark Rd.	Terminus post for ditch
HAR-397	2030 ± 100	Grooved ware settlement, Storey's Bar	Dates the settlement
HAR-774	2030 ± 100	Pit associated with 2nd mill ditches	Dates early use of system?
HAR-399	2020 ± 70	Grooved Ware settlement, Storey's Bar	Dates the settlement
HAR-771	2010 ± 70	Grooved Ware pit outside main settlement	Dates the pit
HAR-401	2010 ± 90	Grooved Ware settlement, Storey's Bar	Dates the settlement
HAR-404	1930 ± 80	Grooved Ware settlement, Storey's Bar	Dates the settlement
HAR-780	1900 ± 120	Around burial, 2nd mill ditch f	Dates early use of system
HAR-409	1860 ± 150	Grooved Ware settlement, Storey's Bar	Dates the settlement
HAR-778	1830 ± 90	2nd mill ditch 8, Newark Rd	Terminus post for ditch
HAR-777	1600 ± 200	2nd mill ditch b, Newark Rd	Small sample
HAR-400	1460 ± 120	From Collared Urn crem, Storey's Bar	Dates barrow phase of Neo ring-ditch

HAR-406	1340 ± 80	Stake in quarry pit, Storey's Bar	Dates late use of pit
UB-676	1280 ± 70	2nd mill ditch 3, Padholme Road	Dates late use of ditch
HAR-3204	1190 ± 80	2nd mill ditch F862, Cat's Water	Dates abandonment of ditch
HAR-775	1170 ± 70	2nd mill ditch n, Newark Rd	Dates associated settlement?
HAR-776	1100 ± 80	2nd mill ditch b, Newark Rd	Dates associated settlement?
HAR-398	1050 ± 70	From well lining, Storey's Bar	*Terminus ante* for Grooved Ware settlement
HAR-784	1040 ± 70	2nd mill ditch 9, Newark Rd	*Terminus ante* for ditch?
HAR-783	1040 ± 80	2nd mill ditch 9, Newark Rd	*Terminus ante* for ditch?
HAR-1971	1030 ± 70	'Industrial Area', Newark Rd	*Terminus ante* for ditch?
HAR-1972	1000 ± 70	'Industrial Area', Newark Rd	*Terminus ante* for ditch?
HAR-781	990 ± 90	2nd mill ditch 9, Newark Rd	*Terminus ante* for ditch?
HAR-782	980 ± 80	2nd mill ditch 9, Newark Rd	*Terminus ante* for ditch?
HAR-1970	960 ± 70	'Industrial Area', Newark Rd	*Terminus ante* for ditch?
HAR-785	940 ± 60	2nd mill ditch 9, Newark Rd	*Terminus ante* for ditch?
UB-677	935 ± 135	Well in ditch 1, Padholme Rd	*Terminus ante* for ditch?
HAR-786	850 ± 80	From 'quarry pit', Storey's Bar	Post-dates abandonment of 'quarry-pit'
HAR-773	790 ± 80	From posthole cut into ditch e	*Terminus ante* for ditch
HAR-407	720 ± 90	From 'quarry pit', Storey's Bar	Post-dates abandonment of 'quarry pit'
HAR-3196	360 ± 60	Stake in bottom of well, Cat's Water	Dates last lining of well
GaK-4198	350 ± 46	Wattle lining of well, Padholme Rd	Dates last lining of well
UB-822	340 ± 125	EIA pit, Vicarage Farm	Dates infilling of pit

on a combination of horticulture and livestock husbandry, with seasonal exploitation of the peats, especially during the months of winter when protein-rich foods were harder to obtain. The settlement pattern is essentially one of extensive, non-nucleated 'log-cabin' occupation (Coles 1976), but in secondary woodland and on terrain that may well have been cleared a number of times previously, during the primary (landnam?) clearance phase.

The wetter conditions of the later fourth and earlier third millennia BC could not have rendered forest clearance by fire particularly effecive. Alder requires conditions far too wet to favour regular clearance by fire, willow must be destroyed below ground level to avoid regeneration and in drier areas shrubs such as hazel would have been proof against sporadic fire clearances (clearance by fire is discussed in Buckland 1979, 13ff). Assuming, for the purposes of argument, that the earliest Neolithic Fen-edge economy was indeed based on livestock and landnam horticulture (or

'long fallow' agriculture — Boserup 1965), it is not improbable that the second, consolidation, phase of the Neolithic also involved repeated clearance of the woodland and shrub cover. This might help account for the apparently sudden appearance of a Late Neolithic phase in which substantial land-management measures are obvious from the very outset. It must also be recalled that the Fen proper would have provided pioneer earlier Neolithic communities with readily available winter food, fodder and fuel and would thus have made it less necessary permanently to clear large tracts of flood-free farm land.

The phase of consolidation can be seen to end with a possible break in occupation. This break seems to coincide with the deposition of the Fen Clay which reached a peak at, and after, 2500 bc (Willis 1961). Two observations support the connection between marine transgression and abandonment of the site. First, there is an apparent gap in the C-14 date sequence (HAR-770, which occurs in the gap, is a small and unreliable sample). Second, obviously diagnostic pottery of Middle Neolithic type (in this area 'Mildenhall Bowls') is absent. The evidence is by any standards slight: the pottery is still poorly understood; there are too few C-14 dates from Fengate and the full effects of the Fen Clay semi-saltwater flooding are also not yet fully understood — especially this far inland. We have seen moreover that settlement along the Fen-edge is generally more dispersed than on the smaller Fen 'islands' and we have also seen that long-fallow agriculture could take longer to clear a given area of woodland than on drier land. It is therefore suggested, given present evidence, that the settlement 'gap' may be more apparent than real.

The environmental effects of the Fen Clay episode must nontheless have been considerable. It is possible, for example, that the destruction, or impoverishment, of the Fen meadows by brackish water, and the deposition of huge expanses of clay-filled creek lands, could have increased the reliance of contemporary communities on the flood-free Fen-edge. Livestock could no longer roam the Fen in summer and the whole community, whether of nuclear family size, or larger, might be forced to live on the margins all year round. Perhaps the Fen Clay floods were the catalyst which hastened development along the Fen-edge. Intermittent long-fallow mixed farming had to give way to more intensive exploitation of the drier lands around the peats which, despite their wet state, were still a natural resource of considerable significance. Abandonment of the Fen-edge was not, therefore, a necessary consequence of the Fen Clay floods. It is also probable that the earliest ditched enclosures at Fengate — those of the Storey's Bar Road subsite — were laid out during this period, when the peatlands were not available for seasonal grazing. The flood-free gravel soils of the Fen-edge thus become the natural focus for the second, Expansion, phase of culture at Fengate.

SECOND PHASE: EXPANSION (MID-3rd TO LATE 2nd MILLENNIA BC)

The economy during this phase appears to have been largely based on the keeping and rearing of livestock: principally cattle, but with sheep/goats. To this end the gravel landscape around the Fen was divided into a series of ditched and probably hedged enclosures. It is suggested in the Second and Third Reports that the ditched enclosures

formed part of a seasonal economic cycle in which much use was made of the summer pastures of the peat Fen (FNG 2, chapter 5). In winter the herds, and with them perhaps a substantial part of the human population, returned to the flood-free pastures of the Fen-edge where, among other factors, pressure on limited, and slow-growing winter grazing necessitated the parcelling-up of the meadowlands which had been created in the later, more rapid, clearances of the previous phase. For the first time we have good, archaeological, evidence for large-scale land management.

Gay Wilson's discussion of the macrobotanical evidence (Appendix 6) has appeared since the publication of the Third Report, and it supports many of the ideas proposed there. Although the number of samples available for study was low, there is some evidence for hedgerow species, and a small deposit of grain (wheat and barley) in one of the enclosure ditches contained very little chaff. Mrs Wilson considers 'that it is hard to escape the conclusion that Fengate's corn supplies were brought in, ready threshed, from elsewhere, perhaps from farms on drier ground farther from the Fens'. It is interesting to note that a similar picture is emerging from palaeobotanical studies of Late Iron and Roman deposits at Maxey, a site in a closely comparable environment (Francis Green, pers comm). Weeds of disturbed ground and arable land were commonest in the Iron Age and Roman periods and reached 'a lesser peak towards the end of the Bronze Age'. This might reflect a period of dereliction before occupation was discontinued, with weeds springing unchecked around the settlement area and the droveways. A closely similar impression is provided by the molluscan evidence where on the Newark Road subsite 'the once maintained open grassland enclosures...became unkempt, with a scrubby vegetation, following the abandonment of the ditch system' (French in FNG 3, 210). Returning to the palaeobotanical study, values of pasture species are high from Early Bronze to Roman times, but there is a slight relative reduction in their importance at the onset of the Iron Age. This might reflect the increased importance of cultivation towards the start of the subsequent phase of Nucleation. In brief, the excavated sample of the second millennium landscape is primarily composed of two elements (laying aside the enigmatic enclosure excavated by Miss Mahany (1969)): a fragment of a Late Neolithic (Grooved Ware) ditched enclosure layout (Storey's Bar Road) and a more extensive tract of a Late Neolithic and earlier Bronze Age ditched field/yard/ paddock system which incorporated numerous droveways. The two elements are discussed at length in the Second and Third Reports respectively.

It is suggested in the Third Report (FNG 3, 169-170) that the two elements form part of the same system of land-use and that the apparently earlier date of the Grooved Ware enclosures is in large part the result of post-depositional factors. It is further suggested that the weathered state of the pottery (FNG 2, 69), especially that from the ditch fillings (the drawable scraps are illustrated in FNG 2, FIG 37 nos 1-9), argues that the features in which they were found were subject to repeated recutting which most probably continued into the Bronze Age. The absence of earlier Bronze Age pottery and flintwork simply reflects the absence of immediately post-Neolithic settlement in that particular, quite small, area. There can be little doubt that the Late Neolithic pottery of the Storey's Bar Road subsite ditches derives from the settlement features enclosed by them; the same must also apply to the second millennium ditches of the Newark Road, Padholme Road, Fourth Drove and Cat's Water subsites. None of the latter subsites, however, happened to contain Late Neolithic settlements, although the second millennium pits in the north-east corner of Newark Road enclosure 3 (dated by HAR-774), which are associated with a ditched droveway, may well be of comparable antiquity. Ditch maintenance has already been discussed at length (eg FNG 2, 59; FNG 3, 74), but in general it appears to have been thoroughly — and regularly — carried out so that shallow or slight, off-centre recuts are, on the whole rare. In certain cases, such as the burial in ditch *f* of Newark Road, the ditch was dug very deep in an early phase and was never subsequently cut through to its original depth; charcoal near the burial in question gave an early radiocarbon date (HAR-780) and provides good supporting evidence for an early date for at least part of the ditch system and indicates the extent of subsequent maintenance.

It is probable that the Fengate ditches were originally laid out as land boundaries to apportion grazing. During the drier conditions of the early second millennium bc there would be no need to dig the ditches particularly deep, as can be seen on Storey's Bar Road. As conditions became wetter, however, the ditches would assume an important drainage function and as winter ground water levels rose, so they would be deepened to cope with the extra water. Under such circumstances it is hardly surprising to discover that the latest recuts are the deepest and that in most cases early, shallower, cuttings have been completely removed. A good example of this is provided by the oak log found in a massive enlargement of F862 on Cat's Water: this wood provided material for the radiocarbon sample HAR-3204 (Appendix 12 and below). In a situation where even deeper recutting must inevitably remove stratigraphic evidence for the origins of the ditched enclosure system, one is forced to fall back on the spatial arrangement of settlement features and their associated ditched enclosures in order to learn about the earlier phases of such a long-lived system of land-management. Arguments concerning the contemporaneity, or otherwise, of the two elements of the ditched enclosures must therefore depend on post-depositional factors, of which ditch recutting and the consequent problems of artifact/ecofact 'residuality' are the most important. These considerations make conclusions based on simple artifact survival irrelevant; they stress, moreover, the importance of understanding an artifact's post-depositional history before it can be used to date the infilling of the feature in which it was found. The latter of the two elements of the ditched enclosure system has been fully discussed in the Third Report and little more need be said here. The earlier Grooved Ware, element was treated in the Second Report, which was written in 1974/5. Six years later, and after a further four seasons of excavation, a few of the original interpretations require modification.

A recent paper (Pryor 1980c) discusses these modifications at length. The basic interpretation still holds good; the phasing and chronology is sound, and the seasonal interpretation of the economy finds additional support in the Third Report. The principal modification, however, concerns the interpretation of the shallow 'pits' of Feature Division 6 (and perhaps, of Division 10 as well). It was thought that these features 'were associated with flint-working'; they were located (FNG 2, FIG 6) in the neighbourhood of, but away from, the ring-ditch settlement area...since sharp flint waste would pose an obvious hazard to people going about their daily tasks' (*ibid*, 155). It is now considered more probable that the shallow, irregularly-shaped, pits of Division 6 represent the truncated remains of a once undulating land surface. The hollows could have been formed by tree roots (Kooi 1974); alternately, man or animals operating in the immediate vicinity of the settlement could also have disturbed the ground. The rubbish (almost entirely broken flint tools or waste) deposited in these hollows was either dumped there deliberately, as secondary refuse, or was thrown there from the settlement area. The evidence does not support the secondary refuse hypothesis, as not only was other domestic refuse (pottery and bone etc) absent, but small flint flakes were lacking, and the tip-lines so commonly encountered in back-filling deposits, were also absent. It would not, therefore, be correct to regard the hollows of Division 6 as representing an 'activity area'.

The idea that ring-ditches of Early Bronze Age date must only be interpreted as the remnants of ploughed-out barrows has a firm grip on the thinking of prehistorians and others. Some (for example, Bamford 1979) have found it difficult to accept that the Newark Road ring-ditch could have had a double use, domestic and funerary, despite the increasing body of corroborative information that has recently been made available (Kinnes 1979). It is important, therefore, to quote a recent, independent, study of faunal bone material from Fengate. This study (La Fontaine 1980) is based on Kathleen Biddick's (FNG 3, appendix 7) report on Newark Road bone and Mary Harman's discussion of the smaller assemblage from Storey's Bar Road (FNG 2, appendix 7). The reassessment is particularly concerned with the distributional aspect of the two bone collections, which it approaches from a behavioural point of view; refuse patterns and pre- and post-depositional distortion are given particular emphasis. The basic statistical technique employed was principal component analysis; this involved several 'runs' through the material, using different configurations of features. The 'Feature Division' system adopted in the Second Report appears to have proved its usefulness in these detailed studies, as it allowed the numerous features that made up the Storey's Bar Road settlement to be broken down into smaller, manageable units for further study.

La Fontaine's conclusions concerning the Storey's Bar Road Late Neolithic and Early Bronze Age bone may be summarised by quoting her report, which is not widely available (La Fontaine 1980, 14): 'Differential distribution of animal bones were clearly marked in Storey's Bar Road between the phase II ring-ditch and the rectilinear enclosures that (mainly) date from phase I. Clear distinctions can be traced for the three large pits given separate feature divisions (pit Y4, pit W17, and well B3) suggesting a specific pattern of refuse for each of these features. Pit Y4, which contained over half the identifiable animal bone present in the site, was consistently highest in the secondary 'edible' division — suggesting its function was specifically the collection of refuse of a secondary nature. Pit Y4 also yielded the largest number of cattle bones. The ring-ditch almost always rated highest in the Primary 'butchery' category, greatly emphasising cow in one case whereas sheep/goat material was stressed in pit W17 — a feature that postdates the ring-ditch itself. While changes through time would be a useful explanation for the ring-ditch/linear ditch dichotomy, sufficient evidence is lacking for an accurate system of phasing that would support such an argument. The continued recutting of the ditches through several phases and the ability of bone fragments to work their way up and down a cultural layer were thought by the excavator (F Pryor) to make any attempts at temporal analysis meaningless'.

The study also provides important supporting evidence for Biddick's discussion of the Newark Road bone collection (FNG 3, appendix 7). In particular, it confirmed that the northern end of Enclosures B and C was a cattle butchery area. 'Two kinds of sheep/goat 'butchery' material occurred in the inner and side ditches of the enclosures (B and C) with cow and pig 'butchery' elements present in the outer ditches' (ibid, 18). The demise of the ditched enclosure system has been considered at length in the Third Report (FNG 3, 186-9). In addition to the radiocarbon dates quoted there, the recent release of HAR-3204 (1190±80bc — see Appendix 12), provides important confirmatory evidence for abandonment on the Cat's Water subsite, at the close of the second millennium bc.

A dispersed pattern of single family settlement in a landscape carefully parcelled-up into ditched plots, arranged within a broader framework on main east-west droves, indicates a degree of social organisation and an intensity of land-use that would not have been thought probable in Bronze Age Eastern England, even ten years ago. The Third Report (FNG 3, 185) concludes that although the communities of second millennium Fengate were dispersed around the ditched fields in small, often short-lived, single-family units there was nonetheless 'a larger society' with, perhaps, a degree of specialization within it. Again, to reiterate the Third Report, 'the important point to emphasise is that a shift from extensive (Consolidation phase) to intensive (Expansion phase) systems of land-use does not necessarily involve increased (hierarchical) social stratification which may be reflected archaeologically by nucleation of settlement'.

The Second and Third Reports have discussed regional comparative material of second millennium BC date at some length and it is not necessary to summarise those discussions here. Nonetheless, there have been some import developments in the region in the two years since the completion of the latter report and these will be considered below.

Turning to recent comparative material from the Fenland the principal discovery of importance was the recognition and subsequent excavation of two barrows at Orton Waterville in the western suburbs of Peterborough by the Nene Valley Research Committee. Excavation is still in progress and full comment must wait until interim reports can be prepared. The barrows are of Neolithic and/or Beaker date and owe their remarkable survival to the alluviation of the Nene floodplain in which they are located. At least one of the barrows has many phases, in part recalling Aldwincle (Jackson 1976b).

The hints of surviving Neolithic and Bronze Age organised landscapes in the Peterborough area mentioned previously (Pryor 1976a, 42-4) have not yet provided any significant new information. Recent work at Maxey has provided indications of possible Bronze Age ditched enclosures, but it is too early to be more precise. The barrow site at Orton Waterville also includes linear ditches which could be of Bronze Age date. Moving slightly further afield, the organised Bronze Age landscape of South Lincolnshire is more problematical: the Billingborough ditched enclosures are now thought to be of Iron Age date (Chowne pers comm), but the enormous quantities of Bronze Age pottery found in surface scatters over large areas of the local Fen-edge indicate a very substantial Bronze Age presence (Chowne 1977). Further work will surely demonstrate that many of the linear cropmarks can be linked to the surface scatters in the manner indicated recently by Burgess (1980, 43).

In southern East Anglia, recent aerial photographs of cropmark sites in south-east Essex suggested possible Bronze Age land division (discussion in Pryor 1976a, 44). It has not been possible to excavate the ditched 'tracks' indentified on aerial photographs, but recent excavation carried out by the Central Excavation Unit has revealed an extensive Bronze Age system of ditched enclosures at Ardleigh (J. Hinchliffe, pers comm). These ditches are probably associated with the cemetery published by Erith and Longworth (1960).

Two other regional developments of importance must also be noted at this point. First, recent excavation by the author and others at Northey are shortly to be published (Gurney 1980). This site, although excavated under salvage conditions, produced linear ditches and pottery that find close parallels at Fengate, just one and a half miles to the west. The layout and alignment of the two parallel ditches at Northey recall Newark Road and the presence of saltern debris in the filling of one ditch again recalls Fengate (Padholme Road). Although a Bronze Age date cannot be confirmed until a radiocarbon sample submitted for assay has been processed, the Northey discoveries suggest that the area of Fen between Fengate and the modern course of the river Nene ('North Brink') was dry prior to the wetter conditions of the first millennium bc. Again if the proposed date for Northey be accepted, it is probable that large expanses of undamaged Bronze Age landscape lie buried beneath the peats and alluvium between Fengate and the modern Nene (ie beneath Flag Fen south of Edgerly Drain).

Second, fieldwork by David Hall in the parish of Haddenham, near Earith, Cambs, has revealed a barrow cemetery comprising over 20 barrows, all of which are partly buried beneath some 2m of peaty alluvium. Preliminary investigations have provided dating evidence: a back-filled pit cut into the tip of one barrow (Ha 3) produced sherds of Late Bronze/Early Iron type and one (non-primary?) cremation produced a fine calcined barbed-and-tanged flint arrowhead, which would indicate an Early Bronze Age or Beaker date (see Hall and Pryor, forthcoming).

The role of field systems in the Neolithic and Bronze Age of Britain and Ireland has received considerable attention in the months following the completion of the Third Report. Much of this increased attention results from the researches of Colin Bowen and Richard Bradley in Wessex, Andrew Fleming and John Collis in Dartmoor and Seamus Cauldfield in the West of Ireland (for convenient summaries see papers in Burgess and Miket 1976; Bowen and Fowler 1978; see also papers by Fleming, Wainwright, Smith and Hammond in Maxfield 1979). In the lowland zone of eastern England the work of Peter Chowne (1977 and 1978) in southern Lincolnshire and Margaret Jones (1974; 1976) in south-east Essex has been particularly influential. This recent work has found expression in two newly published synthesis, both of which devote space to the subject (Bradley 1978, chapter 4; Burgess 1980, chapter 5). It would appear that the role of Neolithic and Bronze Age communities in the formation of the earliest developed landscape is now much better understood than was the case just ten years ago. The important role of trans-humance, Bradley's (1978) 'Rigidly Liturgical Movements', in the early exploitation of marginal lands has also received renewed attention of late (Green 1974; Fleming 1978; Bradley in FNG 2, Appendix 10; FNG 3, chapter 5).

Finally, although west of East Anglia, recent work at Mount Farm, Berinsfield, near Dorchester, Oxon, has produced a large Bronze Age ring-ditch which is associated with burial and cremations. Two possible ditched droves or trackways appear to respect it and an association, on plan at least, seems probable (reported in Selkirk 1979, 110). This arrangement closely echoes the pattern observed at Mucking (M U Jones, 1974).

THIRD PHASE: NUCLEATION (1st MILLENNIUM BC)

Before we consider some of the wider implications of this phase, and thereby continue the discussion begun above, we must first attempt to summarise the available evidence for settlement pattern, land-use and economy. Most of this evidence must derive from the large occupation site on the Cat's Water subsite which forms the principal subject of this report. Although it is about two millennia younger, this settlement area is, in many respects, more difficult to interpret than that on Storey's Bar Road (FNG 2). There are a number of reasons for this; first, and most importantly, Cat's Water was settled, with no apparent change of economy or break in occupation for perhaps four or even five centuries. This settlement pattern was probably all-year round, rather than seasonal, or intermittent, and seems to have taken place within the confines of a comparatively small area. Second, Middle and Late

Iron Age groups in the Peterborough area do not seem, on present evidence, to have made any use of flint tools (Pryor forthcoming). It will be recalled that the distribution of these flints was important to the interpretation of Storey's Bar Road. Thirdly, the Cat's Water subsite is slightly lower-lying than Storey's Bar Road, and archaeological features seem to have been more severely distorted by the known Roman and post-Roman episodes of flooding. If, however, the settlement on Cat's Water presents problems of interpretation, the other Early Iron Age or Late Bronze Age occupation areas at Fengate are even more obscure. We shall consider these briefly below.

On present evidence, the earliest first millennium occupation area is that discovered by Wyman Abbott and published by Hawkes and Fell (1945). Finds were principally located in the 'Gravel pits Settlement Area' of the first two reports (FNG 1, FIG 1; FNG 2, FIG 3; see also C C Taylor 1969, FIG 1), but some are known from workings west of the Car Dyke and as far north as Newark village. It is extremely difficult to locate these finds with any precision, due to the salvage conditions under which they were recovered. Most appear to have been found on land at the same height or very slightly higher than Cat's Water. It is therefore hazardous to attempt a reconstruction of LBA/EIA settlement patterns, as the data is not of the required standard, but one should note (a) the apparent absence of ditches which might have contained pottery of this type and (b) the good condition of sherds recovered. It is always possible that the workmen who provided Mr Abbott with the pottery discarded weathered scraps of undiagnostic shell-gritted coarse wares, and it is also possible that some of the pits could have been ditches revealed in transverse section. However, the comparatively fresh condition of the pottery also indicates that it had been discarded shortly after use, and had probably not lain around in middens, or in surface rubbish tips, for any period of time. Again, the condition of the surviving sherds does not suggest that they derive from redeposited in situ rubbish.

The isolated Late Bronze Age four-post structure from the Newark Road subsite does not appear to have formed part of a larger settlement. It is slightly lower-lying than the broadly contemporary features found by Abbott and this may, perhaps, account for the absence of pits in its vicinity. It should also be noted that the Late Bronze Age was a period of increased wetness at

Fengate so that small differences of height above OD could have been significant.

Turning briefly to the earliest Iron Age on Cat's Water, here again we have an apparently dispersed settlement pattern: there are no buildings and most of the pottery derives from isolated pits, it is generally fresh, unabraded and is found in large pieces, usually without other associated domestic rubbish such as bone, charcoal, daub etc. Hawkes and Fell (1945, 194-5) note that Abbott recorded 'a fact of particular importance', that 'all the archaeological material found in the pits came from deposits within the bottom two feet of their filling, and nearly always from a layer of dark matter at the bottom itself'. The overlying filling was sterile.

Hawkes and Fell suggested that this pattern of deposition resulted from the pits first being used as grain stores, they were then abandoned and filled with rubbish which was subsequently 'sealed over' (we are not told how) by a sterile upper layer. This explanation suggests that a 'good proportion, and not seldom the whole, of the material thus found in the bottom of the pit was in simultaneous use in the period immediately preceding the pit's closing'. The problem with this explanation is simply that ground conditions at Fengate have never favoured the use of underground grain stores, especially in the wetter years of the first millennium BC. What may have applied at Little Woodbury — a well-drained site on the chalk downland — does not apply to the Fen-edge.

The large pits described by Hawkes and Fell are better interpreted as wells in which the dark material at the bottom is still partially waterlogged (note the reference to 'dark matter' rather than wood ash, charcoal etc). 'Sock' wells of this type probably continued in use for decades or even centuries, during which time pottery would have been thrown in them, piece by piece, rather than wholesale. The sterile layer accumulated by natural weathering when the well was abandoned. Many of the 'pit groups' published by Hawkes and Fell therefore represent sherds from vessels that were discarded in open wells (a time-honoured practice), casually, throughout their period of use. If a well had been deliberately filled-in it is probable that it would have been done properly, ie to the top (see for example the well in Cat's Water Structure 54 or that next to the 'quarry pit' of Padholme Road Area XI, F3-FNG 1, 22-29). In short, the nature of the pottery from the original Fengate Early Iron Age pits, and the description of the shape and fillings of the pits themselves suggests that the 'site' — if such it was — consisted of dispersed wells or water holes in the areas of most lush grazing around the then very wet Fen. It is probable that these wells may have been in use for five or six hundred years, from the abandonment of the second millennium ditched enclosures until the establishment, later in the first millennium BC, of the Vicarage Farm and Cat's Water nucleated settlements. Indeed, it is probable that some of these wells had their origins in the full Bronze Age, while others could have continued in use until later Iron Age or Roman times. It would be possible to speculate endlessly as to the length of time that any individual well may have been maintained in use, but a figure in centuries, rather than decades would not conflict with the available evidence. It would moreover reflect the important role of water on an otherwise well-drained gravel site and would help explain the care with which such features were lined, and probably relined, with woven wattle.

The sterility of the layer above the 'dark matter' of the Abbott pits is of considerable interest. The back-filled well on Vicarage Farm, for example, (Area I, F6), was capped by a generally stone-free deposit of finely broken occupation debris (FNG 1, FIG 14, nos 6-21). The back-filling, on the other hand, included large, comparatively fresh sherds, from the lower layers (3-5). It is the tip layers, composed of more or less contemporary topsoil, which indicate the nature of settlement in the area since they probably accumulated within 5-10 years of the original back-filling, as a result of the compaction of the lower layers (this in turn will reflect the quantities of organic material, especially straw, wood etc in the dumped-in deposit). Given this interpretation, the sterility of the upper layers of the pre-War Fengate pits indicates that settlement was not located near the wells, as was the case on Cat's Water and Vicarage Farm. All the pre-War Early Iron Age finds derive from such slowly-accumulated pit deposits and there is still no good evidence for contemporary nucleated settlement in the vicinity, apart, that is, from the somewhat later occupation on Vicarage Farm.

The Vicarage Farm subsite revealed a settlement of later date where the evidence for permanent occupation and nucleation — and with it 'settlement drift' — was better preserved. The settlement on this subsite, however, presents problems of interpretation; most importantly, no structures were recovered. This apparent lack of buildings may be the result of plough-damage, as the topsoil cover over the Cornbrash limestone was exceptionally slight in places (*c* 0.10m). Furthermore, the deposits of alluvium which protected the other subsites was very thin over the central and western edges of Vicarage Farm (ie over most of Area 1 — see FIG 4). The weathered, flaggy, limestone subsoil also proved to be most difficult both to clear mechanically and to clean by hand (two general views of the clearing of Area 1 are given in Pryor 1974d, PLS II and III. It would, of course, be unwise to interpret the settlement pattern at Vicarage Farm in simple evolutionary terms, an intermediate between the dispersed pattern of the earliest Iron Age and the nucleated pattern of the later Iron Age; but there is, nonetheless, evidence for nucleation there, despite the absence of structures (see Chapter 1). The absolute date for the beginning of Vicarage Farm rests on one radiocarbon date alone (UB-822) and this is more recent than the style of the associated pottery would suggest. Early Iron Age (Group 1) pottery from Vicarage Farm is often well broken, is abraded and associated with other domestic refuse such as crushed animal bone, charcoal, burnt clay 'daub' etc. It also occurs over a large, but discrete part of the subsite which must represent the remains of a once considerable settlement (its western extent is lost beneath factory buildings). Stylistically similar pottery from Cat's Water (Group 1) almost invariably derives from isolated pits and there is no evidence for structures. There are, however, no reasons to suppose that the round houses that were most probably used by these communities should not have left any archaeological trace on the Cat's Water subsite, where preservation is good. We must suppose therefore, either that conditions on this low-lying part of the site were too wet for permanent settlement in the earliest Iron Age or, less plausibly, that the settlement pattern was still dispersed. Present evidence would suggest that the large Early Iron Age settlement at Vicarage Farm preceded, and perhaps provided the stimulus for, the Middle and Late Iron Age settlement at Cat's Water. There may have been other nucleated settlements contemporary with Vicarage Farm which also played a part in the formation of the Cat's Water community, but these would probably have been located west of the Car Dyke (ie above the 25-foot contour) and were destroyed by the eastward extension of 19th Century Peterborough.

Given the wetter conditions of the early first millennium BC, it is improbable that significant Early Iron Age settlements lie to the east, undetected, beneath the 3rd Century AD alluvium. Aerial photographic cover is excellent and there is no cropmark evidence for Iron Age settlement in Fengate between the buildings of Peterborough and the thicker deposits of alluvium, towards the modern Fen-edge.

The paucity of archaeological evidence at Vicarage Farm for Middle and Late Iron Age occupation suggests that settlement moved towards the Fen-edge in the later part of the first millennium BC. Again, later Iron Age material is almost completely lacking from the assemblages published by Hawkes and Fell (1945, 222). The isolated wells and water-holes of early first millennium Cat's Water, Newark Road and Abbott's gravel pits lie in a narrow band along the Fen-edge. Perhaps this was the limited extent of winter flood-free grazing in the early Sub-Atlantic period; if this was indeed the case, then most of the permanent settlements associated with the Fen-edge pastures would probably lie above the 25-foot contour, to the west of the Car Dyke, beneath modern Peterborough. As water levels receded, so settlement moved back towards the Fen, first to Vicarage Farm and later to Cat's Water. This explanation, however, assumes a steady fall in Fen water levels throughout the Iron Age which although probable cannot yet be proved (David Hall, pers comm). The move towards the Fen could equally be prompted by economic factors: perhaps the change from animal husbandry to mixed farming in the early first millennium was accompanied by 'an equal and opposite reaction' in which cereal agriculture played an important role. Crops would be grown on higher land and this might have prompted an initial move further 'inland' away from the Fen. Alternately, various purely cultural factors could have influenced the decision to move back from the Fen at the outset of the Iron Age. Further evidence is required to answer these questions satisfactorily.

The explanation so far suggests that the earliest nucleated settlement at Fengate was in Area I of Vicarage Farm, the highest and most westerly point excavated to date. The next and most important area of nucleated settlement is located some 850m to the SE in the Cat's Water subsite, almost the lowest part of the site excavated during the project. Here, in the Middle and Late Iron Age, very approximately between the fourth or third century BC and the mid-first century AD, there flourished a small Fen-edge settlement, positioned on the extreme edge of the seasonally flood-free land, midway between the ten and fifteen foot contours OD.

It cannot be said that the settlement is particularly imposing or important, nor is it apparently fortified; there are no fine stone or timber buildings and the material remains are generally mundane. It has, however, been excavated on a scale sufficiently large to allow at least a partially complete picture of intra-settlement activities to be reconstructed. The main archaeological evidence is provided by an examination of the horizontal distribution of finds within features (above, Chapter 4); this is supplemented by a study of the animal bones (K Biddick, Appendix 6), macro-botanical remains (Gay Wilson, Appendix 5), molluscs and sediments (C A I French, Appendices 2 and 3) and soil phosphates (P T Craddock, Appendix 4). A glance at the general plan (FIG 18) shows that almost half of the structures are located in stratigraphic isolation. In certain cases, for example Structures 3, 16 and 54, it may be possible to associate a structure with a ditched enclosure, which in turn may be associated with the main system of drains. In most cases, however, structures that were originally associated with main drains (for example Structures 10, 16, 18, 32, 33, 49 and 50) have had their stratigraphic association removed by later recutting. The regular maintenance of the most important main drains has made it possible to reconstruct a more detailed phase plan than that offered in FIG 18.

Building entranceway alignment, often a useful guide to phasing, is of little use at Cat's Water, where the majority of structures have entrances facing due east or very slightly south of east. This, surprisingly, is the direction of the bitterly cold Fen winter winds. Some see the prevailing wind as an important factor in determining building orientation, but this explanation ignores the existence of hedges, wattle screens, cob walls, trees etc. More importantly it also disregards the strength of purely social forces — the proximity of parents-in-law may chill more than a brisk Nor'easterly gale.

Estimates of population are probably best reached by considering the last phases of the site; unfortunately, however, the very last phases were probably affected by rising water levels and the picture they give many not be representative of the main phases of the settlement. The last phase of settlement also occupied land already steeped in phosphates from previous phases, and thus presents practical problems in distinguishing buildings used by people from those used by livestock. Again, this is bound to distort any estimate of population. Our discussion will therefore be based on the Late Iron Age settlement of Phase 5. Areas cleared in contiguous parts of neighbouring sub-sites (Padholme Road, Newark Road and Fourth Drove), together with the Cat's Water trial trenches, Areas XI and XII, have produced no evidence for Iron Age settlement, so it is probable that the main settlement area has been accurately located and completely revealed. The only two possible exceptions to this are in the extreme south-east, in the vicinity of Structures 47-50, where Middle Iron occupation may have continued beyond the stripped area. This, however, is a very low-lying part of the site where extensive settlement does not seem probable (further land could not be cleared because of overhead cables). The other area where occupation may originally have extended beyond the stripped area is the north-west, in the vicinity of Structures 4, 14 and 15. It was impossible to extend the trench in this direction, owing to the presence of a modern sewer. It did prove possible, however to maintain a watch on the construction work, and although a few sherds of Nene Valley Grey Ware were recovered, it seems unlikely that any substantial Late Iron Age features were destroyed. A further watching-brief on sewer construction immediately west of, and parallel to, Storey's Bar Road (in the Padholme Road subsite) also proved negative.

Assuming that most large buildings are represented, the maximum size of the Late Iron settlement would have been about 10 buildings. These structures are nos 4, 5, 9, 11, 19, 20, 27, 29, 36 and 53; Structure 41 has been omitted as it is thought to be significantly later than the others; Structures 43, 44 and 52 are too amorphous to merit inclusion, and Structures 24, 35, 37-40 are probably not roofed buildings. The ten buildings listed above are distributed over the central and western part of the settlement area evenly; they appear to respect the layout of main drains that are known to have been open and in use in Late Iron times and there seems, at present, no good reason to doubt that they could all have been occupied at the same time. If it is simply assumed that each one of these structures was used to house people, that they are all strictly contemporary, and that the floor area of each was adequate to serve the needs of a nuclear family, then the maximum population of Late Iron Age Cat's Water would have been about 40-50, of which perhaps 20 would have been adults.

It is interesting to note here that the rough estimate of 4-5 individuals per house accords well with that suggested by D L Clarke for Glastonbury (1972). Clarke based his estimates on the floor areas of the buildings concerned and calculated the populations using the figures of Cook and Heizer (1968), which are derived from studies of aboriginal Californian populations.

We will now examine this gross estimate of population more closely. The discussion that follows is in five parts. First, we will consider the significance and reliability of the archaeological data, most particularly those of finds distribution; second, these data will be used to assign functions to the various structures discussed. The third part of the discussion will consider the results of soil phosphate analyses; this will be followed by a synthesis of the archaeological and phosphate evidence; finally, the original (gross) estimate of population will be appropriately modified.

The analysis of building techniques in Chapter 7 suggests that the open U-shaped penannular ('ring') gullies of the Cat's Water settlement are the eaves-drip drains around the outside of round buildings. These ring-gullies sometimes occur as short arcs (like, for example Structures 4, 5, 29 or 36) and it suggested that these, too, represent the remains of shorter lengths of gully that were placed discontinuously beneath the eaves of round buildings. Wall foundation gullies are known (eg Structures 7, 14 and 54), but these are usually steep-sided, are invariably shallow and are placed about a metre inside the eaves-drip gully. Unfortunately, little is known about the distribution of finds from the eaves-drip gullies of British Iron Age round buildings. Even recent excavation reports have failed to publish distribution plans and we are, therefore, forced to use our own comparative data. The author is currently (Oct 1980) only aware of one published exception to this rule: Hodder *et al's* recent interim account of rescue excavations at Wenden's Ambo, Essex (Halstead, Hodder and Jones, 1978). Unlike the Roman phase of the site, the Iron Age at Wenden's Ambo was neither complex nor multi-phased and it was, therefore, possible to distinguish different types of rubbish deposit reasonably satisfactorily (although the samples of bone and pottery were

small). The main cooking area appears to have been in the region of a three-sided ditched enclosure and the only well-preserved penannular eaves-drip 'showed that the density of potsherds was very high near the entrance, but falls off markedly around the back and sides of the hut'. Unfortunately, the precise position of bone was not recorded at Fengate and consequently an important aspect of rubbish distribution has been lost. It is clear, however, from the Wenden's Ambo study (a) that the round building is a house, and (b) that the gully was an eaves-drip and not a wall trench. There was less bone in the structural ring-gullies than in the pits and ditches of the settlement and this is also true of Fengate. Hodder explains this by suggesting that unpleasant refuse, such as meat bone, was disposed of quickly, away from buildings (dogs must also have helped in this regard), but that the majority of rubbish in the gullies was kicked from the yard surfaces around them. This would help to account for the concentration of material around the doorway, as this was the spot where human traffic was most frequent.

The evidence from Fengate does not appear to offer much support for the distinction made between fine 'table' wares and coarse, scored 'kitchen' wares. Structure 54, for example, which was almost certainly a house, produced enormous quantities of coarse pottery and not one sherd of fine, burnished table ware. Other structures, 20 for example, produced large quantities of fine pottery and comparatively little coarse ware. Both these structures are located in areas where quantities of intrusive and residual material were slight and it is probable that the pattern they present is largely undistorted by previous and subsequent activity in the area. One final point should be mentioned concerning bone; survival of bone in shallower features was noticeably poorer than in deeper pits and ditches; this was probably due to the effects of humic acids in the topsoil and could quite seriously distort the information derived from an analysis of this material. Structure 54 was excavated in detail and large quantities of feature filling were sieved through fine meshes, in an effort to quantify the horizontal and vertical distribution of artifacts and bone. The building was chosen for more intensive study because half of it was exceptionally well preserved. The events surrounding the construction and use of Structure 54 may be briefly summarised (FIGS 75-78; M63-M66). The area chosen for the building was occupied by a larger pit or well (F1593) which was filled-in, probably immediately prior to the construction of the building around it. The material used to fill the pit consisted of large pieces which were deposited in clearly-defined tip lines. Structural evidence for the building consisted of a few postholes, probably associated with the doorway and an internal eaves-drip gully (F47/1503) and internal wall-slot (F1502). The soft, redeposited material in the well soon became compacted, or was worn down, and an *in situ* deposit of floor rubbish (F1501), consisting of finely crushed shell-gritted pottery, bone and charcoal was allowed to accumulate. Eventually the building was abandoned and *de facto* (or abandonment) rubbish was deposited in the eaves-drip gully. This rubbish included an almost complete rotary quern and a crouched human burial. A Late Iron Age main drain (F1505) was subsequently cut through the easterly part of the building.

A study of the horizontal distribution of the rubbish showed that the finely-crushed floor material was poorly represented in either the eaves-drip or wall gullies, although rather surprisingly, the eaves-drip gully contained more of the distinctive floor deposit than the contiguous wall-slot. The distribution of pottery in the two gullies was most dissimilar and the eaves-drip did not show the characteristic heavy concentration of material around the doorway; this could, in part, be explained by the presence, the the north of the entrance, of a crouched burial and, to the south, of a large quernstone. An alternative explanation is that the scatter of pottery south of the entranceway resulted from the passage of people from the building front door to the entranceway, immediately south, through the enclosure ditch (F1504). This pattern of rubbish strongly supports Hodder's suggestion that material in the eaves-drip gully derives from outside the building. The redeposited floor material in the outer gully was quite evenly spread and probably found its way there after the building's abandonment.

Very large quantities of floor deposit were found in residual contexts at and near the bottom of the first phase of the Late Iron main drain which cut through the house site after its abandonment. It was also interesting to note that the second phase of this drain contained less of this material. The detailed investigation was of interest as it demonstrated the major and persistent role of residual material on a multi-period prehistoric site. The artifacts in question were soft, shell-gritted potsherds, and the feature in which they were found was a constantly renewed main drain which must often have held standing, if not flowing water; despite this, the pottery survived to a remarkable extent.

From this discussion it is apparent that the distribution of contemporary artifacts in structural gullies will reflect activities immediately outside the buildings themselves. In general non-contemporary artifacts, in the present case flintwork, do not show a distribution that can readily be attributed to human behaviour (see for example the discussion of finds distribution in Structure 16). Direct evidence for activities that took place inside specific buildings will, on large or multi-period sites, only be derived from the *in situ* rubbish itself. Wallslots rarely contained significant quantities of floor sweepings and, in the present case, could not be used as a reliable guide to the building's original purpose.

Finally, a word of caution is necessary. The Cat's Water subsite is both multi-period and lacks the surface between-structure rubbish spreads, which could provide an explanation of finds distribution within the buildings themselves. The complexity of rubbish distribution on a settlement which, from a strictly archaeological viewpoint is of one period, is well illustrated in a recent paper by DeBoer and Lathrap (1979). Their plan of the surface distribution of rubbish (*ibid*, FIG 46) shows the extent of the information that could have been lost at Fengate. Note, for example, the absence of finds around their thatch drying racks and the large spread of pottery outside, but not within, the 'ceramic' shed.

The archaeological data used to assess the original function of the various buildings encountered is given in detail in the Part I of Chapter 4; a synthesis appears in Part II. The discussion that follows is based on that synthesis.

Patterned distribution of finds, which are thought to be the direct result of human behaviour, were observed in the following Middle Iron round buildings of the two types (continuous and discontinuous gullies) discussed in Chapter 4: Structures 2 (FIG 25); 3 (FIG 27); 6 (FIG 32); 10 (FIG 37); 16 (FIG 43); 17 (FIG 44); 18 (FIG 29); 47 (FIG 64); 54 (FIG 77). Of the structures listed here, Structure 3 had been rebuilt a number of times and had lost the clarity of its original patterning which was retained in its closely-associated exterior enclosure ditch; Structure 17 was represented by a probable wall-slot which did not show any patterning of itself. It was, however, thought that a sharp increase in finds' density in the nearby enclosure ditch around Structure 16, which was broadly contemporary, was most probably associated in some way with Structure 17. Another Middle Iron building, Structure 13 (FIG 39), was rebuilt once and showed a patterned finds distribution in only one of its two phases. Possible patterned finds distributions from Middle Iron round buildings are found in Structures 15 (FIG 41) and 56 (FIG 82). Structure 7 (FIG 34) shows a concentration of finds at the back of the building, away from the door; this may be associated in some way with the neighbouring farm enclosure, Structure 42; otherwise its significance is obscure. Buildings which clearly do not show a patterned distribution of Middle Iron Age finds are Structures 1 (FIG 23); 8 (FIG 25); 12 (no finds); 14 (FIG 41); 32 and 33 (FIG 58); 48 (FIG 66); 50 (no finds).

The ten Late Iron round buildings mentioned at the outset of this discussion did not all show the patterned distributions of finds seen in Structures 4 (FIG 29); 5 (FIG 30); 19 (FIG 45); 20 (FIG 47); 36 (FIG 55). Structure 53 (FIG 74) was dubiously patterned and the remainder — Structure 9 (no finds) 11 (FIG 37), 27 (FIG 45), 29 (no finds) — did not show patterning.

Too much significance should not be attached to this analysis, but it is interesting to compare the figures for the three types of distribution, patterned, unpatterned and doubtful. Patterned distributions accounted for 48% of the Middle and 50% of the Late Iron structures; unpatterned distributions were found in 38% of the Middle and 40% of Late Iron structures whilst doubtfully patterned distributions were observed in 14% of Middle and 10% of Late structures. Put crudely (which the data demands), on artefactual evidence, about half of the Middle and Late Iron structures were probably used as dwelling houses.

Any consideration of the soil phosphate and magnetic susceptibility data (Appendix 4) must allow for the fact that the settlement was long-lived and that as a result clearly defined, discrete concentrations of phosphate were obscured by the general spread of occupation, both human and animal, over several centuries. This is well illustrated by comparing results of the more limited magnetic susceptibility survey with the phosphate samples (FIG 140). One would expect to find areas of enhanced magnetic susceptibility in places where the ground had been subjected to the 'culminative effect of fires and decaying organic material' (M S Tite, Appendix 4). A recent survey at Tadworth in Surrey has shown that such areas represent human occupation (A J Clark 1977). High soil phosphate generally results from animal manure, decaying flesh etc; at Tadworth, an Iron Age 'banjo' enclosure that was less long-lived than Cat's Water, areas of high soil phosphate and areas of enchanced magnetic susceptibility were clearly separated. Cat's Water contrasts with Tadworth, for although the sample is small, the magnetic susceptibility enhancement is coincident with the high phosphate values. Dr Tite suggests that this is because animals were probably being kept in the small stockades surrounding the round buildings.

Dr Craddock's phosphate survey was of great importance, for not only did it discover the Iron Age settlement, which was almost entirely hidden from the aerial camera by the 3rd century AD alluvium (which blanketed the whole subsite), but it also provided important evidence for the way in which the settlement was organised. The general high level of phosphate over the settlement supports the idea that occupation on Cat's Water was far more intensive than for example, on Newark Road. The ephemeral nature of the Romano-British episode is emphasised by the low levels of phosphate along the main Roman droveway surface which crosses the southern part of the main excavated area, from east to west. This contrasts with the high phosphate levels encountered on the trackway surface between second millennium droveway ditches on the Newark Road subsite. Although the northern part of the settlement was not surveyed in the initial, ten-metre grid, the eastern, western and southern edges of occupation were reached. Phosphate levels were appreciably lower beyond the known, usually ditched, limits of the settlement area (FIG 139). A series of spot samples was taken from the stripped C horizon surface. The results were of considerable interest (FIG 142). First, they confirmed the results of the previous B horizon survey (FIG 139) by showing high levels within the main area of settlement, as defined by the principal drainage ditches, and low levels beyond it (the two anomalous samples to the north were probably taken too close to the settlement area). The outline plan used to illustrate the spot phosphate survey (FIG 142) shows the known extent of excavated features in the autumn of 1976, when the survey was undertaken. Some structures, for example 13 and 14 had not yet been discovered and others (eg

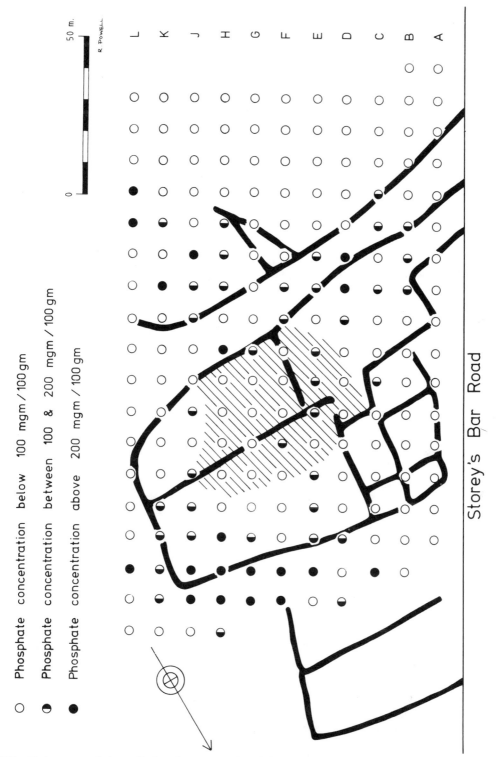

Fig. 138 Cat's water subsite, soil phosphate survey (see P T Craddock, Appendix 4): results of initial (1975), 10m grid, surface survey. Hatching indicates a spread of Roman pottery. Cropmark plan and pottery spread after C C Taylor (1969: FIG 1).

217

15) were not yet fully excavated.

The results of the phosphate survey compare well with those of the finds distribution, discussed above. Taking Middle Iron Age structures first, low phosphate levels were observed inside Structures 2, 3, 16 and (?) 17. These readings agree well with the finds distribution data; the only round building on the eastern edge of the settlement without a patterned finds distribution, Structure 8, did not show a fall-off in phosphate levels in its interior. The Late and Middle Iron Structures 9 and 12, which were superimposed on each other, showed a high phosphate level, as did Structure 11, the Late Iron building superimposed on Structure 10. The location of the Middle Iron Structure 14 showed a high phosphate level, which coincided with its unpatterned finds distribution, although in this case the high phosphate could be due to second millennium activity in the area. Structure 15, also Middle Iron and without a patterned finds distribution, was located in an area of high phosphate. The results of the analyses from Structure 4 were not clear, but Structure 1 showed a high internal phosphate level which agreed well with its finds distribution. The complex of farm structures 24, 37-9 were in an area of high phosphate, but Structure 41, the very Late Iron rectangular building which produced many finds showed a high phosphate concentration. This is probably explained (a) by its late date and (b) by its location at the centre of a Middle and Late Iron ditched enclosure.

We may conclude that the analyses of finds distributions and soil phosphates agree very well. The rather surprising conclusion is clear: animals were kept inside the ditched enclosures, probably in round buildings in which they over-wintered, whereas people occupied identical buildings spaced around the outside of the settlement. Not all buildings around the periphery of the community were used as houses (for example Structures 8 and 42); similarly, not all buildings inside the ditched enclosures were used to accommodate livestock (for example Structures 13, 19 or 20). The general trend is, however, unmistakable.

The construction of round buildings was considered at some length in Chapter 4 and, again, there is little to be gained by repeating this discussion. A previously unrecognised class of round buildings was, however, discovered and it is appropriate at this point to discuss its wider implications. Discontinuous gully round buildings are usually defined by one or more arcs of ring-gully, often forming an approximate semi-circle. They have recently been discussed by Drury (1978), whose evidence is mainly drawn from sites in Essex and Herts. The site at Gun Hill (Drury and Rodwell 1973; Drury 1978, FIG 15) was located on the edge of the Thames, west of Mucking. It was sufficiently near the tidal flats to allow salt extraction to take place and must have been a most exposed site. Its semi-circular ring-gully (dia 9.5m) closely resembles examples from Cat's Water and Storey's Bar Road. Mucking is located atop a gravel ridge and is also a most exposed site, overlooking the Thames estuary; it too, has produced examples of discontinuous ring-gully buildings (Jones 1974, FIGS 3: at grids 950/200; 1050/200; 1140/225; FIG 4, top right). The chalkland site at Barley, Herts (Cra'ster 1961, FIG 4) is a most interesting example of the type: its 'open' side is marked by an absence of pits which otherwise cover most of the area excavated. The evidence that the horseshoe-shaped ditch was used as a wall foundation is not good (compare wall-slots on other chalk sites, for example Winklebury (K Smith 1977); Gussage All Saints (Wainwright 1979, FIG 18)). The absence of pits immediately south of the Barley structure suggests that the building extended into that area; this idea finds support in the distribution of postholes within and to the south of the horseshoe gully (Cra'ster 1961, FIG 4: postholes 6-18).

Round buildings derive their strength and stability from the fact that they are round, so that the roof's thrust is dissipated around the structure. A semi-circular building on the other hand, is inherently less stable, and although Drury (1978, 68) considers that the construction of a roof over such buildings 'need present no difficulties', this is not the opinion of Dr Peter Reynolds who has practical experience of building many round houses (pers comm). Further, many of the Fengate discontinuous arc round buildings, for example Structures 4, 14, 29, 36 occupy about a third or a quarter of a complete circle's circumference. Such buildings would be most unstable. We have seen that Drury's examples from Essex are all located on exposed sites and it is inconceivable that structures with 'essentially open sides, closed only by shutters or door', of lightweight construction, could survive the north-easterly gales of an Essex winter (the open side of the Gun Hill 'semicircular building' faces due north-east, towards the Thames Estuary). Some of the Fengate discontinuous gully arcs, for example Structures 10 and 19,

Fig.

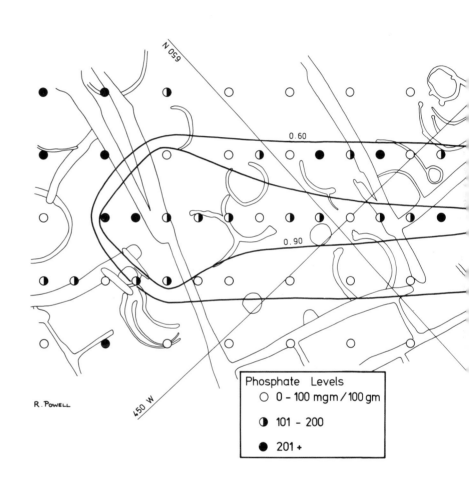

Phosphate Levels
○ 0 - 100 mgm / 100 gm
◑ 101 - 200
● 201 +

R . POWELL

650 N

0.60

0.90

450 W

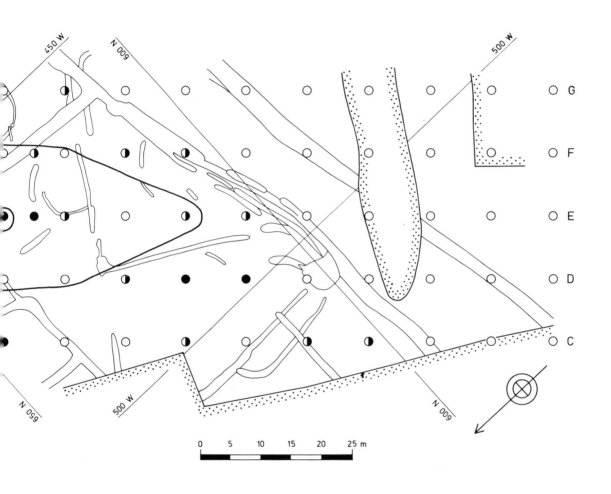

Fig. 140 Cat's Water subsite, soil phosphate survey see P T Craddock, Appendix 4): comparison of phosphate concentration in the 'archaeological layer' (from FIG 289), with results of soil magnetic susceptibility survey (contours represent %C at 0.40-0.70m below surface — for explanation see A J Clark in Appendix 4).

can be shown to have belonged to round buildings, and until positive evidence for a screen wall can be produced 'semicircular buildings' are probably best forgotten.

Finally, attention must be drawn to the many non-circular buildings that must have formed an important component of the original settlement. They have all been considered at length in the discussion of Chapter 4 and little useful can be added here, except to say that with one exception, they were all probably farm buildings of one sort or another (Structures 23-5, for example, may have been stack-stands; Structures 21, 22 etc may be stock pens). The only exception to this interpretation is the rectangular building, Structure 41 (FIGS 113 and 114). This building produced many finds, which were evenly spread throughout the right-angled gully that formed its northern and eastern sides. The phosphate level was high, but, as we have seen, this could be explained by the building's location. In short, it is difficult to assign a function to this structure, but it need not necessarily be a house; the main gully had steep butt-ends and there are no grounds to suppose that the wall continued in the manner indicated by Dr Rodwell (1978, FIG 2).

At this point we must return to the consideration of population which began this discussion. We have seen that the distributional evidence agrees remarkably well with the soil phosphate and magnetic susceptibility studies, and that approximately five out of the ten Late Iron round buildings were houses. Our population estimates must be lowered accordingly. It is salutory to reflect that the large and complex network of ditches, most of which were maintained in use throughout the life of the settlement, was probably dug and maintained, during quiet periods in the farming year, by the adult members of some five families. The suggestion that a large proportion of round buildings and other structures were not used to house people highlights the dangers of estimating population, in lowland Britain at least, from the overall area occupied by, for example, a concentration of cropmarks (see also Sumner 1979); it also renders many typologies of settlement redundant (was Cat's Water, for example, a settlement of Rodwell's (1976, 292) types i or ii?). In sum, the Late Iron population on Cat's Water was probably no more than 20-25 persons who occupied, with their livestock etc, an area of about one hectare. There are good reasons to suppose that the picture in the Middle Iron Age was more

or less the same.

Our discussion has now reached the stage where we have a reasonably reliable impression of the settlement's layout, with livestock mainly at the centre and people around the periphery. We have an estimate, too, of its population in the Middle and Late Iron Age. It is now appropriate to attempt a reconstruction of the ancient environment and economy.

Charles French's examination of the molluscan fauna from two Late Iron main drains (Appendix 6) shows that conditions were wet: '*c* 10-30cm depth of slow-moving water...with scattered marsh vegetation (eg reeds, tall grass, weeds) on the ditch sides'. The conditions are well illustrated in the model made for the project by the Development Corporation's model-makers Eric Ricketts and David Rayner (PLS 27 and 28). This model also shows the ditches within the actual settlement area unaccompanied by hedges, for which there is no evidence, direct or indirect. Apart from the molluscan evidence, there can be little doubt that the ditches were used as drains, since strands of coppiced or pollarded willow had been carefully laid along the bottom of two ditches to form a 'brush drain' (see description and discussion, above; for recent 'bush drains' (sic) see Nicholson 1942, PL VII (David Crowther drew my attention to this reference), see also PLS 15-17, below). The layout of the ditches in small, sub-rectangular enclosures, also suggests that they were used as boundaries. The frequency of ditch maintenance has often been discussed in this and previous reports, and sedimentological evidence for it is given by C French in Appendix 3. The sediment study of the two Late Iron main drains that provided the molluscan samples indicates a complex history of recutting interspersed with possible back-filling, some possible wind-carried deposits and, of course, the ever-present influence of water. There is slight evidence, too for a low bank alongside the ditch F30. Finally, the uppermost, tertiary filling of both ditches was composed of the third century AD flood clay. French notes that 'the wetness of the site in the Late Iron Age must have made occupation precarious at best. This may be one reason for the palimpsest of features, the possible evidence for back-filling, and the frequent recutting of lengths of the enclosure ditches'.

Turning to the macro-botanical evidence, Mrs Wilson (Appendix 5) notes that weeds of arable land and cultivation reach a peak in the Iron Age and Roman periods and that this coincides with cultivated plants as a whole, where 'values range from 1% to 6% of total fossils throughout the Bronze Age and Early Iron Age, rising to around 20% in the Late Iron Age and Roman period'. Cereals were only of minor importance and some of the suggested cultivated plants (for example, celery, mustard, parsnip, thyme) have wild varieties not distinguishable in the fossil state from cultivated varieties. Opium poppy (*Papaver somnifera* L) seeds were found in a Late Iron main drain near Structure 1; this sample also included two apple pips (*Malus sylvestris* Mill). Hedgerow species were low in frequency in the early samples and at the end (Late Iron and Roman). They reach a peak, however, in the Late Bronze Age (samples from the large pit W17, Storey's Bar Road, Area 1 — see FIG 27). Similarly, woodland species have a relatively high frequency in the earliest samples, reach a peak in the Late Bronze Age and are fairly low in Late Iron Age and Roman times. It would seem probable that the increase in hedgerow and woodland species in the Late Bronze Age reflects the abandonment of the second millennium ditched enclosures (FNG 3; Appendix 4). Mrs Wilson notes a 'distinct increase' in the frequency of marsh and water plants at the onset of the Iron Age, during which period conditions were wetter at Fengate than at any other time for which there is evidence. Water weeds (such as duckweeds, stoneworts and starworts) were abundant and 'there is also a wide range of species which inhabit wet mud, shallow water and wet ditches'; these include flag iris, bullrush, rushes, bog bean and water crowfoot.

In the previous, Consolidation phase, there was evidence that cereals were brought onto the site, ready threshed, from outside, as is now believed happened at Maxey in Late Iron and Roman times (Francis Green, pers comm). This is probably what happened at Late Iron Age Fengate, where the Cat's Water settlement is significantly lower-lying than Maxey. Quernstones were evidently curated items of considerable importance, as there is no locally-occuring source of stone for their manufacture; this would account for their comparative rarity on Cat's Water.

It is interesting to note the occurrence of opium poppy in the list of cultivated plants. It would seem probable that this plant was grown to ease the pains of the Fen 'ague' (malaria), but it might also have been cultivated as a source of vegetable oil (Godwin 1978, 156-8). Another possible source of

comfort might have been an infusion made from the bark of willow which was commonly used as an analgesic by poorer people in the Fens, until recent times. Willow, a diverse and useful tree (M Taylor 1981), was a very significant plant to early communities at Fengate: its wood is soft and easily worked, it grows fast and straight when coppiced or pollarded and is pliable, and suitable for basket-making etc. Although the first evidence for its possible coppicing/ pollarding at Fengate is in Late Iron times, it was probably in use slightly earlier (for example the less well preserved 'brush drain' in the enclosure ditch around Structure 16), and there are no good reasons to doubt that it was commonly exploited as early as the Neolithic period (Coles and Orme 1980, 21). Study of the animal bones from Cat's Water was made difficult by the longevity of the settlement and the consequent problems of residuality (Appendix 6). Nonetheless Kathleen Biddick has arrived at some conclusions of considerable interest. She notes that 'the relative abundance of domesticated species based on the fragment counts reveals a complex pattern of animal husbandry' (Table M27). There is a slight preponderance of cattle over sheep which is almost the reverse of that at Ashville, Abingdon (Wilson 1978). This would seem to agree with recent research in the upper Thames where it is suggested that sheep would occur more frequently on slightly higher ground, whereas cattle would be more commonly found on lower-lying sites, such, in our case, as Cat's Water. Biddick points out, however, that the case for such an arrangement has yet to be proved in the lower Nene valley. Horse and pig, on the bone fragment data, appear to have played a reduced role: dog, cat and goat complete the list of domesticated species.

The list of wild species recognised is very varied and it is apparent that wildfowl must have played a significant part in the economy. It must also be noted that the small, thin-walled bones of birds and fish are liable to suffer the erosive effects of soil acids and will be under-represented in the archaeological record at Fengate. It is most interesting, therefore, to record the presence of pike, tench, bream and carp; the list of birds is even more remarkable: 19 species are identified, of which the majority are associated with water (various geese, duck, swans, heron, pelican, cormorant, stork, sea eagle and goosander). There is considerable evidence for the alteration of bone and for butchering practices (PLS 20-26) and

Biddick discusses the butchery of cattle according to the principal cuts involved: skull and mandible; vertebrae and ribs; forelimb and hind limb. These may be contrasted with the study of second millennium butchery practices in the Third Report (FNG 3; appendix 7). Much of the comparative material cited by Biddick derives from the Middle and Upper Thames area; sites such as Ashville Trading Estate, Abingdon and Barton Court Farm. It is greatly to be wished that adequately published prehistoric faunal bone assemblages will soon be available from the East Midlands and East Anglia.

We may briefly summarise the evidence for the economy thus: cultivated plants, which do not appear to have included cereals, were grown on a larger scale than hitherto. Locally-occuring plants such as willow, and perhaps reed may also have been exploited for wicker, wattle, poles, thatching etc. Given the wet conditions that prevailed it would seem that livestock, as hitherto, still dominated the economy and that cattle were perhaps marginally more important than sheep. Fish and wildfowl also provided an important source of protein, particularly during the leaner months of winter. There can be little doubt that the peat Fens would have been impassible in winter and grazing, even in the drier months of summer, would have been restricted to the outer margins (Godwin 1941, 300). The new evidence, discussed in Part I, above, for raised bogs and generally more acid conditions in the Fen, makes the location of Fengate even more important in the Iron Age, when areas suitable for the grazing of livestock would be most restricted. Nutrient-rich water flowing into the Fen basin from the nearby river Nene and its associated creeks, together with water from the base-rich gravels of the lower valley, would have kept the local growth of Sphagnum at bay; it would also have provided nourishment for plant communities along the fringe of the wetlands in Coles' 'zone of fodder production' (1978, FIG 21.1). The second millennium pattern of seasonal movement into the Fen during summer would not have been possible in the Iron Age; perhaps, as an alternative some of the population moved to higher land during the growing season to provide the settlement with supplies of cereals. Unfortunately evidence for this probably lies beneath modern Peterborough. The scale and layout of the Cat's Water farmstead, and the need to maintain its system of drainage dykes in good order however, suggests that a proportion of the community at least, must have lived on the site all the year round. Certainly there can be little doubt that Fengate must have been a very attractive proposition in the winter, with its enormous and varied reserves of fish, fowl and fuel. If grain was obtained by exchange, then the items that the Cat's Water community could have traded would have included fish and wildfowl, willow products, wool, hides, meat and dairy products.

We concluded the discussion of the previous, Expansion, phase with the hypothesis that land-use in the second millennium was intensive, but that the dispersed settlement pattern indicated that the community had not responded to the pressures of intensification by increased social stratification. It was suggested that archaeological evidence for increased social stratification would consist of a pattern in which settlement was nucleated, rather than dispersed. A close examination of the early first millennium settlement data could not confirm the idea, advanced previously, that nucleated settlement was an immediate adaptive response to the environmental changes that lead to the abandonment of the ditched field system. Indeed, nucleated settlements of the early first millennium are so rare in the lowlands of eastern England, that their absence at Fengate must have some wider significance. It is not sufficient to account for the lack by suggesting that they all lie beneath modern Peterborough.

The stimulus that ultimately touched off the change from dispersed to nucleated settlement was most probably associated with the environmental changes of the early first millennium. The effects of so drastic an environmental change on an economy apparently prospering and expanding must have been far-reaching and profound. Perhaps society was able, in the first instance, to adapt to the new environmental conditions as they happened. Fenland communities have always had to live in close harmony with their sometimes treacherous surroundings and would have been swift to move to higher land, perhaps even to clear the tree cover that might still have cloaked the low Nene/ Welland interfluve. One could speculate endlessly on the nature of the initial response to the increased wetness, but it did not cause the site to be abandoned. We can still be reasonably certain that parts of Fengate would have been habitable, even in the wettest of winters and we have good archaeological evidence, in the shape of the Late Bronze Age pottery from the original Abbott pits (Champion 1975), that the site was occupied, albeit seasonally in the early first millennium.

The peat Fen is a vast expanse. During its dry periods it would have provided a huge open range for cattle loosed upon it. We may suppose, as Fleming has recently suggested (1978), that the seasonal movement into open pasture would have provided opportunities for social contact, some of it, no doubt, formalised through ties of kinship. Once, however, the wetter conditions had become established and the areas available for free-range summer grazing had been drastically reduced, the physical opportunities for social contact between different groups would increase. Inevitably, communities moving onto higher land would adopt the already-existing local economy of settled, mixed farming which was, coincidentally, also better suited to the changed conditions along the Fen-edge. Perhaps it was a combination of the changing economic base and an accelerating tendency towards social stratification which led to the nucleated pattern of settlement that was apparently flourishing at Vicarage Farm as early as the fifth century BC.

A combination of factors must have led to the development on the new economic base and altered social order. It would seem, on present evidence, that these developments were a result of purely local stimuli and that an influx of 'immigrants' from elsewhere is highly improbable, whether at the beginning, middle or end of the Iron Age. It is clear that we will never know precisely what caused the local settlement pattern to change in the way it did, and there is still plainly much to learn. We do know, however, the directions in which we should be looking and where we can expect to find the type of information we require.

The Iron Age, and most particularly the Late Iron Age, is the period when British history and prehistory meet. It is a period where scholars often combine the texts of ancient history with a species of prehistory that suspends the accepted rules of archaeology. It is never a simple matter to bring together disciplines that use such dissimilar data, and where political events are concerned it is usually best not attempted. Ancient authorities can, however, be used to provide information on pre- and post-Roman Celtic societies, either in a narrative form (for example Chadwick 1964; Piggott 1968; Ross 1967; 1970) or in a more specific, analytical, form. An example of the latter approach is the important paper by D L Clarke (1972) which reconsidered the lake- or marsh-edge later Iron Age settlement at Glastonbury,

Somerset and its regional setting. It is most fortunate, for our purposes, that Glastonbury is both contemporary with the main occupation at Cat's Water and is located in such a similar environment. It will play an important part in the discussion that follows. Cat's Water and Glastonbury are both multi-phased and must therefore be analysed largely on the evidence of the last period of occupation (Clarke 1972, 807). Both sites produced many buildings (about 56 at Cat's Water; some 90 at Glastonbury), but a close inspection of the vertical stratigraphy only allowed the sure definition of four clearly-defined phases at each site, those at Glastonbury occupying a shorter time-span than Cat's Water. At both sites the location and 'packing' of buildings and other settlement features seems to have been affected by increased, or decreased, wetness of the neighbouring marshland. Glastonbury was consistently larger than Cat's Water: Clarke estimates that the population there fluctuated between 60 and 105. Perhaps the Cat's Water Middle Iron population was slightly greater than the last Late Iron phase, but it is most unlikely to have exceeded 40 individuals at any one time.

The analysis of the Glastonbury structures suggested a variety of types, most of which could be assigned a function; thus we have major houses (usually arranged in pairs), minor houses, ancillary huts, workshop huts, courtyards, baking huts, guard huts, annexe huts, work floors, clay patches, granaries or storehouses, stables or byres, and sties or kennels (*ibid* 814-27). This extraordinary list of structures results from the excavation, some seventy years ago, of a site where the horizontal distribution of many finds was properly logged and, above all else, where organic finds, floor or yard surfaces were preserved intact. The Cat's Water data do not lend themselves to such clear distinction. An analysis based on structure size (Pryor and Cranstone 1978) has been tried, but only with very limited success. 'Major houses', for example, appear, at first glance, to be easily spotted (Structures 3, 4, 6, 7, 13, 15, 16, 18, 20, 54 etc). A closer inspection of the finds distribution and phosphate analyses, however, demonstrates that many had a non-domestic function. Similarly, many of the smaller round buildings, for example Structures 1, 2, 8, 11, 19 appear to have been used either as minor houses or as, perhaps, stables or byres, to use Clarke's terminology. Obvious farm buildings, such as the 'stack-stands' (Structures 24 and 25) or the small enclosures associated with Structure 22, are more readily defined, but again, it is often difficult to be more precise about specific function(s).

These differences aside, it would appear that Cat's Water is about the size of a Glastonbury 'sector' (*ibid*, 808), or very slightly larger. It is therefore particularly significant to note that in its final phase (IV) livestock were corralled in an inner compound where there were 'ample traces of elaborate internal stock fences and baffles'. Clarke (*ibid*, 811) estimates that the combined compounds could have had the capacity to corral more than 1200 Celtic sheep or 300 head of Celtic cattle. Clearly we must be careful not to push the Cat's Water/ Glastonbury analogy too far, but the similarity between the Glastonbury *'sector'* and the Cat's Water settlement is remarkable. The principal difference appears to be that at Glastonbury the groups concerned were actually producing their own cereal crops, for which there is no good evidence at Cat's Water. Clarke suggests that the repeated 'modular' social unit at Glastonbury consisted of two major houses, two minor houses and various ancillary buildings. The houses had adequate floor space to provide shelter for about 20 people, which he sees as the maximum size of the basic social unit. 'Taken altogether the evidence points towards an inturned internally networked, co-operative social unit averaging perhaps fifteen to twenty individuals including males, females, juveniles and adults, ancestrally linked to the unit houses, jointly owning and inheriting property; anthropologically such a unit would normally be a kin group based on a extended family or lineage system.' The Cat's Water evidence is, again, far less clear-cut than Glastonbury and it is impossible to discern a basic kin group module in the site plan. Certainly, paired houses are not immediately evident; if anything large houses, such as 3, 16 and 54, tend to be separated from the rest of the settlement within their own quite independent ditched enclosures. It is, incidentally, instructive to note that the phosphate values inside the ditches around Structures 3 (?) and 16 are high; this might, perhaps, suggest that the enclosures were intended to prevent 'private' livestock from straying into the settlement as a whole; unwanted animal visitors could also be excluded from the areas enclosed.

Finally we come to the question of status hierarchies within the extended family occupying the settlement. Archaeological evidence for hierarchy is very poor indeed: house sizes are remarkably similar, there are no obvious finds of rank-enhancing artifacts (Binford's (1962) sociotechnic component) and, with the very dubious exception of Structure 20 which produced a greater quantity of wheel-made fine wares than other buildings, there are no obviously richer households. The evidence from the burials also fails to suggest the outward trappings of rank, assuming, that is, that in some (perhaps a few?) cases one might expect to find an important person buried, with the symbols of his/her status (Binford 1962). It must be admitted that only a very few inhumations were recovered, but these were all without grave goods of any sort. To quote Clarke again, 'if there is a 'headman' or 'headwoman' then he would appear to have been a 'first among equals', in material terms at least' (*ibid*, 835). One must suppose that the 'headman' or 'headwoman' at Cat's Water was the senior member of the extended family who would not have required symbols of office to maintain his/her position within the small community: such a position would have been enforced by family obligations and the customs of contemporary Celtic society.

FOURTH PHASE: DEMISE (1st AND LATER 2nd CENTURIES AD)

The demise of the Iron Age settlement was most probably due to increased wetness (for evidence see Appendices 2 and 3); but an alternative, historical, explanation is also possible.

It was noted in the Third Report (FNG 3, 154) that there was no physical link between the latest Iron Age phase at Cat's Water and the Fen Causeway which traversed the Fourth Drove subsite from ESE to WNW just a few paces north of the main settlement. A precise date for the construction of the Fen Causeway has still to be established, but the available evidence would suggest that it took place sometime in the third quarter of the first century (FNG 3, 151ff, with refs). The absence of any obvious archaeological connections between the road and the settlement, in the form of, perhaps, subsidiary droves, tracks and associated yards would be most unusual if the two were in fact existing at the same time; certainly settlements associated with the Fen Causeway in the Fen proper are closely linked to it by numerous ditches and trackways (eg Phillips 1970, map 13). If, as has been suggested, the road was probably military and constructed following the Boudiccan revolt of AD 60/1 it could further be suggested that the demise of the Late Iron settlement was a result of that political turmoil (Potter, forthcoming). There is, however, no archaeological evidence to support or refute this hypothesis. The abandonment of the Late Iron settlement could also have resulted from a combination of political, socio-cultural and environmental factors which we do not, as yet, have the evidence to disentangle. However if ground water played a major role in causing the settlement on Cat's Water to be abandoned, society was plainly able to cope with such apparent upheaval. The social structure of contemporary groups may indeed have facilitated movement and while the 'prime mover' may have been environmental, the strength of stimulus required to instigate such a move may only be guessed at, given our poor data. Contemporary social organisation would have played a crucial role in the management of economic and other effects brought about by environmental change.

The available evidence suggests that the Cat's Water settlement was abandoned sometime between the Roman Conquest and Boudiccan revolt. Chronologically the next occupation is found on the Vicarage Farm subsite, around the south and east parts of Area I (FIGS 4 and 5). Pottery from this partially excavated settlement(s) — which probably extended over much of the land between Areas I and II — is thought by Dr Wild (Chapter 7) to belong to the second half of the first century. There may well be some overlap between the final Iron Age phase at Cat's Water and the initial Romano-British presence on Vicarage Farm, but the dating evidence in question, coarse, locally manufactured pottery, is still not fully understood. It is also impossible to determine whether people moved from Cat's Water to Vicarage Farm or whether the latter settlement sprung from the Late Iron Age groups that are known elsewhere in the area.

Evidence for substantial Romano-British occupation at Fengate derives from two independent sources, and it is quite probable that both were broadly contemporary and were also probably culturally and functionally connected. The first element, that of the Cat's Water Romano-British settlement is known from current excavation; the second, that to the south in the 'Gravel Pits Settlement Area' of previous reports (FNG 1, FIG 1; FNG 2, FIG 3; FNG 3, FIG 3), is known from pottery in Peterborough Museum (published in this report, Appendix 10).

The Cat's Water Romano-British phase was most probably short-lived. Dr Hayes' study of the pottery (Chapter 7) suggests a lifespan of perhaps 40 years, centred on the third quarter of the second century, some 100 years after the abandonment of the main, Late Iron, settlement. The pottery evidence accords well with observations in the field. Many of the principal Romano-British ditches follow the approximate alignment of Late Iron ditches, but frequently off-centre, or along an edge (FIG 18). There is no evidence for substantial re-alignment or for modification of the Romano-British ditch system; moreover, Romano-British recuts of Late Iron ditches are often shallower than the original and are separated from them by thick accumulations of flood-borne or edge-derived sediments. Unfortunately, the fillings of the Romano-British ditches contain quantities of residual Iron-Age sherds mixed in with the younger calcite-gritted and Nene Valley Grey wares that are contemporary with the later settlement. The larger quantities of residual pottery argue strongly that much of the bone recovered is also residual and it has not proved possible to separate Iron Age from Roman animal bone, given the small size of the excavated sample. Direct evidence for any change in economy between Late Iron and Roman times is, therefore, lacking. The few waterlogged botanical samples do not, however, suggest that any drastic change took place in the intervening century or so (Appendix 5).

Perhaps the most striking feature of the excavated settlement is its droveway. This feature extends across the Storey's Bar Road subsite (FIGS 8 and 10), under Storey's Bar Road (now Fengate) itself, and onto the Cat's Water subsite where it enters the main excavated area to the SE (FIG 18, see also C C Taylor 1969, FIG 1, no 2). Although much of the evidence has been removed by the Roman recutting of the ditches, there are sufficient lengths of Late Iron Age ditch surviving, beneath and to one side of the later recut, both on Storey's Bar Road and Cat's Water, to indicate the presence of a Late Iron Age phase. The nature of this earlier phase is not altogether clear and there are some grounds to suppose that it might have been discontinuous in places (see, for example the pattern of ditches to the SE of the enclosure around Structure 46, FIG 18). The presence of ditched yards, entered via corner entrances, together with the ditched droveway, strongly suggest that livestock formed an important element in the Cat's Water Romano-British economy. It is, however, difficult, given the nature of the data, to be more specific. Dr Potter's work at Grandford and Stonea generally seems to support the picture that is emerging at Fengate: 'many of the small ditched enclosures, the drove-roads and the empty areas of peat- and silt-land (are) evidence for an intensive stock economy' (Potter forthcoming). Potter would see wool as an important component of the Romano-British Fenland economy, and this would probably hold true for Cat's Water, although the idea cannot be tested.

The rarity of Romano-British settlement features on Cat's Water has been discussed above (Chapter 4, Part II), and it was tentatively concluded that this was the result of post-depositional factors, such as flood-action and ploughing. The water-table particularly in winter, would have been very close to the surface and experience would quickly have shown that posts sunk deep into the ground would not have lasted long. The occupation and structural debris, such as brick and tile, therefore, probably derived from buildings that were either very shallow-set or were placed directly upon the ground surface. It has been noted that many of the Romano-British ditches contain deposits of flood clays (Appendix 2) and it is noticeable that these extend well into the ditch fillings. Although we do not have evidence that occupation was resumed after the episodes of flooding, there can be little doubt that life on Cat's Water must have been precarious during winter, and it is quite possible that the subsite may have been abandoned by men and beasts during wetter seasons.

The second element of Romano-British Fengate is provided by the finds of pottery in Peterborough Museum, published here for the first time (Appendix 10). As with most finds from the 'Gravel Pits Settlement Area', those discussed by Dr Hayes are poorly provenanced. It should be noted, however, that the definitive RCHM volume shows that there were 'Beaker, Bronze Age, Iron Age and Roman Settlements' immediately south-west of the main ditched droveway and a functional connection would seem probable (C C Taylor 1969, FIG 1). The nature of this settlement(s) must remain enigmatic, but the pottery is, in general, broadly contemporary with that from Cat's Water. Perhaps the latter subsite provided a Fen-edge focus for some of the stock-raising activities of the main settlement which was located on slightly higher ground in the 'Gravel Pits Settlement Area'.

We have seen that the ditched fields of the second millennium BC were abandoned and that settlement probably moved onto higher land. Earliest communities of the first millennium probably continued to live in a dispersed fashion, but towards the middle years of that millennium there are indications that changes were afoot: the settlement patterns shows signs of nucleation and there are also indications that mixed farming was becoming increasingly important. Permanent, rather than transhumant, occupation was the norm in the Middle and Late Iron Age at Fengate. The botanical evidence (Appendix 5) shows increased evidence for agriculture (not necessarily involving cereals), but at the same time livestock still maintained an important role in the economy (Appendix 6). Crops, of any type, and livestock must be kept apart, but the evidence for ditched fields is very poor. The RCHM plot of cropmarks (Taylor 1969, FIG 1) shows ditches running at right angles to the main Late Iron and Roman drove immediately SE of the intersection of Padholme Road and Storey's Bar Road. These were investigated in 1972 and only one was shown to be of Roman date (Padholme Road Area XI: see FNG 1, FIG 17, bottom left). The remainder were periglacial features or old stream channels. Similarly, the slightly meandering linear features that traverse much of Storey's Bar Road subsite on the RCHM plan (*ibid*, FIG 1) are not man-made.

Evidence for later Iron Age and Romano-British ditched fields or enclosures is, therefore, very slight. It includes one or two ditches on Vicarage Farm; the features that were once thought to comprise ditches 5 and 6 of the second millennium BC system of Newark Road; and the single ditch, just mentioned, for Padholme Road. This hardly constitutes convincing evidence. Perhaps the agriculture, or horticulture, indicated by the palaeobotanical evidence took place in gardens situated near the ditched enclosure, for which we have no archaeological evidence (but see Farmoor, Lambrick and Robinson 1979, 139). Perhaps crops were grown in areas which were defined by hedges situated outside the main ditched droveway, in the manner of the infield/outfield systems of Medieval times. Again, there is no evidence to support or refute this hypothesis. The Roman settlement pattern at Fengate differs from that of the lower Welland Valley, where the unenclosed landscape of the Iron Age was replaced by an enclosed and apparently well-ordered system of ditched fields and droveways (W G Simpson 1966, 24). Although pit alignments probably formed an important component of the Iron Age landscape in the Welland, there is still no convincing evidence for extensive Iron Age field systems, comparable, for example, with those of Iron Age Wessex. Similarly, the low-lying landscape of the Thames at Farmoor changes from Iron Age to Roman times. Ditched droves and rectangular fields become increasingly common in the latter period, both at Farmoor and at other sites in the area (Lambrick and Robinson 1979). It is still not clear why a similar pattern of events was not also observed at Fengate, where occupation in Roman times seems to have been short-lived and comparatively unintensive. Perhaps this may have been associated with a switch in emphasis slightly further upstream, towards the newly-founded town of Durobrivae (modern Water Newton). On the other hand, an urban centre would have required products that could have been produced, in some abundance, at Fengate. It would again seem that the environment holds the answer to this problem, for the extensive flooding that was so important a feature of the early third century AD would have posed serious problems to communities living at, or below, the fifteen foot contour. Given the undoubted importance of Durobrivae to the local economy, Fengate must still have played its part by providing summer pasture for livestock, together with such Fen resources as willow, fish and wildfowl (Wild 1974, 150-7).

No direct archaeological evidence for the many centuries of human activity that must have taken place on the site between the third century AD and modern times has survived: the recent excavations did not produce a sherd of Saxon or Medieval pottery and the huge amounts of colour-coated Castor wares so frequently encountered elsewhere in the Nene Valley were largely absent. Archaeologically speaking, there is a void between the late second century Romano-British settlement of the Cat's Water subsite and the Enclosure Movement ditches that surround the fields that form the boundaries of the subsites themselves.

PART IV: WIDER CONTEXTS

1. INTRODUCTION: THE DEFINITION OF THE REGION

The introduction to the Second Report outlined the way in which the site could be placed in its contexts. Three levels of analysis were envisaged: an intra-community level (activity areas, the function of different buildings etc), a micro-level (in which the inter-relationships of the various Fengate settlements was considered) and a macro-level, which was to be given over to a consideration of the 'changing relationships of the site, and its various communities, to the surrounding region' (FNG 2, 6). The intra-community and micro settlement patterns of the Grooved Ware and second millennium BC phases have been fully considered, in the Second and Third Reports. Later Bronze Age and Iron Age/ Romano-British intra-community and micro-settlement patterns have been considered in this report (Part III, above). It remains to discuss the macro-settlement pattern of the Iron Age and Roman periods.

The first problem of placing first millennium BC Fengate in a regional setting was the selection of an appropriate area for study. Ideally a contiguous area should have been field-walked as part of the main project (cf Ram's Hill — Bradley and Ellison 1975, chapters 5 and 6). This unfortunately proved impossible for practical and financial reasons. Given the enormous changes in land use that have taken place in the area over the past three hundred years, it is also impossible to attempt site catchment analysis, since the type of data required for such an exercise is unavailable (for modern criteria see Roper 1979). A suitable region may be selected on two grounds: first, it could be homogeneous, 'emphasising the homogeneity and uniformity of elements within the regional boundaries'; second, it could be heterogeneous where 'the inter-relatedness of diverse elements within the regional boundaries' is emphasised (Crumley 1979, 143).

A recent paper (Pryor 1980c), written four months after the final Fengate season, was largely devoted to problems posed by the definition of the region appropriate to the Fengate macro-level study. The paper concluded that a heterogeneous region would best suit the purpose. The area immediately adjacent to the site was not considered suitable, for purely practical reasons; instead it was decided to choose a neighbouring closely analogous area, in this case the lower Welland valley and its adjacent Fen (see also Pryor 1981 for a progress report of this work). The area chosen is very similar to that of the lower Nene valley, some ten kilometres to the south, so comparison should be close. The study of this heterogeneous region is based, at the macro-level, on a series of random aligned transects across the valley. Study at the intra-community and micro-levels will be focussed on two cropmark sites, Maxey and Barnack/Bainton, which are being excavated using methods and techniques that will allow direct comparison with Fengate. Two more seasons of field-work (1980/1 and 1981/2) will be required to finish this survey.

From Bronze to Iron: Local Developments in the Early First Millennium BC

We have seen that the transition period between the latest Bronze and earliest Iron Age is not well represented in the Fengate archaeological record, and it was concluded that much of the evidence for early settlement nucleation lies beneath modern Peterborough. It is, however, an interesting coincidence that there is a similar dearth of early first millennium sites elsewhere in the Fenland, around the western Fen-edge and in neighbouring river valleys. The reasons for this lack of information are not clear, but may reflect the problems we have already discussed with reference to the Early and Middle Neolithic 'void' at Fengate. A dispersed settlement pattern does not leave obvious archaeological traces; the recent discovery, by excavation alone, of the Fengate and Mucking Bronze Age ditched enclosures illustrates this point well. Further, much of the pottery, especially the fine wares, that we now associate with the Late Bronze Age, following excavations such as Runnymede Bridge, Egham (Longley 1976), would once have been placed in the early Iron Age. Flintwork of this period is also poorly understood; indeed, the evidence from Fengate would suggest that there was little or no use of flint on the site after the Middle Bronze Age (Pryor forthcoming). In sum, it seems probable that the scarcity of sites of this important transitional period, both on the Fen-edge and in the river valleys draining into the wetlands, could be more apparent than real. It results from insubstantial features and an inability to recognise pottery, combined with the absence (or extreme rarity) of diagnostic contemporary flint assemblages.

The abundant evidence for Neolithic and earlier Bronze Age activity in the region indicates a considerable population by the commencement of the Late Bronze Age. Detailed field survey by David Hall and colleagues has shown that land between, and including, the upper valleys of the Rivers Ouse and Nene in Northamptonshire and Bedfordshire was cleared of forest during the Bronze Age and very early Iron Age (Hall and Hutchings 1972, 8); indeed Hall would now see this as a conservative estimate and would regard these periods as 'late for actual clearance in many of the intensively settled areas' (pers comm). Good evidence for Bronze Age clearance of the heavy clay lands surrounding the Holme Fen basin has been provided by Godwin and Vishnu-Mittre (1975) and the organised, enclosed, landscape at Fengate strongly suggests clearance of local forest cover, by the start of the second millennium bc. Other, indirect, archaeological evidence for later Neolithic clearance is provided by the barrow fields at Maxey and Barnack in the Welland valley which would have lost their visual impact had they been placed in woodland; this suggestion is given greater weight by recent excavations of the wide (*c* 50m) cursus at Maxey. The two ditches, as they survived, were extremely slight (width *c* 2.0m max depth *c* 0.30m); even if a soil loss of another 0.30m is allowed — and this is a generous estimate — neither ditch is impressive and would have had no visual impact whatsoever in a wooded environment.

The intensity and extent of Iron Age settlement in the Nene valley of Northamptonshire is most impressive. Dozens of sites are known, both from aerial photographs, field walking and a combination of the two (see Hall and Hutchings 1972; C C Taylor 1975; Brown and Taylor 1978; RCHM 1975; RCHM 1979). Sites of the earliest Iron Age (or Ultimate Bronze Age) are apparently very rare: the vast majority of Northamptonshire sites are revealed by surface spreads of hand-made 'scored wares' (usually Middle Iron Age — approximately third to first century BC) or wheel-made 'Belgic' wares (Late Iron Age — post mid-first century BC). The distribution and sudden appearance of these sites requires explanation, and until a better alternative if put forward, it is suggested that the Fengate model for change from the transitional Late Bronze/Early Iron Age to the 'full' (ie Middle and Late) Iron Age can serve as a working hypothesis. Put concisely, it is suggested that the early centuries of the first millennium bc saw a change from an extensive, dispersed, pattern of settlement and land-use, which has left little archaeological trace, to a pattern where settlements were nucleated and where, largely due to environmental factors, some seasonally available marginal land was rendered less accessible. The loss of the resources of the Nene floodplain (principally hay and grazing), which were located in an area cleared of trees only a few generations previously, caused pressure to exploit the higher flood-free terrace gravels to increase. This, in turn, led to increased competition for scarcer available resources which, perhaps exacerbated by a growing population, found expression, at one level, in settlement nucleation and, at another, by the construction of hillforts (Hunsbury, Borough Hill, Arbury Camp etc).

It is, therefore, possible, that 'transitional' Bronze/Iron Age sites may be found beneath deposits of alluvium on the river floodplain, in the manner, for example, of the Orton Waterville barrows. This hypothesis does not require that the whole of the Nene valley be parcelled-up in the second millennium by Fengate-style ditched rectilinear enclosures. Fengate was probably a special case, being located on the edge of exceptionally large and rich summer pastures, with a correspondingly narrow band of flood-free gravel soils. These peculiar circumstances caused extra pressure on

231

winter pasture and hence the elaborate system of land management.

Further up the Nene, the band of seasonally-available floodplain pasture was narrower and the gravel terraces were wider. The pattern of settlement might be less intensive under these circumstances; there would, moreover, be smaller herds (whose size at Fengate would have been in part conditioned by the availability of the enormous Fen pastures nearby) and the light soils of the valley sides would be suitable for cereal cultivation. A more balanced pattern of mixed farming would not have necessitated the large investments of time and effort required to construct and maintain the Fengate ditched droves and enclosures which, on present evidence, are unique in their extent and complexity. This is an explanation based on very slight data and it may prove to be ephemeral. It is, however, of interest to note that recent work in the upper reaches of the Nene has produced evidence of third century AD alluviation on several Romano-British settlements (D. Windell, Northamptonshire Archaeological Unit, pers comm). This accords well with what is known of the same period both at Fengate and in the southern Fenland (Bromwich 1970). We have seen that flood deposits in one period may often conceal evidence for flooding in previous periods. There is widespread evidence for wetter conditions at the onset of the Sub-Atlantic climatic phase and exceptional circumstances preserved deposits of probable Late Bronze Age freshwater flooding on the Fourth Drove subsite (FNG 3, FIG 86). It is quite possible, therefore, that many areas that could be subject to alluviation in Roman times could equally be subject to similar processes in the later Bronze Age — 'flooding (with attendant effects) constitutes a natural process, routinely at work, rather than an anomalous or capricious event'' (Turnbaugh 1978, 605). Such processes, routinely at work along the upper and middle Nene valley, could have affected the numerous, dispersed, family communities that inhabited its floodplain and terraces in the Bronze and earliest Iron Ages. Perhaps similar patterns of settlement and land-use will become more apparent in neighbouring river valleys and along the Fen-edge when the results of recent excavation are made available.

Iron Age sites of the western Fen-edge and its associated river valleys

Reasons for the apparently sudden beginnings of full Iron Age settlement in the Nene Valley could be discussed *ad infinitum;* the explanation offered above is put forward for testing only and has no validity until independent data are found to support it. Having briefly touched on the earliest Iron Age in the region, it remains to consider recent local research into the period and how it relates to Fengate. The discussion will first consider the Peterborough area and the adjacent Welland valley; this is followed by a brief consideration of comparable sites in neighbouring parts of southern Lincolnshire. We then move south, to the Ouse valley of Cambridgeshire and Bedfordshire, before turning to the middle and upper Nene valley for a more detailed discussion.

This section, and the one that follows, are not intended to be comprehensive reviews of the Iron Age, for which the reader is referred to Cunliffe (1978). What follows are selective reviews of recent research into small lowland Iron Age settlements. Special emphasis will be given to site drainage and the way this affects feature morphology; an attempt will also be made to assess the exploitation and availability of seasonal resources, especially of hay and grazing.

Two important comparable sites have recently been excavated in the Peterborough area. The first, known as Monument 97, Orton Longueville, could not be completely stripped and seems to have stayed in use later than the Cat's Water settlement from, perhaps, the late first century BC until the middle of the second-century AD (Dallas 1975). There were three ditched rectilinear yards and the eaves-drip gullies of three round buildings were recovered in the single yard investigated. The yard ditches showed clear evidence for off-centre recutting in a manner reminiscent of Cat's Water. The interim report makes it difficult to judge the size of the community involved, but two, or at most three, nuclear families might have lived within the enclosed area. The second comparable site near Peterborough is at Werrington, just north of the city (Mackreth and O'Neill 1980). This Fen-edge site has many points in common with Cat's Water and Monument 97. It consists of a substantially-ditched rectilinear enclosure and molluscan evidence from the ditch primary and lower secondary filling indicates that it contained alternating phases of standing and slowly moving water (C A I French 1980b). The first phase would appear to be Middle/Late Iron Age; it included the remains of at least three round buildings of which two, very unusually, appear to have been post-built but without an exterior ring-gully to take the run-off from the roof. The largest round building was of more familiar construction with few interior features but it included a continuous and very substantial exterior eaves-drip gully, of a type frequently encountered on Cat's Water (Mackreth and O'Neill 1980, FIG 13). Although disturbed, the best preserved of the two post-built structures seems to have been constructed using two arcs of posts — in a manner reminiscent of the Cat's Water discontinuous gully round buildings. The layout of ditched yards in period two (late first century AD) recalls the Cat's Water Roman yards and the absence at Werrington of domestic features is also noteworthy. The site has produced quantities of organic material from its deep, waterlogged enclosure ditch and should provide valuable comparative material for Fengate. Finally, it is interesting to note that possible early Iron Age pottery (fifth/sixth centuries?) was recovered from an isolated pit which was not associated with the later settlement.

Clearly one pit cannot give evidence for a dispersed settlement pattern, but the similarities with contemporary Fengate are interesting.

The site at Werrington is located on the southern fringe of the Welland valley. Important excavations have taken place further upstream, but publication of these sites is still in progress and until final reports are available we must confine our remarks to a few general observations. Much of the work took place in the early and mid-1960s, ahead of gravel extraction. Pit alignments are perhaps the most distinctive Iron Age features of the lower Welland gravels and their use as boundaries seems in little doubt, since they frequently abut linear ditches (see, for example, W G Simpson 1966, FIG 5; RCHM 1960, 28-31, FIG 6). A pit alignment at Tallington (TF 105081), Lincs produced evidence for a continuous bank alongside the pits, rather than between them, as was suggested in the RCHM survey (1960, 28) (information courtesy of Mrs M U Jones). A precise date for all the Welland Valley pit alignments has yet to be determined, but they are most probably Iron Age and antedate the introduction of wheel-made pottery (RCHM 1960, 28, see also Jackson, 1974). In general, the fields or enclosures they demarcate are large and may well have been further subdivided in a manner that has left no archaeological trace. Fields or enclosures defined by pit alignments near Bainton are enormous: a computer-rectified plot of these cropmarks will be published shortly but, as an example, parts of one enclosure measure about 475m by 500m, or more (Pryor and Palmer, forthcoming, FIG 1). In some respects these enclosures recall the 'ranch boundaries' of the South Downs (Bradley 1971).

Gavin Simpson's important excavations in the lower Welland have already been briefly mentioned. The Tallington barrow cemetery has been fully published (W G Simpson 1976) and excavations in Bardyke Field Maxey (W G Simpson 1962-3) will appear with the present author's current excavation (mainly of the same monuments), following their completion in late summer 1981. In the interim, Mr Simpson has published a synthesis of his results which we have already touched upon (W G Simpson 1966).

An Iron Age enclosure at Maxey (W G Simpson 1966, site 60), presumably part of a farm, produced slag and refractory material from its ditches that indicated 'bronze and iron working on a small scale' (ibid, 18). This accords well with recent results from Cat's Water which are discussed by Dr Craddock in Chapter 6, above. Small-scale smithing and smelting is a common feature of Iron Age settlements of the region, although the evidence for tin working is so far unique to Fengate (a fragment of crucible coated with traces of tin was found in the ring-gully of a Middle Iron building, Structure 1, in Area I of the Storey's Bar Road subsite — see Craddock, sample 1). Preliminary evidence from current excavations at Maxey suggests that cereals were not grown on site, presumably because ground conditions were too wet, but instead were brought in, ready threshed to be ground into flour when required (F Green pers comm). Pollen analysis of samples from a Late Iron/Roman pit (RCHM 1960, FIG 7; W G Simpson 1966, FIG 4) showed a massive preponderance of grasses, but 'pollens of cereals and weeds of cultivation are relatively high' (Dimblelby in W G Simpson 1966, 18). Neighbouring sites at Tallington (nos 35 and 37) produced 'all the Little Woodbury structures…except grain storage pits. Their absence is probably to be explained by the high water table during winter months' (ibid, 18). The cereals grown at site 51 could not have been spring-sown and it is most probable that, as at Maxey, livestock would have played an important part in the economy.

The organisation of the Iron Age and Roman landscape of the lower Welland valley has already been discussed in the broader context of changing local patterns of land-use in the first millennium. At a more micro-level, the recent excavations at Maxey (RCHM 1960, FIG 6, Site 74) have produced about a dozen Iron Age and Romano-British round buildings which are defined by exterior eaves-drip gullies, with walls and other interior features barely set into the ground (Pryor 1981). The small 'hut' — if that is indeed its true function — from Site 35 at Tallington (W G Simpson 1966, FIG 2) is a peculiar feature with haphazardly placed stake-holes sunk into a wide, regularly-proportioned gully, most reminiscent of an eaves drip. Such features do not find ready parallels elsewhere in the region.

Excavations that did not take place under the aegis of the Welland Valley Research Committee have recently been published by Jackson and Ambrose (1978). The site in question, Wakerley, is located upstream of Stamford in the middle part of the Welland valley on a well-drained hillside overlooking the river. Its topographical position is, therefore, quite distinct from Cat's Water. Both sites are of approximately the same size (Cat's Water may be 20-30% larger), but Wakerley has a longer, more substantial, Romano-British occupation than Fengate. The pottery, of Middle and Late Iron Age type, from both sites is closely comparable and the later prehistoric material from Wakerley does not indicate that tht two sites were of significantly different economic status. Wakerley is located near the recently important steel- producing centre at Corby and there is evidence, particularly in the Roman period, for iron production on a much larger scale than, for example, sites further removed from the Northampton Ironstone, such as Maxey site 60 and, of course, Fengate.

The principal contrast between Wakerley and Cat's Water is the morphology of commonly occurring settlement features. At first glance the general plan of the drier site (Jackson and Ambrose 1978, FIG 1) seems similar to Cat's Water: there are several circular buildings, ditched enclosures and a somewhat denser scatter of pits and postholes. Closer inspection, however, reveals important differences. First, the enclosure ditches have sharper corners and are more regular in plan than those at Cat's Water; evidence for frequent maintenance recuts is extremely hard to find, indeed the ditch around the main Iron Age enclosure, A, 'was dug towards the end of the pre-Roman Iron Age and silted up during the early Roman period. There was no evidence of recutting' (*ibid*, 122). The multifarious recuts and off-centre re-alignments that are so important a feature of the Cat's Water ditches are entirely absent at Wakerley. The later site is also liberally sprinkled with postholes and at least five varieties of pits, some of which were probably used for grain storage. The round buildings at Wakerley varied in size, but showed 'a marked uniformity of design' (*ibid*, 133), which involved the weight of the roof being taken on an inner ring of posts while the wall was set in an exterior ring-groove. There was no evidence for an exterior eaves-drip gully. It is probable that the contrasts between the two sites reflects differences in ground drainage.

Having considered contemporary sites in the immediate Fengate region we will now briefly discuss comparable material from slightly further afield, in south Lincolnshire. It should also be noted that a more detailed discussion of material from the sites mentioned below is to be found in the discussion of Iron Age pottery in Chapter 6, above.

The Iron Age in Lincolnshire has been the subject of a recent authoritative study (May 1976) and little useful can be added here, other than to note that of the many sites discussed, all but one (Washingborough Fen, Coles *et al* 1979) have yet to be published in final form. Despite this, the distinction in feature morphology between well drained and poorly drained sites, discussed above, generally seems to hold good. Colsterworth (Grimes 1960b, FIG 6) does not, on the evidence available, appear to 'behave' in the manner of a well-drained site. It is located on limestone (May 1970, 192) and should consequently be well drained. Buildings, however, are highly reminiscent of Cat's Water, defined by penannular and discontinuous eaves-drip gullies, with infrequent internal post settings and possible overflow gullies that could have served to remove surplus water from the eaves-drip trench, in the manner of the Fengate, Newark Road structure (FNG 3, FIG 35), or Draughton, Northants (Grimes 1960b, FIG 5). The published plans also show very few of the scattered pits and postholes which have become such a familiar feature of many well-drained chalkland sites (eg K Smith 1977). On the other hand, there are no substantial interior drainage ditches and the exterior bank and ditch clearly have a defensive purpose.

The important Middle Iron Age settlement at Ancaster quarry illustrates the wet/dry contrast vividly (May 1976, FIG 68): drainage ditches do not appear on the published plan, buildings are not marked by substantial eaves-drip gullies and Little Woodbury-style storage pits abound (*ibid*, 135). Much further north, the later Iron Age site at Dragonby (May 1970; 1976, 182-91) is

located in an area with a high ground water table, as witnessed by the shallow wattle-lined wells that closely recall examples from Fengate (May 1970, PL xxxi). Drainage was always a problem and was undertaken by a network of main drains which linked into smaller, subsidiary 'feeder' gullies. Again, storage pits are rare and, in the earlier phases, a few circular gullies probably define the position of huts. These ranged in size from about six to nine metres in diameter, but the absence of postholes in the gullies or within the areas they enclosed, prevents any reasonable attempt to reconstruct buildings (May 1976, 182). The numerous examples of apparently simple 'huts' from Cat's Water, defined by penannular eaves-drip trenches alone, should greatly assist the notional reconstruction of similar buildings at Dragonby, where the absence of internal features must surely be a result of the high level of the winter water table.

We must now turn out attention from northern Lincolnshire, further south, to the valley of the river Ouse in Cambridgeshire and Bedfordshire. Again, we will confine our remarks to low-lying sites on the river terraces and floodplains.

The area has benefitted from a number of general surveys specifically devoted to the Iron Age. We will briefly consider these surveys and then discuss sites on the Nene/Ouse watershed. Moving downstream, we will next consider sites of the Bedfordshire Ouse, followed by those on the Cambridgeshire (Huntingdonshire) side of the county line, towards the Fen. Turning first to general surveys of the Iron Age in the Ouse valley, and working from the general to the particular, Angela Simco's assessment of the Bedfordshire Ouse valley in the Iron Age (Simco 1973) drew attention to the wealth of material from gravel pits which is reflected in her distribution map (*ibid*, FIG 1). This survey inevitably concentrates on pottery styles and little is said about other aspects of Iron Age life (no doubt a reflection of the data being considered); Simco does, however, point out that the pits from Harrold, to be discussed below, would have been too wet for storage, and the ancient history of the area is also very fully discussed.

The limitations imposed by the data were well presented by Dyer in his later summary (1976b): 'The objects by which we can date the period are limited, and are often old and ill-recorded finds, deposited in the county's museums. Many were found by chance...often in the last century. Excavation has been limited and tends to focus our attention on small areas, rather than present an overall picture' (*ibid*, 7). Dyer's attempt to redress the balance is wholly successful; discussing the earliest (Late Bronze/Early Iron Age) phase he observes that 'arable farming may have been carried out on the chalk uplands, with cattle in the valley bottoms and sheep on the open grassland'. He suggests that two parallel ditches of possible Middle Bronze Age date which are cut by the later linear earthworks known as Dray's Ditches at Streatly, Beds (Dyer 1961, FIG 4, ditches A1 and A2), could have formed the side ditches of a droveway, similar in many respects to those recorded in contemporary contexts at Fengate. Only a very small area was opened, however, so it is uncertain whether the two ditches continued to run parallel for any significant distance; the gap between the ditches is also quite narrow (c 1.4m) and this might argue against a droveway function. The idea is, however, attractive and limited excavation in the area could resolve the matter simply. In the Iron Age proper the Chiltern escarpment was divided into a series of 'territories' by Dray's Ditches; the significance of these territories is not certain, and Dyer (1976) has modified his original contention (repeated in Bradley 1978, 128) that each territory was marked by a central or near-central hill-fort, since some of the excavated hillforts are demonstrably later than Dray's Ditches. Problems are caused by the fact that Dray's Ditches require more extensive excavation, as indeed do the hillforts. It is probable that the Chiltern escarpment could be peripheral to the main distribution of people and sites on the valley floor, and that the hints at territoriality we see preserved along the periphery find their full, and no doubt complex, expression lower down, amidst the fields and paddocks near the floodplains of the slow-moving rivers and along the Fen-edge. Perhaps we will find answers to some of the questions encountered in studies of the chalk hills on lower land, in many cases miles away from the hillforts.

The complex relationship between upland and valley floor has recently been considered by Bradley (1978a, 555-7) who sees transhumance as the connecting mechanism. This may indeed prove to be the case in the early first millennium when the pattern of settlement was dispersed and communities were smaller; it is however hard to visualise wholesale movement in the latter part of the millennium. By Middle and Late Iron Age times the population along the valley floors was large and settlements nucleated; communities living close to the higher valley side, or central river floodplain, would no doubt have exploited these seasonally available lands, but the majority of groups living on the wide expanses of river gravel do not, on present evidence, seem to have led a shifting way of life.

Recent years have seen a shift towards field survey as a means of determining the extent and intensity of settlement. The Ouse valley has been particularly well served in this regard: around the higher reaches and across the interfluve to the Nene valley, Hall and Hutchings (1972) have revealed an extraordinary spread of Iron Age sites of all periods; further downstream Woodward (1978) has successfully related Bronze Age ring-ditches to contemporary settlement debris, thus demonstrating the importance of such low-lying locations before the Iron Age and its supposed land clearances (see also Fadden 1975). This early phase of land-use has recently been investigated by Field (1974) and Green (1974) who make a good case for seasonal exploitation of seasonally available resources, of which grazing is the most

significant. There is, therefore, much evidence that such locations were already cleared, and had probably been farmed for many generations before the start of the Iron Age.

We have claimed above that the low-lying valley floors were the principal areas of Iron Age settlement in Eastern England and we must now draw together the evidence for this. The Ouse valley in Bedfordshire is extraordinarily rich in crop-mark sites (Green 1974; Field 1974), but until recently the settlements have received insufficient attention. In the upper reaches David Hall (1971) has investigated two sites, at Bozeat and Strixton, revealed in his field survey of the Nene/Ouse interfluve. Both belong to the Late Iron Age and the continuous-gully construction of the buildings recalls Cat's Water; larger ditches showed evidence for recutting and although it is doubtful whether either site was occupied for an extended period, surface drainage must have been an important consideration. It is of interest to recall that the Bozeat building still had parts of its floor ('large pebbles and limestone pieces') intact, a phenomenon, as we shall see, that is frequently encountered in the Nene valley.

The gravel site at Radwell in the north of the county was also investigated by David Hall (1973), again under salvage conditions, ahead of gravel extraction. The principal remains were of a substantial Romano-British farm, but as is so often the case, there were also indications of a sizeable pre-Roman presence, which included four Late Iron Age burials, lengths of Iron Age enclosure ditch and a Bronze Age ring-ditch, associated with undecorated pottery comparable with that from Roxton which proved to be a damaged saucer barrow (*ibid*, 69). Neither ring-ditch revealed burials. Further Bronze Age barrows from Radwell have been recently published (Hall and Woodward 1977) and mention was made of Iron Age and Roman features, which will be published at a later date. The site, or rather complex of sites, is clearly of importance.

Salvage work during gravel working at Bromham (TL 017523) in the Ouse valley has also revealed a site of great potential. There is evidence for the production of 'Belgic' pottery and it is thought that the kilns were fired seasonally, for their stokeholes contained bands of wind-blown soil alternating with wood charcoal (Tilson 1973). There is evidence for numerous later Iron Age ditches and no indication for a break between the ultimate Iron Age and the subsequent Romano-British presence. Only one building has been published (Tilson 1975, FIG 1). This would appear to be of Middle Iron date and its post-built construction, with no entranceway arrangement is most peculiar; its size (dia. 1.7m), too, is small for a building. The site is clearly important, but the conditions under which it is being recorded are difficult.

The gravel pits at Wyboston, Bedfordshire (Tebbutt 1957), in the lower reaches of the river, have also produced a complex of Late Iron Age and Roman ditched paddocks on the river floodplain, in a location reminiscent of Farmoor (discussed below). The two round buildings of Late Iron Age date appear to have been constructed using a continuous circular gully; continuous gullies of this sort were thought at Cat's water to have been produced by rebuilding, which may have involved the moving of the doorway. The published phase plan does not make sense unless it is supposed that the Romano-British enclosure ditches were cut along earlier, Late Iron Age ditches, as at Cat's Water. The single schematic ditch section is interesting as it shows at least two periods of alluviation (the 'silt'). The first period was in the Iron Age, the second separated the upper Late Iron Age occupation from the subsequent Romano-British phase. It would appear that the Iron Age occupation ended at the Conquest and that the site lay deserted for a period of at least 60 years (*ibid*, 83). The later occupation seems to have been brief. If allowances are made for the problems experienced in recording features at Wyboston, and it is assumed that the features actually planned represent the bare outlines of the settlement, then the similarity to Cat's Water is striking: both sites ceased occupation at about the Conquest; both were abandoned for several decades and both have a short Romano-British occupation, which involved the recutting of earlier features. It would appear, too, that livestock formed the mainstay of both economies. It is particularly interesting to note (*ibid*, 76) that the farmer of the land stated that it had been flooded in 1947 (see discussion of Farmoor, below), but at no other time within his memory. One wonders how many other Iron Age farms lie buried beneath alluvium along the floodplain, on either side of the Wyboston settlement.

Two years before Tebbutt's salvage operations at Wyboston, J H Edwards undertook more ambitious salvage excavations ahead of gravel extraction, further upstream at Harrold, Beds (Eagles and Evison 1970). Unfortunately, the excavator died before the site's publication and this has clearly led to complications (illustrated by the fact that the otherwise full report lacks a phase plan). There are a number of intriguing features of which the ring-ditches are the most unusual. In size and diameter these ditches recall Bronze Age barrows, but pottery was exclusively Iron Age in type and only two burials were recovered. Seven possible Middle Iron Age houses were discovered and the plan of the trench system used to excavate these features (*ibid*, FIG 3) suggests that annular or penannular eaves-drip gullies defined the buildings, although one cannot be more precise.

More recently, excavation of Ouse gravel sites has been able to take place in a less hurried fashion. Woodward (1977) has carried out rescue work at a complex crop-mark site near Estow Abbey, at Pear Tree Farm (TL 050473), on the terrace gravels of the Great Ouse (Woodward 1977). Iron Age features belonged to the immediate pre-Conquest period. One well-preserved round building (*ibid*, FIG 3, F169) was built in the now familiar pattern of a penannular eaves-drip gully with no obviously recognisable internal features. Features included a substantial rectilinear enclosure ditch which had been recut through an earlier, also Iron Age ring-ditch which Woodward suggests was used for a 'palisade'; this 'palisade' was surrounded by a shallow drip trench. Other features comprised a linear ditch with multiple recuts and a group of circular, steep-sided pits which appear to have been filled-in shortly after being dug; these are interpreted as small gravel quarries. The settlement continued in use well into the Roman period without any apparent break. Woodward notes that 'the evidence from these small rural farm sites, points to a well organised and settled countryside prior to the Roman Invasion' (*ibid*, 35).

Work on a larger scale than Pear Tree Farm has recently been completed by Brian Dix at Odell, on the banks of the river Ouse, some 15km north-west of Bedford (Dix 1979). The site is located just 2.5km east of Harrold and an association between the two cropmark complexes seems most probable; although it is hard to be certain, given the nature of the Harrold material, the latter would seem to be slightly earlier than Odell. The layout of this riverside farmstead strongly recalls Cat's Water: enclosure ditches show evidence for multiple recutting and water was obtained from disused quarry pits and wattle-lined wells — one Saxon well was lined with a finely-made osier basket (*ibid*, 218). Given the height of the ground water table it is interesting to note that Dix records the presence of corn 'silos'; corn must be stored over winter and this, of course, is the time of year when the water-table is highest: other evidence includes querns (which could equally have been used to grind 'imported' grain), drying pits (?) and 'above all the field pattern'. The field pattern at Odell, with at least one substantial drove and numerous corner entrance-ways, points to livestock: some of the smaller paddocks would have made excellent yards for stock control. The location of Odell so close to the Ouse is hardly suited to agriculture; if cereal crops were grown in the Iron Age, then these would have been planted well back from the floodplain, higher on the gravel terrace. Odell is clearly a site of considerable interest, excavated to a high standard, and its publication is eagerly awaited.

Sites in the lower Ouse valley of Cambridgeshire have received far less attention than those in Bedfordshire; many were published in the Huntingdonshire journal, whose disappearance is much regretted. The important complex of cropmarks around Brampton, Huntingdon, were excavated in 1966 (White 1969) but the Huntingdon RDC insisted that excavations must not penetrate below 18 inches (in case it upset subsequent housing!). In addition to Bronze Age ring-ditches, the excavations revealed a rectangular ditched enclosure around three structures. The site is low-lying (below 50ft OD), located near the Ouse and has a sandy and clayey alluvial subsoil which cannot drain very efficiently; this is demonstrated by the fact that the whole area was criss-crossed by modern mole-drains. The single enclosure ditch had a low internal bank of gravel which still survived. The 'huts', if that is what they were, were of scoop-and-post construction of a type unparalleled in the region. The enclosure ditch was slight and the sections suggest that it filled-in naturally; there are no reasons to suppose that such a slight feature had a defensive function and it is best seen either as a ground-water drain or as a means of controlling livestock. The pottery is of Late Iron Age type and the site was not occupied in the Roman period; it would seem therefore, to have been abandoned at about the same time as Cat's Water and Wyboston.

The construction of a pumping station at Houghton, midway between Huntingdon and St Ives, in the Ouse floodplain produced a quantity of Late Iron Age and Romano-British pottery, the former from the filling of a ditch. Clearly this material indicates the presence of a settlement site (Garrood 1942). Settlement in this area was not confined to the flood plain, however, as the discovery of Late Iron Age and Romano-British pottery at Salome (pron 'Salem') Lodge, Leighton attests (Garrood 1939). This site is situated on a poorly draining clay soil on the higher land overlooking the Fen, at about 46m above OD. There is evidence for ditches in both periods and, again, a settlement is indicated.

Our discussion has taken us to the edge of the Fen where there would now appear to be more evidence for Iron Age settlement than had previously been supposed (see, for example, the relevant maps in Fox 1923 and Fox, Burkitt and Abbott 1926). The farm at the edge of the Fen at Woodwalton, Hunts has produced evidence for Iron Age settlement (Garrood 1935, 277). Slightly further south at Monks Wood there are indications of an early Romano-British settlement, with what would appear to be a Late Iron Age component (Garrood 1932, PL 1).

More recently Maisie Taylor has carried out a survey of fieldwork and has shown how much extra information may be discovered by detailed research of this sort (M Taylor 1980). She notes, in particular (*ibid,* 28) 'the increased number of sites on the western Fen edge', concentrated 'in a narrow band around the Fen-edge'. We have briefly indicated the potential of these sites, as recorded in old publications, but modern excavation of at least one is urgently required.

Having briefly considered recent work in the Ouse valley, it is necessary to return north and look at the Nene valley in greater detail. It is a pleasure to introduce this discussion with the important small site at Draughton, Northants, excavated by Professor Grimes who, as Chairman of the Nene Valley Research Committee did so much to encourage early work at Fengate. The site illustrates particularly well some of the characteristics of poorly-drained locations, despite its position on the Northamptonshire Heights, close to

the Jurassic Way, overlooking the valley (OS 1967; Grimes 1951; 1960b). The site was located on impervious boulder clay where surface drainage was clearly a serious problem requiring businesslike solutions. In particular, surface run-off from the roofs and walls of houses was removed either by a short antenna-like ditch leading to a soak away, or, in the case of the largest round-house, it was channelled through an overflow gully about fifteen metres in length which traversed part of the yard surface, passed through the entrance and discharged into the outer ditch (Grimes 1960b, FIG 5). Grimes notes (*ibid,* 23) that 'there were suggestions that the overflow gully had been at least partly covered with slabs'. One of the two smaller buildings (B) was defined by two opposed discontinuous gullies, highly reminiscent of Cat's Water (*ibid,* FIG 5). Despite the fact that Draughton has a substantial rampart and ditch and in surface morphology closely resembles many small upland sites, the details of its layout recall Fen-edge usage and reflect the importance of entirely local factors, of which the most significant is surface drainage.

Following the work of Professor Grimes, recent advances in the Iron Age of the middle and upper Nene owe an important debt to the excavations and publications of Dennis Jackson. We have already mentioned Wakerley and it remains to consider some of Mr Jackson's more significant Nene Valley Iron Age sites (smaller or less complete sites are touched on in Chapter 6).

From the Cat's Water viewpoint, the most significant site published by Jackson is Twywell, near Thrapston, in the middle Nene valley (Jackson 1975). This Middle Iron Age site lies at 225ft above OD on poorly drained marly clay or limestone subsoil in an area known to be rich in Iron Age sites (Hall and Nickerson 1966; Hollowell 1971). In general, the drainage at Twywell was poor, as boulder clay was predominant, but some areas of limestone did drain well. The occupants of the site therefore adopted a 'fail safe' policy in which poor drainage was assumed, regardless of actual soil conditions. This is well illustrated by the three round structures, Huts II, III and V (Jackson 1975, FIG 3) where Huts III and V were on poorly drained clay land, but Hut II, between them, was located on well-drained limestone (Jackson, pers comm). These variable conditions probably account for the numerous pits whose location depends on the height of the winter water-table and the permeability of the bedrock, than on surface drainage. The main enclosure ditches appear to have been frequently recut (eg *ibid,* ditch F226) and the construction of the buildings also recalls Cat's Water practices. Clay-lined shallow pits, interpreted by Professor Hawkes (*ibid,* 66) as dyeing pits, and often located inside round buildings, are more simply seen as 'sinks' used to hold water for general domestic use (*cf* this report Structure 3, FIGS 26 and M35).

Moving from the micro-level to a wider consideration

of the Twywell settlement, Jackson notes (*ibid,* 66) that livestock and pastoralism were important; carbonised grain was found in an early pit (F132), but was not found associated with any other feature and 'no finds suggestive of arable farming were recovered beyond storage pits, the function of which need not necessarily be that of corn storage'. The settlement was located on the interface of permeable (limestone) and impermeable (boulder clay) soils and it is plausibly suggested that the arable fields were located on the limestone lands with, presumably, stock on the heavier soils. The roadway to the site runs along the boundary between the heavier and lighter soils allowing 'immediate access to either one of these areas of exploitation'. It is difficult to estimate the size of the settlement and in view of the suggested dual role of round buildings at Cat's Water, Jackson's original view that the settlement, in its final stages, 'had assumed the nature of a small village' (*ibid,* 67), may need revision. Jackson does, however, note that occupation debris was concentrated in gullies of two houses (Huts II and V) at their entrances (quoted in Williams 1974, 18; also pers comm). If such concentrations were noted in two buildings alone, it suggests that some of the other structures did not have patterned finds distributions and consequently their use as non-domestic buildings is a possibility.

Apart from Twywell there are few truly comparable rural settlements in the Nene valley. Sites such as Irchester (Hall and Nickerson 1966) or Ashton (Hadman and Upex 1975; 1977; 1979), notably successful in Roman times, do not appear to have had particularly humble Iron Age origins. Prehistoric features at both sites have suffered at the hands of their Romano-British successors, but finds from the few ditches that have survived are demonstrably finer than those from Fengate (see discussion in Chapter 6; Iron Age pottery finds from Ashton and Oundle are as yet unpublished, but their quality and quantity are remarkable).

The site at Aldwincle is perhaps best known for its Neolithic and Bronze Age funerary monuments (Jackson 1976b), but the extensive gravel quarry in the flood plain of the river Nene (at its junction with the Harpers Brook, a small tributary) also produced a number of important Iron Age features (Jackson 1977a). The Iron Age phases consisted of three ditched rectilinear enclosures (*ibid,* FIG 5, enclosures B, C and E) together with a complex ditch system. The ditches, numerous pits and the construction of most round buildings are very reminiscent of Twywell, which is somewhat earlier than Aldwincle; structures are defined by external eaves-drip gullies, but with one notable exception. The exception, Hut 2 (*ibid,* PLS 3 and 4, FIG 8) was built in two phases each of whch was of almost the same size, and featured the penannular groove so often associated with an eaves-drip. There was only one ring-gully, and this carried the clear traces of split timbers which originally carried the walls; the roof was carried on posts set irregularly within the building's interior and the expected eaves-drip was absent. This most unusual structure finds no parallel elsewhere in the area and one must look to Wakerley, some 15 miles to the north-west for comparable buildings. The various settlement ditches show evident signs of maintenance and recutting, indeed the modern water table complicated much of the excavation (*ibid,* 13). The height of the winter water table may well account for the 'limited amount of pits found within the enclosure (E)'. One pit contained fragments of bronze, charcoal and fire-reddened soil which the excavator tentatively concludes might be associated with bronze-working. Although only limited excavation was possible, it does appear that the three enclosures were occupied at different times between the first/second centuries BC and the first century AD. Aldwincle, like Moulton Park which we will consider shortly, seems typical of the small, perhaps single family farmsteads which are familiar on aerial photographs of the area (Hollowell 1971).

Moulton Park is the first of two smaller Iron Age settlements excavated ahead of the development of Northampton New Town (Williams and Mynard in Williams 1974). It was not possible to completely strip the site, but efforts were successfully made to determine its original extent (*ibid,* FIG 2). It appears to have been occupied for two, or possibly three phases, the first just antedating the introduction of wheel-made pottery (therefore late second/early first century BC?) the last ending at, or perhaps just before, the Roman Conquest. The site is located about 4.5 kilometres north of the Nene on poorly draining clay soils. All the features typical of such sites were present: round buildings rarely had internal post-settings and were usually defined by continuous penannular eaves-drip gullies or shorter lengths of discontinuous gully (eg *ibid,* FIG 7, Houses 3 and 6; features G36, G38 etc). The buildings themselves sat within three irregularly-shaped enclosures defined by ditches of varying width, which, on surface plan at least, appear to have been kept clear by regular maintenance. Stratigraphic evidence for recutting was hard to obtain owing to the uniformity of the ditch fillings (see, for example, *ibid,* FIG 4 and 5); very careful excavation, did, however, produce clear signs of recutting in one section (c) of the ditch around Enclosure 1 and the authors suggest, quite reasonably, that recutting may not have been localised (*ibid,* 8). At one point the ditch around Enclosure 2 had been bridged by a causeway set on a bed of herringbone masonry, a most unusual find in Iron Age contexts (*ibid,* PLS 3 and 4). Pits were extremely rare and it is interesting to note that pottery was common in the gullies of all six round buildings, 'and in all cases the pottery was most prolific at the entrance; moreover there was also an accumulation of stone at the entrance of houses 2 and 4' (*ibid,* 18). On this evidence it would appear that all the round buildings were used to house people and we must suppose that livestock, if they were over-wintered on site, were accommodated within buildings associated with gullies such as G36, G38, G45 and G46 etc (*ibid*, FIG 7). The excavators estimate the population of this farmstead was at least one nuclear family, and probably somewhat larger at its greatest extent (*ibid*, 18-9). Unfortunately there is little data on which to base a reconstruction of the economy, but the heavy land and the proximity of water and seasonally-available flood-plain pasture would suggest that livestock played a prominent role: the provision of the massively reinforced causeway across the ditch around Enclosure 2 might indicate the presence there of large beasts, such as cattle.

The second later Iron Age settlement near Northampton, Blackthorn, was situated on well-drained sandy soil overlooking the Nene valley; heavy clay soils outcropped roughly 100 metres north of the site (Williams and McCarthy in Williams 1974). It consisted of a double ditched enclosure with a single entrance and an internal area of about a quarter of an acre; settlement features were 'traces of an oval house and 28 pits' (*ibid*, 44). There are inconclusive hints at a post-built entrance structure and it is thought that the two enclosure ditches which are strictly parallel were contemporary. There is no good evidence for a bank either between, outside or inside the two ditches, but collapsed limestone rubble in the southern terminal of the inner ditch could have derived from a revetment wall (or perhaps a road surface?). A shallow open U-shaped gully defined a small (8.5 x 6.0m internal dimensions), slightly 'squashed' oval building. This gully appears to have been the foundation for a wall and the slightly sunken area it surrounded still contained traces of flooring or floor debris ('pottery, bone, black soil and a large quantity of stones overlay the metalled surface and extended slightly over the clear fill of the gully' — *ibid*, 48). The gully was broached by a stone-revetted drain which ran out of the house, through the wall gully and into the inner enclosure ditch. Floor deposits and *in situ* rubbish are now known from a number of sites in the region — a plough ridge preserved partial floor deposits within Hut IV at Twywell (Jackson 1975, FIG 17) and at Cat's Water, trample within Structure 54 caused the loose infilling of a blocked well to compress, thus allowing some floor material to accumulate at a greater depth than usual (FIG 75-78).

Perhaps the most important local Iron Age discovery was at Brigstock, Northants, where Iron Age features survived until very recently as earthworks (Jackson 1979a); floor deposits have been partially preserved and were excavated in 1980 (Jackson, pers comm). Floor deposits or, more correctly, partially preserved floor deposits, are extremely rare on lowland British non-waterlogged prehistoric sites and Northamptonshire must be counted extremely fortunate in this respect (see also Britnell 1974; 1975, FIG 1; Bersu 1977; Lambrick 1978, 118).

One 'floor' of particular interest was discovered during salvage excavations, combined with a watching-brief, ahead of housing development on the outskirts of Wellingborough, at Hardwick Park (Foster *et al* 1977, FIG 9). This 'floor', on the basis of stratified metalwork, would belong to the second quarter of the first century AD, but it is doubtful whether it was in fact associated with a building at all. The whole settlement, which is mainly of later Iron Age date and based around the now familiar pattern of ditched rectilinear yards, is extremely enigmatic, largely due to the difficult conditions under which recording had to take place. Its earliest phase, however, would appear to be Middle Iron Age (Everson 1976).

The ditched enclosures at Hardwick Park are located along a small stream on gently sloping land to the west of modern Wellingborough. The subsoil, chalky boulder clay, is generally poorly draining and there can be little doubt that the numerous enclosure ditches must have had an important drainage function, which is borne out by the fact that many of the enclosures are recut, 'showing constant use and re-use' (Foster *et al* 1977, 58 and FIG 3). Actual ring-gullies were not encountered, but this reflects the difficult conditions in which the work took place, as the quantities of occupation debris strongly indicate that the associated settlement(s) was in the immediate vicinity of the enclosures. The layout of the enclosures is reminiscent of Moulton Park, discussed above.

The small Middle Iron Age settlement at Geddington, Northants, was situated near the river Ise, a tributary of the Nene (Jackson 1979b). The subsoil drained poorly and the single round building encountered was built in the familiar pattern of a recut eaves-drip ring-gully. Some of this recutting appears to have been incomplete and is best interpreted as day-to-day ditch maintenance, as the excavator noticed that the sandy bedrock weathered quickly. It is interesting to record that all the finds from within the ring-guly were concentrated on either side of the entrance (Jackson, pers comm).

We have noted that there is evidence that large tracts of the Nene Valley were cleared of trees by the onset of the Iron Age, and this is confirmed by molluscan analyses at Blackthorn (Evans in Everson 1976). This would agree well with the early date (Late Bronze/Early Iron) of some recently excavated pit alignments (Jackson 1974; 1978), whose significance has been discussed above with reference to the Welland valley (see also D R Wilson 1978).

This brief review of recent developments in the Iron Age of the Nene valley shows that livestock management must have been of considerable significance, especially to communities living near the major flood-plains. Pastoralism, on its own, is not indicated by the available evidence, but the hay and grazing that were so plentiful during the drier months of the year must have played an important part in the local economies. Little can be said concerning communication along the valley, whether in the form of trade, barter or reciprocal

239

exchange to help reinforce social ties and obligations. The evidence is still pitifully thin. Most of the communities we have discussed were small farmsteads of perhaps three or four families, at the most. Material 'luxury' items do not appear to have found their way into later Iron Age rural rubbish deposits, but it is interesting to record the occurrence of Cornish 'Gabbroic' fine ware from a settlement at Weekley, Northants (Jackson 1977b). Weekley is currently the most easterly findspot of this distinctive pottery.

We may summarise the current position of Nene valley Iron Age studies briefly: the later pottery is, on the whole, well understood from a typological point of view (see discussion of Groups 2 and 3, Chapter 6, above). Our knowledge of contemporary stock-raising practices and agriculture is, however, based more on inference than solid data. The Early Iron Age is poorly understood in all respects. The area is extremely rich in potential, as witnessed, for example, by the finds of partially preserved floor deposits, but so far the resources to tap that potential have been lacking. A proper understanding of the Iron Age in any river valley requires that the valley be seen as a whole: interfluve, valley side, terrace and floodplain. At present the Nene valley is seen in four regions: the Fen-edge, the lower, middle and upper reaches of the valley. It is most important that these divisions be removed, for only then will we be able to appreciate the interaction of the various elements that go to make up the region. In short, we must assess the heterogeneity of the valley.

COMPARISONS BEYOND THE FENLAND CATCHMENT AREA

Introduction

This discussion is an attempt to view Fengate in terms broader than the local contexts discussed in preceding sections. Emphasis will be given to the variety of adaptive responses encountered between and within different wetland environments, and the way these are revealed in the archaeological record. Strict chrono-logical or typological links between Fengate and the various regions discussed will not be stressed. The discussion first considers sites in lowland Britain, then moves further afield, to the southern North Sea Basin.

Comparative sites in lowland Britain

Recent work in the Thames valley by the Oxfordshire Archaeological Unit is especially relevant to Fengate and will be considered in some detail. This research has been carried out to a high standard and should serve as a model on which to base future study of the Nene valley. Current work in the Thames valley was preceded by the publication of a synthesis and survey of cropmark sites (Benson and Miles 1974). This survey was fol-lowed, slightly later, by similar surveys further upstream (Gates 1975; Leech 1977).

The Oxfordshire Unit's work in the Thames valley has mainly been confined to the soils of the terrace and the floodplain; some upland soils have been field-walked and surveyed from the air, but this work is still at an early stage (Lambrick 1978). 'The policy of the Unit has been to try to produce fairly complete pictures of a few settlements rather than piecemeal observations of many sites' (*ibid*, 104). Five sites have been selected for special attention and two have already appeared in final published form.

The first site to be published was located on the Thames second terrace gravels at the Ashville Trading Estate, Abingdon (Parrington 1978). In common with many favourably located gravel sites, Ashville included features of more than one archaeological period and we will confine our attention to its substantial Iron Age component. The first Iron Age phase produced evidence for a small approximately circular structure defined by an irregular penannular gully enclosing four post settings (*ibid*, FIG 10). There are parallels for this type of gully at Fengate (FIG 18: structure 47) and elsewhere in the Nene valley (Williams 1974, FIG 28) and Parrington's interpretation — that the structure was a hut or granary — seems entirely convincing. Professor Harding interprets such structures as 'shrines' (1974, FIG 26); here there is no guarantee that the three elements, cremations, four-poster, and ring-gully, are contemporary. The Iron Age 'temple' at Brigstock is built in the manner characteristic of (other) Nene valley round houses (*ibid*, FIG 27). The recutting of the Ashville gully is consistent with its use as an eaves-drip and, again, finds numerous parallels in the Nene valley (see also Harding 1972, FIG 4, Gully A). In general, the pottery from features of Period 1 and at Ashville is very broadly comparable with Fengate Group 1 and the date proposed by DeRoche (in Parrington 1978, 72) — mid sixth to *c* 300BC — also agrees with that proposed for the earliest Iron Age at Fengate. Apart from the single recognisable building, the early Iron Age at Ashville was characterised by a scatter of pits in the south-east corner of the area excavated.

Period 2 at Ashville dates to the Middle Iron Age and is characterised by the building of some 18 round buildings closely comparable with the type found on Cat's Water and elsewhere in the Nene valley: pen-annular gullies vary in diameter from 11.5 to 26m, (markedly larger than Fengate where the maximum diameter encountered was 12m — Structures 6, 13, 18 and 49). Following the discovery of environmental evidence from Farmoor (Lambrick and Robinson 1979, 138) the penannular gullies at Ashville are interpreted as eaves-drip or drainage features; again, this agrees with the interpretation of similar features at Fengate. Internal features, such as wall slots, postholes etc were rare and this is thought to be due to post-depositional factors. One Middle Iron complex of round buildings and associated annexes defined by approximately circular gullies (Parrington 1978, FIG 12) finds a good parallel with the Cat's Water structure complex, comprising structures 21, 22, 34 and 35. The function of these paired buildings and roofed or open annexes is not certain, but an association with livestock seems most probable. Comparable structures are also known from Hod Hill, Stanwick and Farmoor (see Chapter 4). Period 3 at Ashville (Late Iron Age) is marked by a series of small ditched square fields, less than half an acre in size, and isolated pits or postholes are rare.

The general layout of the main Middle Iron Age phase at Ashville is typical of a well drained gravel terrace site: large drainage ditches are absent and there is a characteristic scatter of small pits and postholes. It is interesting to note that the technique of building construction found at Ashville is also suited to poorly drained sites or areas with a high seasonal water table. Two buildings — defined by ditches 19 and 13 — showed an increase in finds' density 'around the entrances' (Parrington 1978, 35). Of special interest is Parrington's observation (ibid, 39) that some of the round buildings were arranged in rows in a similar way to the unexcavated (but probably Iron Age) ditched 'promontory fort' at Dyke Hills near Dorchester-on-Thames (Benson and Miles 1974, 92). Parrington uses an upland model to interpret the settlement's internal organisation. The present author, while acknowledging the Dyke Hills linear arrangement of some ten round buildings is less convinced by the Ashville evidence, where the greatest length of any demonstrable row is just three buildings. The model chosen is not necessarily suited to the Thames terraces and finds no ready parallels elsewhere in the lowlands. This, of course, is not to say that space within the Ashville site was not organised, but merely that the organisation, to judge by simple inspection of the general plan (Parrington 1978, FIG 3), does not appear particularly linear (for contrast compare Cunliffe 1976, FIG 2; Guilbert 1975, FIGS 1 and 2). It is interesting, too, to note that only two buildings showed finds concentrated around the entrance and one might speculate whether some of the other buildings may have been used for non-domestic purposes; perhaps the interior organisation was more 'organic', less linear, than Parrington has proposed. Turning to the environment, Martin Jones' detailed report (in Parrington 1978, 93-110) indicates that a variety of cereal crops were being grown and that there was 'a mature arable environment' at the onset of Period 1. This would, in turn, indicate that clearance was underway, at the latest, by the Middle Bronze Age. In this regard it is of interest to note that the two Middle Bronze Age cremations had been fired with blackthorn and/or hawthorn wood which Jones regards as typical either of regenerating scrubland or, alternatively, of thorn hedgerows. Cereals would have been grown on the terraces and on dry rather stony ground to the north; the latter clay soils were inferior (especially in droughts) to the terrace gravels, but superior to the poorly-drained clay lands to the south. As time progressed it would seem that the two better types of land became less fertile, reflecting a gradual depletion of soil nitrogen, and greater efforts were consequently made to exploit the less suitable soils to the south. The exploitation of these wetter soils is reflected in Period 2 by the importance of the damp-tolerant club wheat and the spike rush (Eleocharis palustris), the latter of which comprises up to 14% of the Period 1 and 2 samples (Jones, ibid, 109). In the Late Iron Age, however, damp tolerant species are far less common and Jones attributes this, most plausibly, to better ground drainage. Evidence for improved drainage is provided by the ditch system which occupies the excavated area in Period 3. This improved land drainage must be seen as an extensive operation of considerable importance.

The Ashville animal bones are given more detailed consideration in Appendix 6 of this report and only a few general points need be repeated here (Wilson et al in Parrington 1978, 110-39). It would appear that sheep and pigs were slaughtered young and that meat was of importance. Cattle and horses were kept for longer and may have been used for dairy products and traction respectively. It is also suggested that sheep were kept on higher, better drained, ground while cattle were principally grazed on the floodplain meadows and on damper ground nearer the river. Ashville shows a considerable preponderance of sheep over cattle, in marked contrast to Farmoor where, although the figures are less pronounced, cattle occur more frequently (Wilson in Parrington 1974, 136). The Cat's Water figures show cattle to be more frequent than sheep and indicate a mix of livestock broadly comparable with sites such as Barton Court Farm on the Thames first terrace, within easy reach of the floodplain meadowland. Meadowland at Fengate would, of course, have been provided by the Fens. Special emphasis has been given to Ashville as this is the type of site which located on slightly higher land, might have complemented Cat's Water at the edge of the Fen. It could have provided the cereals and wool — to name just two important products — that were less readily produced at Fengate; in return, we may envisage dairy products, salt (perhaps, in turn, redistributed from sources located deep within the Fen), hides, fish and fowl being sent to the local equivalents of Ashville, situated on land now covered by modern Peterborough.

The second site published by the Oxfordshire Unit, Farmoor, is located on the junction of the Thames first terrace and the river floodplain (Lambrick and Robinson 1979). The site consists of a number of separate elements, spaced over a much larger total area than Ashville. As at Cat's Water, deposits of alluvium tended to mask cropmarks. Excavation was carried out on an *ad hoc* basis, whenever archaeological features were encountered by the contractors; nonetheless the results, and most particularly the biological analyses, gave a complete and coherent picture. The division between floodplain and terrace is based on the floods of 1947 which reached 203ft above OD in this area (compare Salway 1967, PL VII).

The Early Iron Age at Farmoor is represented by a few scattered pits which need not detain us. The main interest in the site lies in its three Middle Iron Age farmsteads which bear a striking resemblance to elements of Cat's Water. These farmsteads were located well within the floodplain and there is environmental evidence to suggest that they were all subjected to repeated flooding. Each of the farmsteads was occupied for no more than about five years. The round buildings were constructed in the pattern, now familiar, of continuous penannular gullies which 'must have been recut almost annually (or even more frequently)' (*ibid,* 138). There is no doubt, moreover, that the gullies were open and were not used as wall slots. One possible semicircular building is also recorded. It would appear that the principal role of the floodplain settlements was the minding of cattle during the drier months of the year; when conditions became too wet people and livestock would move to the drier land of the terrace nearby. A few carbonised grains show that cereals were consumed, but were not grown on site. The actual settlement(s) which must have complemented the Farmoor summer sites have not been located, but Robinson and Lambrick (*ibid,* 135) suggest that they would have resembled Ashville.

The three very short-lived settlements of the floodplain were abandoned and the site was unoccupied in the Late Iron Age. Occupation was resumed in Roman times after a period of increased alluviation which could be associated with increased agricultural activity and particularly with increased clearance (*ibid,* 126; *cf* Godwin and Vishnu-Mittre 1975, 587). This evidence supports the impression of increased agricultural activity provided by the proposed Late Iron Age drainage operations at Ashville. By Roman times the Farmoor landscape had changed considerably: the floodplain hollows were now filled by alluvium and the Middle Iron Age farmsteads must have been buried too. The landscape was now, apparently for the first time, divided up into ditched (and possibly hedged) fields and paddocks. A substantial ditched droveway led down to the floodplain edge, and there was a small settlement whose principal purpose was the exploitation of floodplain pastures. By Roman times there is botanical evidence for agriculture in the immediate neighbourhood — although its precise location is still uncertain. The Roman settlement also boasted gardens which featured box hedges. There are obvious similarities between features of the Middle and Late Iron Age at Cat's Water and their counterparts at Middle Iron Age Farmoor. First, pits are rare on both sites and the penannular ring-groove pattern of house construction is found on both sites; buildings with annexes or within small enclosures are also frequently encountered. Major drains are absent at Farmoor, as these would have been

ineffective against the severe annual floods, and their maintenance would not have been cost effective. Cat's Water shows no signs of having been flooded while it was occupied and in this respect it differs from Farmoor. In terms of the Fen-edge, we may imagine that sites similar to Farmoor would have been located perhaps half a mile east of Cat's Water in the pastures of the peat Fen proper. Had a Middle or Late Iron Age settlement been located alongside the Romano-British droveway at Farmoor, then the analogy between the two sites would have been closer. Sites of this type are known in the Thames valley, but final publication of recent excavation is still in progress. Two sites that could prove relevant are Hardwick, Mingies Ditch, on the Windrush floodplain, and Appleford, between Abingdon and Dorchester on the first terrace gravels. The former is surrounded by two substantial ditches and there is an attached ditched paddock or enclosure. The plan (Lambrick 1978, FIG 4) shows elaborate entrance arrangements, while the interior contains a number of well-preserved structures including six round buildings (of which no more than four could have been contemporary), two four-post structures, 'and various working areas' (*ibid,* 114). The enclosure, moreover, 'was entered along a gravel road and at one stage there was a gate across the entrance' (*ibid,* 144). Several structural phases are apparent in contrast with the smaller Farmoor enclosures; it is also difficult to suppose that the area was subject to flooding as heavy or frequent as Farmoor. The main surprise, however, is that the Mingies Ditch environment was not open grassland as at Farmoor: 'there was a large element of scrub in the immediate vicinity, including field maple (a species indicating well established scrub, hedges or woodland)' (*ibid,* 114).

Unfortunately, Appleford the site with most in common with Cat's Water, produced little detailed information. The published plan (*ibid,* FIG 5) hints at quite substantial drainage ditches, reminiscent of Cat's Water and 'it seems to be another farmstead consisting of small enclosures but with traces of a droveway and small fields and paddocks' (*ibid,* 114). There are hints at mixed farming, but these will best be assessed in the final report. Finally, the gravel site at Mount Farm has produced full Middle Iron Age ring-groove structures of Cat's Water type, and in Late Iron and Romano-British times was traversed by a number of recut ditches, to judge from the provisional plans (Selkirk 1978, 110).

Before we return to East Anglia, it is salutary to reflect that most of the work just discussed took place within five years. This illustrates the advantages of a rigorously controlled programme of research integrated within a rescue framework. Such programmes pose new questions which must, in turn, be answered by new techniques. The Oxfordshire Unit's pioneering efforts in this direction (for example R Wilson 1978; M Jones 1978) are of great importance and should lead to more precise, cost-effective excavation in the future.

The study of Iron Age settlement in East Anglia has been mainly concentrated in south-eastern Essex, where a number of gravel sites have been excavated ahead of various threats. The best known of these is at Mucking, Thurrock. This enormous project is still under way and it is too early to draw definite conclusions, but a few very general observations are possible (M U Jones 1974; Jones and Jones 1975). The site is located on well drained gravel, high on the terrace overlooking the Thames. Pits occur frequently and ditches appear to have been used more as boundaries than for drainage. There are numerous examples of round buildings, built in the Cat's Water manner with continuous or discontinuous penannular eaves-drip gullies and, in a few exceptional cases, slighter wall slots inside, and concentric with, the external eaves-drip (*ibid,* 186). It is still to early to attempt to reconstruct activity areas within the settlement(s) at Mucking, but a superficial inspection of the plans (eg *ibid,* FIG 3) would suggest that the arrangement of the buildings was non-linear. Many show evidence for rebuilding, in the form of relocated porch and entranceway postholes, and Mrs Jones also notes that 'Increased finds density near the entrance is to be expected, and is surely circumstantial evidence of an open gully, not a wall trench' (*ibid,* 196). The neighbouring Iron Age settlement at Linford (Barton 1962), although generally earlier than Iron Age Mucking, seemed to show a different pattern of settlement, with post-built buildings predominating; the excavation tactics at Linford and Mucking are, however, so very different that is is difficult to compare features from the two sites. Rescue excavations some 18km north of Mucking, at Little Waltham, Essex, have recently been comprehensively published by Paul Drury (1978a). The two main, and probably successive, settlements are of Middle Iron Age date. The main site (Area A) is situated close to the floodplain of the River Chelmer and the underlying subsoil consists of London Clay with sandy gravel and brickearth, overlain by deposits of modern alluvium. This geology has led to the uneven survival of bone and artifacts, the results of variable soil acidity and fluctuating ground water levels. Ground drainage must have been poor, but the slope of the land was such that surface run-off, to the neighbouring stream, would have been sufficient, and does not appear to have necessitated the digging of many drains. The ground, too, is not suitable for use as a soakaway, as is the case at Cat's Water, and this also may account for the otherwise unusual dearth of ditches. One feature of special interest is the 'palisade' ditch surrounding the second main Middle Iron Age settlement (Phase III). This feature did not show direct evidence for timber, in the form of stains or post-packing around voids, but this could in large part be explained by the post-depositional factors just mentioned. The ditch's stepped profile could indicate recutting as much as 'the deliberate digging out of timbers' (*ibid,* 31) and the quantities of stone and gravel which had been dumped in the ditch could also have been used to assist drainage, in the manner of recent gravel-filled land drains. The disturbances of the ditch filling could be the result of recutting.

The constructional techniques used for buildings at Little Waltham changed between Phases II and III; buildings in Period II apparently used their penannular gullies to hold wall posts (see also Lambrick and Robinson 1979, 138). Buildings of the later period were of the more familiar eaves-drip gully type, with internal posts, for walls and roof support, set close to the surface — and generally destroyed by ploughing and other post-depositional factors. It is suggested here that the deep eaves-gully trenches of Period III are a change in building technique necessitated by local wetter conditions. A similar change was observed at Fengate, where during the drier conditions of the earlier Bronze Age round buildings were post-built, whereas, by wetter Middle and Late Iron Age times, walls and internal posts were set high in the ground and buildings were kept dry by the digging of a deep eaves-drip gully, which also lowered the local water table. Given a similar change at Little Waltham, it is somewhat surprising to find that the inhabitants of the later phase settlement, who must have appreciated the role of water in the destruction of timber, surrounded their community with a substantial post-built palisade. Pits are rare in Periods II (*ibid,* table 6) and III (*ibid,* 36), as a result of the prevailing wet conditions (*ibid,* 125).

The division of the settlement into two distinct phases is based on a single stratigraphic relationship, and Drury has found other evidence (ceramic styles and building construction techniques) to support it; and the phasing is indeed plausible. The two periods of settlement represent two farmsteads, occupied for about 100-150 and 50 years each.

Taken as a whole, however, the published archaeological evidence for the Iron Age in Essex is still thin. Apart from the Orsett 'Cock' site, which will be considered below, Little Waltham is the only major rural settlement site to have been recently excavated and published to an acceptable modern standard. A minute sample of Camulodunum was excavated before the War, and, of course, Mucking is in course of publication. Other sites may be added to the list, but many were excavated under difficult conditions (Drury and Rodwell 1973, for example) and environmental evidence is poorly represented.

Drury rightly points out that a major reason for Little Waltham's archaeological importance is that it is located on a clay-rich subsoil, whereas the vast majority of lowland Iron Age sites are found on gravels. Certain lessons learned from poorly-drained gravel sites, or from sites with a high permanent water table must therefore apply. We have noted the absence of storage pits and have suggested that the 'palisade' might possibly be interpreted as an exterior drainage ditch with an associated boundary function, for which there are numerous parallels in Essex and beyond. The well documented change in building techniques could be interpreted as a response to wetter ground conditions, and it would seem that the explanation for the observed changes between Periods II and III need not necessarily be historico-political: increased wetness combined with poor surface drainage. No doubt this may have exacerbated existing social tensions (Drury 1978a, 129), but the archaeological data is still too thin (and biased) for quasi-historical speculation.

The most recently published Iron Age/Romano-British site from Essex is the substantial rectangular ditched Orsett 'Cock' enclosure on the Thames terrace some 2km north-east of Mucking (Toller 1980; Rodwell 1974; Hedges and Buckley 1978, FIG 4 site B). Following earlier sample excavation, the site was interpreted as an early Roman fort (Rodwell 1974), but the more extensive excavations of the Essex County Unit have demonstrated that it is, in fact, a late Iron Age rural settlement with only a reduced Roman phase of a similar, domestic, character. The morphology of the rectilinear ditched enclosures might suggest that in its early phases (Toller 1980, FIG 2, phases 1 and 2) the external ditch served a boundary or drainage function, in the manner of, for example, Fisherwick, Gun Hill, Little Waltham Period III or Werrington. There can, however, be little doubt that the triple ditched enclosure of the later Iron Age phase 4 served a primarily defensive function. The interior structures are of particular interest. Three round buildings (G, L and N) were constructed in and in use throughout the 'Belgic' period and thus provides a counter argument to Rodwell's (1978a) unusual suggestion that 'Belgic' structures were generally rectilinear. Orsett building Q is represented by two opposed discontinuous arcs of ring-gully, closely similar to examples from Cat's Water (eg FIG 18 structures 10, 19 and 56), and provides additional evidence to refute the 'semi-circular building' hypothesis, discussed above. The point need not be over-stressed, but the drastic reassessment of this site also illustrates the dangers of historical speculation.

Moving away from south-east England, Christopher Smith and his team have recently published a series of important surveys and smaller excavations in the area around Fisherwick, Staffordshire. The area contains a number of cropmark sites situated on the lowest gravel terrace of the River Tame, one of the major tributaries of the Trent (C Smith 1979). The approach to the Fisherwick sites emphasises environmental research and detailed surface survey; special attention is paid to the site's role within a wider landscape (C Smith 1977; 1978). The principal site investigated is designated SK 187082 (C Smith 1979, FIG 4). The site is of later (Middle?) Iron Age date, perhaps second or third centuries BC and the parallels cited for 'scored' wares (Banks and Morris in *ibid*, 47) suggest broad contemporaneity with sites such as Twywell, discussed above, and the Middle Iron phases of Padholme Road

and Cat's Water.

The settlement at SK 187082 had two principal Iron Age phases. The first is represented by an indeterminate number of ring-groove houses in which the grooves contained traces of stakes and posts. These features were stratigraphically early and the slight ceramic evidence suggests that they belong within the Iron Age. The ring-groove houses were replaced — and in one case the replacement possibly involved demolition — by a form of construction where the penannular eaves-drip gully was used to drain the interior. There was no direct evidence for a wall foundation slot, but this is explained by the discovery of numerous shaped clay pieces that once formed parts of a mud wall (Samuels in C Smith 1979, 59; FIG 15). It is interesting to note that most of the artifacts found in this part of the site were from ring-ditch terminals and if, as we have argued above, these finds derive from outside the building, then the mud walling pieces found nearby either come from buildings that had fallen out of use or, perhaps more plausibly, they suggest rebuilding, where rejected material was dumped outside the eaves-drip gully, only to be moved back at a slightly later date.

The earlier, ring-groove, episode also sees the construction of a palisade trench, which went out of use in the later period when the principal round building was enclosed within a rectilinear enclosure ditch, broached by a single entranceway. The enclosure ditch is of considerable interest. It showed much evidence for recutting and the upcast appears to have been distributed widely on either side. There was no fence parallel to the ditch, but botanical evidence suggests a laid thorn hedge around the perimeter (*ibid*, 24). The single entranceway through the enclosure ditch was marked by substantial post-settings and there was evidence for the management of livestock. Many of the lower layers of the enclosure ditch were still waterlogged today, and there can be little doubt that one of its original functions must have been drainage. This small, perhaps, single family, farmstead has also produced evidence of metal-working and salt-production.

The change in building technology, from posts set in ring-grooves to eaves-drip gullies and mud walls, and the adoption, in the later phase, of a substantial external drainage ditch echoes Little Waltham, as reinterpreted here. The two sites are, moreover, broadly speaking contemporary. The association of livestock and people is also of special interest and the phosphate survey, although limited in extent, does show higher concentrations towards the centre of the enclosure, presumably where the livestock were fed, milked or over-wintered. The high phosphate concentration also coincides with the ring-gully building which was inhabited by people rather than livestock, an apparent contradiction that is best explained by the small size of the site and its longevity.

Smith (1977, FIG 52) illustrates other examples of Iron Age 'homestead enclosures' similar to Fisherwick

SK 187082, some of which either incorporate ring-gullies into the enclosure ditch or link the two together by a short length of ditch (*ibid,* FIG 2, d and e). This must surely emphasise the drainage role of the ring gullies and, in a least one case, must play down the defensive role of the main enclosure ditches. Smith (1977; 1978) considers that most of the low-lying parts of the Tame and Trent valleys were settled in Iron Age times and that the landscape was, by then almost fully developed, with primary woodland cleared and the land parcelled up by ditches, hedges and droveways. He also emphasises the role of climate which, we have seen, was becoming progressively wetter and colder.

Smith points out that individual river valleys will vary in their physical geography: the Tame, for example, has an uneven, undulating floodplain in which hollows would be gradually filled-in by alluvium. The floors of the river valleys that drain into the Fen, on the other hand, are flatter and present fewer opportunities for flood-free 'island' settlement within the floodplain itself.

The increased use of droveways and large enclosures, sometimes defined by multiple ditches, towards the latter part of the Iron Age, is taken by Smith to indicate increased reliance on livestock, again reflecting the wetter conditions of the later part of the first millennium (C Smith 1977, FIG 5, 59). Closely similar features of Late Iron Age date are known from Lynch Farm, Orton Waterville, immediately west of Peterborough and a similar function is possible. These features lie on the floodplain of the Nene, partially enclosed by a large meander (Challands 1973; C C Taylor 1969, FIG 7). Smith views the organisation of the Iron Age landscape in the Tame/Middle Trent area as being modelled on an infield/outfield system in which cultivated fields were grouped around settlements, with droveways running through the plots to the more open outfield beyond. This model has much to recommend it, but it treats the Iron Age landscape as an essentially new creation, without significant precursors. An alternative view is that the landscape of the lowland river valleys of Britain was, by Iron Age times, a complex phenomenon with a history of at least a millennium's continuous growth and development.

The Fisherwick project is important, not only because it demonstrated the extent of lowland Iron Age settlement in a given region, but because it provided insights into the way the enclosed landscape was actually managed: the significance of hedges was emphasised (C Smith 1978, 98; see also the discussion of Farmoor, Oxon, above); enclosures were considered in their landscape contexts where their role could be properly appreciated. The presence of people and livestock within enclosures, was also pointed out; we have seen that livestock and people occurred together at Cat's Water, and many other sites discussed above have shown evidence for a similar pattern. Proper drainage is as important for beasts as for man, and most enclosed,

drained, settlements in the lowlands would also have held livestock.

Moving south and west, we must briefly consider the marsh-side settlements of the Somerset Levels. D L Clarke's (1972) reinterpretation of Glastonbury (Bulleid and Gray 1911 and 1917) has been discussed in Part III and need not be repeated here. More recently, however, members of the Somerset Levels Project have re-examined the 'sister' site at Meare (Bulleid and Gray 1948-53; Gray and Cotton 1966). This re-examination of the West Village is relevant to the present discussion (Orme *et al* 1981), but mainly from a methodological point of view. The research is still in progress and it would be premature to discuss results in detail at this juncture. No earthmoving machines were used and an area of just 166.5 sq m produced some 20,000 finds. In some respects the recent excavations at Fengate may be compared with Bulleid and Gray's work at Meare which provided a general picture of the settlement, but which posed numerous questions. Infinitely more detailed research, similar to that carried out by the Somerset Levels Project, is required in the Fenland to monitor post-depositional distortion (which at Meare was closely related to the changing peat surface) and to quantify the amount of information that is absent on conventional 'dry land' settlement sites. Despite the dangers of comparing like with unlike, it is apparent that Meare and Cat's Water are contrasting sites, the one occupied intermittently, the other all year round; and although both display a variety of on-site industrial activities, many of which may have been undertaken seasonally, the suggestion that Meare represents a local or regional market centre deliberately located on marginal, no man's land, is attractive. The test of this hypothesis will lie in the discovery and excavation of other sites in similar surroundings elsewhere in the Levels. One specific point deserves mention here, and that is the suggestion that tents were used for houses. Although the area investigated was tiny, the idea gains support from the previous observatons of Bulleid and Gray (1948). Incidentally, this proposal provides an explanation for the unusual absence of structural evidence from within the area enclosed by the Late Neolithic ring-ditch of the Storey's Bar Road subsite.

Finally, we note a few general conclusions that arise from this brief discussion of lowland Iron Age sites. First and foremost, it is essential that lowland sites, of whatever period, be interpreted in their own right. It is misleading, for example, to see them as flat-land hill-forts. Although less readily apparent, the lowlands exhibit a diversity of environment equal to that of the highland zone; initially, therefore, each river valley should be considered on its own. The settlement pattern and land-use practices of individual valleys will depend on a number of factors such as the rate and frequency of flooding, the smoothness of the valley floor, the acidity of the subsoil, the fertility of alluvium and, of course, the nature of neighbouring upland and interfluve. The environment will vary within the valley itself, as is well demonstrated by the subsoil at Little Waltham. Future work must be diachronic: in pre-historic terms the Iron Age in most parts of lowland Britain was the last phase of perhaps two millennia of continuous landscape change and development. That development was carried out by people who lived in social groups and those social groups had their own history and traditions. Such purely social factors would have exercised a powerful influence on the way people managed their surroundings. Studies such as those by the Oxfordshire Unit, or by Smith at Fisherwick, illust-rate just two responses by local groups to their changing lowland environment. If any broad conclusion is emerging it is that in the Iron Age, if not before, lowland communities understood and managed their environment. It was not the other way round. There can be little doubt that regional variations in the relationship of upland and lowland communities pose the most potentially rewarding research topics of British later prehistory.

2. COMPARATIVE SITES IN THE SOUTHERN NORTH SEA BASIN

In order to place later sites in context, and to obtain comparanda for earlier Fengate material, the discussion that follows will first review evidence for Neolithic and earlier Bronze Age wetland settlement in the Low Countries.

Recent studies of Neolithic and Beaker communities in the Rhine/Meuse delta provide an important source of information on the early post-Mesolithic exploitation of a wetland environment. The topic owes much to the work of Dr Louwe Kooijmans whose painstaking approach to the subject, involving macro-scale geographical survey and micro-scale sediment and palaeoenvironmental research, could profitably be employed in this country. We have seen, in Part I, that it is possible to correlate the principal Dutch and British marine transgression episodes and it is also possible to attempt broad 'cultural' correlations with British and Dutch Neolithic groups. The origin of British (Whittle 1977) and Irish (ApSimon 1976) Neolithic culture, and more particularly its regional variants, is still a vexed question, but similarities between contemporary arti-facts on either side of the southern North Sea suggest continuing contact, if not an actual source of Continental inspiration. Close comparisons may be drawn between certain Grimston/Lyles Hill carinated bowls from eastern England and similar vessels of Hazendonk-2 type from the Rhine/Meuse delta (Louwe Kooijmans 1976b).

Before we consider the adaptations of various groups to the wetland environments of the Rhine/Meuse delta, it must be emphasised that the known contemporary sites around the East Anglian Fen-edge, such as Fengate, would have been much drier. Equivalent

Fenland sites must be sought in the peats, on roddons or islands caused by undulations in the underlying Fen floor and many probably lie buried beneath later peats and alluvium. The best known and closest English equivalent of sites such as Hazendonk is Shippea Hill where earlier Neolithic material is found 3m below OD. By contrast, Neolithic Fengate, at perhaps 2-3m above OD would be well clear of actual growing peat, which would still be confined to deeper stream channels (Clark and Godwin 1962; Godwin 1941, 300).

The 'donk' sites of the Rhine/Meuse delta Neolithic provide information on aspects of Fenland archaeology that are still only understood from old or very limited excavations. The 'donken' are early Holocene dunes that are surrounded and partially buried by later deposits. Louwe Kooijman's investigations of 'donken' in the Molenaarsgraff polder (Municipality) are particularly important (1974, 125-168). The interleaved deposits of peats and clay that lapped up to the 'donk' had been subjected to considerable compaction: clays that were deposited in the fifth to third millennia BC had sunk, due to the compression of intercalated peats, from 1.5 to 3.0m each (*ibid,* table 8). It should be noted in passing that compaction of archaeological deposits in the Fenland has yet to be accurately measured and must remain an important, but unquantified, source of post-depositional distortion until further research is under-taken. Compaction and surface erosion, or wastage, are the two elements that combine to cause peat 'shrinkage', as measured, for example, by the Holme Fen post (Godwin 1978, PL 35).

The 'Hazendonk pottery' first described by Louwe Kooijmans in 1974 (FIGS 47-9) is now seen as a late variant of that style and has been renamed 'Hazen-donk-3' (Louwe Kooijmans 1976b, 267). The earlier Hazendonk-1 style and the broadly contemporary settle-ments along the natural sandy levees near Swifterbant, belong in Louwe-Kooijman's (1976b) Neolithic Phase C (3500-3250 bc); Hazendonk-2 falls within Phase D (3250-2700 bc) and at the type site is stratigraphically sealed between deposits of Hazendonk-1 and -3 material. Only the Hazendonk-2 layers, however, appear to be *in situ.* Hazendonk-3 pottery also falls within Phase D and is significantly earlier than perhaps the best known Late Neolithic wetland group of the Low Countries, the Vlaardingen Culture, whose Initial phase falls within Phase E (2700-2450 bc). It should be noted here that (on the basis of a single C-14 date), the Fengate Neolithic house is broadly contemporary with the 'Classical' Vlaardingen of Phase F (2450-2150 bc).

Hazendonk-2 pottery sometimes closely resembles contemporary Grimston/Lyles Hill wares from south and eastern England, and the sites themselves, on either side of the North Sea, are low-lying and often located near water (*cf* Louwe Kooijmans 1976a, FIG 10). It is this locational similarity which, allied to the similarities in material culture, make it easier to accept 'the long distance relationships across the sea' proposed by

Louwe Kooijmans (1976b, 273). We have seen that the Fengate house is later than Hazendonk-2, by some 750 radiocarbon years, and yet the pottery from the house foundation trench is strikingly similar in form and surface treatment to the Dutch material (especially FNG 1, FIG 6, nos 2-5).

Moving forward in time, the Beaker (VBB and BWB) occupation along the Schoonrewoerd stream ridge provides an excellent example of prehistoric settlement in the Rhine/Meuse delta. The area has been fully surveyed and the location of most contemporary sites is known (Louwe Kooijmans 1974, 106). The sandy subsoil of the ridge, is freely draining and was chosen for buildings and permanent settlement. Around the sandy ridge is a belt of clay suited for agriculture, or nearer the marsh fringes, for pasture. Beyond the clay lies the marshland. The stream ridge itself was wooded, prior to the arrival of settled communities, and the clay land supported alder carr, except where it was cleared to make way for agriculture or pasture. Although spread along the ridge, settlement tended to focus around flowing water in the natural break-through channels across the stream ridge. The complex of sites at Albasserwaard was grouped around three break-through channels across the Schoonrewoerd stream ridge (*ibid*, FIGS 18 and 29). While it is speculative to suggest a direct correlation, Louwe Kooijmans's description of the 'ribbon development' along the Schoonrewoerd stream ridge might provide a parallel, not so much for earlier Neolithic as for second millennium groups living along the narrow (?) strip of Fen-edge at Fengate: 'farms were preferably built near open water or on an elevation, while the arable fields were laid out on the somewhat lower intermediate parts of the ridge. The cattle grazed outside there, on the low land adjoining the ridge' (*ibid*, 111).

The discussion of a stream ridge raises the difficulties encountered when crossing the wetlands. Minor waterways were overgrown, convoluted and difficult to navigate in dry seasons and except when frozen are best seen as barriers than routes of communication. Stream ridges and cleared land along the Fen-edge, on the other hand, provided the only readily accessible means of day-to-day communication, especially during wetter periods. During such periods it became necessary to construct trackways, such as those of the Somerset Levels (Coles and Orme 1980 with refs) the Fenland (Godwin 1978, PL 20; Lethbridge 1935; see also Buckland 1979) and, of course the Low Countries (de Laet 1958, PL 25). These trackways represent a rationalised, and probably minimal picture of communication patterns at any period. There was probably a complex network of dry land tracks along the Fen-edge, which branched out in various directions at the point where a marsh trackway reached solid land, or where a stream ridge entered the wetland (Louwe Kooijmans 1974, 111).

The stream ridge was clearly a prime area for settlement. One site close to a break-through channel, where conditions for preservation were excellent, was excavated in great detail. The site, Molenaarsgraaf, like contemporary Fengate, produced evidence both for settlement and burial, dating to about 1700 BC (Louwe Kooijmans 1974, part 4). Bone preservation was excellent and this was fortunate because the excavations revealed three human and one ox burial; as at second millennium Fengate, fish remains were rare in settlement features, despite the thorough recovery techniques employed (Clason in *ibid*, 241). This rarity was the more surprising given the site's location near running water and the fact that the cause of death of one burial was a fish bone lodged in the throat! Another burial contained grave goods that can most probably be associated with fishing. These included three bone fish hooks, four flint tools that could have been used to descale fish, and an antler pick that very closely resembles the antler picks of the British Neolithic and Early Bronze Age. The pick from Molenaarsgraaf grave II was made from shed red deer antler with the second and third tines crudely removed (ie without preparatory grooving). The brow tine is worn at the tip and has longitudinal scratches that (*ibid*, FIG 108) closely resemble the antler pick from Newark Road (FNG 3, FIG 76). This wear pattern could of course be a result of deer, rather than human behaviour; however, be that as it may, neither Fengate nor Molenaarsgraaf are situated on subsoils that would require the use of an antler pick, which is essentially a prizing implement suited to chalk or limestone (but see Dorchester (Atkinson *et al*, 1951, FIG 24)). Louwe Kooijmans suggests that the Molenaarsgraaf implement could have been used as a hoe, or, perhaps more probably in view of its associations, as a fish trap or net lifting hook. If pike were an important element in the diet — and this would seem to be the case at Molenaarsgraaf (*ibid*, 300-4) — then there is much to be said for keeping fingers and hands clear.

Fish waste will generally be disposed of in two areas: scales, fins and tails will be deposited wherever the fish is cleaned; other bones, assuming that the meat is not taken off the bone in advance, will be thrown out with table rubbish and then deposited on a (secondary) heap, or in a pit. The absence or rarity of fish bone at second millennium Fengate or Molenaarsgraaf may therefore be a reflection of rubbish disposal practices.

Certainly, by Iron Age times large fish bones are found with the Cat's Water secondary refuse (Table M27: pike, tench, bream and carp), and it is reasonable to suppose that fish always comprised a significant part of the Fengate diet, particularly during the winter when protein was hard to come by. The apparent rarity of fish material from the Molenaarsgraaf settlement debris is a good example of the distorting effects of Schiffer's (1976) C-(or cultural) transforms, at the time the archaeological deposits were created. The absence of small fish bones at Fengate could also be explained by soil chemical erosion: being the finest bones they would be the first dissolved by soil acids.

The site at Molenaarsgraaf formed part of the 'ribbon development' along a stream ridge. The excavated settlement included two successive oval houses, each over 20m long. There was pollen evidence for cereal agriculture, most probably in the immediate vicinity of the settlement, while slightly further away, on the stream bank itself (but in areas not actually settled by man), grew oak, elm, ash and alder. These 'vacant' areas separated the main elements of the 'ribbon development' which were spaced at intervals of 300 to 1000m, on suitable high ground. Most of the agriculture plots were placed on well-drained soils of the sandy ridge itself, while livestock were confined to the scrub-covered clay lands that separated the 'donk' from the surrounding marshland.

Louwe Kooijmans estimates that each 'occupation unit' along the stream ridge comprised perhaps two households of some 30-60 persons, children included. Each unit probably farmed 4-7ha of land and cattle were the main beasts kept; hunting does not appear to have been significant, but fishing, as we have seen, was probably more important than the archaeological record would allow.

Although there are other Bell Beaker sites in the region (Louwe Kooijmans 1976b), and along the ridge, none have yet been as thoroughly investigated and published as Molenaarsgraaf and little would be gained by discussing them here. The orderly distribution of sites along the stream ridge and their careful exploitation of the various ecological zones: sandy ridge, clay fringes and marshland beyond, surely indicate that the region's abundance of natural resources was well appreciated. Although the environment was not, apparently, put under any strain by these early farming settlements, it was certainly being adequately exploited; as at contemporary Fengate, the archae-ological evidence suggests that land was sufficiently in demand to require that available space be organised.

Somewhat later in time, and further downstream, mainly to the west of the Molenaarsgraaf area, we come to the Vlaardingen Culture which covered most the Rhine/Meuse delta during its 'Classical' phase. Numerous C-14 dates indicate a life-span of 2500 to 2100 bc (Louwe Kooijmans 1974, table 2; 1976b, 280; see also Lanting and Hook 1977, 80-3). Discussion of the Vlaardingen economy will primarily be based on work prior to Louwe Kooijmans's intensive survey of the Rhine/Meuse delta which has shown VL culture sites are not confined to the coastal dunes alone, but are also found on stream banks and 'donken': 'we must assume that still many more VL settlements lie buried in the subsoil on the levee deposits of former rivers at a depth of about 1.50m under the surface' (Louwe Kooijmans 1974, 21; see also FIG 5). The VL way of life may be summarised thus: 'settlements were small and permanently occupied, with rather small rect-

angular houses. On the coast, especially where natural pasture land (salt marshes, shore flats) was available, cattle breeding was the most significant means of subsistence, together with arable farming. In the marshy wilderness hunting and fishing were the prevalent sources of food' (*ibid*, 26).

The coastal dunes landscape was most favourable to settlement: the vast areas of peat marsh were traversed by large rivers whose substantial raised levees would have provided access to the sandy upland to the east. The flood-ridge land provided by the dunes (and levees) has been intensively settled by modern man and archae-ological survival is consequently poor, except in regions where wind-blown sand has buried the ancient levels. Vlaardingen sites of the coastal dunes are located in an environment dissimilar to Fengate and need not detain us here; but it should be noted cattle played an important role in the economy of these communities, since grazing along the well-drained sandy ridges was plentiful and freely available (eg Voorschoten and Leidschendam, Glasbergen *et al* 1967). Agriculture was also practised, but hunting, perhaps because of the grazing nearby, was less important than in the tidal creeks region further inland. Fishing for sturgeon was especially important at Voorschoten.

The Vlaardingen Culture has been shown to have clear evolutionary stages ('initial' — 'classical' — 'degenerate'), which may be distinguished stratigraphic-ally and which may be correlated, more or less, between different sites (see, for example, Voorschoten and Leid-schendam, Glasbergen *et al* 1967; Groenman-van Waateringe *et al* 1968). Studies of VL pottery gain added importance by the recognition, through diatom analysis, that ceramics were made on site, from locally-occuring clays of marine origin (Jansma 1977). A reconsideration of the manufacture and tempering of VL pottery led van Beek (1977) to the view that the devolution from 'classical' to 'degenerate' was not necessarily a synchronous event, but was more probably a process that took place at different times on different sites. He sees this change as a reflection of increasing isolation, perhaps brought on by changes in the environ-ment; the isolation was only broken by the abandonment of the VL settlements, migration, and contact with other, outside groups. This process of evolution could have taken as long as 400 years (*ibid*, 93).

Vlaardingen itself is located behind the coastal dunes in a landscape that was subject to freshwater tidal influence. VL communities living on the 'donken' and stream banks of the peat district further east, continued a way of life substantially the same as that of the Middle Neolithic groups that had preceded them. Recent excavations at the Hazendonk have revealed Neolithic occupation in successive, superimposed layers (Louwe Kooijmans 1978), and although the scale is smaller, the general picture is reminiscent of Fengate: 'in the lowest levels (3400BC) the settled area seems to be small (c 500 sq m). The density of finds increases from the lower layers upwards. In every phase crop cultivation has been proved (pollen), but charred grain occurs mainly in the lower layers. In every period fishing was important in view of the abundant fish remains; sturgeon fishing and hunting (especially of beaver and roe deer) were of considerable importance as late as 2100 BC (Late VL/AOO Beaker)' (ibid, 119).

The economy of the various sites investigated in the freshwater tidal creek area was based on cattle (except at Vlaardingen and Hekelingen where pasture was scarce), with hunting and other domesticated livestock (pig and sheep) of lesser importance. Animal bone evidence suggests that settlements were occupied all-year around (Clason in van Regteren Altena et al 1963, 39ff). It is also interesting to record that 'the absence of fish hooks and harpoons as well as the find of coarse netting at Vlaardingen and the absence of any important number of fish remains, suggests that sturgeon fishery was...important' (ibid, 47). One must be most careful not to under-estimate this resource in the contemporary Fen economy (for VL fish-traps and nets see van Iterson Scholten 1977). The fact that the settlements were probably occupied all year-round is reflected in the quantity of domestic refuse recovered and in the substantial construction (combined with some evidence for rebuilding) of the houses (van Regteren Altena et al 1962, 12, 18). The landscape in the Vlaardingen and Hekelingen region in VL times was arranged around narrow, shallow creeks, perhaps 2-3m deep, with wide (c 30m) sandy levees that are capped with sandy clay material deposited in a freshwater tidal area 'between mean high tide and a slightly higher level' (Pons in van Regeteren Atlena et al 1963, 104). Behind the levee is an area of very soft, perhaps impassible, backswamp which becomes progressively more peaty away from the creek. The levee itself at the time of the VL culture carried a forest cover with elm, ash, maple, oak, hazel and wild cherry; alder would have dominated the vegetation at the backswamp/levee junction, while the backswamp itself was covered by a 'Backswamp wood' of low varieties of willow, together with eutrophic swamp plants such as reed and reedmace.

The landscape was ideally suited to hunting and fishing and the levees were sufficiently wide to allow the efficient exploitation of livestock. Cereals too were grown on the fertile clay soils of the levee, since storm floods were rare during the actual growing season; the pollen record is, however, interrupted from time to time by flood clays in which cereal pollen is not present (Groenman-van Waateringe and Jansma 1969). Cereal agriculture was clearly considered an important resource both in the region of tidal creeks and, as we have seen, in the fluvial clay area further east. The evidence for cereals at Fengate is slight in the second millennium BC, despite the fact that the Fen-edge was well-drained and free from seasonal floods. Given the undoubted importance of cereals to contemporary communities in wetter areas of the Netherlands, we

must not attach too much significance to the admittedly slight, and negative, evidence from Fengate. There can be little doubt that cereals would have played a reduced role, when compared with livestock, both at Fengate as at Vlaardingen and Hekelingen (where querns were also found). It would seem that the role of cereals at Fengate will only be resolved by pollen analysis of buried peats in the neighbouring Fen.

The evidence from the Low Countries illustrates a variety of possible responses to changes in the environment. These responses were often dictated by very small-scale differences in topography and demonstrate the dangers of attempting generalisations about wetlands subject to marine and fluvial influence. Van Beek (1977) and Louwe Kooijmans (1976b, FIG 4) have demonstrated that changes observed in marsh- or fen-edge settlements, when brought about by alterations in the environment, will closely reflect local topography and be conditioned by the precise location of the various settlements. In some cases, for example at Cat's Water, significant differences in height above OD can be as little as 0.50m. Other factors which are harder to recognise may also be crucially important: the blocking of a creek, for example, used for fishing, by wind-blown or alluvial sands (Louwe Kooijmans 1980, 119-21).

We have seen that even in one small region there are a large variety of adaptations to specific wetland environments, of which many are closely comparable with the East Anglian Fenland. We will now consider groups living on drier, better drained, land north of the Rhine/Meuse delta. The brief discussion that follows will first consider Bronze and Early Iron Age settlement on the saltmarsh deposits of Westfrisia.

Research in this area has recently been summarised by Dr Louwe Kooijmans (1980, 124-6). The major published site is of Middle Bronze Age date and is located in the east part of Westfrisia at Hoogkarspel (Bakker et al 1977 with refs). The site can be closely compared with Fengate and is particularly important because of its environmental deposits and, unusual in the Low Countries, because bone has survived in good condition (see, for example, van Mensch and Ijzereef 1977, FIG 6 for bone from the later, but nearby site, currently being investigated at Bovenkarspel). The principal occupation is located on marine deposits of the Dunkirk O transgression (Dunkirk O follows Calais IV, see Louwe Kooijmans 1980, FIG 49), which became habitable before 1300-1200 bc (see 'postcript', Bakker et al 1977, 196). The site at Hoogkarspel-Watertoren ('Watertower') was occupied for perhaps 1-200 years between 1250 and 900 bc; C-14 dates cluster around 1000 bc (early phase) and 700 bc (later phase) (dates are listed in van Regteren Altena 1977, table 1; Lanting and Hook 1977, 144-5).

This rapidly conducted rescue project uncovered several round barrows, part of an associated MBA ditched field system and some of its farmsteads; a peat core was taken from a neighbouring bog and this will provide a control sequence of environmental deposits. The soils of the area had been mapped prior to excavation and it was soon apparent that the archaeological features closely respected the soil pattern. Three phases could be distinguished: 'phase 0, immediately before the sand ridges became inhabited and cultivated; phase 1, when the first settlement and cultivation took place and phase 2 when the black soil layer which fills most ditches and pits was formed and when the main habitation took place' (Bakker *et al* 1977, 192). In phase 0 the landscape consisted of undulating ridges of sand, loam and loam on clay with a high ground water table, subject to tidal influence in lower areas: the western (seaward) edge of the sites includes a break-through channel that cut through sand ridges 'to form a spill-way for water from basins on both sides' (*ibid,* 194). This gully contained a bed of shellfish (just 0.4-0.5m below the surface), typical of a creek in the upper part of the tidal zone.

At Hoogkarspel cultivation seems to have taken place sometime after the natural desalination of the ground, and ploughed fields were most probably placed on the ridges of sand and loam that lay above summer flooding (Bakker *et al* 1977, 196). In phase 1 drainage ditches do not follow the sand ridge contours very closely and this was probably due to the fact that ground shrinkage had yet to throw the sand banks into relief; by phase 2, however, the ground contours were approximately as today's and the drainage ditches closely follow the lie of the land. Lower lying parts of the site formed shallow lakes which later became peat bogs. It will be evident from this brief account of the topographical changes that post-depositional distortion of the archaeological deposits has been very considerable and early in date. Damper ground around the settlement was covered with a type of vegetation (the *Juncetum gerardii* — van Zeist 1974) found in higher parts of salt marshes in a zone only flooded by the sea during storm floods, perhaps a few times a year. Although severely restricted today, the *Juncetum geradii* may originally have been several kilometres wide and possessed 'nearly unlimited potential for grazing' (*ibid,* 333). The area devoted to crops (grown in the summer, they included emmer, hulled barley and flax) was probably located near the settlement itself, but there is evidence to suggest that it became increasingly influenced by freshwater conditions as time passed (Pals in Bakker *et al* 1977). In common with other contemporary Westfrisian Bronze Age settlements, cattle dominated the Hoogkarspel domestic animal assemblage and hunting appears to have been unimportant; pig occurs in significant proportions and fish and shellfish were also eaten (van Mensch and Ijzereef in *ibid*). Houses were rectangular (*c* 26 x 6m), three aisled, with posts set in slots within the freely draining subsoil.

The settlement is remarkable for the presence of numerous, annular, penannular and figure-of-eight gullies which were dug around grain stacks (see Buurman 1979 for botanical evidence). Brandt (in Bakker *et al* 1977, 214) suggests that upcast from the ring-gullies was used to cover the stack, but this seems improbable, given the soil's porous nature; simple thatching would provide a far more effective cover. There are several closely comparable examples of small annular gullies on Cat's Water (Structures 22, 24-5). Elsewhere in Holland crops were stacked in wooden structures, raised off the ground much as they are today, and Brandt attributes the adoption of ring-gully storage at Hoogkarspel (and Bovenkarspel) to a shortage of readily available timber; it is, perhaps, tempting to invoke this explanation for later Iron Age Fengate.

The Hoogskarpel wells bear close comparison with Fengate. They 'are usually cylindrical holes with a mean diameter on the surface of 1m and a depth varying between 150 and 200cm. Often they form part of the ditch system' (Brandt in *ibid,* 214). The enlargement of ditches was also noted at Iron Age Fengate where the uneven profile of many main drains probably resulted from local re-digging to provide a convenient and possibly short-lived supply of water.

We have noted above that the Hoogkarspel ditches followed the lie of the land closely (Brandt in *ibid,* 214ff). This is also true, to an extent, of Fengate where the landscape undulates less: Iron Age and Romano-British ditches in the south-east part of the main Cat's Water excavation all run more or less parallel, carrying water away from the main settlement area to low-lying, perhaps marshy, land outside the area stripped (see the discussion of ditches in Chapter 4). The area partially stripped and excavated at Hoogkarspel was enormous (*c* 500m x 350m) and a variety of ditch-filling types could, consequently, be distinguished. The main distinction was between ditches to the west of the settlement, which had been dug around fields; these contained alternating bands of grey and black soil suggesting interrupted natural silting up, ditches in the main settlement area. These recall Cat's Water: boundaries shift, ditches are constantly redug and include sods, loose soil, settlement debris etc, and efforts are still being made to disentangle the sequence which resembles 'a seemingly random pattern'. Intersections provide some clue to the problem, but many ditches may have been in use at the same time, since they quickly lose their drainage potential when the growth of water plants is out of hand (*ibid,* 215). There is evidence for local recutting or maintenance and the botanical and molluscan data suggest drainage was their primary function.

In a few cases houses could be linked to specific barrows and enclosure ditches and it was possible to arrive at estimates of settlement size (one or two farmyards in use at the same time). Each farmyard had a life of 30-40 years and the total life of the settlement may have been 1-200 years (Brandt and Pals in *ibid,* 223). Bearing in mind that the Hoogkarspel subsoil is, in general lighter than Fengate, that the water table was higher, and that ditches were therefore shallower, it is still remarkable that so small a community could have left such an extraordinary quantity of archaeological features in its wake (*ibid,* FIG 10-14).

Excavations at Bovenkarspel, a closely comparable site nearby, are still in progress and little would be gained by discussing the preliminary results here (see Buurman 1979; van Regteren Altena *et al* 1977). It should be noted, however, that bundles of twigs have been found laid along ditch bottoms; these are usually explained as being crossing points for livestock, but recent farmers in the area used 'brush drains' of the type found at Fengate and it is therefore possible that the supposed 'crossing places' could have had an alternative function (Ijzereef, pers comm).

Although settlements in the 'terpen' district, further north, in Groningen and Friesland are, at first glance, quite distinct from contemporary Fengate, they do represent an interesting adaptation to a not dissimilar environment. Further, they exhibit a diversity of form, size and history that illustrates the variety of potential responses that can be made to uniform and highly deterministic wetland surroundings. This is not the place to attempt a detailed discussion of such a complex subject; instead, a few recently investigated sites will be briefly examined (for a review, with refs to earlier work, see De Laet 1958, 154-57 for a more recent synthesis see Louwe Kooijmans 1980, 127-9).

The raised (mound) settlements of the terpen district of Groningen, in the most north-easterly parts of Holland, were located on various salt marsh deposits that were the result of four marine transgressions, Dunkirk, Ia to IIIa (Louwe Kooijmans 1980, FIGS 49 and 55). The settlements were located on land subject to regular, but not destructive flooding and were protected from the full force of North Sea gales by the coastal barrier dunes. The environment was, therefore, wetter than any discussed above and presented those who wished to exploit it with very special problems, and opportunities. The extraordinary lengths that people went to in order to survive and prosper, in these peculiar surroundings indicate the potential rewards that could be reaped.

It seems that the inhabitants of the different terpen settlements fully understood the micro environments with which they were concerned, since the various vegetation types encountered must be exploited in subtly different ways. The variety of these vegetation types has recently been discussed by van Zeist (1974). Not all terpen settlements were successful: those at Paddepoel (I-III) for example were located on the flat surface left by the Dunkirk Ib marine transgression and only showed three phases of occupation, extending from *c* 200 BC-AD 250. The area is low-lying and on the inner edge of the salt marshes, consequently salt marsh deposits 'would have been deposited to a less high level than more seaward' (*ibid,* 344). This would give rise to wet conditions locally, as river outfalls would be obstructed; this in turn would lead to the dilution of salt water so that for most of the year local water would only have been slightly brackish. The sites themselves were located on wetland adjacent to, but not on, a sandy roddon. The first houses were post-built directly on the flat surface of the marine floodplain; later houses, during the platform phase, were surrounded by ditches and were raised on individual platforms. Soon, the individual platforms became fused into a single settlement terp. The arrangement of the principal buildings was radial, as we shall see elsewhere, and there were numerous post-built outbuildings. The economy was mainly based on livestock, but the serious flooding of Late Roman and Early Medieval times (Dunkirk IIIa) proved too serious a problem and the small settlements were abandoned (van Es 1968). Another short-lived terp was found, by chance, sealed beneath the Medieval Oldehove cemetery. This site, Leeuwarden, was occupied from about 600-400 BC (van Es and Miedma 1970-1). The site was excavated under salvage conditions and only a small part was revealed: the original, flat ground, settlement was not recovered. But the nucleus terp was constructed at NAP (Netherlands OD) and built up to +1m NAP; it was further raised to +3m NAP. Both episodes of mound construction took place in the first century AD and occupation seems to have lasted until the third century. The site was small and consisted of one farmstead, the principal building of which would have sheltered both animals and the farmer's family.

Larger terps were better able to contend with the intermittent inundations, but all had to start from flat ground beginnings. The pioneering large-scale excavation of the small village terp at Ezinge, directed by van Giffen in the early 1930s is of special importance (De Laet 1958; Louwe Kooijmans 1980, with refs). The flat ground settlement consisted of two rectangular houses enclosed within a palisade. The second phase followed swiftly after the flat ground phase and consisted of four buildings, whose layout respected that of the original settlement, but which were raised on a low mound. By early Roman times the mound is greatly enlarged, and heightened, by the deposition of a thick layer of organic material. The buildings still follow the same ground plan, but by now the arrangement is radial. Unlike, for example, Paddepoel, 'wet places with predominantly slightly brackish water were not present in the vicinity of Ezinge' (van Zeist 1974, 348). Botanical samples taken from Ezinge periods 2 (300BC) and 3 (100BC) showed that all mosses found derived from trees only and that, therefore, timber used in the construction of houses and fences were imported from higher, sandy areas to the south (*ibid,* 349). This discovery raises the issue of wetland house construction and the recognition of buildings, or other structures, in sites that have since dried out.

In general, the literature on the British Iron Age has

emphasised substantial, post-built, or gully-defined, constructions which leave clear, if sometimes reduced, archaeological traces (Guilbert 1975). In certain situations, for example Cat's Water, the subsoil is sufficiently freely draining to make it worth digging an eaves-drip, both to remove run-off from the roof, and to lower the water-table indoors. In other situations, however, buildings may be raised on organic platforms, whether of turf or brushwood, and it is difficult to see how their presence would survive archaeologically other than as rubbish scatters or as heightened areas of soil phosphate, or trace elements. Substantial clay walls, when constructed on an organic platform, would not necessarily leave any archaeological remains (see Den Helder — Het Torp in van Zeist 1974). It would, for example, be difficult to reconstruct a convincing case for ancient settlement in the vicinity of the well-known site at Old England, Brentford (Wheeler 1929), had that site been subjected to the type of agriculture one might encounter in a Midland river valley today. Even normally substantial features, such as wells, if cut through the accumulated, mainly organic, make-up of a terp or crannog would leave little or no archaeological evidence once the site had been drained and ploughed. Post-depositional factors such as plough-damage or burial beneath marine or fluvial deposits must account for the surprising absence of raised settlements in East Anglia.

Finally, although livestock played an important part in the economy of the terpen communities, agriculture was still significant. Van Zeist (1974, para 5.2) has discussed the role of cultivated plants in a brackish environment, and since his discussions are relevant to Fengate, and more especially to the deeper Fenland, they will be noted here. Discussing botanical samples from various terpen sites of Iron Age to Medieval date, van Zeist acknowledges that some species could, indeed, be imported from farms in higher parts of the country, perhaps in exchange for meat or dairy products — as is suggested for Cat's Water in the first and second millennia BC. There is, however, plentiful evidence that many species were grown locally and it is doubtful whether surrounding farmers could have supplied such a large terpen population. Van Zeist suggests that archaeologists keep a careful watch for threshing floors on deep wetland sites. Although the area on top of terpen mounds would have been ideally suited to horti-culture or agriculture, it was largely occupied by settle-ment and farm buildings and the remaining area would have been too small: the region around the terp itself must, therefore, have been extensively utilised, despite its sometimes brackish nature. It is usual today to grow crops in newly reclaimed coastal polders, shortly after embankment, the important difference between modern and ancient conditions being that the modern polders are protected from storm floods and spring tides by dykes. Experiments have shown (*ibid*, 365-6) that barley (*Hordeum sp*), flax (*Linum usitatissimum*), gold-of-

pleasure (*Camelina sativa* — grown for its oil), Celtic bean (*Vica faba*, var. *minor*) and probably also oats (*Avena sativa*) may be grown to provide satisfactory yields, provided that no flooding takes place at the growing stage. Flooding at the seedling stage killed nearly all the experimental plants. Long inundations (of several hours) will kill fully grown plants which are also vulnerable when in flower. The experiments suggest, therefore, that it is possible to grow crops in brackish environments provided that plots are sown on the highest parts of an unprotected salt marsh; these areas are, however, vulnerable to winter floods so winter crops would not be expected, unless there was suitable flood-free land available nearby. The availability of flood-free winter growing areas would, of course, be an inducement for communities to settle near the fen or marsh edge (as, for example, the terp at Het Torp, which was situated near dunes at Den Helder; see *ibid*, para 2.1.7).

The brief discussions of sites in the terpen district of the northern Netherlands has stressed the self-sufficiency of communities living in a brackish, apparently inhospitable environment. There is, however, another side to the coin: wetland communities must always depend on those living in drier situations for certain commodities, of which wheat, particularly winter wheat, is an obvious example. Brongers has suggested that 'The number of Celtic fields decreases with the increase in distance from the terp region. This is an argument for the dependence of the terp region upon the Celtic field region' (Brongers 1978, 122). This is not, however, altogether convincing: the greater number of 'Celtic fields' near the wetland may merely reflect increased pressure on land brought about by the larger population that is bound to be attracted to an area that sits on the border of two complementary ecological zones. These marsh-edge groups may well have had close contacts with communities living in the wetlands proper; alternately, they may also have exploited the more marginal wetland soils themselves and would, in fact, have been in direct competition with the terpen settlements. Winter, when crops are safely stored away, is a season when hostility traditionally takes place and it is the season when the terpen settlements would have been naturally defended by encircling flood waters.

Moving briefly to the higher land around the marshy areas, the layout of the admittedly later Celtic fields studied by Brongers (1976) does not recall the ditched enclosures of second millennium Fengate. The Celtic fields discussed by Brongers are comparable with, for example, those of the British chalk downland, in size arrangement and shape, and seem to have been used to delimit fields that were cultivated with an ard. Water seems of greater significance to the users of the Dutch Celtic fields, than their British counterparts.

'Although the Celtic fields were laid out on sand, their location was selected with great care, with particular regard to the height and hydrological situation along the boundary of the chosen terrain. In this way, the water-supply to the occupants of these areas was safeguarded, while the arable land was not over-humid' (*ibid*, 62). Celtic fields were often located on peninsulas or islands within the marsh; outside northern Drenthe, Celtic fields were sometimes located on clay subsoils to take advantage of rain, in the form of surface run-off, as a source of freshwater. The later, Romano-British, ditched fields of the Silt Fens, discussed at length in Phillips (1970), have more in common with counterparts in the Netherlands than the Fengate rectilinear ditched enclosures or paddocks; but even so, the resemblance is not close, either functionally or morphologically (a point that Brongers recognised, *ibid*, 29). Livestock must clearly have played a role in the seasonal cycle of the Dutch marsh-side Celtic fields, but it was probably secondary; perhaps cattle were used to graze and manure fields during fallow periods (*ibid*, 60). Brongers sees the introduction of Celtic fields in the Low Countries, after *c* 600 BC as 'a fundamental change in agricultural technology to meet the growing demands of an expanding economy attended by population increase and perhaps regional specialisation. The important new features introduced...were: multiple course rotation and regeneration of soil fertility by means of humus addition to the fields. The characteristic banks were caused by the removal of clearance debris and exhausted infertile arable soil to the boundaries of the parcels' (*ibid*, 74). Perhaps similar criteria apply to the creation of the Fengate second millennium ditched enclosures, although it is hard to imagine why people should attempt to remove exhausted soil to the field boundaries. Recently, however, Groenman-van Waateringe (1979) has suggested that the banks around the Dutch Celtic fields resulted from the lowering of the main field surface by wind action. She further suggests that the erosion probably took place in the spring, following ploughing and manuring, since the banks around the Celtic fields at Flogeln (briefly discussed below) had high soil phosphate levels.

The enormous survey and excavation project at Texel, the most southerly of the Frisian islands, has already produced information that could be used for comparative purposes when the current British Fenland survey has been completed (Woltring 1975). In particular the reader's attention is drawn to the relationship of Bronze Age barrows and associated settlements and trackways (*ibid*, FIG 11) and the reconstruction of the LBA and EIA landscape, complete with fields, settlements and trackways (*ibid*, FIG 13). Drainage ditches are a special feature of the later Iron Age landscape (*ibid*, FIG 8, nos 8 and 26), where they are only found in low-lying areas. Ditch systems are complex and were probably constructed to drain low-lying meadow and pasture land; this is a use of drains that is not frequently encountered in later Iron Age Britain (this may be due, however to Roman and later alluviation). By Roman and Medieval times the ditch

systems were extremely extensive, as ground water had become a serious problem. These later ditches were frequently recut and are laid-out to follow the contours of the ground. 'It was a matter of repeatedly re-digging and diverting the system' (*ibid*, 31); the parallels with Cat's Water are plain and one must wonder to what extent measures were taken there to raise the ground level of structures such as granaries.

No review of sites in the Low Countries, however, brief, could afford to ignore van Es' comprehensive excavations at Wijster (van Es 1965-7). The site(s) is located on the marsh-edge on the sandy soils of north Holland. The subsoil drains freely, consequently pits, postholes and palisades are numerous. Some 86 buildings were recovered in ground plan 'for the most part they represent large farm buildings, combining the actual house or dwelling with the byre' (*ibid*, 49). One hundred and forty sunken *grubenhausen* were also recovered. The majority of archaeological features post-date the period with which we are concerned, but the site also exhibited the 'double podsol' that is a feature of many sites built on the light wind-borne 'cover sands' of the Groningen area. The first podsol represents something of an 'agricultural catastrophe' which brought about the end of the Zeijen culture *c* 400 BC, when soil exhaustion rendered settlement on the lighter sandy soils almost impossible. There is evidence for very reduced occupation at Wijster from 400-200 BC, but the main settlement did not get under way until after *c* AD 150.

Recent work by Professor Waterbolk (1977) has re-assessed four sites that were occupied in the years between the first and the main phases of settlement at Wijster, ie between *c* 350 BC and *c* AD 100. Like Wijster, the sites are located on freely-drained, generally sandy soils and include a range of settlement features, such as barns, houses, granaries, domestic rubbish, querns etc that suggest full-time settlement and an economic base of mixed farming. The sites are all defended by a rectilinear wall (earth or turf) with inner and outer palisaded revetment; entrances (from 2 to 4 in number) are near the centre of the walls and there are from one to six rows of palisades outside the main wall. These are substantial defended settlements which Professor Waterbolk interprets using a British hillfort model. Certainly there are no comparable sites from similar environments in lowland Britain; although, as we have seen above, such comparisons may be misleading. The sites also have an important ritual component (the presence of a pyre barrow in the vicinity) and the argument that some ultimately gave rise to the Medieval villages, with their clearly defined territories (parishes) is convincing (Waterbolk 1977, 168-70; 1979).

So far this discussion has confined itself to sites in the Netherlands, but the coastal area further north, between the estuary of the Ems and the Danish border, also contains many similar sites and diverse environments.

253

Recent research in this area has been summarised, with references, in two readily-available papers (Schmid 1978; Haio Zimmerman 1978). Little would be gained from prolonged repetition of this work, but one or two points are relevant to the discussion.

The lower Ems estuary was the location for a large-scale government-financed inter-disciplinary study of the pre- and proto-historic archaeology of a comparatively small area (Schmid 1978, FIG 2). The geology and topography were most similar to that of the terpen region north of Groningen, nearby. The archaeology reflects this similarity: at Hatzum, for example, a small 'flat land' settlement of three rectangular houses, which combined accommodation for people and livestock, was located on the salt marsh surface between two rivers. This unit, which included outbuildings, formed part of a larger group of at least six farmhouses but was separated from the larger community by 'wattle-lined boundary trenches'. The site is typical of late pre-Roman Iron Age settlement in the area, both in form and position, being located atop a river bank and covered with silts of the third century BC (Dunkirk Ib) maritime transgression phases; slightly higher land in the Ems valley, on the other hand, sees the development of 'true' terps carrying radially-arranged small villages. These more substantial settlements were able to withstand the later Roman floods.

Another riverside settlement, on the Ems near Bentumersiel, had its naturally well-defended location augmented with palisades, in some respects similar to the defended sites discussed by Waterbolk (1977), and considered above. In common with the northern Dutch defended sites, that at Bentumersiel has produced much evidence for livestock (cowsheds, byres) and cereals (granaries) 'and it is assumed that these settlements have been important for the export of consumer goods, such as cattle and hides, for trade with the Roman Empire or for tributes to the Roman military forces' (ibid, 129). The site also produced evidence for summer corn production and for the growing of crops that can tolerate brackish conditions (for example flax, gold-of-pleasure and Celtic bean). Cattle were only kept in the settlement in summer, whereas in the neighbouring terpen section they were kept indoors over the winter.

Further east, in the coastal district of the Weser valley north of Bremerhaven, the terp at Feddersen Wierde has been the subject of recent, exhaustive, excavations (ibid, 129-37, with refs). It has proved possible to reconstruct the development of the complete terp from its 'flat-land' beginnings, dating to the latter part of the first century AD, via eight stratified and successive villages, raised one upon another, to its abandonment in the fifth century. The various phases can be shown to develop, so that the 'flat-land' phase, for example, develops from five farm units, each consisting of a three-aisled long house containing accommodation for a family and its livestock, to eleven farmyards — before it became necessary to raise the terp in the second century AD. By the third century, there were 23 farm units and there is, by now, evidence for social stratification, in the form of a significantly larger farm unit and 'village hall' set slightly apart from the other buildings and consistently rebuilt in the same spot. The economy was based on mixed farming, with cattle (48.3%) and sheep (23.7%) dominating the list of livestock; crops included barley, oats, beans and flax which were grown on the terp itself and on drier land in the vicinity. This extraordinary site is rendered archaeologically comprehensible by the fact that the main phases are separated by terp make-up. In areas prone to soil exhaustion, or where the expansion of settlement was not constrained by the presence of a mound, a succession of settlements similar to those at Feddersen Wierde would leave a tangle of archaeological features that would be hard to interpret. Fluctuating water levels, whether fresh, salt or brackish, impose order on superimposed deposits that might otherwise be incomprehensible.

The hinterland to the east of the flat clay landscape upon which Feddersen Wierde and other terpen sites sit, is composed of freely-draining sand and loam 'Geest' soils, which form islands interspersed among extensive acid bogs. The islands have been settled since Mesolithic times, and the effects of the different communities on the environment are being studied by pollen analysis. The island of Flogeln, near Bremerhaven has recently been investigated as part of a wider inter-disciplinary research programme into the 'Geest' landscape (Schmid 1978, 137-45; Haio Zimmerman 1978). The settlement differs from Cat's Water in many significant respects (it is larger, somewhat later and positioned on well-drained land), but its location on a wetland island is of considerable significance to the present discussion.

As one would expect from so well-drained a subsoil, drainage ditches are absent, long houses are post-built and in later times it is even feasible to dig grubenhausen. The principal archaeological features date from the first to the fifth centuries AD and, in the earlier part of this period, farm units moved from one location to another, possibly as a result of soil exhaustion. This pattern of 'moving settlement' extends over the main subsequent settlement area and has been revealed by trial trenches in neighbouring Celtic field systems. At the outset of the second century AD the shifting pattern of settlement gives way to a more permanent pattern of nucleated settlement in which some seven farmsteads occupy more or less the same location for about two centuries. Each farmstead is surrounded by a fence and the village also includes an open space. In one phase the settlement comprised some 100-200 people and 320 head of cattle, housed within about 23 aisled buildings which combined the roles of house and animal stall. Cultivated crops included barley, oats and flax. The economy — mixed farming — and the organisation of the basic farm unit was the same in both the shifting and the nucleated phase of settlement.

The reasons for the change in settlement pattern are not altogether clear, but probably reflect changed practices of livestock and land management. One point of interest concerns livestock management: a substantial ditch, some 250m in length, had been dug in a settlement area along the side of a low valley. The ditch bottom was level, so its use as a drain may be discounted and at one end several small feeder ditches carried water to it from nearby springs. One side of the ditch was battered, the other steep and, due to unusual soil conditions, hundreds of footprints of cattle and horses were found leading up to this large and unusual 'watering trough'. The only Fengate feature that remotely resembles it is the large pit W17 of the Storey's Bar Road subsite (FNG 2, FIGS 26-30) which contained a small stagnant pond.

There is abundant evidence that the inhabitants of the 'Geest' island communicated with other groups in the clay lands and beyond via open water and trackways through the bogs. The relationship of Flogeln to such sites as Feddersen Wierde, nearby, is of great interest and is currently receiving attention.

Faced by the wealth of information from the Continent, the sad conclusion of this brief review is that studies of the English wetlands still have far to go before they can make a significant contribution to knowledge of later prehistoric culture in the southern North Sea Basin.

PART V: FIELD TECHNIQUES AND FUTURE RESEARCH

FIELD TECHNIQUES

Details of excavation methods are given in Appendices 1 of the Second and Third Reports; the recording system is described in Appendix 1 of this report and these brief descriptions need not be summarised here. Excavation is a process of discovery that frequently involves changes of tactics and strategy. Aspects of excavation strategy were reconsidered in a recent paper (Pryor 1980c) and that discussion must suffice for present purposes. We are concerned here with a re-assessment of tactics used in the field, within D L Clarke's (1968, FIG 2) 'Sphere of Contextual Analysis'. The discussion that follows will first consider an important case study that has a direct bearing on future work on the Fen-edge. This is followed by suggestions for methodological improvements and how these are currently being put into effect. It became apparent, in the preliminary stages of post-excavation work, that much information was redundant. At the same time it was recognised that despite efforts to standardise data recovery (FNG 2, 169), comparability could not always be assured. There was a subjective impression that dry sieving, while better than no sieving, was far from perfect (Payne 1972) and was prone to personal bias. The importance of field-walking had been appreciated

for a long time, but the thick cover of alluvium prevented this, and the technique of soil phosphate analysis proved an excellent, if somewhat labour-intensive, substitute (Craddock, Appendix 4; FNG 3, appendix 6). Had the funds been available, earthmoving over the whole of the Cat's Water subsite would have been carried out in two operations, the first stopping at the top of the B soil horizon (Craddock's 'archaeological layer'). As it was, areas I-IV were stripped in this way and a few features could be discerned (for example part of the wall trench of Structure 7). Plans were drawn of the B horizon surface at a scale of 1:50 and these have been deposited with the archive. The technique was expensive, as it necessitated the preparation of two cleaned archaeological surfaces, and while the importance of the B horizon cannot be emphasised too strongly (it is discussed by Dr Craddock below), the fact remains that only very few features showed through it. It soon became apparent, for financial reasons, that the settlement could not be completely uncovered if two stage earthmoving was continued, and as the complete stripping of the settlement was a main objective of the project, it was decided to strip the southern part of the excavated area as a single operation.

There are many lessons to be learned from this experience: first, a decision had to be made, and as the project by 1976 had clearly stated research goals there could be no doubt about the appropriate choice. Second, the problem should have been foreseen had sufficient attention been given to such post-depositional factors as alluviation. Third, the buried B horizon was the Iron Age topsoil, more or less distorted by subsequent alluvial action, and it was quite inappropriate to clean it in the hope that features would reveal themselves — which they did not. The surface should have been drawn, but then ploughed and fieldwalked. The whole settlement should have been stripped in two large single operations, as this would not have been much more expensive in gross terms than the method adopted, wherby each Area was stripped separately. The latter method was tailored to the flow of funds which were made available annually. Considerations of cash-flow therefore had an important role in dictating the direction of the research. In future it would be advisable to strip alluviated sites in two operations in which the first surface, the buried soil, was drawn, ploughed (or cultivated) and allowed to weather over winter before being field walked. After winter the surface could be lowered by hand or machine, to a level where features could be seen.

Perhaps the most significant practical lesson to have arisen from Fengate is that redundant information must be kept to a minimum if the final report is to appear within a reasonable time. The alternative — to consign expensively obtained data to a second interment in an unpublished archive — is to admit that archaeologists cannot control the results of their excavations.

SUGGESTIONS FOR FUTURE RESEARCH

The Fengate project has thrown light on a comparatively small part of the western Fen-edge in antiquity. This work has taken almost ten years and has involved the expenditure of almost £100,000, including establishment costs, in-kind contributions from outside etc. It is surely appropriate, after the spending of so much time and effort, to consider what should happen next. The prehistoric archaeology of Fen and Fen-edge is at a most significant stage in its development. Buried landscapes are coming to light and the archaeological potential of the region is slowly revealing itself (Hall and Pryor forthcoming). Somewhat sporadic work is taking place in the lower valleys of the principal rivers draining into the Fenlands, but this urgently needs co-ordination, as does the research work in Lincolnshire and the southern Fenland. Standards of data recovery must be established to allow quantitative comparisons to be drawn between different sites and regions. Environmental evidence from a variety of locations is required to build up a coherent picture of the whole. Above all else, the wetlands of the Fen must not become separated from the Fen-edge, skirtland and lower river valleys that surround them. The 'islands' and uplands around the edge of the great Fen basin must be incorporated within the whole.

We have seen, thanks to work by the Oxford Unit, how the various cultural elements of what Professor Coles has termed a 'concave landscape' may be drawn together while, at the same time, their heterogeneity may also be appreciated. It is this heterogeneity that will provide the subject for future study; we must concern ourselves with changing cultural and environmental relationships in a region where at least a degree of environmental determinism seems reasonably justified. The picture is highly complex; for while it is difficult to generalise, for example, about Fenland vegetation sequences, it is many times harder to attempt broad statements about its human communities. The attempt must, however, be made, and made boldly if, that is, our ultimate aim is Archaeology.

PART VI: A CHRONOLOGICAL GUIDE TO THE FOUR FENGATE REPORTS

INTRODUCTION

Part VI is intended for the student interested in a particular period or topic. It is divided into two parts: the first is a concise descriptive guide to the various periods; the second considers specialists' reports and appendices, under subject headings.

1. PERIOD SUMMARY

Earlier Neolithic

Finds and features of this period were from two main sources: a rectangular house from the Padholme Road subsite and a multiple burial from Cat's Water.

The features of the house are described in the First Report (FNG 1, 6-8; FIGS 4-5); pottery, in the Grimston/Lyles Hill tradition, is described in FNG 1, 8-10 and illustrated in FNG 1, FIG 6. Flints are described in the First Report (FNG 1, 10-13) and Second Report (FNG 2, 7-10) and are illustrated in FNG 1, FIGS 7 and 8. A flake from a Group VI polished stone axe is illustrated in FNG 1, FIG 8. A fragment of a collared jet bead is illustrated in FNG 1, FIG 8 and PL 8. Burnt clay 'daub' from the foundation trenches is considered in FNG 2, 7. Finally, the pottery and the jet bead are discussed by Dr Isobel Smith in the First Report (pottery — FNG 1, 31-33; the bead, 40-42).

The multiple burial was considered in an interim note (Pryor 1976b) and in this report (FNG 4, 19-27; PLS 12 and 13); the skeletal material is discussed by Mr B Denston in FNG 4, Appendix 8.

Other earlier Neolithic finds include two fragments of Group VI axe from ditches of the Vicarage Farm subsite, which may possibly, therefore, be of Neolithic date (FNG I, 14; FNG 4, 129). Finally, a possibly intrusive sherd of Grimston/Lyles Hill pottery was found in a feature of the Grooved Ware settlement, Storey's Bar Road subsite (FNG 2, 91, FIG 37); a few sherds were found in two pits on Newark Road (FNG 3, FIG 57). Earlier Neolithic material was not found on the Fourth Drove subsite.

Later Neolithic

Peterborough pottery was rare. Only three sherds, one from Vicarage Farm and two from Cat's Water are of probable Peterborough type; they are illustrated in FNG 4, FIG 96.

Grooved Ware, flintwork, miscellaneous associated finds and features from Storey's Bar Road form the subject of the Second Report. This material was found in the fillings of ditches and other settlement features on the Storey's Bar Road subsite, Area I. Grooved Ware has also been found in small pits on the Newark Road subsite (FNG 3, FIGS 57 and 58). Padholme Road was the only subsite that did not produce later Neolithic material.

Beaker

Finds of Beaker material have been rare. Despite the clearance of large areas, settlement has not been located on the scale expected; Mr G W Abbott recovered substantial quantities of Beaker pottery from the pre-war gravel workings, and this is reported by Alex Gibson in Appendix 10 of the Third Report. Beaker sherds and flintwork were found in small pits on the Padholme Road subsite (FNG 1, 14-15, FIG 10). The Vicarage Farm subsite produced a few weathered scraps from pits (FNG 4, 129); Newark Road also produced a few sherds from small pits (FNG 3, FIG 59). Weathered Beaker sherds were found in the grave fillings in the Storey's

Bar Road ring-ditch (FNG 2, FIG 37). No Beaker material, however, was recorded from the Cat's Water or Fourth Drove subsites.

Early and Middle Bronze Age

The ditched second millennium enclosures that form the most important Early and Middle Bronze Age component at Fengate were reported in interim form in Pryor 1976a. They are discussed more fully in the Third Report; FNG 4 contains some additional material on the ditched enclosure that could not be included in FNG 3: Chapter 3 considers probable second millennium features on the Storey's Bar Road subsite and Chapter 4, part 2 (FIGS 20, M23-M32), is devoted to details of the second millennium ditches on Cat's Water. Chapter 5 treats finds (mainly pottery and flint) of second millennium date from Cat's Water and Storey's Bar Road. Relevant radiocarbon dates are given in FNG 3 Appendix 12, but an additional date (HAR-3204) is also published in Appendix 12 of FNG 4.

The Storey's Bar Road subsite had a substantial earlier Bronze Age funerary component which is considered in the Second Report (FNG 2, 33-38; 59-62; 97; FIGS 21-25; 37 and 41). Only the Vicarage Farm subsite lacked material of this type and period.

Late Bronze and Early Iron Age

A general discussion of material from these periods is provided in this report, Chapter 6, Part 1, section 4 ('Group 1'). This account contains references to previous reports, which may briefly be reiterated here: the First Report (FNG 1, 15-22; 35-37; FIGS 11-16) contains details of the Vicarage Farm material: the Third Report, (FNG 3, Chapter 2, part IV, section 1) describes Early Iron Age pits from Newark Road (for finds see FNG 3, FIG 61). Similar features from Fourth Drove are described in the Third Report (FNG 3, 151); finds are shown in FNG 3, FIG 89. Finally, features from Cat's Water are described in this report (FNG 4, Chapter 4, 123) and the type series is shown in FNG 4 FIGS M88-M93 (the vessel shown in FNG 1, FIG 14, no 3 is photographed in this report — PLS 1 and 2). There was no material of this period from Storey's Bar Road or Padholme Road.

Middle and Late Iron Age

This period forms the principal topic of this report; Chapter 6 is given over to a general description and discussion of the pottery (Groups 2 and 3) and miscellaneous finds; this chapter also includes references to previous reports which may be summarised here: Middle and Late Iron features are described in chapters 1-4 (Vicarage Farm, Padholme Road, Storey's Bar Road and Cat's Water subsites). The First Report considers material from Vicarage Farm (FNG 1, 15-22) and Padholme Road (FNG 1, 22-29; especially FIGS 20-22) and a general discussion of the Fengate Iron Age is in FNG 1, 35-38. No significant quantities of Middle

and Late Iron Age material were found on the Newark Road subsite.

Romano-British

Material and features of Romano-British date were widespread over the site. A ditched droveway traversed the Storey's Bar Road subsite (FNG 4, Chapter 3, 15); Padholme Road revealed a Romano-British ditch (FNG 1, FIG 17); Newark Road also produced a Romano-British ditch (FNG 3, FIG 44) and the SW corner was traversed by the Fen Causeway (FNG 3, FIG 3). The Fen Causeway crossed the modern road into the Fourth Drove subsite (see FNG 3, Chapter 3 'ditch 10 and associated features'; also FNG 3, FIG 86 and its detailed caption; pottery from the road is shown in FNG 3, FIG 89; the road is discussed in chapter 3: section 2). Numerous Romano-British features were found on the Vicarage Farm subsite (FNG 4, Chapter 1) and the pottery is discussed by Dr J P Wild (in FNG 4, Chapter 7). The Cat's Water subsite Romano-British component is fully described in Chapter 4 of this report; pottery and other finds are considered in Chapter 7.

2. SPECIALISTS' REPORTS AND APPENDICES

1. Radiocarbon dates

See FNG 1: 38; FNG 2: Appendix 13; FNG 3: Appendix 12; FNG 4: Appendix 12.

2. Artifacts

Earlier Neo Pottery (I F Smith), FNG 1: 31-33
Bronze Age pottery fabrics (D F Williams), FNG 3: Chapter 2
Beaker pottery in Peterborough Museum (Alex Gibson), FNG 3: Appendix 10
Iron Age pottery fabrics (D F Williams), FNG 4: Chapter 6
Romano-British pottery from Vicarage Farm (J P Wild), FNG 4: Chapter 7
Roman pottery from Cat's Water (J W Hayes), FNG 4: Chapter 7
Roman pottery in Peterborough Museum (J W Hayes), FNG 4: Appendix 10
Samian ware (Felicity Wild), FNG 4: Chapter 7
Roman mortaria (Mrs K Hartley), FNG 4: Chapter 7
Neolithic collared jet bead (I F Smith), FNG 1: 40-42
Neolithic arrowhead (H S Green), FNG 4: Chapter 4
Microwear study of Late Neolithic flints (B Voytek), FNG 2: Appendix 9
Middle Bronze Age spearhead (D G Coombs), FNG 3: Chapter 2
Analysis of Middle Bronze Age metal (P T Craddock), FNG 3: Chapter 2
Iron Age wooden stake (Maisie Taylor), FNG 4: Chapter 6
Iron Age slags and refractories (P T Craddock), FNG 4: Chapter 6
Iron Age finger ring (M Henig), FNG 4: Chapter 6

Brooches (D F Mackreath), FNG 4: Chapter 6
Coins from Cat's Water (R Reece), FNG 4: Chapter 6

3. Human Bones
Earlier Neolithic burial group from Cat's Water (B Denston), FNG 4: Appendix 8
Early Bronze Age ring-ditch burials, Storey's Bar Road (C Wells), FNG 2: Appendix 8
Bronze Age, from ditches in Newark and Padholme Road (C Wells), FNG 3: Appendix 8
Bronze Age, from ditch on Cat's Water (Faye Powell), FNG 3: Appendix 9
Loose Iron Age bones from Padholme and Storey's Bar Road (Faye Powell), FNG 4: Appendix 7
Iron Age burials from Cat's Water (Faye Powell), FNG 4: Appendix 9

4. Animal Bones
Later Neolithic/earlier Bronze Age from Storey's Bar Road (M Harman), FNG 2: Appendix 7
Bronze Age from Newark Road (K Biddick), FNG 3: Appendix 7
Iron Age, mainly from Cat's Water (K Biddick), FNG 4: Appendix 6

5. Palaeoenvironmental
Bronze Age plant remains from Storey's Bar Road (J R B Arthur), FNG 2: Appendix 3ʼ
Bronze Age wood remains from Storey's Bar Road (Ruth Jones), FNG 2: Appendix 5
Bronze Age pollen from Storey's Bar Road (J H McAndrews), FNG 2: Appendix 6
Soil pH, Storey's Bar Road (F M M Pryor), FNG 2: Appendix 2
Bronze Age sediments, Newark Road and Fourth Drove (C A I French), FNG 3: Appendices 2 and 3
Iron Age sediments, Cat's Water (C A I French), FNG 4: Appendix 3
Bronze Age molluscs, Newark Road (C A I French), FNG 3: Appendix 4
Charcoals, mainly Bronze Age (Maisie Taylor), FNG 3: Appendix 5
Iron Age molluscs, Cat's Water (C A I French), FNG 4: Appendix 2
Palaeobotany, overview, mainly Newark Road, Storey's Bar Road and Cat's Water (Gay Wilson), FNG 4: Appendix 5

6. Site Science
Soil phosphate analyses, Newark Road (P T Craddock), FNG 3: Appendix 6
Soil phosphate and magnetic susceptibility analyses, Cat's Water (P T Craddock), FNG 4: Appendix 4

7. Comparative material
Reinterpretation of Playden, Sussex (Richard Bradley), FNG 2: Appendix 10

8. Concordance etc
FNG 2: Appendices 11 and 12; FNG 3: Appendix 11; FNG 4: Appendix 11

9. Techniques etc
Techniques of excavation, 1971-74, FNG 2: Appendix 1
Techniques of excavation, 1975-78, FNG 3: Appendix 1
Treatment of botanical samples, 1973, FNG 2: Appendix 4
Site recording system, FNG 4: Appendix 1

APPENDIX SUMMARIES
Note

The text of each of the 12 appendices has been placed on microfiche. Five figures (FIGS 138-139 and 140-142) have not been placed on fiche, (a) because of their size and (b) because of the many references to them in the main text. Apart from these five Figures, each appendix is complete, with illustrations integrated within the microfiche text. Tables appear at the end of each appendix. The prefix 'M' is used to denote Figures or Tables on microfiche. The reader is advised to consult the Table of Microfiche Contents at the rear of this volume.

The summaries are intended to give the reader an indication of the reports' contents. Principal results are more fully discussed and are integrated with other data from Fengate in Part III of Chapter 8.

APPENDIX 1 (SEE MICROFICHE PAGES 212-216)

Methods of Recording 1971-78
The first part describes the development of recording systems from 1971-78, with special reference to printed forms, which were introduced in 1974 and developed thereafter. The forms are reproduced in Figs M136-139. The pros and cons of the recording system are considered and suggestions for improvement made.

APPENDIX 2 (SEE MICROFICHE PAGES 217-222)

The Molluscan Fauna from Two Iron Age Ditches at Fengate, Peterborough, Cambridgeshire
by C A I French

This paper discusses molluscs from two ditches of the Cat's Water subsite, Features F30 and F112, near the northern edge of the main settlement. The report includes a detailed species list and closes with an Addendum on recent changes in mollusc nomenclature. The author's principal conclusions may be summarised: The molluscs from F112 suggest a more marshy habitat than F30 which held *c* 10-30cm of slow-moving water with scattered marsh vegetation on the ditch sides. In addition to freshwater 'slum' species, the ditches also included a number of woodland, intermediate and ubiquitous terrestrial species. This small terrestrial fauna was probably living on the ditch sides, above the water's edge.

APPENDIX 3 (SEE MICROFICHE PAGES 223-233)

A Sediments Analysis of the Late Iron Age Ditches at Fengate, Peterborough
by C A I French

This paper begins with a brief discussion of the modern ploughsoil and its formation. The body of the report is given over to a detailed analysis of sediments from the two ditches (F30 and F112) discussed in Appendix 2. The techniques used include determination of soil pH; determination of the alkali-soluble organic matter; determination of the free iron content; and particle size analysis.

The broad conclusions may be summarised as a sequence of events (depths are in cm below the stripped surface):

Ditch F30
1. (85+cm) Initial rapid silting, with hints at an accompanying bank and possible partial back-filling. Ditch held slowly moving water (removed clay and finer silt fraction?), but was subject to periodic drying-out.
2. (72-85cm) Accumulation of lowest secondary fill. Ditch still held water, organic matter and silt (via wind?) accumulate.
3. (66-72cm) Rapid influx of sand and gravel, probably caused by back-filling. This material probably thrown out of nearby ditch F29, immediately north of, and parallel to, F30.
4. (45-66cm) Ditch no longer holds water, but continues to be subject to natural erosion. Lens of ashy material at 55-58cm probably dumped-in from nearby hearth. Ditch now out of use.
5. (45-35cm) Possible third episode of back-filling, possibly as a result of cleaning-out F29 nearby.
6. (0-35cm) Inundation and deposition of flood clay. Third century AD.

Ditch F112
1. (70+cm) Initial rapid filling with some evidence for possible back-filling. Some water, but subject to periodic drying out.
2. (0-70cm) Secondary filling: All secondary filling below 55-60cm was subject to water-sorting. The ditch was recut twice, to south, then to north. Upcast from at least one of these off-centre recuts was thrown into the slowly-filling main ditch. There was also evidence for another, later (15-30cm) episode of back-filling.
3. The tertiary filling of flood clay (C3 AD) dipped into the top of the ditch, but had been removed mechanically at this point.

APPENDIX 4 (SEE MICROFICHE PAGES 234-241)

The Soil Phosphate Survey at the Cat's Water subsite, Fengate 1973-77
by P T Craddock
(with a shorter contribution from M S Tite)

The general conclusions of this report are summarised, in plan form, in the Figures reproduced in the main text (FIG 138-9; 140-142). The report contains a summary account of the analytical methods used and there is a description of the sampling strategy, and the field techniques involved. The distribution of soil phosphate over the excavated area, both before and after topsoil removal is discussed and comparisons are drawn with other sites in this manner. The paper concludes with a general assessment of the technique as a means of site location.

APPENDIX 5 (SEE MICROFICHE PAGES 242-244)

A Report on Plant Macrofossils from Fengate
by Gay Wilson

This paper is a summary report of the author's palaeo-botanical analyses of Fengate material carried out in recent years. A full report of Fengate and other Nene valley sites is in preparation. The report considers Bronze Age deposits from Storey's Bar Road and Newark Road, together with Iron Age samples, mainly from Cat's Water. Main topics discussed are the poor evidence for cultivation, especially in pre-Iron Age levels, the general scarcity of cereals, the (slight) evidence for hedges and the occurrence of woodland plants. There is much evidence for pasture and meadowland and deeper ditches produced aquatic species. The evidence of the flora suggests that the Iron Age was the wettest period at Fengate.

APPENDIX 6 (SEE MICROFICHE PAGES 245-275)

Animal Bones from Cat's Water Subsite, Fengate
by by Kathleen Biddick

This report follows the author's previous study of second millennium material in the Third Report (FNG 3: 217-232). The report considers on-site recovery and analysis procedures. Bone preservation is discussed and modification in antiquity (gnawing, calcination etc) assessed. The relative abundance of species is assessed on a fragment count (Table M32) and Chaplin's (1971) criteria are used to assess minimum numbers of individuals (Table M34). Modified versions of the MNI technique are also employed (Table M30). The distribution of skeletal elements is discussed (based on Table M28) and the age structure of domesticated animals is considered at length, based on epiphyseal fusion (Tables M31-32; FIG M153). Tooth eruption and wear data are also used to arrive at estimates of age structure, for cattle (FIGS M154 and M155) and sheep (FIG M157).

Cattle and sheep mandibles are discussed in some detail (FIGS M154-M159) and comparisons are drawn with Ashville Trading Estate, Abingdon and Barton Court Farm, Oxon. (Iron Age and Roman deposits separately). The sexing of cranial material is considered and special attention is accorded to butchery evidence and patterns (PLS 20-26); comparisons are drawn with butchery patterns previously recorded (Newark Road subsite, FNG 3).

APPENDIX 7 (SEE MICROFICHE PAGE 276)

Human Bones from Iron Age and Roman features of the Padholme Road and Storey's Bar Road subsites
by F V E Powell

This report is a descriptive account of loose human bones from Padholme Road XI, F10; F5 and Storey's Bar Road feature P13.

APPENDIX 8 (SEE MICROFICHE PAGES 277-280)

The Neolithic Human Skeletal Remains from Cat's Water Subsite Feature 1283
by C B Denston

This is a detailed report on the four individuals buried in the communal Neolithic grave, F1283 (Pryor 1976b). Mr Denston's general conclusions are discussed in Chapter 4, Part 1 (earlier Neolithic).

APPENDIX 9 (SEE MICROFICHE PAGES 281-291)

Human Bones from Iron Age and Roman Features of the Cat's Water subsite
by F V E Powell

The first part of this report considers the six inhumations of the Cat's Water Iron Age settlement, which are seen to belong to Whimster's (1977) Group I. All are male, or probably male; 5 are age 17-25, one is adolescent. All were crouch burials.

The second part considers unassociated human bone from a variety of pits, ditches and structures dispersed around the settlement area. The report concludes with a detailed description of three probable Iron Age cremations (F1035, F26 and F27).

APPENDIX 10 (SEE MICROFICHE PAGES 292-295)

Pottery from Fengate in Peterborough Museum
by J W Hayes

This report describes and illustrates (FIGS M302 and M303) hitherto unpublished Roman pottery from Fengate in Peterborough Museum. It is discussed using ware types defined in this report (Chapter 7) and includes descriptions of Nene Valley grey wares, Samian ware and Nene Valley colour-coated ('Castor') wares. Most of the material derives from the Wyman Abbott collections.

APPENDIX 11 (SEE MICROFICHE PAGES 296-306)

A List of Features from the Cat's Water subsite

This codified list itemises every feature from Cat's Water mentioned in the text. Details are given of phasing, function (brief) and location (Grid references). It provides a useful means of access to information stored in the archive.

APPENDIX 12 (SEE MICROFICHE PAGE 307)

Radiocarbon Dates

Details are given of two dates received since the publication of the Third Report (FNG appendix 12). They are fully discussed in Chapter 8, Part III (FIG 137).

BIBLIOGRAPHY

Ackeroyd, A V,
  1972   Archaeological and historical evidence for subsidence in Southern Britain, *Philosophical Transactions of the Royal Society*, series A, 272, 151-69, London
Anderson, J E,
  1969   *The human skeleton: a manual for archaeologists*, National Museum of Man; Ottawa
ApSimon, A,
  1976   Ballynagilly and the beginning and end of the Irish Neolithic, in S J deLaet, ed, *Acculturation and continuity in Atlantic Europe*, 15-30, Dissertationes Archaeologicae Gandensis, Ghent
Armitage, P, and Clutton-Brock, J,
  1976   A system for classification and description of horn cores of cattle from archaeological sites, *J Archaeol Sci*, 3, 329-48
Atkinson, R J C, Piggott, C M and Sanders, N K
  1951   *Excavations at Dorchester, Oxfordshire*, Ashmolean Museum, Oxford
Avery, B W and Bascomb, C L, eds,
  1974   *Soil survey laboratory methods*, Soil Survey Technical Monograph No 6
Abbott, G W
  1910   The discovery of prehistoric pits at Peterborough, *Archaeologia*, 62, 332-52
Bakker, J A, Brandt, R W, van Geel, B *et al*
  1977   Hoogkarspel-Watertoren: towards a reconstruction of ecology and archaeology of an agrarian settlement of 1000 BC, in B L van Beek, R W Brandt and W Groenman van Watteringe (eds) 1977, *Ex Horreo*, 187-225, Amsterdam University
Balkwill, C J,
  1979   The Iron Age assemblages from Darmsden, Hinderclay and Kettleburgh, *Proceedings of the Suffolk Institute of Archaeology and History*, 34, 207-210
Bamford, H M,
  1979   Review of the Second Fengate Report, *Northamptonshire Archaeol*, 14, 133-4
Barker, P,
  1977   *Techniques of archaeological excavation*, Batsford, London
Barton, K J,
  1962   Settlements of the Iron Age and Pagan Saxon periods, *Transactions of the Essex Archaeological Society*, 1, 57-104
Bass, W M,
  1971   *Human osteology: a laboratory and field manual of the human skeleton*, Missouri Archaeological Society, Missouri
Beckmann, C,
  1969   Metallfingerringe der Romischen Kaiserzeit in Freien Germanien, *Saalburg Jahrbuch*, 26, 7-106
Beedham, G E,
  1972   *Identification of the British mollusca*, Pitman Press, Bath
Benson, D, and Miles, D,
  1974   *The Upper Thames valley: an archaeological survey*, Oxfordshire Archaeological Unit Survey 2, Oxford
Bersu, G,
  1977   *Three Iron Age round houses in the Isle of Man*, Manx Museum
Biddick, K,
  1978   Medieval livestock accounts as sources for study of intensive animal management on monastic and lay estates in Great Britain: 1200-1400 AD, paper presented at the Third International Archaeological Conference, Poland, forthcoming in M Kubasiewicz, ed, *Archaeozoological Studies 1*
  1980   Animal bones from the second millennium ditches, Newark Road subsite, Fengate, Appendix 7 in Pryor 1980a
  1981   Animal management and land-use on the Fen-edge, Peterborough: an archaeological and historical perspective, PhD dissertation, University of Toronto
Binford, L R,
  1962   Archaeology as anthropology, *American Antiquity*, 28, 2, 217-25
  1964   A consideration of archaeological research design, *American Antiquity*, 29, 425-41

261

Binford, L R, and Bertram, J,
    1977   Bone frequencies and attritional processes, in Binford, ed, *For theory building in archaeology,* 77-153, Academic Press, London

Bokonyi, S,
    1974   *History of domestic mammals in Central and Eastern Europe,* Akademiai Kiado, Budapest

Boserup, E,
    1965   *The conditions of agricultural growth,* Aldine, Chicago

Brown, H C, and Fowler, P J, eds,
    1978   *Early land allotment,* British Archaeological Reports, 48, Oxford

Boycott, A E,
    1934   The habitats of land mollusca in Britain, *Journal of Ecology,* 22, 1-38

Bradley, R J,
    1970   The excavation of a Beaker settlement at Belle Tout, East Sussex, England, *Proc Prehist Soc,* 36, 312-79
    1971   Stock raising and the origins of the hill fort on the South Downs, *Antiq J,* 51, 8-29
    1978a   *The prehistoric settlement of Britain,* 1st ed, Routledge and Kegan Paul, London
    1978b   Prehistoric field systems in Britain and North-west Europe — a review of some recent work, *World Archaeol,* 9, 3, 265-280

Bradley, R J, and Ellison, A, eds
    1975   *Rams Hill,* British Archaeological Reports, 19, Oxford

Brailsford, J,
    1949   Excavations at Little Woodbury, *Proc. Prehist Soc.,* 15, 156-168

Brewster, T C M,
    1963   *The excavation of Staple Howe,* Wintringham, Yorkshire

Britnell, W J,
    1974   Beckford, *Curr Archaeol,* 45, 293-297
    1975   An interim report upon excavations at Beckford, 1972-4, *Vale of Evesham Historical Society Research Papers,* 1-11

Bromwich, J I,
    1970   Freshwater flooding along the Fen margins south of the Isle of Ely during the Roman period, in Phillips 1970, 114-126

Brongers, J A,
    1976   *Air photography and Celtic field research in the Netherlands,* Nederlandse Oudheden 6, Amersfoort
    1978   The Emmen-Odoorn region in the Iron Age, a study in scale and structure (Summary) in B W Cunliffe and R T Rowley, eds, 1978, 121-2

Brongers, J A, and Woltering, P J,
    1973   Prehistory in the Netherlands: an economic-technological approach, in *Berichten van de Rijksdienst voor het Oudheidkundig Bodermonderzoek,* 23, 7-47

Brothwell, D R,
    1963   *Digging up bones. The excavation, treatment and study of human skeletal remains,* 1st ed, HMSO London
    1972   *Digging up bones,* 2nd ed, Natural History Museum, London
    1967   The evidence for Neoplasms, in Brothwell and Sandison, 1967, 342

Brothwell, D R, and Sandison, A T,
    1967   *Diseases in antiquity,* Springfield

Brown, F, and Taylor C C,
    1978   Settlement and land-use in Northamptonshire: a comparison between the Iron Age and the Middle Ages, in B W Cunliffe and R T Rowley, eds, *Lowland Iron Age communities in Europe,* 77-90, British Archaeological Reports, S48, Oxford

Buckland, P C,
    1979   Thorne Moors: a palaeoecological study of a Bronze Age site, *Birmingham University Department of Geography Occasional Publication,* 8

Buckley, D G, ed,
    1980   *Archaeology in Essex to AD 1500,* Council for British Archaeology Research Reports, 34, London

Bulleid, A and Gray, H St G,
    1911 and 1917   *The Glastonbury lake village,* I and II, Glastonbury Antiquarian Society, Taunton
    1948 and 1953   *The Meare lake village,* I and II, Taunton

Bunch, B, and Corder, P,
    1954   A Romano-British pottery kiln at Weston Favell, near Northampton, *Antiq J,* 34, 218ff

Burgess, C B,
1980   *The Age of Stonehenge,* Dent, London
Burgess, C B, and Miket, R, eds,
1976   *Settlement and economy in the third and second millennia, BC,* British Archaeological Reports, 33, Oxford
Bushe-Fox, J P,
1925   *Excavation of the Late Celtic urnfield at Swarling, Kent,* Research Report of the Society of Antiquaries, 5, London
Buurman, J,
1979   Cereals in circles — crop processing activities in Bronze Age Bovenkarspel, the Netherlands, in U Korber-Grohne, ed, *Festschrift Maria Hopf,* 21-37, Cologne
Carter, H H,
1975   The Animal Bones, in Bradley and Ellison, 1975, 118-22
Case, H,
1970   Neolithic comments, *Antiquity,* 44, 111
Challands, A,
1973   The Lynch Farm complex: the prehistoric site, *Durobrivae,* 1, 22-3
Champion, T C,
1975   Britain in the European Iron Age, *Archaeologia Atlantica,* 1, 2, 127-145
Chaplin, R E,
1971   *The study of animal bones from archaeologial sites,* Academic Press, London
Chatwin, C P,
1961   *British regional geology: East Anglia and adjoining areas,* 4th ed, Institute of Geological Sciences, HMSO, London
Cherry, J F, Gamble, C, and Shennan, S, eds,
1978   *Sampling in contemporary British archaeology,* British Archaeological Reports, 50, Oxford
Chowne, P,
1977   Some recent finds of Bronze Age pottery from South Lincolnshire, *S Lincolnshire Archaeol,* 1, 24-25
1978   Billingborough Bronze Age settlement: an interim note, *Lincolnshire Hist Archaeol,* 13, 15-24
Churchill, D M,
1970   Post-Neolithic to Romano-British sedimentation in the southern Fenlands of Cambridgeshire and Norfolk, in C W Phillips, ed, *The Fenland in Roman times,* 136-146
Clark, A J
1977   Geophysical and chemical assessment of air photographic sites, appendix to J Hampton and R Palmer, Implications of aerial photography for archaeology, *Archaeol J,* 134, 187-191
Clark, J G D,
1933   Report on an Early Bronze Age site in the South-Eastern Fens, *Antiq J,* 13, 264-96
1960   Excavations at the prehistoric site at Hurst Fen, Mildenhall, Suffolk, 1954, 1957 and 1958, *Proc Prehist Soc,* 26, 202-45
Clark, J G D, and Fell, C I,
1953   The Early Iron Age site at Micklemoor Hill, West Harling, Norfolk, and its pottery, *Proc Prehist Soc,* 39, 1-40
Clark, J G D, and Godwin, H,
1962   The Neolithic in the Cambridgeshire Fens, *Antiquity,* 36, 10-22
Clark, R M,
1975   A calibration curve for radiocarbon dates, *Antiquity,* 49, 251-66
Clarke, D L,
1970   *Beaker pottery of Great Britain and Ireland,* Cambridge University Press, 2 vols
1972   A provisional model of an Iron Age society ánd its settlement system, in D L Clarke, ed, *Models in Archaeology,* 801-70, Methuen, London
Clarke, R R,
1960   *East Anglia,* Ancient Peoples and Places series, Thames and Hudson, London

Coles, J M,
  1965   The archaeology of the Cambridge region: prehistory, in J A Steers, ed, *The Cambridge region,* British Association for the Advancement of Science, London
  1976   Forest farmers: some archaeological, historical and experimental evidence relating to the prehistory of Europe, in S J deLaet, ed, *Acculturation and continuity in Atlantic Europe,* 559-66, Bruges
  1978   The Somerset Levels: a concave landscape, in H C Bowen and P J Fowler, eds, *Early land allotment,* British Archaeological Reports, 48
Coles, J M, and Hibbert, F A,
  1975   The Somerset Levels, in P J Fowler, ed, *Recent work in rural archaeology,* 12-26, Moonraker Press, Bradford-on-Avon, Wiltshire
Coles, J M, and Orme, B J,
  1980   *Prehistory of the Somerset Levels,* Somerset Levels Project, Cambridge and Exeter
Coles, J M, Orme, B J, May, J, and Moore, C N,
  1979   Excavations of Late Bronze Age or Iron Age date at Washingborough Fen, *Lincolnshire Hist Archaeol,* 14, 5-10
Cook, S F, and Heizer, R F,
  1965   *Studies on the chemical analysis of archaeological sites,* University of California Publications in Anthropology 2, Berkley and Los Angeles
  1968   Relationships among houses, settlement areas, and population in aboriginal California, in Chang, K C, ed, *Settlement archaeology,* 79-116, National Press Books, Palo Alto
Corcoran, J X W P,
  1967   Excavations of the chambered cairns at Loch Calder, Caithness, *Proc Soc Antiq Scotland,* 98, 1-75
Corder, P, *et al*
  1961   The Roman town and villa at Great Casterton, Rutland, Third Report, Nottingham
Cotton, M A, and Frere, S S,
  1968   Ivinghoe Beacon excavations, 1963-5, *Rec Buckinghamshire,* 18, 187-260
Coy, J,
  1975   Iron Age cookery, in A Clason, *Archaeozoological Studies,* 426-30, Elsevier, Amsterdam
Craddock, P T,
  1980   The soil phosphate survey at the Newark Road Subsite, Fengate, Appendix 6 in F M M Pryor, 1980a
Cra'ster, M D,
  1961   The Aldwick Iron Age settlement, Barley, Hertfordshire, *Proc Cambridge Antiq Soc,* 54, 22-46
Crumley C L,
  1979   Three locational models: an epistemological assessment for anthropology and archaeology, in Schiffer, M B, ed, *Advances in archaeological method and theory,* 141-173, Seminar Press, London
Cunliffe, B W,
  1966   The Somerset Levels in the Roman Period, in A C Thomas, ed, 1966, 68-73
  1968   Early Pre-Roman Iron Age communities in Eastern England, *Antiq J,* 48, 175-191
  1976   Danebury Hampshire: second interim report on the excavations 1971-5, *Antiq J,* 56, 198-216
  1978   *Iron Age communities in Britain,* 2nd ed, Routledge, London
Cunliffe, B W, and Rowley, R T, eds,
  1978   *Lowland Iron Age communities in Europe,* British Archaeological Reports, S48, Oxford
Dallas, C,
  1975   A Belgic farmstead at Orton Longueville, *Durobrivae,* 3, 26-7
Darby, H C,
  1940   *The Medieval Fenland,* David and Charles, reprinted 1974
  1956   *The draining of the Fens,* 2nd ed, Cambridge University Press
Davidson, G R,
  1952   *Corinth XII, the minor objects,* Greece
de Boer, W R, and Lathrap, D W,
  1979   The making and breaking of Shipito-Conito ceramics, in C Kramer, ed, *Ethnoarchaeology,* 102-38, Columbia University Press, New York
de Laet, S J,
  1958   *The Low Countries,* Ancient Peoples and Places series, Thames and Hudson, London
Dix, B,
  1979   Odell: a river valley farm, *Curr Archaeol,* 66, 215-218
Dolling, H,
  1958   *Haus und Hof in westgermanischen Volksrechten*

von den Dreisch, A,
1976   *Das Vermessen von Tierknochen aus vor-und fruhgeschichtlichen Siedlungen,* Institut f. Palaoanotomie, Domestikationsforschung und Geschichte der Tiermedizin, Munchen

Drury, P J,
1978a   *Excavations at Little Waltham 1970-71,* Council for British Archaeology Research Reports, 28
1978b   Little Waltham and pre-Belgic Iron Age settlement in Essex, in B W Cunliffe and R T Rowley, eds, *Lowland Iron Age communities in Europe,* 43-76, British Archaeological Reports, S48, Oxford
1980   The Early and Middle phases of the Iron Age in Essex, in Buckley, ed, 1980, 47-54

Drury, P J and Rodwell, W,
1973   Excavations at Gun Hill, West Tilbury, *Essex Archaeol Hist,* 5, 48-112
1980   Settlement in the Later Iron Age and Roman periods, in Buckley, ed, 1980, 47-54

von den Driesch A, and Boessneck, J,
1974   Kritische Anmerkungen zur Widerristhohenberechnung aus Langemassen vor-und fruhgeschtilicher Tierknochen, *Suagtirkunde Mitteilungen,* 22, 325-48

Ducos, P,
1968   L'origine des animaux domestiques en Palestine, *Publications de l'Institut de Prehistoire de l'Université de Bordeaux,* memoire no 6

Dyer, J,
1961   Dray's Ditches, Bedfordshire, and Early Iron Age territorial boundaries in the Eastern Chilterns, *Antiq J,* 41, 32-43
1976a   Ravensburgh Castle, Hertfordshire, in D W Harding, ed, *Hillforts: later prehistoric earthworks in Britain and Ireland,* 153-161, Academic Press, London
1976b   The Bedfordshire region in the first millennium BC, *Bedfordshire Archaeol J,* 7-18

Eagles, B N, and Evison, V I,
1970   Excavations at Harrold, Bedfordshire, *Bedfordshire Archaeol J,* 5, 17-56

Eidt, R C,
1977   Detection and examination of anthrosols by phosphate analysis, *Science,* 197, 1327-1333

Ellis, A E,
1941   The mollusca of a Norfolk Broad, *Journal of Conchology,* 21, 224-243

Ellison, A, and Harriss, J,
1972   Settlement and land use in the prehistory and early history of southern England: a study based on locational models, in D L Clarke, ed, *Models in archaeology,* 911-962, Methuen, London

ELE Catalogue
1978   *ELE Catalogue,* 5th Ed, 204-234, ELE Ltd, Frogmore Road, Hemel Hempstead, Hertfordshire

Elsdon, S M,
1975   *Stamped Iron Age pottery,* British Archaeological Reports, 10, Oxford

Erith, F H, and Longworth, I H,
1960   A Bronze Age urnfield on Vinces Farm, Ardleigh, Essex, *Proc Prehist Soc,* 35, 178-192

Evans, J G,
1972   *Land snails in archaeology,* Seminar Press, London

Evans, G E,
1969   *The farm and the village,* paperback ed 1974, Faber and Faber, London

Evans, R,
1979   The early courses of the River Nene, *Durobrivae,* 7, 8-10

Everson, P,
1976   Iron Age enclosures at the Queensway Health Centre Site, Hardwick Park, Wellingborough, *Northamptonshire Archaeol,* 11, 89-99

Ewbank, J M, Phillipson, D W, Whitehouse, R D, and Higgs, E S,
1964   Sheep in the Iron Age: a method of study, *Proc Prehist Soc,* 30, 423-26

Fadden, K,
1975   A field-walking exercise in the Ampthill area, *Bedfordshire Archaeol J,* 10, 1-4

Fell, C I,
1936   The Hunsbury hill-fort Northampton — a new survey of the material, *Archaeol J,* 93, 57-100

Field, K,
1974   Ring ditches of the Upper and Middle Great Ouse valley, *Archaeol J,* 131, 58-74

Field, N H, Matthews, C L, and Smith, I F,
1964   New Neolithic Sites in Dorset and Bedfordshire, with a note on the distribution of Neolithic storage pits in Britain, *Proc Prehist Soc,* 30, 352-81

Fleming, A,
1978   The prehistoric landscape of Dartmoor Part 1: South Dartmoor, *Proc Prehist Soc,* 44, 97-123
Folk, R L, and Ward, W C,
1957   Brazos River Bar: a study in the significance of grain-size parameters, *Journal of Sedimentary Petrology,* 27, 3-26
Foard, G,
1978   Systematic fieldwalking and the investigation of Saxon settlement in Northamptonshire, *World Archaeol,* 9, 357-74
Foster, P S, Harper, R, and Watkins, S,
1977   An Iron Age and Romano-British settlement at Hardwick Park, Wellingborough, Northamptonshire, *Northamptonshire Archaeol,* 1977, 12, 55-96
Fowler, G,
1933   Fenland waterways, past and present, South Level District, Part I, *Proc Cambridge Antiq Soc,* 33, 108-128
1934   Fenland waterways, past and present, South Level District, Part II, *Proc Cambridge Antiq Soc,* 34, 17-33
Fowler, P J, ed
1975   *Recent work in rural archaeology,* Moonraker Press, Bradford-upon-Avon, Wiltshire
Fox, C,
1923   *The archaeology of the Cambridge region,* Cambridge University Press
Fox, C, Burkitt, M C, and Abbott, G W,
1926   Early man, *Victoria County History — Huntingdon,* pt 4, London
French, C A I,
1980a   A sediments analysis of second millennium BC ditches at Newark Road subsite, Fengate, Peterborough, Cambridgeshire, in Pryor, 1980a, 190-202
1980b   The molluscs from the Werrington enclosure, *Durobrivae,* 8, 26-7
Frere, S S,
1972   *Verulamium excavations,* Vol I, Research Report of the Society of Antiquaries, 28, London
Frere, S S, and St Joseph, J K,
1974   The Roman fortress at Longthorpe, *Britannia,* 5, 1-129
Gallois, R W,
1979   *Geological investigations for the Wash water storage scheme,* Institute of Geological Sciences Report, 78/19, HMSO, London
Garrood, J R,
1932   A Romano-British village in Huntingdonshire, *Transactions of the Cambridgeshire and Huntingdonshire Archaeological Society,* 5, 89-101
1935   Stone and bronze implements, objects from Castle Hill Farm, Wood Walton, *Transactions of the Cambridgeshire and Huntingdonshire Archaeological Society,* 5, 275-7
1939   Iron Age and Romano-British site at Salome Lodge, Leighton, *Transactions of the Cambridgeshire and Huntingdonshire Archaeological Society,* 6, 66-74
1942   An Iron Age and Roman site at Houghton, *Transactions of the Cambridgeshire and Huntingdonshire Archaeological Society,* 6, 155-8
Gates, T,
1975   *The Middle Thames valley: an archaeological survey of the River Gravels,* Berkshire Archaeological Committee Publications, 1
Gibson, A M,
1979   Bronze Age pottery from the collections of the City Museum and Art Gallery, Peterborough, *Northamptonshire Archaeol,* 14, 89-91
Gingell, C J and Schadla-Hall, R T,
1980   Excavations at Bishops Canning Down 1976, in R T Schadla-Hall, and J Hinchliffe, eds, *The past under the plough,* HMSO, London
Glasbergen, W, Groenman-van-Waateringe, W, and Hardenberg-Mulder, G M,
1967   Settlements of the Vlaardingen Culture at Voorschoten and Leidschendam (I) and (II), *Helinium,* 7, 3-31, part I, 97-120, part II

Godwin, H,
   1941   Studies of the post-glacial history of British vegetation: parts III and IV, *Philosophical Transactions of the Royal Society,* London, B, 230, 233-303
   1968   Introductory address, in J S Sawyer, ed, *World climate from 8000 to 0 BC,* 3-14, Royal Meteorological Society, London
   1975   *The history of the British flora,* 2nd ed, Cambridge University Press
   1978   *Fenland: its ancient past and uncertain future,* Cambridge University Press
Godwin, H, and Clifford, M H,
   1938   Studies of the post-glacial history of British vegetation: I Origin and stratigraphy of Fenland deposits near Woodwalton, Huntingdonshire, II Origin and stratigraphy of deposits in Southern Fenland, *Philosophical Transactions of the Royal Society,* London, B, 229, 323-406
Godwin, H, and Vishnu-Mittre,
   1975   Flandrian deposits of the Fenland margin at Holme Fen and Whittlesey Mere, Hunts, *Philosophical Transactions of the Royal Society,* London, B, 270, 561-608
Godwin, H, and Willis, E H,
   1961   Cambridge University natural radiocarbon measurements III, *Radiocarbon,* 3, 60-76
Grant, A,
   1975   The use of tooth wear as a guide to the age of domestic animals, in B W Cunliffe, *Excavations at Portchester Castle I: Roman,* Society of Antiquaries Research Report, 32, 437-450
Gray, H St G, and Cotton, M A, eds,
   1966   *The Meare lake village,* vol III, Taunton, privately printed
Green, H S,
   1974   Early Bronze Age burial, territory and population in Milton Keynes, Buckinghamshire, and the Great Ouse Valley, *Archaeol J,* 131, 75-139
   1976   The excavation of a Late Neolithic settlement at Stacey Bushes, Milton Keynes, and its significance, in Burgess and Miket, 1976, 11-28
   1980   *The flint arrowheads of the British Isles,* 2 vols, British Archaeological Reports, 75, Oxford
Grimes, W F,
   1951   The Jurassic Way across England, in W F Grimes, ed, *Aspects of archaeology in Britain and beyond,* 144-171, Edwards, London
   1960a   *Excavations on defence sites, 1939-45: mainly Neolithic-Bronze Age,* HMSO, London
   1960b   Settlements at Draughton, Northamptonshire, Colsterworth, Lincolnshire and Heathrow, Middlesex in S S Frere, ed, *Problems of the Iron Age in Southern Britain,* 21-28, Institute of Archaeology Occasional Papers, 11, London
Groenman-van-Waateringe, W,
   1979   Nogle aspecter af Jernalderens agerbrug i Holland og NV Tyskland (with English summary), in H Thrane, ed, *Fra Jernalder til Middelalder,* Odense University
Groenman-van Waateringe, W, and Jansma, M J,
   1969   Diatom and pollen analysis of the Vlaardingen Creek: a revised interpretation, *Helinium,* 9, 105-117
Groenman-van Waateringe, W, Voorips, A, and van Wijngaarden-Bakker, L H,
   1968   Settlements of the Vlaardingen culture at Voorschoten and Leidschendam, ecology, *Helinium,* 8, 105-30
Guilbert, G C,
   1975   Planned hillfort interiors, *Proc Prehist Soc,* 41, 203-221
Gurney, D A,
   1980   Evidence of Bronze Age salt production at Northey, Peterborough, *Northamptonshire Archaeol,* 15,
   forthcoming   Romano-British salt production on the western Fen-edge — a reassessment, *Proc Cambridge Antiq Soc*
Hadman, J and Upex, S J,
   1975   The Roman settlement at Ashton near Oundle, *Durobrivae,* 3, 13-15
   1977   Ashton, 1976, *Durobrivae,* 5, 6-9
   1979   Ashton, 1977-8, *Durobrivae,* 7, 28-30
Hains, B A, and Horton, A,
   1969   *British regional geology: Central England,* 3rd ed, Institute of Geological Sciences, HMSO, London
Haio Zimmerman, W,
   1978   Economy of the Roman Iron Age settlement at Flogeln, Kr Cuxhabe, Lower Saxony: husbandry, cattle farming and manufacturing, in B W Cunliffe and R T Rowley, eds, 1978, 147-165

Hall, D N,

1971   Pre-Roman Iron Age sites at Bozeat and Strixton, Northants, *Bedfordshire Archaeol J,* 6, 17-22

1973   Rescue excavations at Radwell Gravel Pits, 1972, *Bedfordshire Archaeol J,* 8, 67-91

Hall, D N, and Hutchings, J B,

1972   The distribution of archaeological sites between the Nene and Ouse valleys, *Bedfordshire Archaeol J,* 7, 1-16

Hall, D N, and Nickerson, N,

1966   Sites on the North Bedfordshire and South Northamptonshire border, *Bedfordshire Archaeol J,* 3, 1-6

1968   Excavations at Irchester 1962-3, *Archaeol J,* 124, 65-99

Hall, D N, and Pryor, F M M,

forthcoming   The Haddenham barrow field: a preliminary note on recent discoveries

Hall, D N, and Woodward, P J,

1977   Radwell excavations, 1974-5: the Bronze Age ring ditches, *Bedfordshire Archaeol J,* 12, 1-16

Hall, D N, Evans, R and Switzer, R

1980   Acid peat in the Cambridgeshire Fenlands, *Proc Cambridge Antiq Soc,* 70

Hallam, S J,

1961   Wash coast-line levels since Roman times, *Antiquity,* 35, 152-4

1970   Settlement round the Wash, in Phillips, 1970, 22-113

Hamilton, J,

1978   A comparison of the age structure at mortality of some Iron Age and Romano-British sheep and cattle populations, in M Parrington, ed, 1978, 126-133

Halstead, P, Hodder, I, and Jones, G,

1978   Behavourial archaeology and refuse patterns: a case study, *Norwegian Archaeological Review,* 11, 118-131

Harcourt, R A,

1974   The dog in prehistoric and early historic Britain, *J Archaeol Sci,* 1, 151-75

Hardin, M A,

1979   The cognitive basis of productivity in a decorative art style: implications of an ethnographic study for archaeologists' taxonomies, in C Kramer, ed, *Ethnoarchaeology,* 75-101, Columbia University Press, New York

Harding, D W,

1972   *The Iron Age in the Upper Thames Basin,* Oxford University Press

1974   *The Iron Age in Lowland Britain,* Routledge Kegan Paul

Harris, E C,

1975   The stratigraphic sequence: a question of time, *World Archaeol,* 7, 109-121

1979   The laws of archaeological stratigraphy, *World Archaeol,* 11, 111-117

Harris, L E,

1952   Sir Cornelius Vermuyden and the Great Level of the Fens. A new judgement, *Proc Cambridgeshire Antiq Soc,* 45, 17-27

Hartley, B R,

1957   The Wandlebury Iron Age hill-fort excavations of 1955-6, *Proc Cambridgeshire Antiq Soc,* 50, 1-27

Hawkes, S C,

1976   A late-Roman nail-cleaner with peacock, *Durobrivae,* 4, 17-18

Hawkes, C F C, and Fell, C I,

1945   The early Iron Age settlement at Fengate, Peterborough, *Archaeol J,* 100, 188-223

Hawkes, C F C, and Hull, M R,

1947   *Camulodunum,* Research Report of the Society of Antiquaries, 14, London

Hedges, J, and Buckley, D,

1975   Excavations at a Neolithic causewayed enclosure, Orsett, Essex, *Proc Prehist Soc,* 44, 219-308

Henkel, F,

1913   *Die Romischen Fingerringe der Rheinlande,* Berlin

Hesse, P R,

1971   *A textbook of soil chemical analyses,* London

Hills, R L,

1967   *Machines, mills and uncountable costly necessities — a short history of the drainage of the Fens,* Goose, Norwich

Hodge, C A H, and Seale, R S,

1966   *The soils of the district around Cambridge,* Memoirs of the Soil Survey, Harpenden

Hoffman, M,
    1964   *The warp-weighted loom*

Hollowell, R,
    1971   Aerial photography and fieldwork in the Upper Nene Valley, *Bulletin of the Northamptonshire Federation of Archaeological Societies,* 6

Horton, A, Lake, R D, Bisson, G, and Coppack, B C,
    1974   *The geology of Peterborough,* Report of the Institute of Geological Sciences, 73/12, London

Howard, M M,
    1961-62 The early domestication of cattle and determination of their remains, *Zeitschrift fur Tierzieuchtung und Zuchtungsbiologie,* 76, 252-64

Hughes, M J, Cowell, M R, and Craddock, P T,
    1976   Atomic absorption techniques in archaeology, *Archaeometry,* 18, 19-37

Jackson, D A,
    1974   Two new pit alignments and a hoard of currency bars from Northamptonshire, *Northamptonshire Archaeol,* 9, 13-45
    1975   An Iron Age site at Twywell, Northamptonshire, *Northamptonshire Archaeol,* 10, 31-93
    1976a   Two Iron Age sites north of Kettering, *Northamptonshire Archaeol,* 11, 71-88
    1976b   The excavation of Neolithic and Bronze Age sites at Aldwincle, Northamptonshire, 1967-71, *Northamptonshire Archaeol,* 11, 12-70
    1977a   Further excavations at Aldwincle, Northamptonshire, 1969-71, *Northamptonshire Archaeol,* 12, 9-54
    1977b   Petrology of Iron Age pottery from Weekley, *Northamptonshire Archaeol,* 12, 183-4
    1978   A Late Bronze Age — Early Iron Age vessel from a pit alignment at Ringstead, Northamptonshire, *Northamptonshire Archaeol,* 13, 168
    1979a   Note on Brigstock (SP 925842), in Archaeology in Northamptonshire 1978, *Northamptonshire Archaeol,* 14, 102
    1979b   A Middle Iron Age site at Geddington, *Northamptonshire Archaeol,* 14, 10-16

Jackson, D A, and Ambrose, T M,
    1978   Excavations at Wakerley, Northamptonshire, 1972-75, *Britannia,* 9, 115-242

Jansma, M J,
    1977   Diatom analysis of pottery in B L van Beek *et al,* eds, 1977, 77-85

Jelgersma, S,
    1966   Sea level changes during the last 10,000 years, in Sawyer, 1966, 54-71

Jones, M,
    1978   Sampling in a rescue context: a case study in Oxfordshire, in Cherry *et al,* eds, 1978, 191-205

Jones, M U,
    1974   Excavations at Mucking, Essex: a second interim report, *Antiq J,* 54, 183-199
    1976   The Mucking excavations 1976, *Panorama* (Journal of Thurrock Local History Society), 20, 34-43

Jones M U, and Jones, W T,
    1975   The crop-mark sites at Mucking, Essex, England, in R L Bruce-Mitford, ed, *Recent archaeological excavations in Europe,* 133-187, Routledge, London

Keepax, C, and Robson, M,
    1978   Conservation and associated examination of a Roman chest and evidence for woodworking techniques, *The Conservator,* 2, 35-40

Killip, I M,
    1970   Spades in the Isle of Man, in A Gailey and A Fenton, eds, *The spade in Northern and Atlantic Europe,* 60-66, Ulster Folk Museum, Queen's University, Belfast

Kinnes, I A,
    1979   *Round barrows and ring-ditches in the British Neolithic,* British Museum Occasional Papers, 7, London

Kooi, P B,
    1974   De Orkaan van 13 November 1972 en het Onstaan van 'Hoefijzervormige' Grondsporen, *Helinium,* 14, 57-65

La Fontaine, R G,
    1980   An analysis of animal bone distribution from two prehistoric sites, M Phil Dissertation, Cambridge University

Lamb, H H, Lewis, R P W, and Woodroffe, A,
    1968   Atmospheric circulation and the main climatic variables between 8000 and 0 BC: meteorological evidence, in J S Sawyer, ed, *World climate from 8000 to 0 BC,* 174-217, Royal Meteorological Society, London

Lambrick, G,
   1978   Iron Age settlements in the Upper Thames Valley, in B Cunliffe and R T Rowley, eds, *Lowland Iron Age communities in Europe,* 103-20, British Archaeological Reports, S48, Oxford
Lambrick, G, and Robinson, M,
   1979   *Iron Age and Roman riverside settlements at Farmoor, Oxfordshire,* Council for British Archaeology Research Report, 32
Lanting, J N, and Mook, W G,
   1977   *The pre- and protohistory of the Netherlands in terms of radiocarbon dates,* C-14 Laboratory, Groningen
Leaf, C S,
   1935   Report on the excavation of two sites in Mildenhall Fen, *Proc Cambridge Antiq Soc,* 35, 106-27
Leech, R,
   1977   *The Upper Thames in Gloucestershire and Wiltshire: an archaeological survey of the river gravels,* Committee for Rescue Archaeology in Avon, Gloucestershire, and Somerset, Survey 4, Bristol
Leeds, E T,
   1922   Further discoveries of the Neolithic and Bronze Ages at Peterborough, *Antiq J,* 2, 220-37
Lethbridge, T C,
   1953   Burial of an Iron Age warrior at Snailwell, *Proc Cambridge Antiq Soc,* 47, 25-37
Lindquist, S O,
   1974   The development of the agrarian landscape on Gotland during the Early Iron Age, *Norwegian Archaeological Review,* 7, 6-32
Longley, D,
   1976   Excavations on the site of a Late Bronze Age settlement at Runnymede Bridge, Egham, *London Archaeologist,* 3
Louwe-Kooijmans, L P,
   1974   The Rhine/Meuse delta, *Oudheid-Kundige Mededelingen,* 53-54, Leiden
   1976a   The Neolithic at the Lower Rhine, in S S de Laet, ed, *Acculturation and continuity in Atlantic Europe,* 150-173, Dissertationes Archaeologicae Gandensis, Ghent
   1976b   Local developments in a Borderland, *Oudehiedkundige Mededelingen uit het Rijksmusuem van Oudheded te Leiden,* 57, 227-297
   1980   Archaeology and coastal change in the Netherlands, in F H Thompson, ed, 1980, 106-133
Mackreth, D F, and O'Neill, F
   1980   Werrington: an Iron Age and Roman site, *Durobrivae,* 8, 23-25
Mahany, C M,
   1963   Fengate, *Curr Archaeol,* 17, 156-7
Matthews, C C,
   1976   *Occupation sites on a Chiltern Ridge, Part I: Neolithic Bronze Age and Early Iron Age,* British Archaeological Reports, 29, Oxford
Maxfield, V A, ed,
   1979   Prehistoric Dartmoor in its context, *Transactions of the Devon Archaeological Society,* 37
May, J,
   1970   Dragonby: an interim report on excavations on an Iron Age and Romano-British site near Scunthorpe, Lincolnshire, *Antiq J,* 50, 222-245
   1976   *Prehistoric Lincolnshire,* History of Lincolnshire Committee, Lincoln
McGrail, S,
   1978   *Logboats of England and Wales, parts i and ii,* British Archaeological Reports, 51, Oxford
Miller, S H, and Skertchly, S B J,
   1878   *The Fenland past and present,* Longmans Green, London
Modderman, P J R,
   1973   A native farmstead from the Roman period near Kethel, municipality of Schiedam, Province of South Holland, *Berichten van de Rijksdienst voor het Oudeidkundig Boedmonderzoek,* 23, 149-158
Moroney, M J,
   1956   *Facts from figures,* 3rd ed, Pelican Books, Harmondsworth
Murphy, J, and Riley, J P,
   1962   A modified single solution method for the determination of phosphate in natural waters, *Analytica Chimica Acta,* 27, 31-6
Needham, S, and Longley, D,
   1979   Egham: a Late Bronze Age settlement and waterfront, *Curr Archaeol,* 68, 262-7

Nicholson, H H,
    1942   *The principles of field drainage,* Cambridge University Press
O'Connor, B,
    1975   Two groups of prehistoric pottery from Kettleborough, *Proc Suffolk Inst Archaeol,* 33, 231-240
Orme, B J, Coles, J M, Caseldine, A E and Bailey, G N,
    1981   *Meare Village West 1979,* in J M Coles (Ed), Somerset Levels Papers 7, pp 12-69
OS
    1967   *Map of Southern Britain in the Iron Age,* Ordnance Survey, reprint 1967, Chessington, Surrey
Parrington, M,
    1978   *The excavation of an Iron Age settlement, Bronze Age ring-ditches and Roman features at Ashville Trading Estate, Abingdon, Oxfordshire, 1974-76,* Council for British Archaeology Research Report, 28
Payne, S,
    1972   Partial recovery and sample bias: the results of some sieving experiments, in E S Higgs, ed, *Papers in economic prehistory,* 49-64, Cambridge
    1973   Kill-off patterns in sheep and goats: the mandibles from Asvan Kale, *Anatolian Studies,* 23, 281-303
Peacock, D P S,
    1971   Roman amphorae in pre-Roman Britain, in M Jesson and D Hill, eds, *The Iron Age and its hillforts,* 161-188, Southampton
Perrin, R,
    1980   Pottery of 'London Ware' type from the Nene Valley, *Durobrivae,* 8, 8-10
Phillips, C W, ed,
    1970   *The Fenland in Roman Times,* Royal Geographical Society Research Series, 5, London
    1980   Archaeological retrospect I, *Antiquity,* 54, 110-117
Piggott, S,
    1962   *The West Kennet long barrow,* HMSO, London
    1968   *The Druids,* Ancient People and Places series, Thames and Hudson, London
Plog, F T,
    1974   *The Study of prehistoric change,* Academic Press, London
Potter, T W,
    1976   Valleys and settlement: some new evidence, *World Archaeol,* 8, 207-219
    forthcoming   *Excavation at Grandford, March*
Provan, D M J,
    1971   Soil phosphate analysis as a tool in archaeology, *Norwegian Archaeological Review,* 4, 37-50
Pryor, A,
    1978   The Car Dyke, *Durobrivae,* 6, 24-5
Pryor, F M M,
    1974a   Two Bronze Age burials near Pilsgate, Lincolnshire, *Proc Cambridge Antiq Soc,* 68, 1-12
    1974b   Fengate, *Curr Archaeol,* 46, 332-38
    1974c   *Excavation at Fengate, Peterborough, England: the first report,* Archaeology Monograph 3, Royal Ontario Museum, Toronto
    1974d   *Earthmoving on open archaeological sites,* Nene Valley Archaeological Handbook, Nene Valley Research Committee, Peterborough
    1976a   Fen-edge land management in the Bronze Age: an interim report on excavations at Fengate, Peterborough 1971-4, in C B Burgess and R Miket, eds, *Settlement and economy in the second and third millennia BC,* British Archaeological Reports, 33, 24-49, Oxford
    1976b   A Neolithic multiple burial from Fengate, Peterborough, *Antiquity,* 50, 232-3
    1977   Fengate 1976, *Durobrivae,* 5, 14-16
    1978a   *Excavation at Fengate, Peterborough, England: the second report,* Archaeology Monograph, 5, Royal Ontario Museum, Toronto
    1978b   Three new Bronze Age weapons, *Durobrivae,* 6, 14-16
    1980a   *Excavation at Fengate, Peterborough, England: the third report,* Northamptonshire Archaeological Society Monograph 1, Royal Ontario Archaeology Monograph 6, Toronto and Northampton
    1980b   Raising the dead, *Durobrivae,* 8
    1980c   Will it all come out in the Wash? Reflections at the end of eight years digging, in J Barrett and R J Bradley, eds, *Settlement and society in the British Later Bronze Age,* British Archaeological Reports, 83, 483-500, Oxford
    1981   Plough-damage and post-depositional distortion: recent research at Maxey, Cambridgeshire, in J Hedges, ed, *Archaeology and agriculture, Case Studies from Essex,* Essex County Council, Chelmsford

forthcoming   Report on the flints in J P Wild, ed, *Report on Nene Valley Research Committee's excavations at Longthorpe, Peterborough*

Pryor, F M M, and Cranstone, D A L,
    1978   An interim report on excavations at Fengate, Peterborough, 1975-77, *Northants Archaeol* 13, 9-27

Pryor, F M M, and Palmer, R
    forthcoming   Aerial photography and rescue archaeology: a case study, *Aerial Archaeol*, 5, 1981

Raftis, J A,
    1957   *The estates of Ramsey Abbey,* Pontifical Institute of Medieval Studies, Toronto

Ralph, E K R, Michael, H N M, and Han M C H,
    1973   Radio-carbon dates and reality, *Museum Applied Science Centre for Archaeology Newsletter,* 9, 1-20, University of Pennsylvania

Ravensdale, J R,
    1974   *Liable to floods,* Cambridge University Press

Royal Commission on Historical Monuments
    1960   *A Matter of time: an archaeological survey,* HMSO, London
    1975   *An inventory of the historical monuments in...North-East Northamptonshire,* HMSO, London
    1979   *An inventory of the historical monuments in...Central Northamptonshire,* HMSO, London

Rees, J W,
    1968   Morphologic variation in the mandible of the white-tailed deer, *(Odocoieleus virginianus):* a study of population skeletal variation by principal component analysis, *Journal of Morphology,* 127, 113-35
    1969   Morphologic variation in the cranium and mandible of the white-tailed deer *(Odocoeleus virginianus):* a comparative study of geographical and four biological differences, *Journal of Morphology,* 128, 95-112
    1971   Mandibular variation with sex and age in white-tailed deer *(Odocoieleus virginianus)* in Canada, *Journal of Mammalogy,* 521, 223-26

Renfrew, C, ed,
    1974   *British prehistory: a new outline,* Duckworth

Reynolds, P J,
    1974   Experimental Iron Age storage pits: an interim report, *Proc Prehist Soc,* 40, 118-131

Richmond, Sir I A,
    1968   *Hod Hill, volume 2,* British Museum, London

Rodwell, W J,
    1974   The Orsett Cock cropmark site, *Essex Archaeol Hist,* 6, 13-39
    1976   Coinage, oppida and the rise of Belgic power in South-Eastern Britain, in B W Cunliffe and R T Rowley, eds, *Oppida in barbarian Europe,* 181-367, British Archaeological Reports, S11, Oxford
    1978a   Buildings and settlements in South-East Britain in the Late Iron Age, in B Cunliffe and R T Rowley, eds, *Lowland Iron Age communities in Europe,* 25-41, British Archaeological Reports, S48, Oxford
    1978b   Relict landscapes in Essex, in Bowen and Fowler, eds, 1978, 89-98

Roper, D C,
    1979   The method and theory of site catchment analysis: a review, in M B Schiffer, ed, *Advances in archaeological method and theory,* 119-140, Seminar Press, London

Ross, A,
    1967   *Pagan Celtic Britain,* Routledge, Keegan and Paul, London
    1970   *Everyday life of the pagan Celts,* Batsford, London

Salway, P,
    1967   Excavations at Hockwold-cum-Wilton, Norfolk 1961-1962, *Proc Cambridge Antiq Soc,* 60, 39-80
    1970   The Roman Fenland, in Phillips, 1970, 1-21

Sanders, C,
    1972   The Pre-Belgic Iron Age in the Central and Western Chilterns, *Archaeol J,* 128, 1-30

Sawyer, J S, ed,
    1966   *Proceedings of the International Symposium on world climate,* 8,000 to 0 BC, Royal Meteorological Society, London

Schiffer, M B,
    1976   *Behavioural archaeology,* Seminar Press, London

Schlabow, K,
    1976   *Textilfunde der Eisenzeit in Norddeutschland*

Schmid, P,
    1978   New archaeological results of settlement structures (Roman Iron Age) in Northwest German coastal area, in B W Cunliffe and R T Rowley, eds, 1978, 123-145

Seale, R S,
1975   *Soils of the Chatteris district of Cambridgeshire,* Soil Survey Special Survey, 9, Harpenden
Shackley, M L,
1975   *Archaeological sediments: a survey of analytical methods,* London
Sieveking, G de G, Longworth, I H, Hughes, M J, Clark, A J, and Millet, A,
1973   A new survey of Grime's Graves, Norfolk, *Proc Prehist Soc,* 39, 182-218
Silver, I A,
1969   The ageing of domestic animals, in D R Brothwell and E S Higgs, eds, *Science in archaeology,* Thames and Hudson, London, 283-302
Simco, A,
1973   The Iron Age in the Bedford region, *Bedfordshire Archaeol J,* 8, 5-22
Simmons, B B,
1977   Ancient coastlines around the Wash, *S Lincolnshire Archaeol,* 6-9
1979   The Lincolnshire Car Dyke, *Britannia,* 10, 183-196
1980   Iron Age and Roman coasts around the Wash, in F H Thompson, ed, 1980, 56-73
Simpson, W G,
1962-3   *Welland Valley Research Committee Report 1962-3,* Council for British Archaeology, London
1966   Romano-British settlement on the Welland gravels, in C Thomas, ed, *Rural settlement in Roman Britain,* 15-25, Council for British Archaeology Research Report, 7, London
1976   A barrow cemetery of the second millennium BC at Tallington, Lincolnshire, *Proc Prehist Soc,* 42, 215-240
Sjoberg, A,
1976   Phosphate analysis of anthropic soils, *Journal of Field Archaeology,* 3, 447-454
Skertchly, S B J,
1877   *The geology of the Fenland,* Memoirs of the Geological Survey, HMSO, London
Small, A M,
1977   *Monte Irsi, Southern Italy,* British Archaeological Reports, S20, Oxford
Smith, C,
1977   The valleys of the Thame and Middle Trent, their population and ecology during the late 1st millennium BC, in J Collis, ed, *The Iron Age in Britain,* 51-61, Sheffield University Press
1978   The landscape and natural history of Iron Age settlement on the Trent Gravels, in B W Cunliffe and R T Rowley, eds, 1978, 91-102
Smith, C, ed,
1979   *Fisherwick,* British Archaeological Reports, 61, Oxford
Smith, I F,
1956   The decorative art of Neolithic ceramics in South-Eastern England and its relations, unpublished PhD thesis, Institute of Archaeology, London
1974   *The Neolithic,* in C Renfrew, 1974, 100-136
Smith, K,
1977   The excavation of Winklebury Camp, Basingstoke, Hampshire, *Proc Prehist Soc,* 43, 31-130
Smith, R A,
1927   Pre-Roman remains at Scarborough, *Archaeologia,* 78, 179-200
Sparks, B W, and West, R G,
1965   The relief and drift deposits, in Steers, 1965, 18-40
Spratling, M G,
1974   The dating of the Iron Age swan's neck sunflower pin from Fengate, Peterborough, Cambridgeshire, *Antiq J,* 54, 268-9
Steers, J A, ed,
1965   *The Cambridge region,* British Association for the Advancement of Science, Cambridge
Sumner, W M,
1979   Estimating population by analogy: an example, in C Kramer, ed, *Ethnoarchaeology,* 164-174, Columbia University Press, New York
Tatton-Brown, T,
1977   Excavations at Highstead, near Chislet, *Archaeologia Cantiana,* 92, 236-8

Taylor, C C,

1969   *Peterborough New Town, a survey of the antiquities in the area of development, part 1*, Royal Commission on Historical Monuments, London

1975   Roman settlements in the Nene Valley: the impact of recent archaeology, in P J Fowler, ed, *Recent work in rural archaeology*, 107-120, Moonraker Press, Bradford-upon-Avon

Taylor, M,

1979   A survey of prehistoric sites North of Cambridge, *Proc Cambridge Antiq Soc*, 69, 21-36

1981   *Wood in archaeology*, Shire Publications, Princes Risborough

Taylor, T P,

1979   Soil marks near Winchester, Hampshire, *J Archaeol Sci*, 6, 93-100

Tebbutt, C F,

1957   A Belgic and Roman farm at Wyboston, Bedfordshire, *Proc Cambridge Antiq Soc*, 50, 75-84

Thomas, A C, ed,

1966   *Rural settlement in Roman Britain*, Council for British Archaeology Research Report, 7

Thompson, F H, ed,

1980   *Archaeology and coastal change*, Society of Antiquaries Occasional Paper, (new series), 1, London

Tilley, C Y,

1979   *Post-glacial communities in the Cambridge region*, British Archaeological Reports, 66, Oxford

Tilson, P,

1973   A Belgic and Romano-British site at Bromham, *Bedfordshire Archaeol J*, 8, 23-66

1975   The excavation of an Iron Age hut circle at Bromham in 1971, *Bedfordshire Archaeol J*, 10, 19-24

Tite, M S,

1972   *Methods of physical examination in archaeology*, 7-57, Academic Press, London

Tite, M S, and Mullins, C,

1971   Enhancement of the magnetic susceptibility of soils on archaeological sites, *Archaeometry*, 13, 209-221

Toller, H S,

1980   An interim report on the excavation of the Orsett 'Cock' enclosure, Essex: 1976-79, *Britannia*, 11, 35-42

Trotter, M, and Gleser, G C,

1952   Estimation of stature from long-bones of American whites and Negroes, *American Journal of Physical Anthropology*, 10, 463-514

Turnbaugh, W A,

1978   Floods and archaeology, *American Antiquity*, 43, 4, 593-607

Tylecote, R F,

1976   *A history of metallurgy*, 1st ed, The Metals Society, London

United States Department of Agriculture

1951   *USDA, Soil Survey Manual*, United States Department of Agriculture Handbook Number 18

Van Beek, B L,

1977   Pottery of the Vlaardingen culture, in van Beek et al, eds, 1977, 86-100

Van Beek, B L, Brandt, R W, Groenman-van Waateringe, W, eds,

1977   *Ex Horreo*, IPP, Amsterdam

Van Es, W A,

1965-7   Wijster: a Native village beyond the Imperial Frontier, AD 150-425, *Palaeohistoria*, 11, 1-595

1968   Paddepoel, excavations of frustrated Terps, 200BC-250AD, *Palaeohistoria*, 14, 187-352

Van Es, W A, and Miedma, M,

1970-1   Leeuwarden: a small terp under the Oldhove Cemetery, *Berichten van de Rijksdienst voor het Oudheidkundig Bodemonderzoek*, 20-1, 80-117

Van Iterson Scholten, F R,

1977   Rope and fishing tackle, in van Beek *et al*, eds, 1977, 135-143

Van Mensch, P J A, and Ijzereef, G F,

1977   Smoke-dried meat in prehistoric and Roman Netherlands, in van Beek *et al*, eds, 1977, 144-150

Van Regteren Altena, J F, Bakker, J F, Clason, J A, Glasburgen, A T, Groenman-van Waateringe, W, Pons, L J,

1962   The Vlaardingen Culture, I-III, *Helinium*, 2, 3-35, (I), 97-103, (II), 215-243, (III)

1963   The Vlaardingen Culture, IV-V, *Helinium*, 3, 39-54, (IV), 97-120, (V)

Van Regteren Altena, J F, van Mensch, P J A, Ijzereef, G F,

1977   Bronze Age clay animals from Grootebroek, in van Beek *et al*, eds, 1977, 241-254

Van Zeist, W,

1974   Palaeobotanical studies of settlement sites in the coastal area of the Netherlands, *Palaeohistoria*, 16, 223-371

Wainwright, G J,
    1979   *Gussage-All-Saints: an Iron Age settlement in Dorset,* Department of Environment Archaeological Reports, 10, HMSO, London

Waterbolk, H T,
    1977   Walled enclosure of the Iron Age in the North of the Netherlands, *Palaeohistoria, 19, 97-172*
    1979   Siedlungskontinuitat im Kustengebiet der Nordsee swischen Rhein und Elbe, *Probleme der Kustenforschung im sudlichen Nordseebebiet,* band 13, Hildesheim

Webster, G,
    1974   *Practical archaeology,* 2nd, ed, Black, London

Wheeler, R E M,
    1929   Old England, Brentford, *Antiquity,* 3, 20-32
    1936   *Verulamium: a Belgic and two Roman cities,* Research Report of the Society of Antiquaries, 11, London
    1943   *Maiden Castle, Dorset,* Research Report of the Society of Antiquaries of London, 12
    1954a   *The Stanwick fortifications, North Riding of Yorkshire,* Research Report of the Society of Antiquaries, 17, London
    1954b   *Archaeology from the earth,* Penguin Books, Harmondsworth

Whimster, R,
    1977   Iron Age burial in Southern Britain, *Proc Prehist Soc,* 43, 317

White, D A,
    1969   Excavations at Brampton, Huntingdonshire, 1966, *Proc Cambridge Antiq Soc,* 62, 1-20

Whittle, A W R,
    1977   *The earlier Neolithic of Southern England and its continental background,* British Archaeological Reports, S35, Oxford

Wild, J P,
    1970   *Textile manufacture in the Northern Roman provinces,* Cambridge University Press
    1974   Roman settlement in the Lower Nene valley, *Archaeol J,* 131, 140-170

Wilhelmi, K,
    1977   Zur Funktion und Verbreitung dreieckiger Tongewichte der Eisenzeit, *Germania,* 55

Wilkes, J J, and Elrington, C R, eds,
    1978   Roman Cambridgeshire, *Victoria County History, Cambridgeshire,* Volume VII

Williams, P W,
    1969   The geomorphic effects of ground water, in R J Chorley, ed, *Introduction to fluvial processes, 108-123,* Methuen, London

Williams, J H,
    1974   *Two Iron Age sites in Northampton,* Northampton Development Corporation, Archaeological Monographs, 1, Northampton

Willis, E H,
    1961   Marine transgression sequence in the English Fenland, *Annals of the New York Academy of Science,* 95, 368-376

Wilson, D M,
    1976   *The archaeology of Anglo-Saxon England,* London

Wilson, D R,
    1978   Pit alignments: distribution and function, in H C Bowen and P J Fowler, 1978, 3-5

Wilson, R,
    1978   Sampling bone densities at Mingies Ditch, in Cherry *et al,* eds, 1978, 355-61

Wilson, R, Hamilton, K, Bramwell, D, and Armigate, P,
    1978   The animal bones, in Parrington, 1978, 110-39

Woltring, P J,
    1975   Occupation history of Texel, I: the excavation of Denberg: preliminary report, *Berichten van de Rikjsdienst voor het Oudeidkundig Bodermonderzoek,* 25, 7-36

Woods, P J,
    1969   *Excavations at Hardingstone, Northamptonshire,* 1967-8, Northampton
    1971   Excavations at Brixworth, Northamptonshire 1965-1970: the Romano-British villa, Part 1, *J Northampton Mus Art Gallery,* 8, 1ff

Woodward, P J,
    1977   Excavations at Pear Tree Farm, Elstow, Bedfordshire, *Bedfordshire Archaeol J,* 12, 27
    1978   Flint distribution, ring ditches and Bronze Age settlement patterns in the Great Ouse Valley: the problem, a field survey technique and some preliminary results, *Archaeol J,* 135, 32-56

NOTES
For plates please turn to page 279

NOTES

NOTES

Plate 1   Early Iron Age bowl from Vicarage Farm, Area I, F6, layer 4, showing holes for handle attachment. *Photo Royal Ontario Museum*

Plate 2   Wrapped wooden handle of Early Iron Age bowl illustrated in Plate 1. *Photo Royal Ontario Museum*

Plate 3   Close-up view of saw-cut in an alder log from the bottom of the Middle Iron Age quarry pit, F1, Padholme Road, Area XI. Width of cut: 0.40m.

Plate 4   Padholme Road subsite: general view, looking NE, of the Middle Iron pit complex of Area XII. Scale in half metres.

Plate 5   Storey's Bar Road subsite, Area I: general view of Structure 1, looking SW. Scale in half metres.

Plate 6   Aerial view, looking NW, of the Cat's Water (foreground) and Newark Road (middle distance) subsites. *Photo by S G Upex, Nene Valley Research Committee.*

Plate 7　Aerial view (from SW) of Storey's Bar Road and Cat's Water cropmarks. The ring-ditch in the centre foreground is of Late Neolithic date; the ditched diagonal droveway and yard system to the right (NE) are Late Iron Age and Roman. *Cambridge University Collection: copyright reserved.*

282

Plate 8 Cat's Water subsite: northern end of main excavated area, with N to the left; Structure 16 is at top, centre. *Photo S G Upex, Nene Valley Research Committee.*

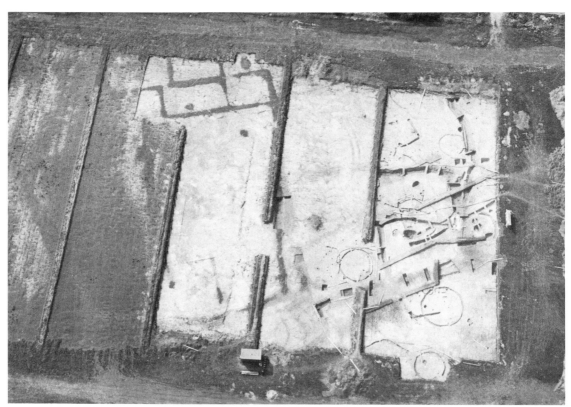

Plate 9   Cat's Water subsite: aerial view of the 1975 excavations (Areas I and II), with N to the right.
Photo S G Upex, Nene Valley Research Committee

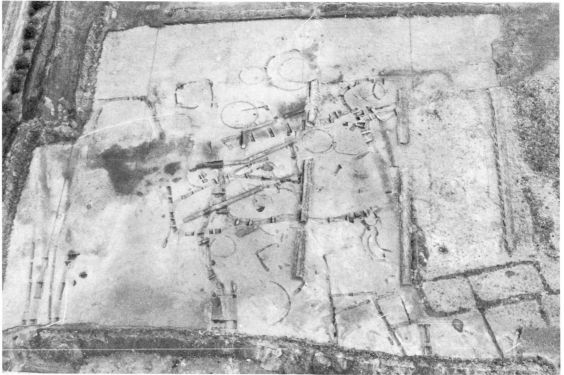

Plate 10   Cat's Water subsite: aerial view of 1976 excavations (Area I, II, and IV), with N to the left.
Photo S G Upex, Nene Valley Research Committee

Plate 11   Cat's Water subsite: aerial view of the 1977 excavations (mainly Area V). The weed-covered dark area was excavated in 1975; N is towards top left. *Photo by S G Upex, Nene Valley Research Committee*

Plate 12   Cat's Water subsite: earlier Neolithic multiple burial, general view, with Body 1 in the foreground. Scale in half metres.

Plate 13   Cat's Water subsite: earlier Neolithic burial; close-up view of flint leaf arrowhead lodged between ribs 8 and 9 of Body 1. Scale in inches and centimetres.

Plate 14   Cat's Water subsite, Structure 54: plate showing comparative sizes of sherds from the filled-in pit, F1593 (left), and the trampled floor deposits of F1501 (right).

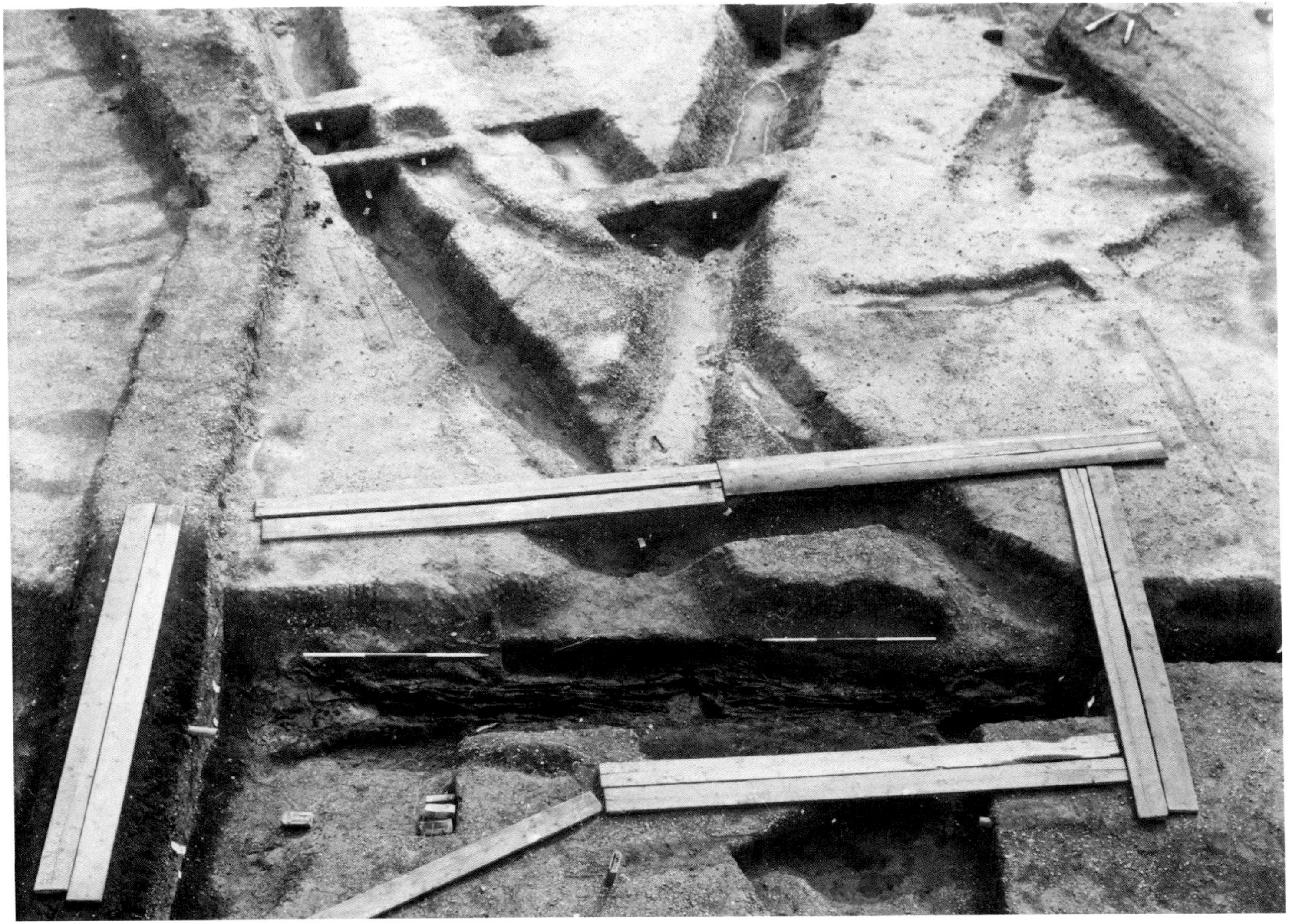

Plate 15   Cat's Water subsite, Late Iron 'brush drain': distant view, from NE (for location sketch see Fig 84). Scales in half metres.

Plate 16   Cat's Water subsite, Late Iron 'brush drain': view from W. Note modern land drain pipe protruding from section; the dark layer at the top of the section is the Roman flood clay deposit. Scales in half metres.

Plate 17   Cat's Water subsite, Late Iron 'brush drain': close-up view of osiers, showing parallel arrangement. Scale in half metres.

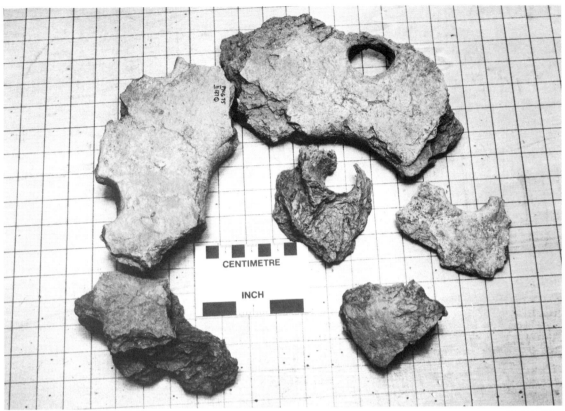

Plate 18   Fragments of probable Iron Age clay oven (see also Fig 119). Cat's Water subsite, Area II, F1137, layer 1 (Grid 402W/669N)

Plate 19   Detail of stamped and rouletted decoration on a Romano-British bowl, Cat's Water subsite, F412, layer 2. See report by J W Hayes, Chapter 7 (catalogue no. 34). *Photo by D R Crowther*

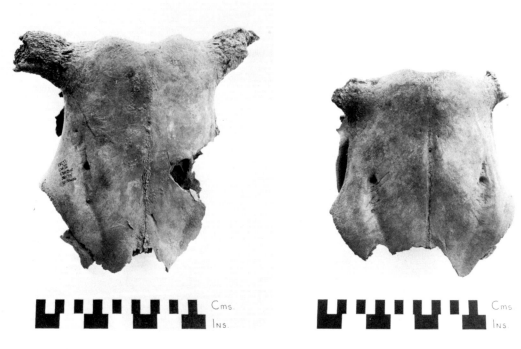

Plate 20   Cat's Water subsite, faunal bone report (for more information see Appendix 6): cattle skulls.
         Photos by Rupert Watts

291

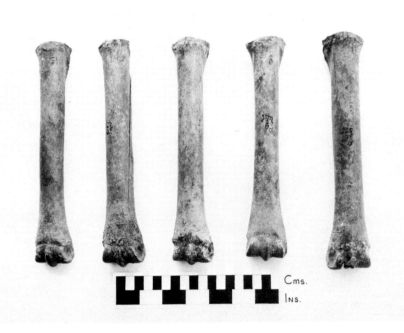

Plate 21   Cat's Water subsite, faunal bone report (for more information see Appendix 6): horse mandibles and metapodia. *Photos by Rupert Watts*

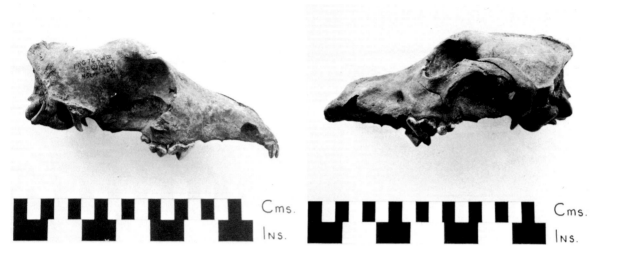

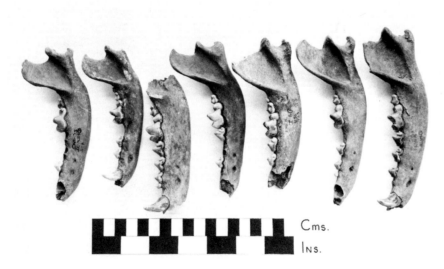

Plate 22   Cat's Water subsite, faunal bone report (for more information see Appendix 6): dog skulls.
Photos by Rupert Watts

Plate 23   Cat's Water subsite, faunal bone report (for more information see Appendix 6): fox skull and other material. *Photo by Rupert Watts*

Plate 24   Cat's Water subsite, faunal bone report (for more information see Appendix 6): sheep skull,
sheep/goat and goat horn cores. *Photo by Rupert Watts*

Plate 25   Cat's Water subsite, faunal bone report (for more information see Appendix 6): pathologies.
Photos by Rupert Watts

296

Plate 26 Cat's Water subsite, faunal bone report (for more information see Appendix 6): worked material.
Photos by Rupert Watts

297

Plate 27 Reconstruction of the central part of the Cat's Water Middle Iron Age settlement, with Structures 6 (foreground) and 12; the main drain junction is that of F1006 and 1086. *Model (by Eric Ricketts and David Rayner) and photo courtesy of Peterborough Development Corporation*

Plate 28   Another view of the Cat's Water model (see also plate 27) with Structure 12 in the foreground; the main drain is an early phase of F1006. *Model (by Eric Ricketts and David Rayner) and photo courtesy of Peterborough Development Corporation.*

LIST OF MICROFICHE FIGURES

LIST OF MICROFICHE TABLES